China and Europe

What are the likely long-term implications of this shift to Asia for the cities and regions of Europe? To just 'wait and see' cannot be the response, nor the hope that the attractiveness of Asia will diminish over time and that the economic growth will slow down. Will Europe be able to retain its economic power?

There is a need to think about possible futures for the cities and regions of Europe when industrial production is reduced, when high-tech and bio-tech industries do not compensate for the loss of industrial jobs, when Europe's supremacy in financial services is eroding, or even when Chinese capital is investing in Europe to exploit the territorial capital of the 'old' continent.

China and Europe address the challenges for the cities and regions of Europe that may be the consequences of such development trends. Contributions by policy-makers and academic observers will prepare the ground for debating the dimensions 'economy', 'knowledge and culture', 'environment and mobility', 'quality of life', and 'governance' of this challenge.

Klaus R. Kunzmann is an honorary professor of the University of Cardiff and Professor Emeritus at the University of Dortmund. **Willy A. Schmid** is Professor Emeritus of the Institute for Spatial and Landscape Planning of the Swiss Federal Institute of Technology (ETH) Zurich. **Martina Koll-Schretzenmayr** is a lecturer at ETH Zurich and managing editor of the international planning journal disP.

Regions and cities

Series editors:

Ron Martin *University of Cambridge, UK*
Gernot Grabher *University of Bonn, Germany*
Maryann Feldman *University of Georgia, USA*
Gillian Bristow *University of Cardiff, UK*

Regions and Cities is an international, interdisciplinary series that provides authoritative analyses of the new significance of regions and cities for economic, social and cultural development, and public-policy experimentation. The series seeks to combine theoretical and empirical insights with constructive policy debate and critically engages with formative processes and policies in regional and urban studies.

China and Europe

The implications of the rise of China for European space

**Edited by Klaus R. Kunzmann,
Willy A. Schmid and
Martina Koll-Schretzenmayr**

LONDON AND NEW YORK

First published 2010
by Routledge
2 Park Square, Milton Park, Abingdon, Oxon OX14 4RN

Simultaneously published in the USA and Canada
by Routledge
711 Third Ave, New York, NY 10017

Routledge is an imprint of the Taylor & Francis Group, an informa business

First issued in Paperback 2011

© 2010 Selection and editorial matter, Klaus R. Kunzmann,
Willy A. Schmid and Martina Koll-Schretzenmayr; individual chapters,
the contributors

Typeset in Times by Wearset Ltd, Boldon, Tyne and Wear

British Library Cataloguing in Publication Data
A catalogue record for this book is available from the British Library

Library of Congress Cataloging in Publication Data
A catalog record for this book has been requested

ISBN13: 978-0-415-55060-4 (hbk)
ISBN13: 978-0-203-87273-4 (ebk)
ISBN13: 978-0-415-51658-7 (pbk)

Contents

Figures

Tables

Contributors

Louis Albrechts is Professor Emeritus and Special Guest Professor at the Department of Architecture, Urbanism and Planning, Catholic University of Leuven, Belgium. His research interests include: the practice and nature of strategic spatial planning, the link between plan and implementation, planning as a creative process, issues of power in planning, the gap between plan-making, political decision-making and implementation, sustainability in strategic planning, and diversity in planning. He has published widely about these issues in international journals and linked his theoretical work with innovating practices.

Tridib Banerjee is Professor in Urban and Regional Planning at the University of Southern California's School of Urban Planning and Development He has focused his research, teaching and writing on the design and planning of the built environment and the related human and social consequences. In particular, he is interested in the political economy of urban development, and the effects of globalization in the transformation of urban form and urbanism from a comparative international perspective. His current research includes implementation of smart growth policies, converting brown fields to affordable housing, designing for residential density and walkable communities, and transit-oriented development.

Jef van den Broeck is a spatial planner/designer, Honorary Professor at the University of Leuven, Belgium (since 1998), and Honorary Lecturer at the University College Henry Van de Velde in Antwerp (1978–2005). His main research areas are spatial planning and design at all scales and policy levels, strategic (structural) planning, integrated area focused planning and spatial quality. He is promoter of a running (2005–9) research programme 'SP2SP' (Spatial Planning to Strategic Projects) which should result in four PhDs as well as in policy recommendations concerning the development and realization of strategic spatial projects. He was co-founder and director (1973–97) of Studiegroep Omgeving, dealing with planning and design, architecture and topography.

Philippe Doucet is an architect-engineer and obtained his MSc degree at the Faculty of Applied Sciences of the University of Louvain (Belgium). Specialized in urban and regional planning, he started his career as a researcher and then became a civil servant in the Walloon spatial planning administration. During his four-year posting at the European Commission, he spearheaded the development of the European Spatial Development Perspective and contributed to the launch of INTERREG IIC. Thereafter, he spent almost eight years as Head of the INTERREG IIC NWMA and IIIB North West Europe Joint Technical Secretariats. More recently, he set up GEPHYRES, a consultancy specializing in European and cross-border territorial development. He is recognized as a fully fledged expert in European territorial cohesion and cooperation issues. Combining programme management field practice and theoretical thought; he has taught, published and given lectures on the same topics. He has initiated original lines of thought about key notions such as transnational issues and intensity of cooperation.

Andreas Faludi is Professor in Spatial Policy Systems in Europe at Delft University of Technology. His special interests are planning theory and methodology, the study of Dutch strategic planning and of European and comparative planning. He has done commissioned research for the Centre for Environmental Studies, London (1974–7), the Association of Dutch Municipalities (1977), the Dutch Ministry of Finance (1982/3), the S.O.S.-network of Dutch growth centres (1989–90), the Scientific Council of Government Policy (1997) alongside several projects for the Dutch National Spatial Planning Agency and for the Dutch Organization for Fundamental Research.

John Friedmann has been appointed an Honorary Professor in and continues as Professor Emeritus in the School of Public Policy and Social Research at UCLA. He was Founding Professor of the Program for Urban Planning in the Graduate School of Architecture and Planning at UCLA, and at various times between 1969 and 1996 served as its head for a total of 14 years. In 1988, he was given the American Collegiate Schools of Planning Distinguished Planning Educator Award. International recognition for his achievements includes Honorary Doctorates from the Catholic University of Chile and the University of Dortmund. His publication record includes 15 individually authored and 11 co-edited books, as well as 150 chapters, articles and reviews. Prior to coming to SCARP, he was a Professorial Fellow in the Faculty of Architecture, Building and Planning of the University of Melbourne. He is currently involved in research on urbanization processes with special reference to China. His most recent books include *Empowerment: A Theory of Alternative Development* (1993), *Cities for Citizens: Planning and the Rise of Civil Society* (with Mike Douglass) (1996), *The Prospect of Cities* (2002), and *China's Urban Transition* (2005). Friedmann is married to Leonie Sandercock, Professor of Urban Planning and Social Policy, who joined the SCARP faculty in July 2001.

Marco Keiner is Director of the Environment, Housing and Land Management Division at the United Nations Economic Commission for Europe (UNECE).

2000–6 he has been Assistant Professor, Senior Researcher and Lecturer for Spatial Planning at ETH Zurich and the University of Innsbruck. He was also head of the Sustainability Research Group of the Institute for Spatial and Landscape Planning (IRL) at ETH Zurich.

Herbert Kemming studied economics and social psychology in Bochum and Siegen, Germany, and has a university degree in economics. He has been working for the Research Institute for Regional and Urban Development since 1980 and is Deputy Director and head of the ILS Department 'Mobility and Land Use' (formerly Transport Research). At ILS Herbert Kemming worked in the field of urban and regional planning, economic development of cities and mobility and transport. His specialities include mobility management, mobility and transport in metropolitan areas, public transport, cycling and walking, pricing and fiscal measures in transport, city logistics, integrated land-use and transport development, social aspects of mobility, mobility of young people and of the elderly.

Robert Knippschild, PhD in Spatial Planning, currently works as Project Manager and Lecturer at the Leibniz Institute of Ecological and Regional Development in Dresden, Germany, in the fields of European Spatial Development Policy and cross-border cooperation planning processes.

Martina Koll-Schretzenmayr is Senior Researcher in the Network City and Landscape at ETH Zurich. She studied geography, history, urban and spatial planning at the University of Augsburg, the TU München and ETH Zurich. She gained a PhD in Spatial Planning on the Redevelopment of Brownfield Sites (1998) at ETH Zurich and has researched and written on urban redevelopment, socio-spatial transformation of metropolitan regions, and real-estate development.

Thomas Krueger is Professor for Urban Project Development at the HafenCity University Hamburg. He studied spatial planning in Dortmund and urban design and planning in Hamburg. His PhD at Technical University focused on the economic structure of cities. He gained practical experience in various fields of planning and real-estate development as head of the department for concept development of the development company of the state Schleswig-Holstein.

Klaus R. Kunzmann is Professor Emeritus in European Spatial Planning at the University of Dortmund. He studied architecture and urban planning at the Technische Universität München (1967) and obtained his doctoral degree in urban planning from the Technische Hochschule in Vienna/Austria (1971). From 1971 to 1974 he was working with consulting engineers, partly in Düsseldorf and in Bangkok/Thailand, before he was appointed to be the founder Director of the Institute of Spatial Planning of the School of Planning at the University of Dortmund, a position which he held until 1994. Klaus Kunzmann has been a Visiting Professor at the Institut Français d'Urbanisme of the Université Paris VIII (1990), at the ORL-Institute of the ETH Zürich/ Switzerland (1992), and at the Graduate School of Architecture and Planning of the University of California, Los Angeles (1993). He has also been a Visiting Fellow at the Technion Haifa/Israel (1992) and the Tinbergen Institute/Rotterdam (1995). His research fields mainly concern comparative spatial planning in Europe and spatial restructuring of traditional industrial regions. Over the past five years his research has focused on the role of creativity and cultural industries for endogenous regional development. Over the past 20 years Klaus has been project leader on numerous research and policy projects for various German ministries at the federal and the *Länder* level, for the council of Europe and the European Commission. Other research projects have been supported by research grants from the German Research Society, the Anglo-German Foundation for the Study of Industrial Society and the Agnelli Foundation. Moreover, he has been a frequent consultant to German Technical Assistance projects in developing countries.

John Lovering is Professor of Urban Development and Governance and member of the Urban and Regional Governance Research Group at Cardiff University. His research and teaching interests lie in the many aspects of the interconnections between changing 'ways of seeing' (discourses and ideologies); changing policy biases (especially those impacting on the development of employment, cities and regions); and the political structures through which these are connected (the state and other institutions of authority, including the universities, religious institutions, social hierarchies, etc.): urban development and governance; the cultural industries and urban 'regeneration'; labour-market structure and change at various scales; regional economic development and policies; the Welsh economy; industrial restructuring (especially in the defence industry); theories of globalization and their policy implications; international political economy; the history and theory of the state; the philosophy of social research, Marxism poststructuralism, critical realism; the development of Turkey and Istanbul.

Simon Miles is a consultant on public policy and international development, focusing on the areas of institutional analysis and capacity development, policy-making, planning, development and administration. He has worked in over 50 countries for governmental, non-governmental, local, national and international agencies. He has advised on environmental, natural resource, socio-economic and technological policies and programmes, with an emphasis on their integration. This work has assisted countries to move towards sustainable development and to adapt their human resources and labour markets to respond to rapid global changes.

Achim Prossek studied geography and German literature. He is Research Assistant at the Faculty of Spatial Planning, the Technical University in Dortmund.

Angelo Rossi taught regional economics and environmental economics at ETH Zurich, the University of Zurich and the University of Fribourg. The focus of his research was the spatial development and economic growth of urban systems in developed countries. Since his retirement, he works as consultant on these topics for government agencies and private firms.

Willy A. Schmid is Professor Emeritus for Landscape and Environmental Planning at ETH Zurich. His main fields of research are ecological planning: support of integration of environmental considerations in the (spatial) planning process; infrastructure and spatial development: support-informed decision-making in the context of infrastructure planning and urban development: advancement of planning tools and instruments: facilitating decision-making and monitoring changes to our environment by means of planning tools and instruments relying on state-of-the art technology, mainly on three-dimensional visualization.

Alain Thierstein is Professor of Spatial Planning at TU München. His areas of interest are regional and territorial development, urban and metropolitan development, sustainable regional development, innovation and regional policy, cross-border cooperation and policy evaluation.

Ivan Turok is Professor of Urban Economic Development and Director of Research in the Department of Urban Studies, University of Glasgow. He has researched and written extensively on city and regional economic development, social cohesion, labour markets and urban regeneration, and advised the United Nations, OECD, European Commission and UK government. Ivan led the integrative case studies of Glasgow and Edinburgh under the Economic and Social Research Council's CITIES: Competitiveness and Cohesion Programme. He is the co-author of *The State of English Cities* (2006); *Changing Cities: Rethinking Urban Competitiveness, Cohesion and Governance* (2005); *Twin Track Cities* (2004), *The Jobs Gap in Britain's Cities* (1999) and *The Coherence of EU Regional Policy* (1997).

Michael Wegener was Director of the Institute of Spatial Planning and Professor at the Faculty of Spatial Planning of the University of Dortmund until 2003, and is now a partner in Spiekermann & Wegener, Urban and Regional Research, Dortmund. His main research fields are urban and regional development, European urban systems and trans-European networks. His specialization is urban and regional modelling, in particular of the land-use transport interface in cities and regions and the regional impacts of European transport infrastructure projects and policies.

Introduction[1]

Klaus R. Kunzmann, Willy A. Schmid and
Martina Koll-Schretzenmayr

Information on China and its rapid economic development has grown explosively in recent years. Even before the wide coverage of the Olympic Games' locations and projects, the popular press and visual media were full of reports about developments in China and about Chinese activities in Europe. In particular the spectacular development of architecture and cities in China has raised great interest far beyond that in architectural and planning journals. The popular and specialized business journals are full of features and reports about business development in China, about business opportunities and the huge Chinese market. Advertisements promote business services for enterprises intending to participate in Chinese economic growth or promise higher yields from capital investments in the Chinese financial market. Almost monthly new German–Chinese, French–Chinese or British–Chinese associations are established to accommodate the growing number of individuals and firms wishing to benefit from the huge market. Chinese communities all over Europe are growing. Chinese scientists are much welcomed at European universities and research institutions; and an increasing number of Chinese students, still admiring the image of European institutions of higher education or attracted by generous scholarships from national governments, such as the German government's prestigious Merkel Fellowships, are enrolling in European universities. Even Chinese as a language is booming among European students, who wish to increase their chances in the slowly globalizing job market. Some kindergartens and primary schools have even introduced Chinese classes to meet a demand expressed by parents or growing Chinese communities in European cities. China has become a European passion.

At the turn of the twenty-first century China is an economic global power. Favoured by globalization processes, new information and communication technologies and the logistic revolution, China's economic growth is having an increasing impact on economic development elsewhere in the world, particularly in 'old' Europe. The economic repercussions can be felt and seen at many locations. European port cities (such as Hamburg, Rotterdam, Antwerp and Naples) are handling growing numbers of containers from China and increasing numbers of containers return with sophisticated European products to supply Chinese industries and higher-income upscale consumers. European financial centres

(London, Frankfurt, Paris) are aware of the growing importance of China's role in world finances. European engineers, architects and planners are greatly involved in ambitious Chinese projects. French luxury brands sell well on the Chinese market and French architects are among the winners of this internal European competition for contracts from influential city mayors, who wish to gain eternal fame from fancy urban monuments. European mayors and civic leaders forge twin-city arrangements with Chinese cities to prepare the ground for business co-operation. Local economic development agencies in Europe make great efforts to attract Chinese investment to the metropolitan region in order to participate in the economic success story of the Asian giant. Chinese modern art is experiencing impressive success on the global market. Chinese production complexes are also increasingly thriving in Italy, France, Spain and Romania and even in North Africa. And while Chinese students have discovered Europe as a place to learn, Chinese tourists travelling around Europe in five, seven or ten days, already outnumber Japanese travellers. All this has certainly slowed down as a consequence of the crisis in the global financial system. But it has not come to a standstill.

European response to these changes wavers between cheering the new market opportunities and painting the Chinese peril on the wall, as indeed happened once in a while during the last century. But unless local conflicts are heating up local politics, as in Milan, Naples or Paris, metropolitan regions are either not yet aware of the Chinese challenges or regard them with much serenity. Although Chinese challenges to urban development in Europe may still be negligible, it makes sense for European metropolitan regions to think now about their likely urban implications.

At present it is mainly Chinese low-cost production, both in China itself and in Chinese production clusters in ethnic enclaves in Europe which is alarming labour organizations. However, in the near future other questions will be crucial, such as: Will all of these European industries, now flourishing due to the insatiable Chinese market, continue to do so, or will they be challenged by high-quality Chinese products? Will all the profitable contracts, off which hi-tech industries, such as Airbus, Alsthom or Siemens currently live so comfortably, be phased out? Will the European motor-vehicle industry continue to benefit from exploding mobility in China or will China export cheaper eco-cars to Europe? Will technological advancement and design quality remain the most essential asset of European industries? Will Chinese higher education, research and development make the country fully competitive with European universities within less than a generation? These questions and the answers to them will have implications for economic development and employment in metropolitan regions in Europe, whether they be the locations of the car industry, or, whether they still benefit from local fashion, design or environmental technology clusters. And they will have consequences for employment and quality of life, and, in the end, even for the traditional European model of tamed, socially responsible capitalism.

How should, how could metropolitan regions in Europe face such challenges? Should and can European cities prepare for Chinese investments? Should they wait for social unrest in the rapidly polarizing China after the 2008 Olympics and the flagging of the Asian sandstorm? Or, should they rather strengthen their own local and regional economic circuits in order to become less and less dependent on the global division of labour? Such questions will be elaborated and explored in this compendium.

The future of metropolitan regions in Europe

Globalization, new technologies, international capital flows and global logistics have already had a significant impact on spatial (or territorial) development in Europe. Spatial development in Europe has been influenced by European market-led economic policies, which have clearly promoted the further concentration of economic development processes in metropolitan regions, and indirectly prioritized core areas over peripheral areas and large city-regions over small- and medium-sized cities. Trends of spatial concentration in Europe have additionally been aggravated by demographic change. Europe's population is ageing. Influenced by urbanization, better education and changing values, fertility and reproduction rates are declining. As immigration from regions outside Europe is discouraged, population all over Europe, at least in the decades to come, will stagnate or even further decline, despite the fact that most national governments, although without much success, try to encourage families to have more children, and to find politically and socially accepted solutions to migration.

The trends reported in official EU and most ESPON (European Spatial Planning Observatory Network) documents show that the spatial structure of Europe is changing. While the core regions of the continent continue to grow, rural and peripheral regions, which do not benefit from the positive effects of globalization, are declining. Following the goals and principles of the Lisbon Agenda to maintain Europe's competitiveness against North America and Asia, national governments are concentrating their efforts on strengthening metropolitan regions. Aiming to overcome national boundaries and creating a strong single European market, their efforts are undertaken in the context of most of the EU's and national sectoral policies, such as transportation, innovation and competition.

By and large, spatial development in Europe is characterized by three mega-trends, namely: metropolitan concentration, spatial specialization and fragmentation, and polarization.

Metropolitan concentration

Most economic growth in Europe occurs in metropolitan regions, mainly in the capital city-regions of the 27 member states of the European Union. These metropolitan regions are the hubs of European infrastructure networks and the preferred location of the qualified young, creative and mobile labour. Property markets flourish in these city-regions; their flagship projects and events attract continual media interest. Knowing that it is almost impossible to reverse this trend, public policy-makers opt rather to promote active strategies of metropolitan growth and development in order to strengthen the aspired international competitiveness of their national metropolitan regions.

Spatial specialization and fragmentation

The logic of globalization and economies of scale is causing spatial fragmentation at the European as well as at the national or metropolitan level. The structurally justified division of labour favours the clustering of specialized production and services at selected locations and defines and determines the respective location factors. This results in spatial archipelagos, mono-functional, although globally interwoven enclaves, which are the life and workspaces of people who traditionally reside and work in such 'islands' or who have chosen to live there temporarily. These enclaves comprise the attractive financial centres in core cities, the gentrified former inner-city areas, semi-agricultural suburbs, edge cities and the post-industrial districts of new technopoles or backwater areas.

Polarization

The market-driven economy in the EU is an effective mechanism in fostering sustainable economic growth and is gradually reducing disparities within Europe. The economic gap between the richer and the poorer member states is slowly narrowing down, bringing the former eastern European countries closer to the more affluent member states in western and northern Europe. However, while national disparities between countries diminish slowly, the disparities within countries, regions and cities are increasing almost synchronically. Here, the Lisbon Agenda and EU cohesion jargon clearly contradict each other, while the Gothenburg Agenda seems an effort to disguise political priorities for market-driven neo-liberal policies. There is common belief that such policies tend to increase spatial disparities at the cost of less 'talented' or neglected looser regions. In the end, the promised trickle-down effects may not work and polarization at all spatial levels in Europe will become the unintended – or even the accepted – consequence.

Metropolitan concentration, spatial specialization and fragmentation and spatial polarization are the major spatial consequences of globalization and technological change. The fierce competition for investment, talent and creativity promoted by policy advisors, business consultants, researchers and ambitious city leaders among metropolitan regions in Europe seems to have nurtured a kind of metropolitan 'fever' – a fashionable academic discourse of metropolitan regions. This metropolitan fever has resulted in the emergence of ambitious development projects, ornate architecture and impressive bridges, as well as the establishment of mega-events to attract tourists and media. Promoted by local economic development agencies, who see a chance to maintain existing or even to create new jobs, to find new owners for bankrupt enterprises or investors for various types of brownfield projects, this European metropolitan fever has, combined with the growing interest in China, triggered off a fierce competition for Chinese investment between metropolitan cities. Clearly, no metropolitan region in Europe can neglect the Chinese card.

Chinese challenges for metropolitan city-regions in Europe

The rise of China as a world power and as an economic powerhouse has considerable political and economic implications for the European economy, as well as for all European countries and ones that will penetrate beyond the widely stated consequences of globalization and technological changes. However, the implications for metropolitan regions in Europe are mainly indirect, i.e. they are caused by changing local and regional economies, affecting employment and access to jobs and these changes, obviously, cannot be attributed to developments in China alone. It is rather the magnitude of China-related influences which is causing and accelerating local and regional changes. The resulting challenges for metropolitan development in Europe can be briefly sketched as follows.

Cheaper labour and lack of qualified engineers

The Chinese competition felt most in Europe is primarily a consequence of cheaper production costs in China due to much cheaper labour costs. These huge cost differences force many European enterprises to form joint ventures with Chinese enterprises, to outsource some links in their production chains and to relocate the labour cost-intensive parts of their production to China. There they benefit from low wages, low environmental and social regulation, and additionally gain easy access to the booming Chinese market with hundreds of millions of consumers.

Such developments compel changes in the style of production in European enterprises as mass production is increasingly shifted to China, with negative consequences for the lower-qualified sections of the European workforce, while the demand for higher-qualified labour grows. In Germany, for example, enterprises increasingly bemoan the lack of qualified engineers, while unskilled low-paid workers find it hard to get a job. As a consequence, metropolitan regions aim to attract qualified labour with higher salaries and better urban amenities and by doing so they more or less unconsciously drain peripheral regions of their mobile qualified labour force. This vicious circle is a particular burden for all non-metropolitan regions.

Evolving Chinese production clusters and infringement into urban backwaters

It is little known that an increasing amount of 'Chinese' clothing is actually being produced in Europe. Chinese entrepreneurs in Italy, Spain, Portugal, Romania and Bulgaria run enterprises that produce cheap fashion goods, employing Chinese and other migrant labour on minimum-wage contracts. A place notorious for a concentration of such enterprises is Prato, a small Italian town in the metropolitan region of Florence, where 15,000 Chinese are working and living, legally and illegally. These production areas are in turn linked to inner-urban districts of Rome, Milan, Naples or Catania, and even inner Paris, and represent the focal points of comprehensive logistic chains for wholesale distributors, who deliver their products to small sweatshops all over the continent. Occasionally these enterprises even subcontract single models from international brands, such as Armani or Gucci, and by doing so they learn how to increase their productivity and quality. Eventually, in the longer run, and with perceivable growing wage disparities in Europe, these production clusters may further grow in cheap-labour regions, and render imports from China superfluous. In the longer run, one could imagine that it will be cheaper to produce 'Chinese' textiles in the backwaters of European metropolitan regions than in the Chinese mainland, i.e. nearer to the market and the consumers.

Logistic challenges

Due to the rapidly growing logistic flows between Europe and China, logistic hubs which specialize in European–Chinese linkages have emerged all over Europe. They include the ports of Hamburg, Antwerp, Rotterdam and Le Havre in the north or Naples and Gioa Taouro in the south, which have been successful in attracting a number of European–Chinese businesses. In this way, Hamburg (*Hanbao*) has become the main entry point for goods from China. As a result, since 2005 the city has witnessed a strong interest in the highest take-up of logistics property in Germany and unprecedented levels of investor interest. Occupier demand is emanating from the German logistics operators, who are keen to provide storage and distribution space for the increasing export trade from Germany as well as the growing number of Chinese shipping companies entering the port. As a result the leasing market has seen growth of around 50 per cent with a steady rise in rents. It is estimated that Hamburg is the home of 10,000 Chinese, who live and work there formally and informally. By hosting annual 'China Days', the City of Hamburg demonstrates the importance Chinese–German linkages and co-operation have for the local economy. Likewise in the south of Europe in Italy, demand for warehousing space has surged around the southern Gioa Taouro port where new logistics space is being developed, again as a result of the growing trade with Asia and China.

From all international airports in Europe, the number of non-stop flights from and to China is growing annually. In 2008 German Lufthansa offered 58 flights a week from Frankfurt and Munich to China with Beijing, Shanghai, Shenzhen and Hong Kong as destinations. The international airports of London, Paris and Copenhagen are experiencing similar demand. Aiming to benefit from the booming China-to-Europe flows of goods, a Chinese investor is in the process of acquiring one of the former Soviet military airfields in Parchim in former East Germany, halfway between Berlin and Hamburg, to develop the brownfield site as a logistic centre and offer regular freight connections from Germany to China. Another ambitious project is the aim of the German *Bundesbahn* (German Federal Railways) to modernize the existing railway line between Berlin and Beijing to speed up freight services between Germany and China.

The logistic boom has had considerable repercussions on port cities and port facilities. Both European and Chinese investors express high demands for storage space for outgoing and incoming freight, for storage facilities, and for real estate at strategic port locations. Metropolitan regions with booming ports (such as Hamburg, Rotterdam or Antwerp) are eager to promote their comparative location advantages. There, playing the China card has become an essential dimension of city politics.

Chinese inward investment in Europe

Chinese corporations and investors are currently searching throughout Europe for profitable investments. Wherever they can, they purchase enterprises, which are, for whatever reasons, for sale, and which hold patents for modern technologies. The number of such 'Chinese' enterprises in Europe is growing gradually. This development has become a new challenge for local economic development agencies that have to learn to communicate with such new, foreign owners, who practise different styles of communication.

One particular tale concerns the acquisition of a modern steelworks in Dortmund, Germany, by a Chinese investor. In 2002 Chinese workers came to Dortmund to dismantle the steelworks and prepare its components to be shipped by ocean-going vessels and overland trains to Lian Yun Gang in China, where the steelworks has been rebuilt, and where, since 2006, it has produced quality steel for the Chinese motor vehicle industry. An artificial lake is now under construction on the former site of the steelworks in Dortmund. This lake will be the heart of a totally new middle-class suburb in Dortmund, which is being developed together with a new technology park for creative industries. Without the ambitious and unique Chinese project, the modernization of the city would not have had such an unusual incentive to convert a rundown industrial district into a modern city quarter.

Chinese motor vehicle production and technological advancement

In the long run, the rapid development of Chinese automobile production will become a serious challenge for European cities, where automobiles represent a prime source of revenues, such as Saarlouis, Turin, Sochaux, Antwerp, Ingolstadt, Rüsselsheim (near Frankfurt) or Wolfsburg. Automobile production in China is a priority project of the Chinese government both to help satisfy consumer demand in the country and to modernize Chinese industrial production as a whole. With the growing expansion of production, quality improvement and cheaper labour, together with an abundance of engineers from Chinese or Anglo-American elite universities, the Chinese motor vehicle industry will become a serious threat to European corporations, who with their manifold joint ventures, are key players in the promotion of mobility in China, and the production of cars for a huge national market, and increasingly for export.

There is much speculation about the long-term effects on single European locations. The opinions range from 'no worry' to 'serious threat', depending on geo-political scenarios, on the estimates of future labour costs in both macro-regions and on the price of petroleum. Resource constraints and global warming may force Chinese producers to shift rapidly to energy-saving technologies. Pressed and supported by the government they may be able to offer affordable energy-saving cars on the global market earlier than their European competitors.

The popular belief is that it is mainly cheap labour that is enabling China to flood the world market with cheap products. But this theory that Europe will remain the main provider of high technologies may prove wrong in the medium run. Given the enormous development of high-technology parks and cities all over the country, and the promotion of higher education and research in innovative technologies, China one day, like Japan, may become a leader in selected fields of highly sophisticated machinery and equipment and an equal competitor on the world market.

Chinese tourism. With increasing family income and education, growing numbers of Chinese citizens wish to travel abroad. Europe, obviously, for which travel visas are easier to get, has become a prime target. In recent years Chinese tourist groups have become a popular feature in European cities, following in the footsteps of Japanese tourists, who started to explore European cities during the last quarter of the twentieth century. In contrast to their Asian neighbours, Chinese tourists, as a rule, do not feel comfortable with European cuisine. They prefer to eat Chinese food in Chinese restaurants. Consequently, Chinese restaurants are opening up and flourishing at locations where tourist targets attract visitors from China. With this new generation of visitors, the local character of such locations tends to change.

Implications

All of the above-mentioned 'Chinese' challenges to Europe have one thing in common. They add to the number of Chinese who already live and work in Europe, who send their children to European schools and universities, and attend cultural events, such as concerts or art exhibitions. While schools are of key concern to families, Chinese communities, so far, do not show much interest in getting involved in local political decision-making and participatory processes. While they contribute to a higher visibility of Chinese faces, signs and products in the European environment, their clear focus is on surviving, making money, being successful, getting access to Chinese food and on giving their children a better grounding.

The old image of 'Chinatowns' in London, Liverpool, Amsterdam or Paris, with their Chinese restaurants and specialized food shops, no longer reflects the general dimensions of Chinese visibility in European cities, which has become something new. While the traditional Chinatown tourist spots remain what they were, attractive targets for young city tourists searching for cheap food, the new Chinese economic activities are spread all over cities across Europe and not just in metropolitan regions. The new Chinatowns, as can be seen in Milan, Rome, Naples or Paris, are more like urban quarters where small Chinese wholesalers and stores sell their products together with many related services from real-estate and travel agencies, to hairdressers, authentic restaurants, food shops and dentistry. While property owners may benefit from the renting power of Chinese businesses, local indigenous shops often cannot survive due to the higher rents they have to pay. In such quarters conflicts between local citizens and the new migrants are unavoidable and city governments, as a rule, are not prepared to handle such conflicts. They are just too unfamiliar with the socio-cultural and economic dimensions of changes in such quarters. And, so far, not much research on 'cosmopolitan' local economic development has been done to improve the knowledge base.

China and metropolitan regions in Europe: three scenarios

There are many ways to depict the possible future development of European metropolitan regions within the framework of the European territorial trends as briefly sketched above. Numerous scenarios have been written in the past decade speculating about possible social and economic developments in cities and regions. In the following section of this introduction some speculative deliberations on possible implications of China's rapid economic growth on metropolitan regions in Europe are presented. These speculations are elaborated in the context of three scenarios:

1 *China: After the Olympics* portrays a situation, where political and social developments have considerable repercussions on local economies in Europe.
2 *Slowpark Europe* describes the metropolitan regions of Europe as attractive tourist destinations for myriads of Chinese tourists.
3 *European partnership* illustrates the potential gains from close co-operation between European and Chinese knowledge industries.

However, the most obvious scenario has been omitted. It would sketch in the trends of developments during the last decade. On the one side, the export of technologies, engineering and business services, as well as the export of high-quality consumer products to China will continue, the shift of mass production to the country will increase, although wages in China may also go up. On the other side, Chinese interest in targeted investments in Europe will rise further and co-operation projects between European and Chinese enterprises will become increasingly common, negatively impacting employment opportunities and the European labour market even more seriously.

Scenario one: China after the Olympics

Until the 2008 Olympics in Beijing and the Shanghai Expo 2010 things will go on as usual. No major changes will occur, although there will be more and more internal (social) and external (economic and political) pressure on the Chinese government, i.e. value of the Chinese currency, resource conservation and democracy. Both will contribute to maintaining the present status in order not to alarm the international media. The Tibet issue and the earthquake of 2008 had already raised tensions and shown a new nationalism among proud Chinese communities at home and abroad.

During the second decade of the twenty-first century, things may change. The construction boom will slow down or even come to an end, causing unemployment of casual workers as well as the educated labour force. Very likely, the Chinese economy will lose some of its steam in the 2010s. One outcome could be that the export of luxury goods from Europe to China will fade away, with implications for local economies in those European metropolitan regions, where they are designed, produced, marketed or traded. This will happen once members of the new middle class in China experience a dwindling purchasing power as their salaries are frozen, while food and living costs rise.

Supported by worldwide sympathy (and the vested interests of US institutions) groups from the civil society, students and knowledge workers will articulate their social, ecological and economic concerns, and their dissatisfaction with growing disparities. They will request more social and environmental initiatives and ask the government for more freedom. The reaction of the government is still unpredictable. Most probably, whatever happens, conditions will change. Regulations will either again become tighter to avoid social unrest or the government will remove control and repression, opening the system for new social and political experiments. Both potential reactions will have considerable repercussions for European–Chinese economic co-operation.

Another issue in China with implications for European–Chinese relationships will be the growing shortage of natural resources and the degradation of the environment, whether water provision, air pollution or soil degradation. Unless new resource-conserving technologies soon become available for mass production, these may force the government to restrict motorized private transportation with major implications for car ownership and car use. This in turn will have further effects on metropolitan development and the construction industry and again on related technologies and products imported from Europe. Motor vehicle production clusters in Europe may be affected by such developments as along with locations that had been comfortably relying on the success of their exporting industries or services. Similarly, for various political and financial reasons the number of students and scholars, who were coming to Europe may decline, forcing European universities to review their policies, or, particularly in Britain, to reformulate their business strategies.

There is much evidence in this scenario that development in China will slow down. And where European industries and their forward and backward service linkages relied on and benefited from the rapid economic growth in China, they too will have to adapt to a slower pace.

Scenario two: **Slowpark Europe**

While China and its neighbours in East Asia with their unlimited human resources, have the potential to take over most of the globe's industrial production, particularly mass production, much of Europe's territory may become a kind of a large theme park for history and culture, filled with attractive small and medium-sized cities, 'gown towns' providing excellent post-graduate and post-doctoral education in inspiring environments and attractive landscapes where food and wine is being produced and consumed. *Slowpark Europe*, as it could be called, would become a continent of cultural and creative industries and related educational institutions, a preferred target for cultural tourism and learning holidays. Based on more than 2,000 years of tradition, *Slowpark Europe* is a splendid museum of music, dance, architecture, theatre, the arts and languages. The chance to learn about and experience the related crafts, technologies and cultural activities will motivate Chinese students and scholars to visit Europe.

Assuming that China's economic growth endures and that the Chinese middle class will continue to favour Europe as a territorial location for learning and relaxing, *Slowpark Europe* is a leisure paradise, rich in theme parks, eco-golf ranges and yachting grounds, a landscape of second homes and nature reserves, a safe home for senior citizens, a perfect place for inspiring sabbaticals and academic workshops, a centre for traditional herbal medicine, a breeding ground for rare plants and animals. As 'Eurowood' it also represents a good stage for history movies and soap operas.

Slowpark Europe may continue to be a target for passing holidaymakers or even for those investing in second homes in Italy, France or Sweden. Servicing these target groups will become the main sector of employment. This will have repercussions on qualifications as well as attitudes. Southern European regions, with their long tourist traditions, may benefit more from such developments than the industrial regions of the north. In the end, even agricultural production in Europe may witness an unexpected renaissance, not as the source of the production of biofuel for the Chinese middle class, but of a rich variety of food and wine to be exported to Asia. *Slowpark Europe* is a laboratory for sustainable integrated food systems. A large number of slow cities form a dense network of liveable and walkable cities. The attractive diverse European landscapes are a valuable asset, which have been preserved by quality-conscious and responsible planners and politicians.

With declining export rates, most inhabitants of *Slowpark Europe*, particularly the lower and middle classes, will have to live with slightly lower income levels and lower pensions. The consequence of this, however, will be a reduction in consumer power, which in turn will reduce holiday expenditures and result in less investment in property, cars and luxury goods. Forests and nature parks will expand into areas where population decline has caused the gradual erosion of regional economies and public infrastructure.

Scenario three: China, a partner in Europe

The growing economic and financial power of China will eventually lead to even closer co-operation, mutual exchange and gradual integration of the two economies. One dimension of such integration could be that Europe may become a profitable production site for Chinese corporations, where European and Chinese engineers, scientists and managers co-operate closely. This may be achieved at those locations in Europe where Chinese investors have bought up unprofitable enterprises. Instead of dismantling such enterprises and exploiting their technologies for production in China, they may in the end benefit more from continuous expertise and quality concerns of European labour, once they have decided to continue production in Europe for European markets, just subcontracting the less sensitive parts to Chinese enterprises.

In order to accommodate the interest in producing in Europe, single metropolitan regions may also consider developing special Chinese enterprise zones for Chinese firms, adjacent to technical universities attracting considerable numbers of Chinese engineering students. Such enterprise zones could also accommodate Chinese technology parks, where European and Chinese scientists work together in developing new products for global markets. Even outlets of the huge Chinese technology parks, which already exist in Beijing, Xi'an and Shanghai, may be an option for metropolitan regions in Europe wishing to further strengthen their Chinese profile. For qualified Chinese labour which increasingly shows a growing interest in coming to Europe, this would be an additional incentive. And it would solve the shortage of engineers as continually expressed by the respective industries, in Germany, Switzerland and elsewhere in Europe.

One area where Chinese–European co-operation in technological development may become a future-oriented venture could be the development of energy-saving and zero-emission eco-cars, which are urgently required to protect the environment in the huge Chinese mega-cities, once mobility restrictions materialize. Such cars may in the end be produced in joint ventures at locations, where the European motor industry will suffer due to increasing imports from China.

Another field of Chinese–European scientific co-operation could be the development of efficient and affordable translation software, which may challenge English as the global *lingua franca*. Used in little receivers, like the iPod, such technology, transmitted via (Chinese and European) satellites (similar to the GPS systems) would enable easy communication between partners in native languages, without being forced to take the English detour. In a world were cultural regionalism may be an alternative to an excessively globalized world, such a revolutionary technology would break the hegemony of the Anglophone world and change the world once more.

Policy conclusions

What then can European metropolitan regions do when faced with the challenges sketched above? Can they prepare for the challenges arising from the growing

Chinese presence in European metropolitan cities, from the various real, perceived and mistaken implications of China's economic growth for local economies?

Dealing with the growing manifestation of Chinese presence in Europe requires, first, to acknowledge that the issue goes beyond anecdotal evidence, and to prepare for a better understanding of ongoing cultural, social and economic changes. This needs a much better insight into ongoing local development processes, a better knowledge of cultural differences and competent communication with the single individual of the community or official representatives of the new urbanites from East Asia – how many Mandarin- or Cantonese-speaking professionals, for instance, are currently in European city governments? It also requires careful approaches beyond 'yellow peril' attitudes, as covered so intensively in popular business media. Little research has been done in the past to explore the various dimensions of a growing Chinese presence in European metropolitan regions and the immediate peripheries. The outcome of such research may help to formulate adequate policy responses.

Dealing locally with the negative effects of globalization – and the repercussions of economic and political development in China is one of the facets of globalization – is much more complex. As a rule, metropolitan region governments are limited in what they can do to react to globalization. They can neither halt globalization processes nor can they develop strategies independent from regulations, policies and strategies at upper tiers of government, at national or European level. While anchoring the city(-region) firmly into global networks and integrating their local economies in worldwide trade, commodities, capital and communication flows, they would be well advised to sustain and strengthen their endogenous economic base as much as possible.

The less the local metropolitan economy depends on developments and markets elsewhere, the better this can be for the local economy. Given their larger population potential and a considerable metropolitan consumer power, they have a good chance to balance the relationship between global and local economies and gradually increase the share of local against global markets, by questioning the ultimate rationale of economies-of-scale and division-of-labour rationales, when sustaining local economies and caring for local communities. For instance, just to take two examples: holistic metropolitan policies could strengthen regional food production systems to reduce the dependence on global imports of fish, meat, fruits or vegetables. Obviously, this would require the reinvention of urban agriculture, as well as the promotion of regional food to strengthen local consumer markets; second, promoting local family businesses and limiting the gradual internationalization of shopping precincts could be another metropolitan policy, to strengthen the local embeddedness of shops and shop owners as well as local identity and a regional profile. In the context of metropolitan strategic planning, targets could be set for such policy directions and actions be identified to contribute to their gradual realization. In this way it would also make sense to develop risk-minimizing spatial portfolios to balance local, regional and global concerns and to strengthen higher education and knowledge industries within the metropolis, linked to or even focused on such ambitions.

For some time all the metropolitan regions in Europe have been engaged in a continuous profiling and branding of their locations based on their own local cultural, social and economic potentials. In such a context cultural traditions and urban heritage will gain further importance as economic assets for future urban and regional economic development. In their striving for global media coverage, some metropolitan regions, assisted by trendsetting architectural media and juries, believe that they need the same tourist-attracting flagship projects designed by the celebrated international architects which their urban competitors have already built. While they do not stop preaching the paramount importance of maintaining a local identity, they do not realize that the same stylish international museum, opera or waterfront development – a kind of *Guggenheim-Mania* – has just the opposite effect, as it leads in the end to a kind of globalized uniform cityscape.

Two more ongoing academic and political discourses may help to strengthen endogenous regional development in Europe. First, despite all the academic controversies about the threat of global warming, low-carbon cities have become a new paradigm for city development, driven by the gradual exhaustion of oil reserves and rocketing oil prices, new urban concepts, which discourage individual inner-urban car mobility and favour the return to a mix of land uses are winning increasing political and popular support. This is also a consequence of another ongoing discourse. Second, the fashionable paradigm of the creative city is the perfect motivation to promote re-urbanization, the importance of urban high-density development and mixed land use to accommodate the revival of integrated home-and-work life spaces in metropolitan regions.

However, one thing should be kept in mind: sustainable local employment cannot be achieved with local economic development strategies focusing on broad export initiatives. The global market is too vulnerable to guarantee continuous local economic growth. The scenarios described above have demonstrated that conditions can change daily in the aftermath of geopolitical developments. Europe's metropolitan regions have to remain a life space, where all citizens can enjoy a high quality of life, access to education and lifelong learning, with selected bridges linking the region to the world, which is still a long way off for most Chinese metropolitan regions.

China is certainly no threat to Europe. Through rapid economic growth, the emergence of a multi-million consumer market, and the gradual evolution of innovative knowledge industries, based on Confucian values, China will become a global power, which will force Europe, already labelled as an 'old' Europe to explore new paths to a sustainable future, sustainable in its economic as well as in its ecological, social and cultural meaning. In between the United States in the West and China in the East, Europe and its metropolitan regions will have to develop their own cultural and social approach. The European social model, which is a vision of a society that combines sustainable economic growth with good living and working conditions, has to be sustained. This implies affordable access to education, full employment, good-quality jobs, equal opportunities, affordable housing, social protection for all, social inclusion, and involving citizens in decision-making processes at all tiers of government in Europe. China's economic growth is a warning and a challenge for cities and regions in Europe not to sacrifice that model on the market of globalization. Europe has to play the *European* card in order to maintain its role in the world.

Note

1 This introduction is based on an article published by Klaus R. Kunzmann in *Town Planning Review*, 79(2–3), 2008, pp. 331–46. The authors are most grateful to the publisher, who has given permission to reproduce the article in this compendium.

Part I

China

A challenge for European policy and spatial planning?

1 Pathways towards a new world order

China's challenge to the European Union

John Friedmann

This book is focused on the implications of China's economic rise for the cities and regions of Europe.[1] Many readers will therefore think it odd that I should give a political twist to this topic by introducing the term world order. In my view, Europe lacks coherent meaning except in a political sense, and if you agree with this, then the question immediately presents itself: in the decades ahead, what sort of Union is capable of responding effectively to the multiple challenges that China's emergence as a global power will pose for the world? Although primarily a question for the European Union, it is also, and in a broader sense, a question about the kind of world we need as a political framework for the actions that Europe's cities and regions will have to take if they wish to take up this challenge. A wave of the hand in the direction of globalization is not enough.

Allow me to summarize the gist of this chapter in a few words.

At present, we live in a uni-polar world in which the United States of America is the unchallenged global hegemon. Having no check on its own power, the US sees itself as a law unto itself or, to be more precise, as standing *above* the law of nations. Unchecked, it can and unfortunately does act as it will, intervening in world affairs according to its own understanding of its collective interests.

China's rising economic power is perceived by the global hegemon as a threat to its own unrestricted power, as a competitor for world domination. Projecting into the future, China's growing economic power will inevitably convert into political and military power as well, thus re-creating the bi-polar world that we lived through for the half-century when American confronted Soviet power, and the Cold War was construed as a contest that in the long run only one side could win. It was also a contest that, time and again, brought us to the edge of nuclear Armageddon. In the end, it was the internal collapse of the Soviet Union that led to the uni-polar world of today which, insofar as it is effectively challenged by China, is an unsustainable world order.

But as experience has taught us, a bi-polar world is a dangerous world capable of erupting into a full-scale global war at any time. It follows that a multi-polar world of great powers promises stability. In the foreseeable future, there are only two potential centres of power capable of exercising restraint on the global hegemon and its principal competitor, China. The first is the European

Union, the second is India. With a projected population of 1.5 billion by mid-century, the Indian federation will be the largest country in the world, its economy growing apace, albeit at a slower rate than China's. As a functioning liberal democracy, India is already the world's largest but appears to have little interest in seeking global power. Its primary aim is political stability in South Asia, a region over which its influence extends. India will thus perforce have a key role in helping to shape a new world order geared to peace and prosperity. But in the remainder of my chapter, I will say no more on this subject.

My primary focus here is Europe or, more precisely, the European Union. At the present time, the EU is a hybrid of what are respectively called inter-governmentalism and supra-nationalism. The constitutional project of the EU which would have strengthened its supra-national aspect was rejected by France and Holland in public referenda and has been put on hold, perhaps to be revived some day in a new form. At the moment, therefore, the EU's inter-governmental aspect predominates as it tries to coordinate the economic affairs of its 25 – soon to be 27 – member states. An important economic entity, the EU is a huge potential market for the world. But its economic growth is placid at present, and its energies are currently stretched to the limit by the commitments, including financial ones, to integrate the 12 new member states into the Union and to work towards eliminating the huge economic (and cultural) disparities that character-ize the enlarged Union. Even so, as a prime economic power in the world, the European Union is strategically located to become, if it chooses to play its hand, a third political pole in the world, capable of restraining the remaining world powers while taking its own initiatives.

Another element, however, is still missing for the completion of a multi-polar world-order model. The model I propose is informed by a world-systems per-spective which, following Immanuel Wallerstein, classifies world regions into three categories: core, periphery, and semi-periphery. So far, I have addressed only the question of the three major core regions comprising the global system at present, the US (the global hegemon), China (the principal challenger for global leadership), and the European Union (a potential third force in global politics). But what of the global periphery and semi-periphery, the by-passed and lagging economic regions of the world only tangentially incorporated into the circuits of global capital and without much bargaining power? As we learned during the Cold War era, some of these will fall directly into the spheres of influence of one or another of the two or three core regions of the global system, others (such as certain Middle Eastern and Central Asian countries) will for strategic reasons be more hotly contested.

The world periphery poses a great threat to global stability. Some peripheral countries are recruiting grounds for Islamic jihad warriors (e.g. Yemen, Egypt, Palestine), some erupt from time to time into genocidal madness (Rwanda, Liberia, Kampuchea), some are governed by corrupt authoritarian, even tyranni-cal regimes (North Korea, Myanmar, Zimbabwe), some, as regions within nation states, engage in long-term secessionist, often violent struggles (southern Sudan, the Tamil Tigers of Sri Lanka, Kosovo), some revert to atavistic systems of governance and become what are known as failed states (Somalia, Afghanistan). Collectively, the world periphery is the primary source of the illicit global trade in arms, drugs, and people which flourishes whenever world order breaks down.

To avert these outcomes, some means must be found to give an effective voice to the billions of people who are condemned to live under conditions of peripheral disorder. Their voices can be heard effectively only within the framework of the United Nations and its multiple agencies for health, education, human rights, development, food and agriculture, peacekeeping missions, and so forth. Although the United Nations is a weak organization at present, it is also an absolutely essential institution for a just, peaceful, sustainable world. To turn it into a more effective instrument of global governance, it will need to be greatly strengthened. But this topic goes beyond the present essay and will have to be addressed on another occasion.

In the remainder of these brief remarks, I propose, first, to sketch a scenario in which China attains its position as a global power by mid-century. Second, I want to suggest some propositions about the European Union and what it needs to do in order to become something more than a multinational market characterized by a common currency, customs union, an integrated transport system, unhampered movements of labour across national frontiers, and so forth. Europe is, of course, already something more than a common market. Its Copenhagen accession criteria (1993) give a good sense of what this 'more' consists of. A country wishing to join the European Union must, first of all, be located *in* Europe. Once this is established – and where the boundaries of Europe are drawn is ultimately a political decision – the following additional criteria must be satisfied:

- stability of the institutions guaranteeing democracy, the primacy of law, respect for human rights, as well as the respect for and protection of minorities;
- the existence of a viable market economy, the ability to withstand competitive pressure and market forces in the internal market of the Union;
- the ability of the applicant country to accept its obligations as a member of the Union and to implement the Community rights and obligations in its national legislation.

All of these criteria, and the actual institutions through which they are implemented concern matters that are *internal* to the Union. They tell us nothing about the EU's possible political role in global politics, including the United Nations which, as its name suggests, is composed of nations ranging in size from a few tens of thousands to more than 1.3 billion people, each of which claims at least nominal sovereignty. My comments will therefore be primarily concerned with Europe's role as a potential 'super-power' in the world rather than with its internal policies though, of course, the two questions are interrelated.

Finally, I will address some of the issues with which we are chiefly concerned: the challenge of China's rise to Europe's cities and regions. But I will do so in the context of my multi-polar world-order model.

I turn now very briefly to consider the question of the extent to which China's challenge as a global power should be taken seriously.

The challenger: China as a global power?

Most commentators on reform-era China are bedazzled by the sustained high economic growth rates over the past 20-odd years and the country's capacity to supply much of the world's manufactured goods. But does becoming the world's Number One export platform translate, willy-nilly, into global power? Actually, more than half of China's exports are now produced by foreign-owned firms, and a large proportion of these exports is in assembly trade in which foreign firms import components for final assembly into products that are later re-exported (Dullien 2005: 126). Assembly manufacturing is, in the language of economists, efficiency seeking, and as the price of local labour rises relative to other countries, firms are likely to shift their operations elsewhere. This may well be the fate of many of China's FDI-financed firms (ibid.).[2] Consequently, it may be reasonable to ask whether China's 'economic miracle' can be sustained over the longer term, and further, whether the country's *political* stability is secure.

Unfortunately, to answer such questions is to juggle contingencies that cannot be foreseen, and subjective judgments will not only bias any prognosis but may turn out to be wrong. Still, some informed judgments must be made, if only as scenarios. Sebastian Dullien's answer is that any foreign-capital flight may well be replaced by what he calls *market-seeking* enterprise, that is investments that stake their fortune on opening up China's *domestic* markets. In line with this expectation, he suggests a series of policy measures to ensure that such a turn in the application of foreign capital would come to represent a net gain for China's economic growth (Dullien 2005).

Dullien's focus is quite limited, however, especially when we consider that in 2001, foreign direct investments in China constituted only a shade over 10 per cent of fixed capital formation with the remainder coming from domestic savings and loans (ibid.: Figure 1).[3] A broader analysis is therefore necessary to answer my initial question: what is the likelihood that China's long-desired quest for global power will succeed?

I will proceed as follows. First, I want to take a quick look at China's relative position in East Asia, particularly with regard to demographics and its implications. Second, I will review China's development goals as revealed in recent policy statements, commenting on their feasibility. Third, I will identify what I regard as the People's Republic of China (PRC)'s Achilles heel in pursuing its goals over the next half-century, suggesting that sustained economic growth in a socialist market economy also requires political changes which, if they are not forthcoming, may seriously disrupt the long-term scenario of successful modernization and global power.

The United Nations' long-term population projections portray what in many ways is a troubling scenario (United Nations 2006). China's future population is shown to be levelling off, rising only slightly over current levels by mid-century, or from 1.3 to 1.4 billion.[4] In sharp contrast to this, Japan's population is projected to decline from 128 to 112 million over the same period, the *combined* population of the two Koreas to fall from 70 to 68 million, and the Russian Federation to suffer a precipitous drop from 143 to 111 million, all this against a median projected *increase* in world population of 2.5 billion, *with most of this growth concentrated in the global periphery*, the group of countries and regions that is the principal source of world disorder today. To me these numbers suggest, first, that by 2050 the global periphery will continue to be mired in poverty; second, that the Russian Federation and Japan are rapidly aging societies, their energy directed more to preserving what they have rather than to playing leading and always risky roles in global policy; and third, that the sheer bulk of China's demographic profile which, despite its continuing one child-per-family policy, is still a relatively young though maturing population, suggests a society prepared to vigorously assert itself in world affairs.

I turn now to consider China's current policy objectives. My sources here are a recent authoritative essay by Bi Jiyao, Deputy Director of the Institute for International Economic Research under the National Development and Reform Commission of the PRC (Bi 2005) and the 'CCP Central Committee Proposal on the 11th Five-Year Programme on National Economy and Social Development' approved by the Fifth Plenum of the 16th CCPCC on 11 October 2005 (CCP Central Committee 2006).

Bi Jiyao refers to China's 'new concept for development [which] gives priority to human development [the "people first principle"], emphasizes environmental and socially sustainable development, and insists on an overall and coordinated development of the economy, society and its people' (Bi 2005: 112). Within this general framework, China expects to quadruple its nominal 2000 GDP level from US$1.2 to 4.8 trillion and triple income per capita from $940 to a nominal $3,000,[5] achievement of these goals would place China among the middle-income developing countries as currently classified by the World Bank. The point of all these numbers is to illustrate the determination of the PRC government to continue promoting a steady 7 per cent plus growth rate up to at least 2020 and, it is safe to assume, a declining but still accelerated rate thereafter. In short, as an integrated nation state, China is set to break out of its peripheral economic status and reach developed-country status within the next two generations.

To attain this goal for one-fifth of the world's population, China, according to official policy, needs to rebalance its development along five dimensions. They are: (1) the relation between urban and rural development to ensure the proportionate development of the latter, (2) equitable growth of the country's macro-regions to ensure the proportionate development of China's western and northeastern regions, (3) the relationship between humans and nature to ensure sustainability,[6] (4) the relationship between an economy driven by participation in the global economy and the expansion of internal markets,[7] and (5) the relationship between economic and social development by accelerating social development in all its aspects[8] (ibid.: 115–18). The sense expressed in these 'balances' points to the need continually to assess ongoing developments and to rebalance their dynamic relationships. I believe that the Chinese state has demonstrated that it possesses the requisite steering capacity to guide national development successfully through the dangerous shoals of modernization.[9]

It is nevertheless important to acknowledge that China's march towards the future has an Achilles heel that renders the country vulnerable to serious disruption of its quest.[10] I call it the *disarticulation of China's political class from the people*, that is to say, the growing distance between the perceptions of the political class as it monitors the country's development and the sentiments, hopes, fears, and aspirations of its citizens, especially those residing in rural areas.

There is empirical evidence, I would argue, that this distancing (though perhaps not yet complete disarticulation) is already taking place, partially rooted in the Party-state's fear that granting more autonomy to a nascent civil society is to invite social 'chaos'. I refer here, for instance, to the growing numbers of civil-unrest episodes which, in a recent count, have risen to a reported 86,000 and have often been handled with considerable lack of sensitivity by public security forces (to put it mildly), resulting in the arrest, beatings, and even the death of many participants regardless of the merits of their grievances.

Political leaders' outdated understanding of the people not as rights-bearing citizens but as the homogenized 'masses' who must be led towards a brighter future by the clear-headed modernizers of the CCP is another indicator of this 'distancing'. In the recent CCP Central Committee policy statement on the 11th Five-Year Plan there is repeated mention of the 'masses' and the need for 'social management', as for instance in this passage:

> To build a harmonious socialist society, it is imperative to strengthen social construction, perfect the social management system, and strengthen the social management order featuring leadership by party commitments, responsibility by government, co-ordination in society, and public participation. It is necessary to properly handle the relationships among different interests and earnestly resolve issues involving interests of the greatest concern and practical significance to the masses, by focusing on expanding employment....
>
> (CCP Central Committee 2006: 258)

Or in the following excerpt:

> It is necessary to strengthen the comprehensive management of social order, continue to push forward the construction of a prevention and control system for social order, intensively to carry out activities aimed at creating models in maintaining peace and order, crack down hard on various crimes in accordance with the law, preserve national security and social stability, and ensure that the masses live and work in peace and contentment.
>
> (ibid.)

Similar stilted language – a language indicative of a frame of mind – is found in subsequent pages which suggests little inclination to open up new spaces of democracy beyond already existing institutions (village elections, people's congresses, urban residents' committees). It is of course conceivable that the Party's understanding of itself and its relation to an emerging civil society and to such fundamental civil rights as freedom of speech and assembly will undergo further changes over the course of the next few years. At present, however, there is little evidence of an impending democratic transition. The danger of disarticulation therefore persists and is likely to grow more serious.

A comprehensive positive assessment of China's prospects for global power must therefore be tempered by some words of caution. If modernization is to go forward in a relatively open economy, it will have to make room for a more active civil society or, to put it another way, for the greater articulation between Party-state and what we can expect to be an increasingly assertive civil society, with more autonomy granted to the latter as well as to already existing political institutions such as the National People's Congress and its affiliates at the provincial, municipal, and district levels.[11]

Given this scenario, what challenges does China's emergence as a global power and its inevitable challenge to American hegemony bode for the European Union and, within that context, for Europe's cities and regions? It is to a consideration of this question that I now turn.

As I argued in the introduction to this essay, my aim here is to explore the possibilities of a multi-polar world beyond expected bi-polar tensions between the US and China, with particular emphasis on the potential role of Europe. But progress towards a new world order would involve not only this but two major structural changes. The first, of course, is the ability and willingness of the European Union to assume the leadership role of a third power block, thus avoiding the likelihood of another 'cold war' era punctuated by localized 'hot wars' in regions of competition over global resources, such as Iraq. The second is to work assiduously with the countries and regions of the global periphery to give them a vital stake in global prosperity. This second structural transformation to enable a new world order goes beyond the scope of the present discussion. But initial steps towards a solution of the first problem should be regarded as a precondition for making substantial progress on the second.

What role for Europe in the coming world order?

The European Union has gradually evolved from a trade body into an economic and political partnership of 25 states, soon to be further enlarged with the accession of Romania and Bulgaria. If one thinks of the Union as a single political entity, its dimensions are indeed impressive: at nearly four million square kilometres, it is the seventh largest trading area in the world; its combined population of 460 million ranks third after China and India; its GDP of $12.3 trillion represents a fifth of the GWP (gross world product); and its per capita income of $26,900 is a shade higher than America's.

These overall dimensions are not very meaningful, however, and as an organization of nation states, the EU has many weaknesses, especially when we think of its capacity to further evolve into a third mega-power, a counterweight to China and the United States. Despite its Parliament, the EU is in no sense a state but a *sui generis* political entity, the joint product of realist inter-governmental diplomacy and idealist supra-nationalist aspirations, whose two dozen plus states continue jealously to guard their individual sovereignties.[12] Evolving out of the former Common Market and formally established in 1992, the EU has grown fast and now consists of three so-called pillars: economic cooperation, primarily a supra-national institution; a Common Foreign and Security Policy; and Judicial Cooperation in Criminal Matters. The latter two, however, are no more than loose inter-governmental arrangements with relatively little power. The constitutional treaty which was to merge this tripartite division into a single coordinated body, though approved by 13 member states in 2005, was badly defeated in public referenda in both France and the Netherlands and is currently on hold. But more on this later.

As a family of nation states, member countries display an extraordinary diversity, on a scale perhaps equalled or surpassed by that of India. There are 20 official languages in the EU along with three working languages (English, French, German). And even though Christianity continues to be the dominant religious orientation, it comes in many variants, such as Roman Catholic, Lutheran, Anglican, Methodist, Baptist, Orthodox Christian, Mormons, and dozens of others. Of late, large numbers of Muslims (again of various persuasions) have moved to Europe and their numbers would swell if Turkey and Bosnia-Herzegovina were to become full EU members in the future as has been proposed. In economic size, Europe is dominated by five countries: Germany, the UK, France, Italy, and Spain, with Poland, which occupies sixth rank, having a GDP that is only half of Spain's and one-fifth of Germany's (measured in PPP dollars that adjust nominal dollar amounts to the cost of living in each country).

Furthermore, there is a steep income gradient that runs generally from west to east and from north to south, measured in PPP dollars, with Ireland's per capita income of $43,000 on the one hand and Latvia's $8,400 on the other, a ratio of roughly 1 to 4.[13] Similarly, comparing Denmark and Greece, the income gradient runs from $36,000 to $23,500, north to south. In short, huge regional inequalities are built into the recently expanded Union, inequalities that will take decades to even out. On the positive side, low-income countries in Europe have registered more rapid income growth on average than the Union's 2005 unimpressive rate of 1.5 per cent, though this can be misleading. Poland's economy, for example, has surged ahead in recent years, but its unemployment is still at 17 per cent of the labour force, almost double the EU's average of 9 per cent. Finally, although the euro has gained on the US dollar since its inception, it is the accepted currency in only 12 countries, competing with 13 national currencies in circulation, notably the pound sterling.

The very idea of a united Europe is hotly contested. Many Britons, for example, have little confidence in a continental alliance, preferring the UK's historical links with Anglo-America. As Euro-sceptics, they are joined by the Poles and Czechs, among others. Norwegians and perhaps unsurprisingly also the quintessential go-it-alone Swiss have stayed out of political Europe altogether, while maintaining close economic ties with the EU. France and Germany have been the standard bearers of a Euro-centric alliance, which is why the rejection of the constitutional treaty by French voters came as a shock to the country's political class. And when it comes to the question of enlarging the European Union to the east and south, the very idea of 'Europe' becomes at best a fuzzy one. As a schoolboy in Austria, I was told that Europe ends at the Ural Mountains, but if we include only whole countries, such as the Russian Federation, 'Europe' would nominally extend from Dublin to Vladivostok on the Pacific Ocean! And then, what about Turkey, which for some time now has insistently been knocking on Europe's door? And if Turkey should be admitted one day, would it be outrageous to consider Israel and perhaps Lebanon as worthy candidates for EU membership? In the end, as I said earlier, Europe is a political, not a geographic concept, and as a political concept, it will always be open to contestation.

One of the debates about the European Union as a political entity concerns its military presence. The draft constitutional treaty foresaw a small strike-force for rapid deployment in so-called peacekeeping and similar missions. But this modest militarization, which would have little strategic value in a potential crisis, is possible only so long as NATO provides the necessary security shield for Europe. But NATO is arguably a tool of American power: its military operations are firmly under American command. It comes as no surprise, therefore, that when the US government decided to invade Afghanistan supposedly as punishment for not handing over Osama Bin Laden as the world's number-one terrorist, that NATO forces rallied behind the Americans and sent battle troops to that distant, inhospitable land. NATO forces also got involved in the air war against Serbia, again under American command, to force that country to desist from its invasion of Kosovo. In short, NATO is not, *sensu stricto*, a military arm of the European Union but rather of the hegemonic power and its European and North American allies, including, among others, Germany, Canada, and France.[14]

Europe, in short, is seriously divided on the question of its own future. These divisions are nowhere more evident than in a political analysis of the defeat of the constitutional treaty in France and the Netherlands, and of the current positions on the steps which should be taken next. In a cool-headed policy analysis by Ettore Greco, 'And Yet It Moves: The European Constitutional Debate One Year Later', these positions are clearly identified.[15] I have briefly summarized them in the following.

1   Proceeding pragmatically with a focus on economic reforms (e.g. Tony Blair).
2   Abandoning the goal of an ever closer Union and to return to 'intergovernmentalism' as the *modus vivendi* (e.g. Václav Klaus, President of the Czech Republic, Lech Kaczyński, President of Poland).

3   Saving the constitutional treaty in its entirety (Austria, Belgium, Germany, Italy, Luxembourg, Spain – all of which approved the treaty, Spanish voters with an impressive majority of 77 per cent).
4   Pushing for the informal application of parts of the treaty (e.g. Jacques Chirac and Dominique de Villepin).
5   Renegotiating the treaty and to resubmit it to a vote, possibly in a greatly slimmed down version (this position is supported in several public opinion polls).
6   Working on the consolidation of a core group of integrationist countries (e.g. the 12 countries that have accepted the European currency).

Greco's own view is that a renegotiation of the text of the constitutional treaty is inevitable. A shorter text, he argues, would be more comprehensible to ordinary citizens, but could incorporate the bulk of the institutional innovations envisaged in the constitutional treaty as well as the charter of fundamental rights. He hopes that the countries that have already ratified the treaty will launch a common initiative soon and reactivate the diplomatic process of institutional reform.

Steps towards a more united Europe

Europe's future lies in the balance. It can reject the road to greater unity, returning to a Europe of nation states that live under the umbrella of American military might and will thus inevitably be drawn into an American–Chinese conflict one or two decades from now, or it can choose a road that will enable Europe to gain an independent voice in foreign policy capable of exercising restraint on American power and helping to bring about a more stable world order. There is no way of knowing which way Europe will turn, though I remain cautiously optimistic. But assuming that the EU will opt for greater unity rather than less, and therefore assuming something along the lines of the positive scenario suggested by Greco, what should the European Union do now, once it has adopted a revised constitutional treaty? The sources of Europe's present weakness will not be easily resolved, but they can be resolved over time, thus creating the preconditions for a foreign policy independent of America's.

It is quite clear in my mind that a strong Union requires a moratorium on further territorial expansion. The 12 new members, soon to be 14, need to be properly integrated into a Europe whose geographic bulk lies to the west, physically through transport and communication links, economically through a new territorial division of labour, and culturally through the gradual discovery of a common European identity over and above traditional national identities. Integrating the new member states must become the over-arching European project over the next several decades. Meanwhile, China needs to be engaged. I will therefore offer a few ideas about how this might be done.

Engaging China

Beyond expanding economic relations, there are principally three policy areas for strengthening relations with China that will help the European Union to nudge China towards a more stable world order even as the PRC struggles with its own enormous problems. They are cultural exchange, scientific collaboration, and a strengthened role for cities and regions in the development of both China and Europe. I will conclude with a few words on each of these.

Cultural exchange is perhaps the most important of the three, because mutual engagement requires a deep cultural understanding of the respective societies.

The intensive study of Chinese language, culture, and history must be further and better incorporated into European schools and universities, and this will require funding programmes to enable students to travel in both directions, learning about Europe and China at first hand and thus, one may hope, enhancing mutual understanding. European students need exposure to the diversities of Chinese reality, and vice versa. Promoting the study of the Union's three official languages in China, and teaching a primer on the European Union in future European cultural centres located in some of China's major cities would be an aspect of this exchange. The model I have in mind are the branches of the Goethe Institute and the Alliance Française which are successfully maintained in many of the world's major cities. China should, of course, be encouraged to establish similar cultural centres in Europe.[16]

Scientific collaboration could represent a second approach in this multistranded effort to weave the fabric of Sino–European relations. This could be done through various already existing research institutes, or through new institutes focusing on global concerns particularly in the environmental area, with an emphasis on alternative energy sources, and/or specific environmental problems (water, sustainable energy, desertification, forest management, etc.) which are of special interest to China.

The third and last pathway to the future concerns the role of cities and regions in a project of 'engaging China'. Cities articulate regional economies with the global.[17] Continuing a medieval tradition, European municipal governments are elected bodies but have only limited powers and financial resources. If the European Union should adopt a revised constitutional treaty, an expected result of further centralization at the European level would be a general expansion of municipal and/or regional powers (Brenner 2004). Within the framework of the European Union, both cities and regions will compete against each other for a share of global capital markets, but they will compete unequally. For many years to come, Western city-regions will outperform those in the East. In addition to intercity competition, we can also expect the appearance of *intercity networks* both within the Union itself and beyond its boundaries, particularly with their active trading partners (Brenner 2004: 286–94).

It is in this context that European city-regions would be well advised to engage their Chinese counterparts, similarly concerned with their own future under conditions of continuing modernization. Opportunities can be created for specific joint undertakings, based on the comparative advantage of one or the other city. A striking example of such a project is the extended partnership between Zurich and the capital of Yunnan Province, Kunming.[18] Evolving gradually over a period of more than 20 years, a key role was played by the ETH Zurich (Swiss Federal Institute of Technology) in an advisory capacity on transport planning and urban heritage conservation. According to the authors,

> The current achievements rely very heavily on the relationship of trust between experts and public officials from the twinned cities, as well as on study trips organized for decision-makers to European cities.... Due to shared experiences on the same city level collaboration with specialists on both sides has proved to be a very successful approach.
>
> (Feiner *et al.* 2002: 67)

Overall, the project has forged new links between two major cities of Europe and China, links that can be expected to yield positive results for its participants beyond the concrete achievements in transport management and heritage conservation. To my mind this experience is worthy of further study and could well be used as a model for similar ventures between city-regions in the EU and Chinese partner cities. Such ventures, for example, on sustainability issues, undertaken in the same spirit of mutual learning, would help to strengthen relations between Europe and China, recovering a millenial trading relationship between these two poles of the Eurasian continent (Frank 1998).

Notes

1 I have not attempted to update my information on both China and the European Union from what was available to me in 2006. The precise numbers that I cite have changed for example with the enlargement of the EU following accession of Romania and Bulgaria in 2007, but the overall picture I draw of both entities is essentially unchanged as of mid-October 2008 when final revisions were made to this text.
2 The 'elsewhere' doesn't need to be in other platform countries with lower wage costs; it may also be in one of China's interior provinces.
3 Its peak was reached in 1994 when FDI's share of capital formation stood at around 17 per cent. Since then, the percentage share has steadily declined.
4 According to the State Council's 'White Paper on Population' (2000), the government will seek to hold mid-century population to 1.6 billion, with population declining thereafter. See www.cpirc.org.cn/en/whitepaper.htm (accessed 8 July 2006).
5 China's per capita income in 2004, reckoned in PPP dollars was 7,600 which is 4.4 times higher than its nominal value of over $1,700. The PRC's Human Development Index ranks 85 out of 177 countries. Its corruption perception index of 3.2 (out of a possible 10) is also about middling, ranking 78th out of 158 countries surveyed (see the Transparency International website for 2005).
6

> In order to achieve coordinated development between the economy, society, population, resources and the environment, China needs to live its economic growth efficiently: to advocate healthy lifestyles and consumption behaviour, actively engage in economizing resources and strengthen ecosystems construction and environmental protection so as to increase the potential for a sustainable development.
>
> (Bi 2005: 117)

7

By fully participating in globalization, China will not only continue to take in foreign capital, advanced technology, as well as expertise to develop hi-tech industry and transform traditional industry. China will also go abroad to expand regional economic cooperation and tap international markets and resources.

(ibid.)

8

Compared with its economic development, China has lagged behind in the reform and development of education, science and technology, public health care, social security system, and the people. In comprehensibly building a prosperous society, it is imperative for China to accelerate social development in all its aspects.

(ibid.: 116)

9 This conclusion is not universally shared. In a recent article by Jude Howell (2006), for example, the author takes pains to show the many ways the Chinese central state has failed in its endeavour to guide national development. Comparing the PRC to Japan, South Korea, and Taiwan, she finds that rather than being a 'developmental' state firmly in charge, the Chinese state is 'polymorphous'. To put her conclusion more colloquially, Beijing is losing its grip on the economy and lacks the capacity to rebalance the country along any of the five dimensions to which it aspires.

10 China's environmental problems are another potential source of disruption but their impact is more difficult to assess. See Lo and Xing 1999; Ho and Vermeer 2006.

11 Another danger on the 'long march' of China's modernization is the harsh words reserved in the CCP prolegomenon to the 11th Five-Year Plan for Taiwan's ambition to 'declare its independence.' At the time of writing (July 2006), there appears to be no immediate danger that the PRC will employ force to bring Taiwan into its orbit. It is conceivable, however, that under certain conditions cross-straits violence will erupt, not for any 'rational' reasons, but because of 'irrational passions' capable of being aroused by events that no one can now foresee and which would inevitably draw the US and perhaps other countries (Japan?) into a major East Asian conflict.

12 In legal terms, member states remain the 'master of treaties' in the sense that the Union does not have power to transfer *additional* powers from states unto itself without their agreement through further international treaties.

13 With approximately $10,000 each, Romania and Bulgaria have lower per capita incomes than even Poland.

14 For basic information on the history of NATO, see the wikipedia website.

15 See www.brookings.edu/fp/cuse/analysis/greco20060427.pdf (accessed 14 May 2006). Greco is Deputy Director of the Institute of International Affairs in Rome.

16 According to the *Frankfurter Allgemeine Zeitung* (FAZ 2006), China has opened 60 Confucius Institutes since 2004 worldwide for the study of the Chinese language as well as workshops on calligraphy, lectures, and other events. This number is expected to rise to 100 in the near future. In addition, China is establishing cultural centres (*Kulturzentren*) in a number of major metropolises, including one in Berlin that is expected to cost €93 million.

17 Some European city-regions are virtual city-states, such as Barcelona/Catalunya, Dublin/Ireland, Riga/Latvia, Malta, Luxembourg, Prague/Czech Republic, among others.

18 For a detailed account of its history, see Jacques P. Feiner *et al.* (2002) 'Priming Sustainability: The Kunming Urban Region', *DISP*, 151: 59–67, accessed at NSL Network City and Landscape: DISP-Online, 16 May 2006. See also Carl Fingerhut and Ernst Joos (eds) (2002) *The Kunming Project: Urban Development in China*, Basel and Boston: Birkhäuser.

References

Bi, J. (2005) 'China's New Concept for Development', in United Nations Conference on Trade and Development (ed.) *China in a Globalizing World*, New York and Geneva: United Nations: 105–24.

Brenner, N. (2004) *New State Spaces: Urban Governance and the Rescaling of Statehood*, Oxford: University Press.

CCP Central Committee (2006) 'Proposal on Formulating the 11th Five-Year Programme for National Economic and Social Development', *China Quarterly*, 185 (March): 243–63.

Dullien, S. (2005) 'FDI in China: Trends and Macroeconomic Challenges', in United Nations Conference on Trade and Development (ed.) *China in a Globalizing World*, New York and Geneva: United Nations: 125–54.

FAZ (2006) 'Offensiv: Welches Bild von China zeigen Pekings Konfuzius-Institute?', *FAZ* Issue, 13 July 2006.

Feiner, J. P., Salmeròn, D., Joos, E., and Schmid, W. A. (2002) 'Priming Sustainability: The Kunming Urban Region', *DISP*, 151: 59–67, accessed at NSL Network City and Landscape: DISP-Online (accessed 16 May 2006).

Fingerhut, C. and Joos, E. (eds) (2002) *The Kunming Project: Urban Development in China*, Basel and Boston: Birkhäuser.

Frank, A. G. (1998) *ReOrient: Global Economy in the Asian Age*, Berkeley: University of California Press.

Greco, E. (2006) 'And Yet It Moves: The European Constitutional Debate One Year Later', available at www.brookings.edu/fp/cuse/analysis/greco20060427.pdf (accessed 3 October 2008).

Ho, P. and Vermeer, Eduard, E. B. (eds) (2006) 'China's Limits to Growth: Greening State and Society', special issue, *Development and Change*, 37(1): 255–71.

Howell, J. (2006) 'Reflections on the Chinese State', *Development and Change*, 37(3): 273–98.

Lo, Fu-chen and Yi-qing Xing (eds) (1999) *China's Sustainable Development Framework: Summary Report*, Tokyo: United Nations University/Institute of Advanced Studies.

State Council (2000) 'White Paper on Population', available at www.cpirc.org.cn/en/whitepaper.htm (accessed 8 July 2006).

United Nations (2006) *World Population 2004* (wall chart), New York: United Nations, Department of Economic and Social Affairs, Population Division.

2 The impact of China's development

Is there a need to alter land-use and transport policy in Europe?

Herbert Kemming

Introduction

Raising awareness of the global impact of the developments in China

Thinking, and worrying about, the impact that the rapid developments in China will have on the global environment and the global economy is not new. In the field of transport, environmental NGOs as well as researchers and others have previously warned against the fast increase of motorization in China and have asked for new strategies for the automobile industry and for transport policy in the developed countries as well. The main idea was that if developed countries pursued a path of development that recognized the environmental need to avoid global warming and could show that this strategy would be economically successful, the threshold countries would accept such a path and would follow.

These warnings did not yet have consequences for the behaviour and strategies of the most important stakeholders – industry and policy-makers. Therefore, the initiative to organize an international conference on the topic of the consequences that Chinese development would have for Europe was an excellent idea for promoting discussion on this issue. Here in Europe we often think about global consequences, such as global warming, but this topic remains rather abstract. Very often, we have the feeling that rich countries are able to handle the problems and avoid the impact of global effects on their own country. By and by it becomes clearer that global warming will affect all countries, even the rich ones, and that the developments in China will change the global markets for raw materials, energy, etc., and simultaneously the development of other threshold countries (www.sternreview.org.uk (accessed 3 October 2008)); UNEP 2007: iiif., 2f.; Steiner 2007: 1ff.).

The economic boom in China and resulting problems

The economic growth in China is without precedent. Over the last 15 years, the growth rate was about 9 per cent a year (see Figure 2.1). With regard to the economic growth, experts have called the twenty-first century the 'Chinese century' (Eberl 2004: 14).

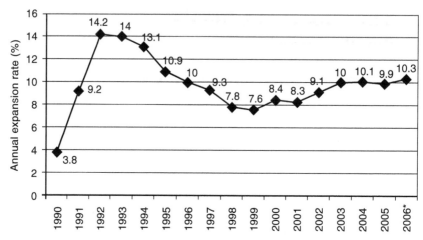

Figure 2.1 Chinese gross domestic product (*1st quarter of 2006) (source: www.stats. gov.cn (accessed 3 October 2008), bpb 2006: 19).

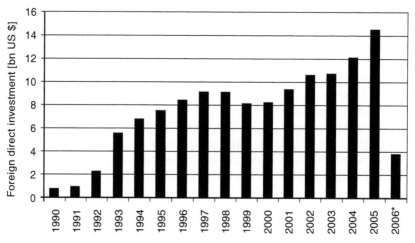

Figure 2.2 Chinese foreign direct investment (*January–April) (source: www.stats.gov. cn (accessed 3 October 2008)).

The main factors of this development are a cheap workforce and a growing domestic market; these factors make China a highly attractive target for direct foreign investment (see Figure 2.2), e.g. direct investments in 2004 represented 8 per cent of worldwide investments (Sieren 2005: 14).

The export surplus in 2005 added up to US$32 billion, despite the high imports of raw material (Sieren 2005: 14). The structural change of the Chinese economy is a success but also a burden. The share of agriculture in domestic income decreased from 31 per cent in 1990 to 15 per cent in 2004 (bpb 2006:

12). Simultaneously, many farm workers lost their jobs. Many people moved from the rural areas to urban areas, primarily in eastern China (Böhn 2005: 7).

A challenge to solve manifold problems simultaneously

One negative side of the dynamic economic development is environmental damage. In general, there are the same problems as in every developing country. But the Chinese development is unique: China is the world's most populous nation and rapid development means that all problems arise simultaneously. Air pollution is one of the biggest problems. According to the World Bank, 16 of the 20 most polluted cities in the world are in China (Sieren 2005: 32, referring to the World Bank). One main factor is the use of dirty and sulphurous domestic coal. Another problem is the severe lack of water. Estimates say that the economic loss resulted from environmental damage is about 8 per cent a year (Vorholz 2005: 73), about equal to the growth rate of the economy.

A second main problem is the limited energy supply. Even today, China has to import 60 per cent of its energy needs. In 2005, China consumed 250 million tons of oil, 8 per cent of the world market, and was thus the second largest consumer in the world (bpb 2006: 14). And China's demand will continue to increase rapidly.

A third main problem is the East–West divide. For more than 20 years, the state has allowed inhabitants of the rural areas to move into the cities. Cheap artisans, dealers and migrant workers were the basis for the fast development into a private economy in the agglomerations. The rural areas did not gain much from this economic development. The average income in rural areas in 2004 was €283 and in urban areas €908 (bpb 2006: 35).

Global impact of China's development

The analysis of the need for action by European stakeholders will focus on three effects of China's development: global warming, shortage of energy resources and rising energy prices. Currently, the increase in energy consumption and CO_2 emissions is dominated by burning coal. In future, oil consumption and its respective CO_2 emissions will take a higher and higher share because of increasing individual motorized transport.

Global warming

At this stage, China is the second largest source of carbon dioxide emissions in the world (see Figure 2.3).

Looking at the stationary sources of CO_2 China turned out to be one of the three biggest global CO_2 emitters in the world, after the US and Europe. Within the time period from 1990 to 2000, China had the largest increase of CO_2 emissions in the world, caused primarily by road transport (see Figure 2.4).

Currently, the motorization level (i.e. car density) in China is still rather low

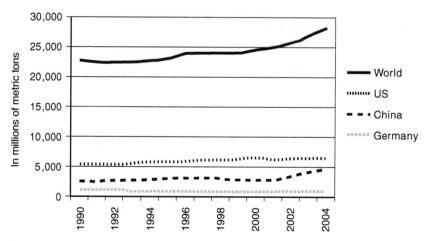

Figure 2.3 Carbon dioxide emissions 1990–2004 (Mt) (sources: www.bmwi.de (accessed 3 October 2008), Deutsche BP 2006: 9ff).

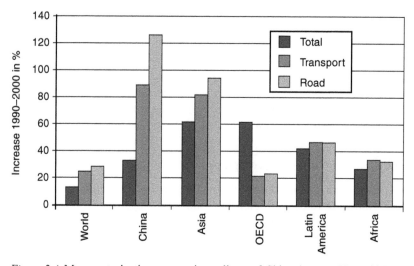

Figure 2.4 Mass motorization as a major polluter of China (source: Naoyuki Hasegwa, Ministry of Land, Infrastructure and Transport of Japan, as cited in Dalkmann 2005).

(see Figure 2.5), but if China were motorized to the same degree as Germany, there would be twice as many cars in the world as there are today.

Over time, we have to expect progressive growth of the Chinese car fleet (see Figure 2.6). The main reasons will be increasing available incomes and cheaper cars (Zhang 2003: 20ff.)

Additionally, the impact on the world oil markets as well as the local and regional environment have to be taken into account.

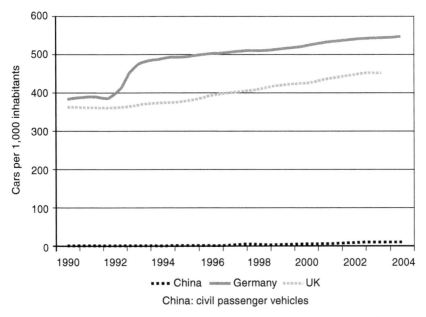

Figure 2.5 Car densities in different countries (source: www.vda.de (accessed 3 October 2008)).

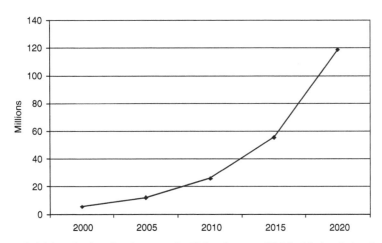

Figure 2.6 Motorization development in China (source: Walsh, National Academy of Sciences, Tsinghua University, as cited in Dalkmann 2005: 7).

Shortage of energy resources

Under current circumstances, we cannot expect that China and other threshold countries can go on the way they are. A main reason will perhaps not only be the horror scenario of global warming, but the fact that the available energy reserves are limited. According to Figure 2.7, the oil, gas and uranium reserves will be exhausted within this century. Additional resources are available, but mining is not possible under today's technical and economic circumstances.

Besides the limited availability of energy, the limitation of other raw materials is also relevant.

Rising energy prices

A high demand for goods while supply is limited will mean higher prices on the world market. For years we have seen rising energy prices, and especially over the last few years, oil prices have increased continuously (see Figure 2.8).

Opportunities for Europe to avoid possible consequences

Probable consequences of China's development

If these developments actually take place, continuing global warming and the probable lack of energy and increase in its price will have severe consequences,

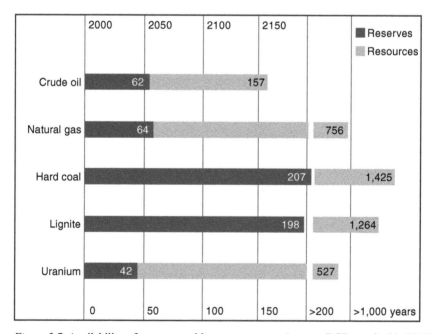

Figure 2.7 Availability of non-renewable energy sources (source: BGR, as cited in BMU 2007).

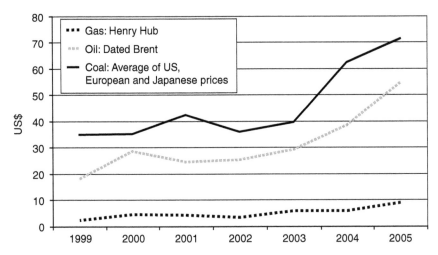

Figure 2.8 Rising energy prices (source: Deutsche BP 2006: 3).

for Europe as well. It is obvious that the world has to be prepared for the declining availability of fossil fuels and rising energy prices. Nobody will be able to stop threshold countries from further growth. But, it will be necessary to slow down the increase in energy consumption and global warming and to decouple CO_2 emissions from economic growth in the world economy. Here the community of states has to find a way. Currently, the developed countries are not very credible when they ask threshold and developing countries to reduce energy consumption and CO_2 emissions without setting a good example for such a solution.

Taking increased energy prices in the future as a fact, we can expect that transport will become more and more expensive with effects such as reduced car use and transport effort (vehicle kilometres) and a decrease in the accessibility of suburbanized and rural areas. Also within agglomerations, there will be areas with poor accessibility to services and public transport. These effects will increase the impact we already expect from demographic development: fewer people and older people with reduced mobility; shrinking rural areas far away from the agglomerations with access to only rather poor public transport. From these developments, we can particularly expect both a social and an economic impact.

There will be a strong need for strategies to maintain a good, accessible supply of shops, health care, etc., near home locations (which enable people to walk and cycle there), as well as good access to public transport. In the long run, we will have to strengthen dense and mixed land-use structures and find ways to redesign the settlement structures of city-regions and urban landscapes.

Opportunities

The threshold countries will take advice from the developed countries only if these can show that economic growth is feasible in a sustainable way. This means that the main ecological, economic and social needs are recognized. As the United States is currently not willing to reduce its energy consumption, Europeans have an outstanding responsibility – and opportunity.

Looking at transport policy, the main problems are: increasing vehicle kilometres (transport effort) and emissions. Making transport sustainable means to decrease the transport effort (fewer vehicle km) and reduce emissions (per km) while ensuring mobility and accessibility. The challenge will be to ensure development in places where a high quality of life (including mobility as well as shelter from pollution), social inclusion and high site quality for companies to enable economic growth can be realized. A big problem arises from freight transport. But this chapter focuses only on passenger transport.

Making transport more sustainable is a big challenge for public authorities. Measures they can implement are planning, constructing and operating infrastructure, supplying mobility services, legal and regulatory measures, and/or pricing and fiscal approaches. Additionally, they can influence and motivate institutions and stakeholders such as companies and organizations, hospitals and schools and others to ensure their own mobility and make it more sustainable. People can be influenced to be mobile in a more sustainable way and the mobility climate can be improved.

The only promising chance for influencing the global impact of the development of threshold countries is in implementing innovative solutions at home and being able to demonstrate that they work, that they ensure quality of life and help to guarantee economic growth. But doing so means, in addition, having an advantage in the worldwide competition between the regions of the world.

Tackling main driving forces of transport growth: urban sprawl, mobility behaviour and the strategies of the economic sector

One main cause of the growth of transport effort is urban sprawl, combined with car-oriented behaviour among the people and economic developments that include growing incomes and the strategies of the automobile industry, for example. The everyday regions where people live and act have expanded considerably over the past few decades. Manifold factors have influenced this development. But currently, land-use structures at the local and regional levels, especially within agglomerations, have not only resulted in mixed-settlement structures with city centres, but also in so-called urban landscapes in and between cities. Many people do not live and work in centres where they can find a complete supply of services for their everyday lives. Settlement densities have decreased and spatial functions get more and more separated. Both factors make an attractive public transport less economically feasible. Less density also means decreasing demand for and a withdrawal of services.

Additionally, in an ageing society, suburban areas and neighbourhoods grow older, i.e. people continue to live in the same neighbourhoods as they become older despite the fact that services become hard to access without a car. In this respect as well, a decrease in density intensifies the above-mentioned effects.

Anticipating a situation where transport will become more and more expensive and keeping in mind the impact of demographic developments and economic driving forces, the need for integrating land-use and transport planning will increase. Workable centres have to be strengthened or developed. Land-use policy objectives such as high density, mixture of functions, and good access to public transport, all well-known aims that have very often been neglected by planners in the past, will have to undergo a revival. This will support public transport, walking and cycling, as well as a neighbourhood supply of every day goods. But we have to be realistic: we cannot simply reconstruct our land-use structure. In a spatial mixture of growing and shrinking areas, it will be a long-term task to change the settlement structures.

To enable integrated land use and transport planning at the city or city-region level, integrated planning instruments are needed. Constructing and operating the infrastructure should not prefer car use but prioritize alternatives. Fiscal and financial rules, for example, road pricing or tax advantages for sustainable travel behaviour, have to support this integration. In the transport sector, car use (i.e. especially single car driving) has to be reduced. Helpful instruments include, for instance, pricing policies, reallocating public space primarily to sustainable modes, fulfilling the specific needs for walking and cycling (e.g. shortcuts/short routes, road safety, safe and weather-independent bicycle parking, etc.). It is not possible to go into detail here, but it seems useful to focus on three topics which include currently non-exhausted potential:

1   reduction of petrol consumption of cars;
2   strengthening alternatives to single car use;
3   mobility management as a transport demand-oriented approach.

The first topic needs action at a high political level despite the, at least in Germany, resistance of the automobile industry. The second topic needs to improve the infrastructure as well as services. The third topic asks for more information and organization as well as cooperation and new services to directly influence the transport demand.

Reduction of petrol and diesel consumption

The European Union discussion on maximum CO_2 emission standards for cars in early 2007 reminded us of the fact that the German automobile industry will fail to meet its commitment to reduce CO_2 car emissions to 140 grams per kilometre by 2008 (FR 2007). Over the last 25 years, there has only been a slow reduction in car petrol and diesel consumption (see Figure 2.9).

A basic reason for increased CO_2 emissions is the increasing number of all-terrain and sports utility vehicles whose consumption often exceeds ten litres per 100 km. Energy-efficient vehicles are rather expensive and have failed in the market. Usually, the automobile industry argues that people want to buy these cars rather than the economical ones. The interests of the automobile industry

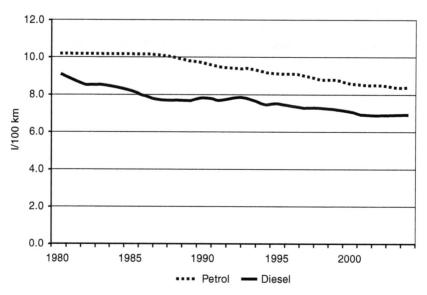

Figure 2.9 Average consumption of petrol and diesel vehicles 1980–2004 in Germany (source: DIW 2006).

and the consumers match each other well. Therefore, a regulation at the European level is needed.

Looking at the limited carbon resources, the further development of alternative drives and cleaner and renewable fuels should be included. The European industry does not seem to be so keen on investing money in this field. However, from the market success of Toyota's hybrid cars in the US, the other competitors could learn that these initiatives can generate profit (WR 2007).

Optimizing the transportation system: creating multi- and intermodal options

A precondition for changing mobility behaviour from single car driving towards both more efficient car use and recourse to other modes of transport is a good supply of alternatives. There are different options:

- The multimodal option where people opt for different modes for different trips according to the circumstances (e.g. walking or cycling on short trips, carpooling with colleagues for work or taking public transport to a city centre).
- The intermodal option for the combination of different modes on a single trip.

Despite the fact that on average a significant share of transport effort in Europe is done by car, there are still regions and cities where alternatives exist, e.g. cycling. This could be an example for demonstrating a policy that tries to change the trend away from more and more car use. A few examples from Germany and North Rhine-Westphalia may exemplify successful strategies for strengthening cycling.

The Federal Transportation Ministry set up the National Cycling Plan (*Nationaler Radverkehrsplan*) for 2002–12. It aims to demonstrate opportunities to develop and strengthen cycling as part of a sustainable transport system by creating implementation strategies as well as recommended actions to create a bicycle-friendly climate in Germany (BMVBS 2002). The federal government sees itself as a catalyst and moderator in fostering cycling, whereas (due to federalism) the main responsibility lies at the regional and local level. As an important success factor, framework conditions should be improved to plan and implement measures for fostering bicycle use within a complete system. To tap more of the potential of cycling in Germany, learning from other European countries like the Netherlands, appeared to be helpful.

The number of federal state programmes as well as local activities shows the role of North Rhine-Westphalia as the forerunner of all German federal states in fostering bicycle use. Since 1978, the federal state has invested money in bikeway infrastructure and other cycling facilities. Since then, the number of programmes and initiatives was successively raised. In 1993, the network of bicycle-friendly cities in North Rhine-Westphalia (*AG Fahrradfreundlicher Städte und Gemeinden in NRW*) was founded. In September 2004, the network included 32 cities and four counties. These are forerunners with a high share of cycling and/or the will to increase it substantially. The city of Münster, for example, has a cycling share of more than 40 per cent of all trips. Four years later the programme '100 bicycle stations in NRW' (*100 Fahrradstationen in NRW*; MVEL 2004a) was launched. Security of parked bicycles is good in Germany, with bicycle stations existing in many German cities at the interchanges. The bicycle station in Münster offers parking facilities for approximately 3,300 bicycles as well as additional services such as repairs and rental. In September 2004, 51 bicycle stations existed in North Rhine-Westphalia and more are expected in the future. In 2002, the federal state started to install a country-wide uniform signposting system to help cyclists easily find the shortest and most scenic routes (MVEL 2004b). A web-based route finder for cycling has been set up which can not only help in planning cycling tours but can also be accessed on tour by GPS on mobile PDAs. It includes not only bicycle routes, but also interchanges, especially with public transport (www.radroutenplaner. nrw.de).

Other federal states are also developing signpost systems and web-based cycling route finders, for example, Bavaria. There are always specific regions and cities where cycling has traditionally enjoyed a big share of trips due to a particular mobility culture, for instance, the northwest of Germany near the Netherlands or cities like Münster, Freiburg i.Br. or Bremen. Current examples show that fostering cycling can be successful even if there is only a small share of cycling and framework conditions are poor. Leipzig offers a very good example in this respect. This city successfully increased the modal share of cycling from 5 per cent in 1991 to 13 per cent in 1999. In close cooperation with stakeholders, such as the cyclists' association (ADFC), the city implemented a bundle of measures (plans, installation of a tool to assess the impact of transport measures on cycling, traffic calming, reconstruction of crossings, public-awareness measures, dedicating a share of the city budget to cycling measures, etc.) (NAPOLI 2004). In this way, the city was able to exploit its cycling-friendly framework conditions of a flat topography, a compact and dense urban structure, a green belt surrounding the city centre and a high number of students.

A second promising example is CarSharing and CarPooling. According to the usual understanding in continental Europe, CarSharing is understood as renting a car for a (short) time from a CarSharing company or association. Generally the customers pay a registration fee and a time- and kilometre-related fee for single trips. CarPooling is joint use of a car, for example, by colleagues for journeys to work. There are organizations that offer matching systems to help people find others for common trips. Large companies may also offer such matching systems to their employees.

According to a recent study, the potential of CarSharing in Germany is esti-mated at about 1.5 million users, although in fact only around 100,000 people per day currently use CarSharing (Öko-Institut 2004: 13ff.). The most important reason restraining its growth is a lack of knowledge. In Germany, CarSharing is available in 260 cities with altogether 1,450 CarSharing stations. The number of CarSharing users is increasing dynamically (up 14.5 per cent from 2006 to 2007). There are negotiations between CarSharing providers and local transport companies to establish its better integration into the public transport system. Fur-thermore, strengthening the role of CarSharing is the aim of an amendment of the Federal Road Traffic Act, which should allow city authorities to assign parking spaces for CarSharing vehicles in public road space (bcs 2007).

In North Rhine-Westphalia, 14 CarSharing providers run 285 CarSharing sta-tions in 43 cities. Since 2002, DB CarSharing has been running as a subsidiary company of German Rail based on a franchise system together with other Car-Sharing companies. Generally, CarSharing is available mainly in large cities: 83 per cent of all cities in North Rhine-Westphalia with more than 100,000 inhabit-ants have one or more CarSharing station/s related to a high population density. This ratio declines with a declining number of inhabitants so that only one of 216 cities with less than 25,000 inhabitants has CarSharing provision.

CarSharing is more and more popular in public and private organizations, for example, the city administration of Münster established CarSharing for its busi-ness trips, abolishing company cars and reimbursement for private-car usage. The main impact was a strong reduction in vehicle mileage and an annual saving of €120,000 (LOGIBALL (undated)).

Several organizations in Germany offer CarPooling matching systems. The commuter network North Rhine-Westphalia (*Pendlernetz NRW*) is being intro-duced in many cities and counties in the federal state; today 35 counties and big cities (Bürgerservice Pendlernetz NRW 2005). The important PR tasks are supported by the Ministry for the Environment of North Rhine-Westphalia. The objectives are to reduce costs for commuters as well as parking space for the companies in order to relieve the road system from congestion and to protect the environment.

The *Pendlernetz* was created in 2002 mainly driven by local- agenda working groups. Financial contributions from the cities and counties as well as funding from the federal state enabled the establishment of the web-based matching system and the operating costs. The main focus of the project is on the high number of commuters (about 3.5 million people in North Rhine-Westphalia every day) and the fact that 80 per cent of them use their private cars. While for every trip on average 1.2 people sit in one car, this rate is about 1.04 people per car on commuter trips. Increasing this rate is the main objective. Currently, there are attempts to broaden the system, for example, to include event traffic (NAPOLI 2004; www.nrw.pendlernetz.de (accessed 3 October 2008)).

Recently, the *Pendlernetz* was further extended so that networks exist in the agglomerations Stuttgart and Rhine-Main (Bürgerservice Pendlernetz NRW 2005).

The two examples of modal policies show that improve alternatives to single car use display a multimodal approach. In the following, the intermodal approach is addressed.

For realizing intermodality, i.e. combining different transport modes on a single trip, some main requirements have to be fulfilled:

- interconnected and interoperable networks and interchanges;
- door-to-door information, integrated tariffs and ticketing;
- integration of long-distance travel and first/last urban mile;
- baggage handling.

The integration of modes within public transport should also be included.

Alternatives to (single) car use need an optimized supply of passenger transportation over all elements of the chain of a trip from door to door and a complementary supply of information, ticketing, luggage handling etc. If people have access to a car, and no other reasons press them to change their behaviour, they normally will not feel disposed to choose other modes if these conditions are not fulfilled.

Regarding intermodality, there are strong disparities on the national level. The best conditions can be found in northwestern Europe (http://europa.eu.int). In other European regions, we encounter partly a lack of knowledge regarding the market, the behaviour and the impact, and partly a lack of awareness. Intermodality is not a fast-selling item. The main challenge when realizing intermodality is to ensure cooperation in a market that is an increasingly competitive environment. There, moderation and improving framework conditions are necessary.

The following presents some information on implementing intermodality in Germany. The success of intermodal transport solutions (not only) in passenger transport depends very much on reliable opportunities to switch between modes. To ensure reliability within the public-transport system, North Rhine-Westphalia implemented integrated, synchronized timetables (*Integraler Taktfahrplan*) for the rail system with attractive connections at the interchange stations. This system was first developed in 1995 and has been improved step by step.

In Germany, almost all local and regional public-transport connections have been integrated into the door-to-door information system HAFAS used by German Rail and based on an agreement on data exchange. German Rail's transport information system is well accepted and used by many long-distance passengers, and therefore can be seen as the most important German passenger-information system. A rather good integration of long-distance and regional/urban travel information including walking and public transport has already been achieved within this system. It includes maps and enables a comparison of travel costs by different modes (e.g. rail, car, bicycle), a feature rarely found elsewhere in Europe.

There are efforts to further improve these information systems, for example, by including real-time information which can be used on a trip. At the regional level, public-transport associations also offer door-to-door information (addresses, stop names), as well the 'Smart number for bus and rail' (*Die schlaue Nummer für Bus und Bahn*: www.schlaue-nummer.de).

The Ruhrpilot, a new means of real-time information implemented in the Ruhr agglomeration, combines data regarding all transport modes and projects them on one platform. About 500 control points measure the road loading and give information about congestion. Data from German Rail and other local transport companies give information about delays in public transport. Both delays and congestion are taken into account for the routing, which simultaneously shows trip options via car and public transport. All this information can be obtained via Internet, mobile phone or navigation system. *Ruhrpilot* is a project run by a public-private partnership (Projekt Ruhr 2005).

As in other European countries, efforts have been made in the field of electronic ticketing like smart cards. Such systems not only make travelling in a travel chain more convenient, but also make it easier to obtain necessary data for the task of revenue sharing, which is a critical point in cooperation between different transport operators.

A good example in Germany of an interoperable transport system between urban and national rail (tram-train) exists in Karlsruhe, where urban trams and regional light rail can run on the same railway tracks. This links the city centre with the outlying region without the previously needed change at the main railway station which is located outside the city centre. This so-called *Karlsruher Model* has been quite successful and can be found in other cities as well.

Another innovative service offered in Germany is Call-a-bike, undertaken by DB Rent, which is available in some major cities such as Berlin, Frankfurt, Cologne and Munich. Bicycle rental is offered to passengers of German Rail, particularly on long-distance trips. Call-a-bike currently has around 50,000 registered clients.

Influencing transport demand by Mobility Management

Mobility Management (MM) is not yet a common approach, but it is not in use in all European countries. Therefore, it seems to be necessary to define it first.

> Mobility Management is a concept to promote sustainable transport. At the core of Mobility Management are 'soft' measures (e.g. information or coordination of existing user services), which enhance the effectiveness of 'hard' measures within urban transport planning (e.g. new tram lines, new roads and new bike lanes). Mobility Management measures (in comparison to 'hard' measures) do not necessarily require large financial investments to change mobility behaviour and may have a high benefit–cost ratio.
>
> Mobility Management is primarily a demand-oriented approach to transport. Its aim is to support and encourage a change of attitude and behaviour to reduce single car use and to strengthen sustainable modes of transport. Cooperation between public and private institutions enables solutions that fulfil public as well as individual objectives in mobility and transport. Mobility Management measures are based on information, communication, organization, coordination, and promotion.
>
> Mobility Management measures need to be integrated into bundles of measures which can additionally include planning, constructing and operating infrastructure, supplying mobility and further services, legal and regulatory measures, and/or pricing and fiscal approaches to gain enhanced synergistic impacts.
>
> In order to design and implement Mobility Management strategies or measures within a holistic marketing approach, the needs of the target groups have to be explored; products, services or messages have to be defined; prices have to be fixed; and communication strategies have to be developed. Information can be provided to the public or to a defined target group within a campaign to change attitudes or mobility behaviour. Alternatively, information on concrete products or mobility services can be delivered to a single person or a target group to motivate them to use or buy these products or services.
>
> (www.max-success.eu)

MM has been developed in Europe according to the Transport Demand Management (TDM) approach, which has been developed and implemented since the Clean Air Acts in the United States. The forerunner country in Europe was the Netherlands (with primarily a top-down approach). In Germany, a similar approach was developed (with a bottom-up approach). Within projects funded by the European Commission, the approach has been developed further. Currently, several European countries use MM, primarily the UK, Sweden, the Netherlands and Switzerland.

Despite the fact that there is no national MM policy in Germany, as in the other countries mentioned above, there are many activities in this field primarily organized by local stakeholders such as towns and cities, companies and organizations, mobility service providers and NGOs. In the following, there is a short overview of different fields where MM has been implemented. Taking the state of development that currently exists, there is still great potential for achieving more sustainable transport. Promising fields are mobility centres, corporate mobility management, hospitals, schools and housing areas:

- Mobility Centres (MCs) in passenger transport provide local or regional services such as multimodal information and advice, public-transport tickets, organization of demand-oriented public transport, rental of bicycles, etc. Nowadays, some MCs also offer tourism and recreation information or information for disabled people and provide consulting to schools or companies. The portfolio of MC services can differ between centres. Past initiatives to develop a corporate design for all MCs in Germany ultimately proved unsuccessful. As of 2005, there are about 50 mobility centres and about 20 public-transport service centres in operation in Germany (www. mobilitaetsmanagement.nrw.de).

- Corporate (or Company) MM (CMM) is understood as a site-oriented MM operated by companies, authorities, administrations and other kinds of organizations. In Germany, the approach of CMM has been implemented by many different companies, as well as by public or private organizations. Cities that have been innovators in this field were Bielefeld and Münster, and currently Munich, Freiburg i.Br. and Dresden. A survey within a recent national research project on CMM in Germany[1] shows the variety of implemented measures as well as the level of implementation. Concerning commuting, a high level of implementation can be found, e.g. for cycle parking, time organization and cloakrooms/showers (Kemming et al. 2007). Additionally, employers are interested in implementing, for example, job tickets and carpooling. More than 40 per cent of the organizations studied offer their employees the private use of company cars; with regard to sustainability, a counterproductive measure.[2]

- MM for hospitals is an interesting special case of CMM. Due to their mostly integrated sites in or near city centres, hospitals are often confronted with huge accessibility and parking problems. Employees as well as patients, visitors and goods transport or delivery services compete for scarce space. There are several good practice solutions in this field in Germany; one of them is the big hospital in Bielefeld-Bethel, which had already started CMM in 1996.

- MM at schools is being implemented more and more often in Germany, but still at a common low level. On the basis of a sharpened public perception of road-safety problems, especially for children, and the knowledge that early learning of sustainable behaviour as a child will influence mobility behaviour of the later adults, the Board of School Ministers (Kultusministerkonferenz) decided in 1996 to establish mobility education in schools in Germany. This can be understood as a starting point for MM at schools in

Germany. Currently, many local or school initiatives all over Germany are implementing MM. This development has been supported by initiatives of NGOs (e.g. Verkehrsclub Deutschland), research projects at the national level, information platforms (e.g. www.mobilitaetsmanagement.nrw.de), and regional implementation efforts, e.g. in North Rhine-Westphalia, while implementing measures of the road-safety programme.

- MM in the field of housing is of especial interest because the home residence is the most important origin and destination of trips. MM and mobility services offered there can be an important leverage point to influence mobility behaviour. In this way, people can be supported to live in car-free housing areas (www.wohnen-plus-mobilitaet.nrw.de). Mobility services afforded residents by housing companies in close cooperation with public-transport companies, CarSharing and other service providers and cities can be a means to reduce single use of cars. In Germany, several housing companies offer such services. Main elements of these service packages are CarSharing and rebated resident's tickets (*Mietertickets*), but there are also bicycle parking lots with, in some cases, repair services, rental bicycles or trolleys, delivery services, neighbourhood buses, etc. (www.wohnen-plus-mobilitaet.nrw.de).

Conclusions

In the global economy, there are close interrelationships between the developments in developed and threshold as well as in developing countries. Obviously, the economic growth and energy consumption of a large country such as China will influence the global energy market. The main effects will be a reduction of time in which we will be able to use fossil energy and rising energy prices. These effects are not avoidable. Europe has to be prepared for this development. New policies and strategies are necessary for a high-energy-price situation. In land-use and transport policy, this means reducing the need for transport, by re-steering land-use development towards higher density, a mixture of functions and close access to public transport, among other factors. Such a strategy will also strengthen centres at all levels as well as walking and cycling, important factors for ensuring social inclusion.

Besides the economic interrelations, global warming is a phrase that expresses the close interdependencies between the development of different countries and regions in the world. There is an obvious clash of interests between the threshold countries such as China and the developed countries in Europe. The developed countries fear for their supremacy in the global economy and for the welfare of their inhabitants if they reduce CO_2 emissions significantly. Additionally, they fear the environmental, economic and social consequences of progressive global warming. On their side, threshold countries understand energy consumption as a precondition for economic growth and increasing the welfare of their population. For them, avoiding global warming is not at the top of their agenda.

Developed countries can convince threshold countries to reduce energy consumption and CO_2 emissions only if they show in practice that sustainability is a way to get competitive in the global economy, that high quality of life and radically increasing energy efficiency on one side and economic growth on the other are not mutually exclusive. This chapter identifies sustainability strategies for the transport sector which can increase energy efficiency and should feature in the general transport policy of all European countries. In implementing these strategies, Europe can show that this can also be a matrix for China.

Notes

1 Conducted for the Federal Transport Ministry in Germany.
2 To avoid misunderstanding, it should be noted that there is no information about how many employees in these organizations have been offered the private use of company cars.

References

Böhn, D. (2005) 'China zwischen Wachstumsdynamik und sozialen Verwerfungen', *Praxis Geographie* 35, 4–9.

Bundesministerium für Verkehr, Bau und Stadtentwicklung (BMVBS) (2002) *Nationaler Radverkehrsplan 2002–2012 FahrRad!, Maßnahmen zur Förderung des Radverkehrs in Deutschland*, available at www.bmv.de/Anlage/original_9153/Nationaler-Radverkehrsplan-2002–2012-FahrRad.pdf (accessed 18 June 2007).

Bundesministerium für Wirtschaft und Technologie (BMWi), available at www.bmwi.de/BMWi/Navigation/root.html (accessed 20 May 2007).

Bundesministeriums für Umwelt, Naturschutz und Reaktorsicherheit (BMU), available at www.unendliche-energie.de/documents/1-Weltenergie.pdf (accessed 6 June 2007).

Bundesverband CarSharing (bcs) (2007) *CarSharing in Deutschland verzeichnet wiederum ein erfreuliches Wachstum der Nutzungszahlen. Bundespolitik würdigt Entlastungspotenziale der CarSharing durch Gesetzesinitiative*, press release, 19 March, Hannover: bcs.

Bundeszentrale für politische Bildung (bpb) (2006) 'Volksrepublik China', *Informationen zur politischen Bildung* 289, Bonn: bpb.

Bürgerservice Pendlernetz NRW (2005) *Mobilisieren Sie Ihren Betrieb: Fördern Sie Fahrgemeinschaften*, Rheine.

Bürgerservice Pendlernetz NRW, available at www.nrw.pendlernetz.de/ (accessed 3 October 2008).

Dalkmann, H. (2005) 'Zukünftige Rolle des Pkw in einem nachhaltigen Verkehrssystem', Automobilkongress für Unternehmen und Wissenschaft an der Ruhr-Universität Bochum, available at www.ruhr-uni-bochum.de/autokongress2/download/beitraege/dalkmann-gruppe5.pdf (accessed 12 June 2007).

Deutsche BP (2006) *Energie in Zahlen – BP Statistical Review of World Energy 2006*, Berlin: BP.

Deutsches Institut für Wirtschaftsforschung (DIW) (2006) *Verkehr in Zahlen 2006/2007*, Hamburg: Bundesministerium für Verkehr, Bau- und Wohnungswesen.

Eberl, U. (2004) 'Die Megacity des 21. Jahrhunderts', *Pictures of the Future – Die Zeitschrift für Forschung und Innovation, Frühjahr*: 14–15.

EU-Projekt MAX, available at www.max-success.eu (accessed 18 June 2007).

Europäische Kommission, available at http://europa.eu.int/comm/transport/intermodality/passenger/studies_en.htm (accessed 18 June 2007).

Frankfurter Rundschau (FR) (2007) 'Klimaziel rückt in weite Ferne', *Frankfurter Rundschau* 27 February.

Informationsnetzwerk, 'Wohnen plus Mobilität', available at www.wohnen-plus-mobilitaet.nrw.de/wohnen_ohne_auto/index.html (accessed 18 June 2007).

Intergovernmental Panel on Climate Change (IPCC), available at http://arch.rivm.nl/env/int/ipcc/pages_media/SRCCS-final/graphics/jpg/large/Figureper   cent20TS-02a.jpg (accessed 12 June 2007).

Kemming, H. *et al.* (2007) *Weiterentwicklung von Produkten, Prozessen und Rahmenbedingungen des betrieblichen Mobilitätsmanagements*, Concluding report, Dortmund.

LOGIBALL [undated] *Betriebliches Mobilitätsmanagement*, Münster: Stadt Münster.

Ministerium für Verkehr, Energie und Landesplanung des Landes Nordrhein-Westfalen (MVEL) (2004a) *Fahrradstationen in NRW – eine Idee wird Programm*, Düsseldorf.

Ministerium für Verkehr, Energie und Landesplanung des Landes Nordrhein-Westfalen (MVEL) (2004b) *Fahrradfreundliches Nordrhein-Westfalen. Meilensteine der NRW-Radverkehrsförderung*, Düsseldorf.

NAPOLI (2004) *Umsetzung und Akzeptanz einer nachhaltigen Verkehrspolitik – NAPOLI: Forschungs- und Entwicklungsvorhaben im Auftrag des Bundesministeriums für Verkehr, Bau- und Wohnungswesen (FOPS-Projekt Nr. 70.695/2002)*, Abschlussbericht, Dortmund.

National Bureau of Statistics of China (NBS), available at www.stats.gov.cn/english/ (accessed 20 May 2007).

Öko-Institut (2004) *Bestandsaufnahme und Möglichkeiten der Weiterentwicklung von Car-Sharing*, Schlussbericht, Freiburg.

Projekt Ruhr GmbH (2005) *Ruhrpilot. Mobilität der Zukunft für die Metropole Ruhr*, Essen.

Radroutenplaner NRW, available at www.radroutenplaner.nrw.de (accessed 14 June 2007).

Sieren, F. (2005) *Der China-Code. Wie das boomende Reich der Mitte Deutschland verändert*, Berlin.

Steiner, A. (2007) *Message on World Environment Day*, available at www.unep.org/wed/2007/downloads/documents/ED_Message2007.pdf (accessed 14 June 2007).

Stern reviews on the economy of climate change, available at www.sternreview.org.uk (accessed 18 June 2007).

Transferstelle Mobilitätsmanagement, available at www.mobilitaetsmanagement.nrw.de (accessed 18 June 2007).

United Nations Environment Programme (UNEP) (2007) *GEO-Year Book 2007*, Nairobi: UNEP.

Verband der Automobilindustrie (VDA), available www.vda.de/de/aktuell/statistik/index.html (accessed 10 June 2007).

Vorholz, F. (2005) 'Eine Last für die Menschheit', in V. Ullrich and E. Berié (eds) *Der Fischer Weltallmanach aktuell, Weltmacht China*, Frankfurt a. M: 72–5.

Westfälische Rundschau (WR) (2007) 'Spritsparende Autos bringen Toyota Rekordgewinne', *Westfälische Rundschau* 10 May 2007.

Westfälische Verkehrsgesellschaft mbH (WVG), available at www.schlaue-nummer.de (accessed 18 June 2007).

Zhang, Y. (2003) *Vergleich der Verkehrsentwicklung in deutschen Großstädten und Shanghai sowie Herleitung von Handlungserfordernissen*, Munich: TU München, Lehrstuhl für Verkehrstechnik.

3 Will China's thirst for oil affect accessibility and mobility in the regions and cities of Europe?

Michael Wegener

Introduction

Some 20 per cent of mankind commands 80 per cent of the world's wealth and is responsible for 80 per cent of greenhouse gas emissions. This inequality is growing. Since the 1970s, the per-capita income of the industrialized countries has grown by a factor of ten, whereas that of the developing countries has only tripled.

Yet, this traditional division of the world into rich and poor countries is collapsing. In particular, four so-called developing countries, Brazil, China, India and Russia, have two-digit growth rates of their economies and in a few years will produce more than North America and Europe taken together. The globalization of markets for goods and services will destroy millions of jobs in today's industrial countries and lead to hitherto unknown distribution conflicts.

The reaction of the rich countries is to face global competition by enforced growth in key technologies and strict barriers to immigration. Politicians and economists ignore the fact that in order to avoid mass unemployment, it is necessary to replace not only the jobs lost through global competition but also those lost through rising productivity. The growth rates necessary for this would be enormous.

But another multiplication of production, consumption and resource use by the rich countries by a factor of ten as in the last 30 years would exceed the resources of the planet. Today, it is already foreseeable that if the energy consumption of the world continues to grow only as it has in the past, the known deposits of fossil fuels would be exhausted before the end of this century. If, however, one adds the growing energy demands of Brazil, China, India and Russia, they will be depleted in only a few decades. Similar constraints apply to other raw materials.

In addition, there are the challenges of climate change. Climate researchers agree that to avoid the worst implications of climate change, a reduction of worldwide greenhouse gas emissions by 50 per cent is necessary. For today's industrialized countries, this means a reduction of 80 per cent. Even with the most optimistic assessment of the potential for energy conservation and increasing energy efficiency, such a reduction is incompatible with continued economic growth.

However, only a few politicians and scientists are taking serious account of this situation. Only a few countries meet the target set by the United Nations to spend 0.7 per cent of their national product on development aid. Mainstream neo-liberal economic theorists continue to put their stakes on further deregulation of international trade and unconstrained economic growth. There are virtually no theories, concepts or visions of how a sustainable economic order might be developed without continued material growth in the richest countries of the world.

This chapter focuses on one aspect of this larger issue, energy scarcity, and the particular role of China. It starts with facts and forecasts about the past and likely future of China's economic development, energy consumption and greenhouse gas emissions and their likely implications on world energy prices, and, derived from that, accessibility and mobility in the regions and cities of Europe. It reports results of the EU-funded research project STEPs (Scenarios for the Transport System and Energy Supply and Their Potential Effects) in which the likely effects of scenarios of energy scarcity on accessibility and economic performance of regions and cities, as well as on daily mobility and residential and firm location in metropolitan areas in Europe, were explored.

China and transport energy

In the last 30 years, world energy consumption has more than doubled, and more than 90 per cent of all energy used is fossil (US Department of Energy 2007). Petroleum accounts for 36 per cent of energy consumption. It is expected that the year when oil extraction will reach its maximum ('peak oil') is very close – oil production in all non-OPEC countries has already peaked. However, energy demand has more than doubled since 1970 and is expected to grow by another 50 per cent until 2030, mainly because the standard of living in developing countries, in particular, in China and India, will come close to that of today's industrialized countries (IEA 2007). This means that the petroleum resources known today will be exhausted before the end of this century. With declining supply and increasing demand, energy prices will rise. In mid-2008, the price of crude oil on the world market reached nearly US\$150 per barrel, and only because of the economic crisis it dropped for a short period below US\$50.

Oil remains the most important fuel for transport because there are few alternatives that can compete with its energy density. Transport accounts for two-thirds of the total projected growth in oil consumption until 2030. There is no indication that it will be possible to decouple economic GDP growth from growth in transport; in particular, freight and air transport are expected to grow at the same rate or faster than the GDP. Experts believe that, because of the ultimate depletion of oil resources, political instability in the Middle East and growing energy demand from fast-developing countries such as China and India, energy will continue to become more expensive in the long run.

China is now second only to the US as an energy consumer. China's energy consumption grew by 60 per cent between 1990 and 2003, compared to 15 per cent in the European Union. But China's energy intensity (the amount of energy it needs to produce one unit of GDP) is five times that of the US. China's oil imports are expected to grow by a factor of almost four until 2030. China's car ownership stands at 30 million cars or 24 cars per 1,000 persons today, compared to 470 in the EU. Car ownership and car traffic in China are expected to grow by 20 per cent annually in the near future.

The growth in energy consumption is closely linked to the debate about climate change. The Kyoto Protocol of the United Nations Framework Convention on Climate Change, adopted in 1992, sets mandatory targets for the reduction of greenhouse gas emissions in comparison to 1990: 5.2 per cent worldwide, 8 per cent for Europe and no reductions for developing countries, including China and India. The Kyoto Protocol has been in force since 2005; to date, it has been signed by 170 countries. On 9 March 2007, the EU heads of state signed a resolution to achieve 20 per cent less energy, 20 per cent renewable energy and 20 per cent less carbon dioxide (CO_2) emissions by 2020. The British Prime Minister announced on 13 March 2007 that Great Britain will reduce its greenhouse gas emissions by 26 points to 32 per cent by 2020 and by 60 per cent by 2050. On 9 June 2007, the political leaders of the G-8 summit committed their countries to aim for a reduction of greenhouse gas emissions by 50 per cent by 2050.

But, according to the latest report of the United Nations Intergovernmental Panel on Climate Change (IPCC 2007), this is not enough. In order to reach the worldwide 50 per cent target, today's industrialized countries will have to cut down their greenhouse gas emissions by 80 per cent in order to allow the developing countries to expand their economies. The responsibility of the rich countries as the heaviest energy users to lead the way in reducing greenhouse gas emissions was also behind the compromise resolution of the Bali Climate Change Conference in December 2007. The 80 per cent target results from a simple calculation. Today, average greenhouse gas emissions worldwide amount to four tonnes per capita, the sustainable amount being two tonnes. To reach this target, the United States will have to reduce its energy consumption and CO_2 emissions by a factor of ten and the European countries by a factor of between five (Germany), four (Spain, Italy) and three (France) – and China by a factor of two.

It is hard to say which of the two will hit faster, energy scarcity or the requirements of climate protection. But they will both work in the same direction: energy for transport will become more expensive, either through political conflicts or simply because oil is running out, or through government-imposed taxes on fossil fuel or vehicles or through user fees, such as emission permits or road pricing.

This chapter reflects on the likely consequences of non-marginal fuel price increases in regions and cities in Europe:

- Regions. Modern economies depend on cheap transport. Deregulation of international trade has made worldwide supply chains feasible. The growing integration of markets has intensified flows of passengers and especially freight. Just-in-time production relies on efficient up-to-the-minute deliveries. Globalization of enterprises and financial flows requires face-to-face communication across continents. Without worldwide tourist flows, many developing countries would remain in poverty. If cheap transport were no longer available, will all that end? Will regional economies be seriously affected, and if so, which regions will suffer more, the central prosperous regions, which today enjoy high levels of accessibility and mobility, or the peripheral regions, which critically depend on access to far-away markets?

- Cities. The modern city is based on mobility. The railway, and later the automobile, made the vast expansion of cities into metropolitan areas possible. Because transport was fast, efficient and cheap, households could afford to leave the medieval city and enjoy life in the suburbs or countryside and still travel to work in the city. Only much later did retail, services and manufacturing follow their customers or employees to the suburbs creating the fragmented urban–rural landscape surrounding most of our cities today. The price for the suburban arcadia is high: declining city centres, loss of open space, long travel times and growing emissions of greenhouse gases, air pollutants and traffic noise. Moreover, it ignores the imperative to reduce greenhouse gas emissions in order to avoid or at least slow down climate change, and, it ignores the fact that cheap mobility will not be here forever. With severe increases in mobility costs, will location choice and mobility patterns change in response to rising transport costs? Will suburban lifestyles and settlement patterns become unsustainable and have to be abandoned? Or are European cities resilient and flexible enough to accommodate even severe changes in transport cost?

This chapter is based on the EU 6th Research and Technology Development Framework project STEPs (Scenarios for the Transport System and Energy Supply and Their Potential Effects). The project examined the impact of different scenarios of fuel-price increases, resulting market responses and different combinations of policy interventions in the fields of infrastructure and technology, travel demand regulation and land-use control on regional economic development and travel patterns, the environment, accessibility and land use in metropolitan areas. For this, the project used several European and urban/regional simulation models (STEPs 2006). The results of the SASI model of regional economic development (Wegener and Bökemann 1998; Bröcker *et al.* 2004) and the Dortmund model of urban land use and mobility (Wegener 1998; Lautso *et al.* 2004) are presented here.

Scenarios

The project developed a set of scenarios combining different rates of consumer fuel-price increases with three sets of policies (see Table 3.1):

Table 3.1 STEPs scenarios

Policy	Fuel-price increase		
	+1% pa	*+4% pa*	*+7% pa*
Do nothing	A-1*	B-1	C-1
Business as usual	A0	B0	C0
Infrastructure and technology	A1	B1	C1
Demand regulation	A2	B2	C2
All policies	A3	B3	C3

Note
*Reference scenario.

- *A scenarios*. The A scenarios assume consumer fuel price increases by 1 per cent per annum in real terms (or about one-third between the base year 2005 and the target year 2030), a very optimistic view in the face of recent fuel-price increases. The Reference Scenario A-1 is a true do-nothing scenario: i.e. it is assumed that no government policies to respond to the changes in energy prices are implemented, however, it is assumed that technical innovation and market response will lead to moderate reductions in energy use of cars, lorries and trains. The business-as-usual Scenario A0 assumes that already planned road and rail projects will be implemented, that progress in energy efficiency, emission control and alternative fuels is made as in the past and that there is no change in land-use policies. The infrastructure and technology Scenario A1 assumes that large-scale road and rail projects are implemented and significant efforts to promote energy efficiency, emission control and alternative fuels are made. The demand-regulation Scenario A2 assumes strong disincentives to car travel and goods transport on roads through speed limits, road pricing and higher petrol taxes, supported by incentives for public transport use and land-use development at rail stations or substitution of work trips by telework. The combination Scenario A3 combines the policies of Scenarios A1 and A2.
- *B scenarios*. The B scenarios assume real consumer fuel-price increases of 4 per cent per annum (or +167 per cent until the target year 2030), which is still less than recent increases. Except for the assumed higher fuel prices, the B scenarios are the exact counterpart of the corresponding A scenarios, including the assumptions about the diffusion of energy-saving and alternative vehicles.
- *C scenarios*. The C scenarios are based on the assumption that consumer fuel prices will grow dramatically by 7 per cent per year, or almost fivefold, until 2030, a pessimistic scenario in which, besides the growth in fuel consumption by China and India, the diminishing fossil-fuel resources are taken into account. Again, Scenario C-1 is a do-nothing scenario in which no policy response is assumed. However, the remaining C scenarios assume a stronger policy response than the corresponding A and B scenarios. Sce-

nario C0 assumes that governments attempt to compensate their economies for the high costs of transport through tax rebates and even subsidies (as in the case of aircraft kerosene), even at the expense of less investment in high-speed rail. Scenario C1 invests more in transport technology to promote energy-saving cars and trains and more alternative vehicles. Scenario C2 employs heavy fuel taxes and road-user charges to save fuel by reducing travel by all modes. In addition, Scenario C2 applies strict anti-sprawl land-use policies allowing development only on brownfield sites in the inner urban areas of the three largest cities in the metropolitan area. Scenario C3, which applies the policies of Scenarios C1 and C2 together, is the strongest imaginable policy response.

Results

In this section, the results of the two simulation models, the European model and the urban model, for the 15 scenarios are presented. Each diagram shows the development of one indicator. The heavy black line represents Reference Scenario A-1. As the scenario policies are introduced only after 2006, all scenarios have the same historical path as the Reference Scenario until 2006. After that, each scenario is represented by a different line identified by its scenario code.

European regions

Figure 3.1 shows the impact of 15 scenarios on *accessibility*. In the past, regional accessibility has grown continuously because of the infrastructure development

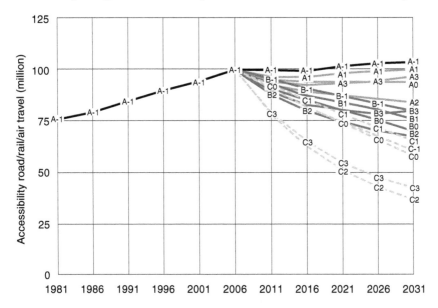

Figure 3.1 SASI model results: accessibility road/rail/air travel 1981–2031.

and the removal of political, social or cultural barriers through European integration. Even in Reference Scenario A-1, which assumes no network development or acceleration of modes in the future, accessibility grows slightly because of the underlying assumptions on further European integration.

All scenarios have a significant impact on accessibility. The effects vary with the scenario assumptions on fuel-price increases and the different forms of policy intervention. In all scenarios, accessibility is below the Reference Scenario. This is to be expected for the do-nothing Scenarios B-1 and C-1 as their fuel-cost increases are higher than in Scenario A-1. But none of the policy scenarios is able to compensate the effects of the fuel-price increases. This is so because, in all policy scenarios, road transport is made even more expensive by road pricing. This is also true for policy scenarios in which rail is favoured either by assumptions on network development and an increase in speed (as in the infrastructure and technology Scenarios A1, B1 and C1) or through a reduction of rail fares per km (as in the demand-regulation Scenarios A2, B2 and C2). Even the combination of both (in Scenarios A3, B3 and C3) does not compensate for the loss in accessibility because of the massive policies against car and lorry use in these scenarios. The magnitude of the negative impact depends primarily on the assumptions about fuel cost.

The reduction in accessibility through higher transport costs affects all regions in Europe. However, the different policy scenarios result in different spatial patterns of accessibility change. The infrastructure Scenario A1 even leads to gains in accessibility in several regions of the new member states, in regions of the Nordic countries and in Spain. Even in combination with the more drastic policies against car use in the combination Scenario A3, some regions gain in accessibility compared to Reference Scenario A-1. The overall spatial pattern is similar in the same policy groups in the B and C scenarios. However, the decrease in accessibility is larger, and there are no regions with accessibility gains.

The *economic* impact predicted by the fuel-price and policy scenarios of the SASI model are presented in Figure 3.2. In all scenarios, the economic growth of the past continues in the future. There is no scenario that leads to additional growth; all policy interventions slow down economic growth. Whereas in the Reference Scenario A-1 the average GDP per capita in 2031 is about €38,000, the combination of high fuel-price increases and strong policy response, as in Scenarios C2 and C3, leads to an average GDP per capita of only about €34,000, more than 10 per cent less than in the Reference Scenario.

This loss of economic prosperity is not evenly distributed across the continent. If one isolates the effects of fuel-price increases by comparing only scenarios with equal policy combinations, such as Scenarios B0 with A0 and B1 with A1, the regions in the new EU member states and the northern and southern periphery suffer more from the fuel-price increases because they have to spend more to reach their far-away markets. The consequence is increased out-migration from these regions to more prosperous regions in the European core. In absolute terms, however, the prosperous central regions lose more because they spend more euros per capita on transport and mobility.

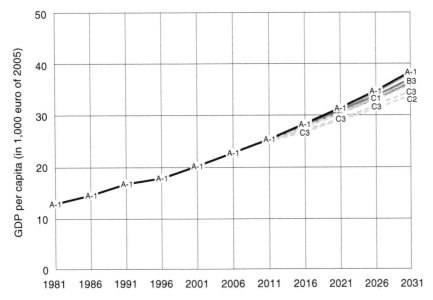

Figure 3.2 SASI model results: GDP per capita 1981–2031.

If one includes the effects of the policy scenarios, the picture is slightly different. In Scenario A1, which is a combination of moderate fuel-price increases, some infrastructure network development and only modest additional cost to road transport, some regions have a better economic performance than in Reference Scenario A-1. The benefiting regions are nearly all located in the new member states or in the two accession countries, Bulgaria and Romania. However, in the remaining A scenarios and the B and C scenarios, there are no regions with higher GDP per capita than in the Reference Scenario, i.e. the higher rates of fuel-cost increases are not compensated by the policies considered in the scenarios.

Metropolitan regions

The Dortmund model developed at the Institute of Spatial Planning of the University of Dortmund (IRPUD) was designed to study the impact of policies from the fields of industrial development, housing, public facilities, land use and transport. The model study area is the metropolitan area of Dortmund with a population of 2.6 million. Exogenous inputs are forecasts of total regional employment and net migration of the metropolitan area and global policies (taxation, regulation) and local policies (land use, transport).

In the application for STEPs, the forecasts of total employment in the study region were adjusted to the forecasts of the SASI model. This was done by adjusting the regional employment control totals of the Dortmund model to the GDP forecasts of the SASI model for the ten NUTS-3 regions of the Dortmund

Table 3.2 Dortmund metropolitan area: GDP effects

Policy	Fuel-price increase		
	+1% pa	*+4% pa*	*+7% pa*
Do nothing	A-1*	B-1	C-1
	0.	−2.5	−5.2
Business as usual	A0	B0	C0
	−1.5	−4.1	−5.7
Infrastructure and technology	A1	B1	C1
	−1.0	−3.5	−4.6
Demand regulation	A2	B2	C2
	−2.8	−5.1	−10.6
All policies	A3	B3	C3
	−1.7	−3.9	−9.3

Note
*Reference scenario. Per cent values indicate differences to Reference Scenario in 2031.

metropolitan area. As in the SASI model, all fuel-price and policy scenarios result in lower regional GDP per capita than in Reference Scenario A-1: the SASI model predicts GDP per capita in these regions between 1 per cent (Scenario A1) and 10.6 per cent (Scenario C2) lower than in the Reference Scenario in 2031 (see Table 3.2). These reductions in economic activity affect employment, non-residential construction, household incomes and work trips and transport emissions in the Dortmund model.

The scenarios were run from 1970 to 2030. All scenarios are identical until 2005, with the first policies becoming effective in 2006. In Figures 3.3 to 3.6, as in Figures 3.1 and 3.2, the heavy black line represents the Reference Scenario; each thinner line represents one policy scenario identified by its scenario code.

The first thing to note is that all assumed further fuel-price increases and policies work in the same direction: they constrain *mobility*, despite the fact that some policies are intended to compensate or at least mitigate the negative effects of increasing fuel prices. In no case are these counter-policies strong enough to compensate for the fuel-price effect.

Figures 3.3 and 3.4 emphasize that fuel-price increases have a major impact on travel behaviour. In all scenarios, the share of public transport trips goes up and that of car trips goes down compared with Reference Scenario A-1. As expected, the magnitude of the impact is a function of the degree of the price increase, and, in general, the policies applied reinforce the price effect. If the policies are combined with land-use policies, as in Scenarios A2 and A3, B2 and B3 and C2 and C3, people again make more trips by foot or bicycle, public-transport use returns to levels common in the 1950s and car travel to what it was in the 1970s.

In Scenarios C2 and C3, car use is reduced to less than 10 per cent of all trips. That may appear a rather extreme response of the model. However, in these two scenarios in 2030, a litre of petrol costs €22 at the petrol stations in today's

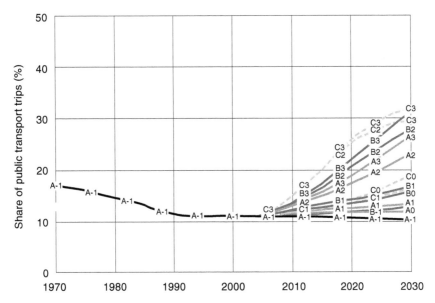

Figure 3.3 Dortmund model results: share of public transport trips 1970–2030.

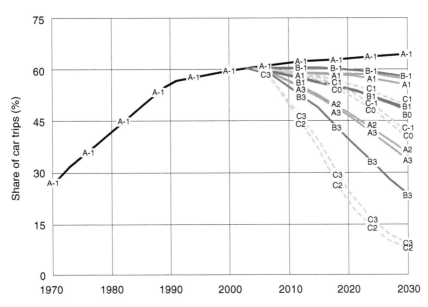

Figure 3.4 Dortmund model results: share of car trips 1970–2030.

money and almost €40 including inflation. At the same time, household incomes in the Dortmund metropolitan area grow by about 10 per cent less than in Reference Scenario A-1 according to the SASI model. This makes it impossible for households to increase their travel budgets in order to maintain their present level of mobility. In particular, long-distance car commuters will have only two choices: to travel to work by public transport or to move closer to their place of work.

The distance-reducing effects of fuel-price increases can also be seen in Figure 3.5, which shows average trip distances. If one looks at the fuel price only in Scenarios A-1, B-1 and C-1, the results are consistent with expectations. As fuel prices go up, travel distances go down. However, it is instructive to relate this decline to the growth in travel distances in the last three decades. Average trip lengths have grown by 40 per cent since 1970: travel distances per capita per day have more than doubled and person-km by car have quadrupled. In scenarios A3, B3 and C3, average trip distances start to rise again after 2020 because faster trains and buses offer travel alternatives not available in Scenarios A2, B2 and C2.

With the assumed reductions in fuel consumption per car-km, car fuel consumption and *emissions* can be calculated. Transport emissions are calculated using speed-related emission functions and information about the changing composition of the vehicle fleet.

Figure 3.6 shows the results of the calculation of emissions of greenhouse gases from transport per capita per day based on the traffic flows by vehicle type and speed predicted by the Dortmund model.

CO_2 emissions from transport have grown continuously in the past because of the combined effect of growing transport volumes and the trend towards larger

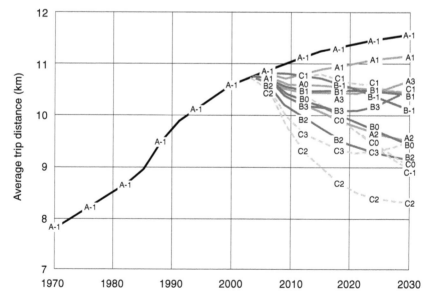

Figure 3.5 Dortmund model results: average trip distance 1970–2030.

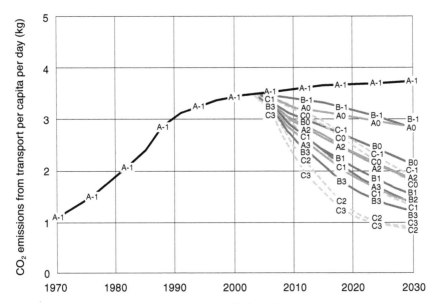

Figure 3.6 Dortmund model results: CO_2 emissions from transport per capita per day 1970–2030.

cars that consume more fuel, which has more than offset the effect of decreasing fuel consumption per vehicle. Transport CO_2 emissions have grown in the past and will continue to grow, though to a lesser degree, in Reference Scenario A-1. All scenarios have a significant impact on future CO_2 emissions, i.e. they lead to strong reductions. Within each of the three scenario groups with identical assumptions about fuel price, the demand-regulation scenarios (A2, B2, C2) are more effective than the infrastructure and technology scenarios (A1, B1, C1), in other words, advances in fuel efficiency without restrictions on car use are not sufficient to achieve more sustainable urban transport. The combination of infra-structure and technology with demand-regulation policies and rigorous anti-sprawl land-use policies (A3, B3, C3) leads to the largest reduction, which is in line with earlier model results (Lautso *et al.* 2004). Most of the scenarios result in CO_2 emission levels per capita below CO_2 emissions in 1990.

The fuel-price increases and policies assumed in the scenarios also have a significant impact on car ownership. In all scenarios, car ownership is lower than in Reference Scenario A-1, where car ownership, which has almost tripled since 1970, continues to grow to more than 700 cars per 1,000 inhabitants. In the fuel-price only Scenarios B-1 and C-1, it grows only slightly less, and even in the demand-regulation Scenarios A2, B2 and C2, car ownership remains at a level higher than today because these measures do not affect the costs of owning a car. In the technology Scenarios A1, B1 and C1 (and consequently also in Scenarios A3, B3 and C3), the higher costs of alternative vehicles are assumed to affect the cost of owning a car. The result is that in these scenarios car ownership goes down by about 40 per cent to less than 450 cars per 1,000 inhabitants, the level of the late 1980s.

It is common knowledge among urban planners that the massive outflow of people to the suburbs over the last few decades would not have been possible without the automobile and cheap fuel. In fact, suburbanization has gone hand in hand with the growth of car ownership and the decline of fuel prices in real terms. If, as in the scenarios examined in STEPs, fuel prices grow and car ownership goes down, will people leave the suburbs and return to the cities?

The simulations with the Dortmund model show that this cannot be expected without policy intervention. The investments of suburban households in home ownership are so large that even significant increases in the costs of car travel will not induce them to give up their house and move back into a flat in the inner city – as long as they have alternatives, such as travelling by public transport or choosing a job nearer to their home. Only in extreme cases of long-distance commuting from rural areas in which there are neither acceptable public-transport connections nor job alternatives, will a move be the only choice. The effects of the fuel-price increase and associated policy scenarios on the distribution of population and employment in the urban area are therefore negligible except in the scenarios in which land-use policies are applied (A2, A3, B2, B3, C2, C3).

However, Figures 3.3 to 3.6 show that scenarios with strong anti-sprawl land-use planning perform better in terms of environmental quality and sustainability and are better prepared to cope with fuel shortages and high fuel prices.

Conclusions

Which main messages about the spatial impact of increases in fuel costs and related policy responses can be taken from the results of the two models?

The simulations with the SASI model show that fuel-price increases and related policy responses have a strong negative impact on accessibility in all scenarios. The magnitude of the negative impact depends on the rate of fuel-cost increases. The transport-related policies do not improve the situation. Even worse, most of the policies, in particular, those with demand regulation, contain so many additional costs for road, and to a lesser degree for air transport, that average accessibility in the policy scenarios is lower than in the corresponding fuel-cost only scenarios. The improvements of rail transport are not strong enough to compensate for the cost increases in the two other modes. In summary, the SASI model suggests that fuel-price increases lead to notably lower levels of accessibility and that policies that try to influence demand make the situation even worse. This results in levels of accessibility not only lower than in the Reference Scenario, but even lower than today.

The combined scenario simulations with the SASI and Dortmund models show that the assumed fuel-price increases and policy responses have a strong negative impact on the economy and daily mobility in the metropolitan area. Once again, the magnitude of the negative impact depends on the rate of fuel-cost increases, with transport-related policies not improving the situation. Most of the policies, in particular, those aiming at demand regulation, contain so many additional costs for car travellers that average accessibility in the policy scenarios is lower than in the corresponding fuel-cost only scenarios. The improvements in public transport are not strong enough to compensate for the cost increases in car travel. This again results in levels of accessibility not only lower than in the Reference Scenario, but even lower than today.

These constraints in mobility lead to significant changes in daily travel behaviour. In all scenarios, the long-term trend towards more and longer trips and more trips by car is stopped or even reversed. Average travel distances per capita return to the level of the 1990s, average travel distances by car to the level of the 1980s and before. There is a renaissance of walking and cycling trips, and the number of trips by public transport more than doubles or even triples. The share of car trips declines to levels last experienced in the 1970s.

These changes in travel behaviour are not voluntary, but forced responses to severe constraints and, in most cases, imply a substantial loss of quality of life. As mandatory trips, such as work and school trips, can less easily be changed, the reductions in trips and trip distances mostly affect voluntary trips, such as social or leisure trips, and every such trip not made means a friend not visited, a meeting not attended or a theatre performance or soccer match not seen. Rising costs of transport also mean financial stress for most households and families who sell their cars and still have to spend more on travel than before, although their income grows less and housing becomes more expensive.

The positive side-effects of the reduction in traffic caused by rising fuel prices are its effect on the environment. Every car trip not made, and every kilometre shorter the remaining trips are, means fewer greenhouse gases, less air pollution and fewer accidents. In addition, the efforts to develop more energy-efficient cars and alternative vehicles stimulated by the fuel-price increases and related policies contribute to the positive environmental balance. From the point of view of achieving the Kyoto objectives, high fuel prices are the best possible prospect. However, the price paid for this success, both in terms of money and quality of life, is substantial, and ways to alleviate the hardships in these two dimensions have yet to be found.

Even large fuel-price increases do not lead to a voluntary return to the inner cities. European cities contain a huge potential for internal reorganization through better coordination of activities. High-density, mixed-use urban structures result in significant further reductions in fuel consumption without unacceptable loss of quality of life.

To mitigate the hardships and maximize the benefits of higher fuel prices, regions and cities need integrated and long-term land-use and transport strategies that include a combination of pricing policies directed at car users with moderate public-transport fares, public-transport infrastructure investments to improve speed and service and a regional spatial development plan supporting living near central areas, in satellite cities or along public-transport corridors.

Integrated land-use and transport strategies for whole metropolitan areas require a high degree of consensus and cooperation between the core cities and suburban municipalities. Moreover, they require a strong regional planning system and efficient mechanisms of horizontal and vertical coordination between government departments and levels, a broad public debate between researchers, policy-makers, stakeholders and citizens and strong efforts to raise public awareness of the importance of preparing regions and cities for an energy-scarce future by promoting more sustainable modes of transport, regional economic circuits and less car-dependent settlement structures.

Acknowledgement

The author is grateful to the STEPs team, in particular, his colleague Klaus Spiekermann, for permission to report on their common work.

References

Bröcker, J., Meyer, R., Schneekloth, N., Schürmann, C., Spiekermann, K. and Wegener, M. (2004) *Modelling the Socio-economic and Spatial Impacts of EU Transport Policy*, Deliverable D6 of IASON (Integrated Appraisal of Spatial Economic and Network Effects of Transport Investments and Policies), Kiel/Dortmund: Christian Albrechts University of Kiel/Institute of Spatial Planning.

IEA – International Energy Agency (2007) *World Energy Outlook 2007 – China and India Insights*, Paris: IEA, available at www.iea.org/Textbase/npsum/WEO2007SUM.pdf (accessed 27 August 2008).

IPCC – Intergovernmental Panel on Climate Change (2007) *Fourth Assessment Report 2007: Synthesis Report. Summary for Policy Makers*, available at www.ipcc.ch/pdf/ assessment-report/ar4/syr/ar4_syr_spm.pdf (accessed 3 October 2008).

Lautso, K., Spiekermann, K., Wegener, M., Sheppard, I., Steadman, P., Martino, A., Domingo, R. and Gayda, S. (2004) *PROPOLIS. Planning and Research of Policies for Land Use and Transport for Increasing Urban Sustainability*, Final Report, Helsinki: LT Consultants, available at http://www1.wspgroup.fi/lt/propolis (accessed 3 October 2008).

STEPs (2006) *Transport Strategies under the Scarcity of Energy Supply*, Final Report of the Project 'Scenarios for the Transport and Energy Supply and Their Potential Effects' (STEPs), A. Monzon and A. Nuijten (eds), The Hague: Bucks Consultants International, available at http://www.steps-eu.com/ (accessed 3 October 2008).

US Department of Energy (2007) *Annual Energy Outlook 2007 with Projections to 2030*, Washington, DC: Energy Information Administration, available at www.eia.doe.gov/ oiaf/archive/aeo07/index.html (accessed 3 October 2008).

Wegener, M. (1998) *The IRPUD Model: Overview*, available at http://irpud.raumplanung. uni-dortmund. de/irpud/pro/mod/mod_e.htm (accessed 3 October 2008).

Wegener, M. and Bökemann, D. (1998) 'The SASI Model: Model Structure. SASI Deliverable D8', *Berichte aus dem Institut für Raumplanung 40*, Dortmund: Institut für Raumplanung, Universität Dortmund, available at www.raumplanung.uni-dortmund. de/irpud/pro/sasi/ber40.pdf (accessed 3 October 2008).

4   Fear of the East

How the rise of China is being used to rationalize undemocratic and inappropriate planning in Europe

John Lovering

Introduction

Leading European politicians have for some time pointed to the apparently inexorable economic rise of China as a major challenge to Europe. If the future of European incomes, jobs and well-being depends on 'competitiveness', then the rise of a new and growing source of cheap exports, and a magnetic new competitor in the search for mobile capital, is surely a challenge indeed – or even a major threat.

In 2005, Peter Mandelson, speaking in Beijing, ran through the usual ritualistic numbers associated with the Chinese boom: a third of world growth since the year 2000 has come from China. China's foreign exchange reserves are 17 times larger than the UK's. Of China's three million graduates each year, 250,000 are engineers. Within 15 years, China will consume more than Saudi Arabia's current entire oil production. In ten years, there will be 160 million cars on Chinese roads. China already consumes around a third of world steel and its own production of steel increases each year by the equivalent of half the total Japanese steel output. Chinese economic growth has averaged around 9 per cent for 28 years. But his point was to insist that:

> The truth is Europe can compete in the new world, but it involves a process of restructuring and adjustment in which there will inevitably be losers as well as winners within the EU itself. But it was always thus, given that economic dynamism, technological change and human creativity are the source of Europe's high levels of prosperity.

For Mandelson, the member-state governments behind him, and the EU bureaucracy in general, 'China' is a signifier reinforcing the validity of the Lisbon agenda for 'economic reform and growth', which crystallized under the influence of the BBA trio, Blair, Berlusconi and Aznar. In this spirit, the European Commission promises 'to deepen the EU's economic relationship with China (and other Asian countries), utilizing market access to each others' markets and stimulating the flow of investment. This is a priority for the Barroso Commission over the next three years.'

At home, this means more urgency in the 'debate on the future of the European social model'. The position of the Mandelsonians on this debate is well known, albeit wrapped in euphemisms:

> our social, regional and industrial policies all need to be updated to adjust to the speed of economic change. These reforms promise more competitiveness, and rapid spatial change. So there will be more losers, in social and geographical terms. So Mandelson adds that 'we need more explicit policies to address the problems of the losers' from globalization and to tackle the new inequalities that globalization brings.

The European Commission's job is to lead such thinking and help spread good practice across our continent. In 2004, Romano Prodi announced 'another ambitious 5-year project aimed at further integrating China into the world trading system'. An indicative budget of €250 million was planned for the period 2002–6.

Against this background, the development of at least a discourse concerning European Spatial Development has begun to make a prominent mark on the EU's documentation and on its websites. Much of the debate about this amongst planners has concerned the likely effectiveness of the agreements signed at Hannover in September 2000, and the relationships between the EU and national competences (e.g. Faludi). The more important issue here is the extent to which the principles underpinning this development conform to the Lisbon vision and Mandelson's insistence that China should signify 'the same, only more so'. As Klaus Kunzmann noted a few years ago (1996), the future of spatial development in Europe will be profoundly shaped by the influence of such thinking.

The main ingredients of the Lisbon package are well known. Under the rubric of the need to address competitiveness, social cohesion and environmental sustainability, it is allegedly imperative that Europe develops a knowledge economy and that cities, and increasingly city-regions, become more pro-active economically and socially and thereby improve that mysterious property known as their competitiveness. This has become the dominant discourse in certain policy circles, spread as a result of the growing demand for and supply of resonant policy ideas on the part of what I call the urban or regional 'service class' (Lovering 2003).

The resulting documents, webpages and strategic comments often seem to have done more to license the growth of American-style urban boosterism than to generate empirically well-informed and analytically well-balanced urban-regional analysis and strategies. But, in a governance-environment climate dominated by influences from above rather than democratic pressures from below, they have been welcomed by their purchasers as demonstrating that they are 'performing governance' in an acceptable manner. They do not offer much to the question that is the spur to this book: What is the significance of the rise of China for European planning? The proliferation of such quasi-research says more about the impoverished intellectual environment of planning policy than about the realities of China, Europe, or jobs or cities.

Interestingly, analyses by academic economists tend to generate rather different impressions than do the statements of European Commissioners or the endlessly repeated bullet points of high-profile consultants. First, they point to the many very peculiar contingencies that have underpinned recent Chinese–European economic relations, with the implication that is highly unlikely that these will persist uninterrupted for another 28 years. More important in the present context, they suggest that the impact of Chinese growth on economic and especially employment trends in Europe is likely to have been, and to continue to be, much less dramatic than is often suggested. On the one hand, there are no clear criteria whereby 'vulnerable' and 'invulnerable' jobs can be identified, therefore, the current discourse of the knowledge-based economy is somewhat misplaced. And on the other, much employment in Europe (and elsewhere) never has been, is not, and will not be in or dependent on globally traded sectors where 'the threat of China' is a relevant consideration. The loss of jobs in Europe in recent decades has been a result of processes largely unrelated to globalization, and particularly to the export success of China. The main causes of recent job change in Europe lie in policy choices made in and by European political leadership at national, urban-regional, and, increasingly, at supranational levels.

These considerations suggest that if planning in European cities and regions is to respond appropriately to the rise of China while also fulfilling its remit to be socially responsible and forward-looking, a rather different set of scenarios and policy options needs to be considered than is currently the case. This is especially so at the level of European Commission thinking about spatial development and at the (somewhat autonomous) level of urban governance. Both of these are excessively influenced by simplistic economic assumptions. It is intellectually and ethically inadequate to assume, whether with Peter Mandelson and the European Commission, or Michael Parkinson and a small herd of urban and regional consultants, that the lesson of the rise of China is that European authorities must try harder

> to fill the Lisbon Agenda and become more 'competitive' in the sense in which this intrinsically empty term is currently deployed. In sum, much more thinking needs to be done to develop strategies which prioritize sustainable job creation, minimize fossil fuel use, and maximize localization.
>
> (Woodin and Lucas 2004)

The contingencies of the current growth of China

Bretton Woods II

Much attention has been given to the sheer scale and rapidity of the Chinese economic take-off. Far less attention has been given to the conditions that have made it possible.

First among these are the extraordinary international financial arrangements that have arisen as a result of explicit and implicit collusion between the world economy's main financial players. At the core of these is the sustained over-spending of US consumers and government, which has for several years gener-ated a current-account deficit of 6 per cent of the GDP. The rest of the world subsidizes US consumption by some £1.7 billion a day. This is sustained by a continual inflow of funds primarily from East Asia, with China making a major contribution. In the early 2000s, three Deutsche Bank economists identified this as what they ironically dubbed the 'Bretton Woods II' system (Dooley *et al.* 2005). Just about the only thing all agree on is that it will not last indefinitely. This system is inherently less stable than the original Bretton Woods regime. It lacks a gold conversion constraint on the reserve currency (the dollar). Any of the partner nations at any time could act unilaterally and disrupt the relationships that keep the system going

In the (possibly long) meantime, the Bretton Woods II system accounts for much of the current remarkable economic prominence of China. The global financial system, maintained by the deliberate actions of both Western and Asian governments, means that the dollar (and currencies linked to it) is overvalued, and the yuan is correspondingly undervalued. This enables the US to continue to spend well beyond its means (i.e. to maintain high consumption and virtually no savings). This in turn helps maintain high Chinese (and Japanese) exports. Exports to the US alone accounted for about 9 per cent of Chinese GDP in 2000 and 12 per cent in 2004.

The fact that commercial price signals are well out of line with 'real eco-nomic costs' also means that the costs to firms of setting up business in China are much lower than they would be in a more genuinely 'free market' system. This underpins the recent incentives for multinational companies to locate pro-duction for Western markets in China (which was first and most energetically recognized by Japanese companies). Foreign-funded companies accounted for 2 per cent of China's merchandise trade in 1986. By 2000, this had risen to 48 per cent (Li 2002: 4).

The Bretton Woods II system also means that European workers engaged in the traded sectors (manufacturing and, increasingly, service industries subject to inroads by multinationals) face exaggerated disadvantages (compared to those they would face if the financial system was shaped less by the collusion of a small set of nation-state leaders).

Overall therefore, the recent pace of global transfers of jobs, and indeed the wider phenomenon of neo-liberalism, is premised not on the working out of some 'naturalistic' processes as theorized in traditional liberal economic theory, but on the highly 'un-naturalistic' relationships created by the contemporary international state system. Within this, the key role is played by the peculiarities of the (mostly undemocratic) political institutions, the class structure, and the influence of particular ideologies of modernization in half a dozen states (Murphy 2006). The neo-mercantilism of the US government and the European Union (both dominated by multinational corporate interests), and the anxiety to maintain high growth rates of employment to absorb rural migration and prevent social disruption in China are fundamental factors.

The US is seeking, in effect, to reduce its debt by a slow gradual devaluation. Those holding dollars know that their chances of redeeming them at current value are minimal. If the dollar falls by 33 per cent, Asian countries will lose over US$600 billion. In effect, therefore, some of the profits of Chinese industry are being given away to American consumers for there is little hope that they will be fully repaid. That this arrangement is attractive to the Chinese government (and other East Asian lenders) says much about the political economy of those regimes, and the urgency with which their ruling elites prioritize the maintenance of high rates of economic growth (Murphy 2006).

The failure to develop indigenous motors of demand

This points to a second distinctive feature of the current Chinese boom. Unlike virtually every other country that has experienced decades of sustained growth, working groups have not seen their wages rise significantly. The much vaunted reduction of poverty in China reflects the decline of the peasantry (although it remains vast) rather than the growth of working-class incomes. The Chinese people are as yet far from reaching even the levels of income that Japan, Korea and Taiwan experienced at the *beginnings* of their 'take-offs' (Glyn 2006: 89). The very low average income of working people in China means that only a small proportion are able to buy the products they produce (although this is a significant number in absolute terms, some 60 million, and for the superficial observer this can create, especially in glamorous urban shopping centres, the impression of dynamism, and of 'Westernization'). In a less flippant perspective, China is clearly not yet within sight of creating the kind of Keynesian domestic motor of growth that propelled Western countries during the Golden Age of Capitalism.

If we project the economic growth of China on the optimistic assumption that recent five-year average growth rates of GDP and population can be cheerfully extrapolated to 2050, GDP per capita will still be but a small fraction of today's European average (see Figure 4.1).

For the foreseeable future, then, Chinese growth will not be based on the kind of 'horizontal accumulation' (Hymer 1972, or Fordist pattern that generated the enormous improvement in working-class standards of living and productivity in the West from the 1950s to 1970. The Chinese government requires a high growth rate to generate some ten million jobs per year, and this can only come (in the absence of a radical change in direction) from further exports. But the ability of China to continue to increase its export competitiveness at recent rates is a matter of considerable uncertainty. All the more so, as Chinese exports are currently radically overproduced, in the sense that profit levels are low and many products are selling at near cost.

In short, the recent redistribution of jobs via foreign direct investment (FDI) and 'offshoring' to China is contingent on many specificities, many of which are unlikely to last. Many observers of China, even those who have not taken into account these economic factors, have suggested that the country's future integrity is in doubt (Gittings 2005; Chang 2002). There is no space to explore

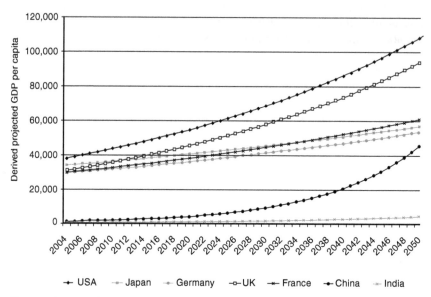

Figure 4.1 Per capita income extrapolated from recent growth and population trends.

these arguments here, only to note that many clouds gather on the Chinese horizon. Meanwhile, the intensity of FDI, offshoring, and global job relocation to China, rooted in the exceptional cost attractiveness of Chinese workers (and cities) to multinational corporations (MNCS), are likely to diminish significantly in future years.

The relatively modest impact of China on European economic development and employment

Whatever its future prospects, it is widely believed that globalization, and the rise of Chinese exports in particular, has been the main cause of employment change in the US and 'Old Europe'. The assumption is that employment is driven by world trade. And, as even the Nobel Prize-winning (and generally neo-classical) economist Paul Samuelson agrees, there are no good reasons to believe that market forces, in response to the rise of a major competitor such as China, will generate a new pattern of Ricardian specialization that will leave sufficient jobs in the former advantaged countries (Samuelson 2004).

The policy lessons drawn from such considerations are, however, based on a massively oversimplified model of economic change and the nature of contemporary globalization that has been curiously influential in the planning community (thanks, perhaps to books such as Castells 1991 and Borja *et al.* 1997. The origins of this can be traced back to the early 1990s, when the European Union was beginning its evolution away from a Franco-German and broadly social-democratic conception towards the more neo-liberal model we have today.

The myth of the immobility of smart labour

In the early 1990s Robert Reich, later to become Clinton's labour advisor, pub-lished *The Work of Nations* (1991). This set out a neat typology of jobs intended to identify those that would be vulnerable to increased competition (globaliza-tion) of the kind that the rise of China now supposedly embodies. Reich reck-oned that routine manufacturing jobs would be the most easily 'competed away' by lower-cost competitors. This would leave two categories: The first, face-to-face services (making coffee, cleaning tables, nail studios), which, he insisted, promised little growth. Therefore, the future of high-quality employment could only be secured by the second category, 'symbolic analysts' (a term sufficiently vague to embrace every conceivable form of commercializable creativity: artists, hi-tech engineers, innovators of all types).

By the late 1990s, the Reich typology (thanks in no small part to New Labour in Britain) had become embodied in the discourse of the 'knowledge economy'. In Europe, the ascendancy of this term reflected a fundamental shift in the nature of the European polity, which followed the end of the Delors era, and the reori-entation of the emergent European employment strategy between the early and late 1990s (the story is told in Lovering 1998). The early commitment under Delors to develop a labour-market strategy to compensate for the vicissitudes that would inevitably follow the adoption of the Single Europe Act was already weakening at the Essen Summit in 1994. By the 1997 Amsterdam Summit, it had mutated into a 'Resolution of the European Council on Growth and Employ-ment', which was recognizably neo-liberal in principle, jettisoning any residue of 'Keynesian macro-economics' – and by the time of Lisbon, the mutation was complete.

The discursive link, European economic competitiveness and employment, is now centred in the knowledge economy. But this is a slogan rather than a strat-egy based in any kind of rigorous economic analysis. The idea that a shift towards a knowledge economy makes European jobs more secure, despite Peter Mandelson, Manuel Castells, or Michael Parkinson, lacks theoretical or empiri-cal support. As Green European parliament critics of neo-liberal globalization recently pointed out in the context of debates over China, there is no field in which 'knowledge' necessarily imparts geographical fixity. Hi-tech 'symbolic analytical' jobs may well prove to be as susceptible to global relocation as low-tech ones; there is nothing about IT skills, medicine, or infotainment (including the now-fashionable 'cultural industries' in the sense that they have been cele-brated by Richard Florida) that inherently lends them territorial fixity. The sug-gestion that the development of a knowledge economy will weld competitiveness and employment sustainability is mere rhetoric. It fetishistically shifts attention onto the technical character of a job (the qualifications and 'smartness' involved) and away from the determinants of the geography of labour markets.

This has been particularly evident in some locations. In the US, for example, despite huge apparent increases in smartness and knowledge, as measured by the level of qualifications, the 'economy's ability to provide "good jobs" has fallen since the late 1970s by 25 to 30 per cent' (Schmitt 2005: 3). Closer to home, one of the most globalized regions in the EU is Wales. There 20 years (and half a billion pounds) of regional assistance has significantly raised skills, qualifications and productivity in the foreign-owned manufacturing sector. Welsh manufacturing output in value terms is at a historic high, and the foreign-owned sector largely accounts for this. But employment fell by 36 per cent between 1995 and 2005 (a rate of collapse as severe as that of the infamously catastrophic years of job losses in coal and steel under Mrs Thatcher). *All* the new jobs in the Welsh economy have come from entirely unrelated sectors, such as distribution services, banking, and, above all, public administration, health and education.

What an emphasis on knowledge does more clearly, however, is address some the most vociferous demands of the most powerful voices in economic strategy in Brussels: namely multinational corporations. It is no accident that the demand for a knowledge-economy bias was first articulated in the corridors of Brussels by the European Roundtable of Industrialists (Balanya *et al.* 2000). It subsequently became the staple fare of Commissioners and the legions of urban and regional-policy consultants and think-tanks whose business depends on proliferating the cognitive and normative biases favoured by dominant institutions. But the substance behind these slogans is thin, and often contentious, for the orthodox Mandelsonian response to the rise of China is based on tendentious reasoning. The policies proposed hold out no serious promise of creating sustainable high-quality employment on a significant scale.

The rise of China will continue to be an important factor bearing upon economic strategizing in Europe. But its significance is far more ambivalent than the currently dominant discourse suggests. First, Chinese exports have high import context, some of which will continue to come from Europe. Second, the growth of Chinese exports (and of attractiveness to FDI) at recent rates is unlikely to be sustained because Bretton Woods II is unlikely to be sustained. Third, the effects of increasing demands for imported energy are likely to create some capacity constraints. The energy dimension of this is noted below. With this exception, however, Chinese growth is mainly significant for Europe only to the extent that European employment policies make it so. In other words, the key factor relevant to this book is not developments in China at all, so much as it is policy thinking in European cities and regions. It is here, rather than in Shenzhen or Beijing, that the main problems for European workers and citizens, and thence in principle for planners, are to be found.

The main determinants of European employment are homemade

Economists' attempts to quantify the effect of globalization on job losses in Northern countries have almost always generated very undramatic results. This is because other factors have invariably turned out to be more important.

In quantitative terms, the competition from China (or anywhere else, such as India) has influenced only a very small part of European employment change.

This is because manufacturing and tradable services are only one – shrinking – layer of the employment 'cake', especially at the urban level. The development of employment in Europe has been determined by factors of a totally different order. Although competition from China or from EU accession countries has accounted for some individual, and highly visible, cases of factory closure, invoking globalization as the explanation merely short-cuts the explanation. It fails to explain why the jobs lost have not been replaced by others. Cheaper foreign wages in China or anywhere else do not in themselves explain the lack of local demand to reutilize the labour so released for other activities.

The decline in manufacturing employment and the polarization of labour markets is only in small part due to external competition and much more to domestic policy shifts (Glyn 2006; Baker and Schmitt 1999; Etxezarreta *et al.* 2003, etc.). The growth of European service industries has also failed to generate the job content of its American equivalents (Glyn *et al.* 2004).

A large literature has demonstrated that the main cause of the European jobs crisis, and the urban and regional adjustments which are a consequence, has been the changed macroeconomic strategies of European governments (on which EU-level strategy has had an increasing influence). Contrary to the suggestions by Mandelson, Blair, Brown, Merkel, Chirac, *et al.*, the main causes of recent changes in European employment and the related urban-regional disruption are to be found in the policies adopted at the level of European member states. Glyn (2006) and Schmitt (2005), for example, have consistently found that macroeconomic changes initiated by governments within Europe must bear the bulk of the blame for recent labour-market imbalances. The primary cause of the new spatial unevenness in Europe is its abandonment since the 1980s of the social compact between organized capital and labour and the 'neo-liberalising turn' in many dimensions of public policy in all countries. It is this that has played the main role in the loss of manufacturing (low-skill) jobs and also the shift to consumer-spending-driven, property-market-oriented urban regeneration.

Why do less-qualified workers suffer more unemployment?

The popularity of the Reichian notion that there are some kinds of jobs that are intrinsically vulnerable to foreign (now Chinese) competition has often been allowed to obscure the real dynamics of employment change in Europe. The fact that it is low-qualified employees whose jobs have been lost does not necessarily demonstrate that all but knowledge-economy jobs are vulnerable to globalization (so the latter should be targeted for support). There are theoretical and empirical reasons to believe that it is far more likely to indicate instead a general shortage of jobs, together with the emergence of new queuing processes. On the labour-supply side, these involve the use of formal qualifications as labels, and on the demand side, the increasing willingness of employers to use credential criteria in selection. Education research shows that there is no systematic relationship over time between countries in education, economic growth, and employment (Wolf 2002). But there is plenty of evidence of a growth of the use of qualifications to rank job seekers.

Little of this is evident in the urban and regional policy orthodoxies regularly reproduced by European Commission documents and the consultants whose claims resonate with the Commission's policy preferences. Many reports on city competitiveness merely list the percentages of qualified people, as if the knowledge-economy significance of this is self-explanatory. It is not.

For a decade and a half, Europe has suffered a chronic shortage of jobs. This is expressed more in the rise in economic inactivity than in unemployment, the former and latter accounting for two-thirds and one-third, respectively, of the growing employment gap compared to the US (Glyn *et al.* 2004: 3). Job shortages underlie the polarization of the labour market and the rise of qualifications as 'queue markers'. Education is popular at the individual level, not because it imparts skills, but because it improves the beneficiaries' chances of getting ahead of the competition (Wolf 2002). Planning which seeks to reproduce these tendencies may merely reinforce divisive policies, rather than improve productivity. Prudent planning would seek to diminish the incentives for such queue-jumping.

What does this mean for planning?

The economic paradigm to make the European Union 'the most dynamic and competitive-knowledge-based economy in the world by 2010' embedded in the Lisbon Agenda is not only implausible (as recent Commission statements have admitted). It has major, and retrograde, implications for planning. The argument here seeks to suggest that the cognitive and normative assumptions underpinning the Lisbon Agenda's scenarios are based less on fact than on ideology; less on evidence than on *a priori* theory. Many economic and social analyses imply, in fact, that it is the economic strategy embodied in the Lisbon Agenda, rather than the rise of China, that is responsible for exacerbating polarization in the labour market, exacerbating migration flows, creating a slate of 'shrinking cities', and entrenching social divisions and deepening ethnic/cultural antagonisms even in more prosperous ones.

As Klaus Kunzmann has argued (1996), different scenarios for the determinants of European economic development have radically different implications for planning. The hegemony of the kind of thinking encapsulated in the Lisbon Agenda implies the further development of recent spatial trends, leading to a far-reaching reconstruction of European space. But, if the analysis above is reasonably correct, this reconstruction is one shaped by particular special interests and elite prejudices rather than by technological and economic necessities or sustainable possibilities. The spatial reflection of European neo-liberalism marginalizes the provisions for welfare and sustainability in any deeper sense than that of the survival of competitiveness in the market. This is rationalized by discourses claiming the inevitability of current trends and advocating glorified versions of the traditional planning mode of 'predict and provide'. But the 'predict' element here is based not on any serious economic analysis but on the unchallenged hegemony of particular and partisan policy orthodoxies (Glyn 2006). The European Spatial Development Strategy (ESDS) is perhaps the most unabashed example of this kind of reductionism.

The ESDS seeks to promote a polycentric urban system and a new rural–urban relationship, centred on increasing consumption of energy for transport, especially in the form of the car. It anticipates low-density greenfield development around the increasingly gentrified core of towns and cities, and suburbanization along broadly American lines. Much of the discussion on European spatial development by planners (e.g. Faludi) has concentrated on questions of the competence of the EU *vis-à-vis* national governments. But far more important are the implausibility of the techno-economic imperatives it embodies and the undesirability of the scenarios it proposes. Spatial development along the lines that this kind of thinking encourages would seem set to intensify the emergence of Kunzmann's (Euro-megalopolis, with smatterings of Theme Park Europe and perhaps Virtual Europe, but precious little sign of a Europe of sustainable regions (see Figure 4.2).

The assumptions underpinning the 'fear of China' versus the reality of urban and regional development

In the short to medium term, the crucial weakness of the model which many influential authorities would have planners adopt in response to the alleged challenge of China lies in the labour market. From the heights of the European Commission to the most remote local authority, there is an almost total absence of serious empirical analyses of the real drivers of labour-market change in European regions and cities. This is partly a result of the absence of local research capacity. But it also reflects the ubiquitous absence of local political pressures to give voice to alternatives, and the pressure to be seen instead to conform to centrally generated discourses. One effect of this has been the (costly) tendency for policy-makers to invoke the authority of branded consultants. This has often, I suggest, had disastrous effects in terms of limiting cognitive and normative horizons.

The real economic motors of urban development are, in general, very different from those portrayed in the neo-liberal orthodoxy endorsed by the European Commission and the most commonly used consultants (e.g. Parkinson 2005). In fact, 'Most economies are still dominated by locally produced goods, and even where an economy appears to be open, such as Belgium or Ireland, its trade is, in fact, dominated by either regional producers or a sub-set of them' (Edwards 2006: 14). Contrary to mountains of glossy publicity celebrating urban development, and the international academic authorities whose work they often cite (e.g. Sassen 1991), the growth of employment in most West European cities in recent years has been driven only to a very modest extent by externally traded (and high-profile) sectors. Awareness of the real history of urban development and urbanism has all too often been dissolved by the acid of neo-liberal ideology. For the city remains, in economic terms, mainly a space of *localized* interaction and exchange. In the UK, the public sector has been, despite neo-liberalism, an

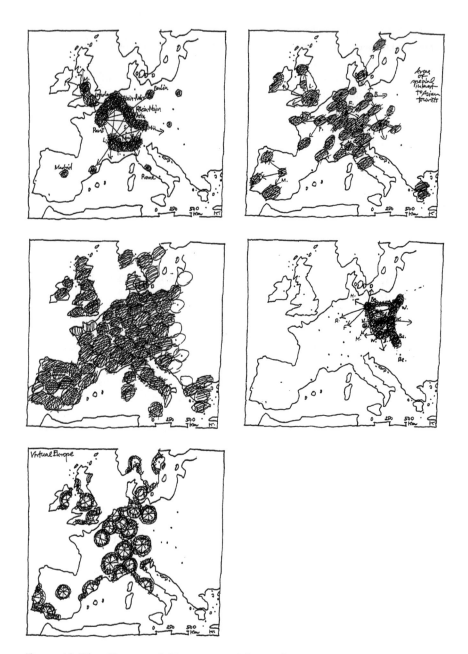

Figure 4.2 Klaus Kunzmann's European spatial scenarios.

irrepressible provider of localized services using local input (mainly of people) (Glyn 2006). And, it has been the main source of increased employment in the past decade.

This has been entirely overlooked in most of the recent literature on urban development, especially that ostensibly concerned in identifying appropriate policy. It is overlooked in the dominant Mandelsonian 'must try harder' interpretation of the significance of China for Europe.

In the medium to longer term, the main weakness is environmental. The spatial restructuring that Lisbon Agenda thinking encourages is increasingly anachronistic. It promotes an American style of economic and social geography, a development that was viable only in an era of (deceptively) cheap oil. Sometime around now the oil peak will pass, having exhausted half of all global oil reserves. Future oil costs are set to rise until for many they will become unaffordable. Here at least the 'threat' of China is real, for its escalating energy demands will inevitably intensify oil-cost pressures on European consumers. Since there is, as yet, no foreseeable plausible substitute, planning that seeks to construct cities, regions, and countries as if we were still living in the era of the American Dream can only be described as short-sighted, if not simply irresponsible.

The stirrings of an alternative interpretation

These were some of the issues raised in the debate in the European Parliament last year concerning the challenge of China. In more imaginative circles, this stirred demands for a breakaway from the narrow ideological orthodoxies which have hampered economic and spatial policy debates in Europe since the early 1990s. The China Factor would, some argue, trigger a much needed rethinking of the premises of planning orthodoxy in Europe, since it draws attention to the mounting certainty of resource and environmental constraints, and the social dysfunctionality of current models of development.

These debates suggest that the greatest threat arising from the rise of China is that it will help legitimize the strategies for socio-economic, and thence, spatial development that most of Europe has been following since the mid-1990s. That promises to create, by mid-century, a continent of polarized cities, extreme juxtapositions of wealth and poverty, conflictual cultural identities, spectacular consumerism and guarded public space, endemic violence and ubiquitous fear, all tottering on fragile economic pillars, loomed over by impending ecological disaster.

From globalization to localization

The key principle underpinning alternative approaches is a rebalancing of globalization with localization. While this has been around in the geographical and policy literature for some time (e.g. Lovering 2001; Hines 2000), it has been almost taboo in official circles. In recent years, the advantages of considering localization have been recognized in the case of food, but generally in ways that have rendered a partial and unchallenging 'special case' anchored in the supposed special character of the commodity in question. In fact, the issues raised by the challenge of localization are of far more general significance.

'The rise of China' is at present a floating signifier that has mainly been captured by those who wish to advocate more corporate-oriented globalization along recent neo-liberalizing lines. The extreme reductionism of the dominant discourse concerning China could be a spur to a rethinking of the fundamental purposes and methods of planning, opening up the chances of re-democratizing it by making it a space of popular engagement with the fundamental issues of social and environmental possibilities in the first half of the twenty-first century.

To this end, planners would need to develop new cognitive and normative habits, expressed in new indicators. The development of 'sustainable economic welfare indicators', or 'genuine progress indicators', for example, could be a potent tool in opening up new ways of assessing the benefits of competing proposals (Munday and Roberts 2006). Like all indicators, these are not technocratic solutions so much as ways of putting the issues in front of the electorate. A precondition for such a widening will be to draw the recent trend to proliferate intellectually vacuous but politically partisan agendas under the rubrics of 'competitiveness indicators' and the rhetoric of knowledge management, knowledge regions, innovative regions/cities, etc. to an end.

In terms of the labour market, serious strategy would require a wholly new approach designed to illuminate the working of labour markets from both supply and demand sides. This will require empirically focused research into the points of entry, blockages, and 'ladders', which determine the distribution of opportunities in the territorial labour market. A key policy area across Europe must be the question of how to create more and better jobs in the service sector, for these are underdeveloped compared to the US: 'A reason for Europe's inability to absorb workers released from agriculture and industry could be the degree of mismatch between labour supply and job vacancies associated with the growing role of services' (D'Agostino et al. 2006: 17).

This approach would also entail a reevaluation of different kinds of jobs, in a spirit very different from that of Robert Reich's globalization-centred categorization. Indeed, the Lisbon Agenda's disdain for McJobs, and that of many urban and regional authorities seeking to promote the chimeras of competitive, high-status, creative, or knowledge-economy jobs is entirely misplaced. For 'it is precisely McJobs that many EU countries lack: jobs that offer pathways to work for the young, unskilled, women and the old' (Gavin Cameron and Fawcett 2005: 14). The aim of a labour-market strategy should be to create an array of jobs and to ensure there are systematic non-discriminatory bridges between them. The EU's current neo-liberal agenda predominantly casts employment strategy in terms of corporate factor costs (demand side) considerations, not in terms of the social need for jobs (supply side). In a more appropriate approach, 'lifestyle' jobs would be celebrated and encouraged, not denigrated and ignored (as is the case in the strategy of the Welsh Assembly Government, for example)

Conclusion: avoiding a new orientalism

Numerous commentators point to the current rapid economic growth of China as a major challenge to Europe, especially in terms of employment. China is presented as confirmation of the inescapability of the pressures of globalization. This is fuelling a reemphasis on what has in recent years become a neo-liberal policy orthodoxy. European cities and regions must develop new structures, institutions, and discourses converging on a redefinition of the key problem planners must face. Planning strategies must converge with other policies designed to enhance space competitiveness. To this end, they must enhance the development of the knowledge economy, develop new frameworks for knowledge management, work to develop 'smart skills, smart companies, and smart places'. Economic strategy should converge with social and cultural strategies to encourage entrepreneurship, innovation, and the production of commercializable knowledge. In the European Union, these have been formally inscribed in the form of the 2000 Lisbon Agenda.

The analysis sketched in this chapter suggests that this approach is radically oversimplified, invokes implausible theories of economic development, and rests on insufficient empirical evidence. China is invoked as a signifier of the validity of a preexisting set of cognitive and normative assumptions which have numerous analytical, practical, and ethical flaws. In reality, the rise of China does not necessarily imply the arrival of any of these scenarios or the necessity of these supposed imperatives. This rhetorical use of China amounts to a new kind of orientalism, in which an elite Western construction of a global 'other' represents little more than a mystification of interests based entirely here in the 'us' of Europe.

Planners, who tend to work in a research-impoverished environment subject to powerful institutional and ideological influences, have been particularly prone to taking on these discourses uncritically. In so doing, they have often unwittingly come to serve a particular partisan set of interests, rather than the interests of the present and future communities they ostensibly serve. And, a small industry has emerged to exploit the 'market for ideas' which has largely had the effect of reproducing tendentious analyses of globalization, and an authoritarian set of global norms for planning strategy. It is not in the general interest that they should continue to act as chambermaids in the neo-liberal hotel.

The rise of China could, and should, create space for a less tendentious and more balanced debate over economic development prospects and the range of possible policy imperatives.

Bibliography

Baker, D. and Schmitt, J. (1999) *The Macroeconomic Roots of High European Unemployment*, Washington, DC: Economic Policy Institute.

Balanya, B., Doherty, A., Hoedeman, O., Ma'anit, A., and Wesselius, E. (2000) *Europe Inc. Regional and Global restructuring and the Rise of Corporate Power*, London: Pluto Books.

Borja, J. and Castells, M. with Belil, M. and Benner, C. (eds) (1997) *Local and Global: The Management of Cities in the Information Age*, London: Earthscan.

Cameron, G. and Fawcett, N. (2005) 'Economic Policies for Growth and Employment', *Dept. of Economics Discussion Papers* 249, Oxford.

Castells, M. (1991) *The Informational City*, Oxford: Blackwell Publishers.

Chang, G. (2002) *The Coming Collapse of China*, Munich: Random House.

D'Agostino, A., Serafin, R., and Ward-Warmedinger, M. (2006) 'Sectoral Explanations of Employment in Europe: The Role of Services', *European Central Bank Working Paper* 625, Frankfurt: ECB.

Dooley, M., Folkerts-Landau, D., and Garber, P. (2005) *International Financial Stability: Asian Interest Rates and the Dollar*, Bonn: Deutsche Bank.

Edwards, T. H. (2006) 'How Globalised Really Is European Trade?', *Discussion Paper series* 2006–10, Department of Economics, Loughborough: Loughborough University.

Etxezarreta, M., Grahl, J., Huffschmid, J., and Mazier, J. (2003) *Full Employment, Welfare and a Strong Public Sector: Democratic Challenges in a Wider Union*, European Economists for an Alternative Economic Policy in Europe, available at www.memo-europe.uni-bremen.de (accessed 27 August 08).

Gittings, J. (2005) *The Changing Face of China*, Oxford: Oxford University Press.

Glyn, A. (2006) *Capitalism Unleashed*, Oxford: Oxford University Press.

Glyn, A., Salverda, W., Moller, J., Schmitt, J., and Solloboub, M. (2004) *Employment Differences in Services: The role of Wages, Productivity and Demand*, DEMPATEM Working Paper, Amsterdam: University of Amsterdam.

Hines, C. (2000) *Localisation: A Global Manifesto*, London: Earthscan.

Hymer, S. H. (1972) 'The Multinational Corporation and the Law of Uneven Development', in J. N. Bhagwati (ed.) *Economics and World Order*, London: Macmillan.

Kunzmann, K. R. (1996) 'Euro-megalopolis or Themepark Europe? Scenarios for European Spatial Development', *International Planning Studies* 1: 143–63.

Li, Y. (2002) *China's Accession to WTO: Exaggerated Fears?*, New York: UNCTAD.

Lovering, J. (1998) 'Globalisation, Unemployment, and "Social Exclusion" in Europe: Three Perspectives on the Current Policy Debate', *International Planning Studies* 3: 35–56.

Lovering, J. (2001) 'The Coming Regional Crisis (and How to Avoid It)', *Regional Studies* 35: 349–54.

Lovering, J. (2003) 'MNCs and Wannabees: The Regional "Service Class"', in N. J. Phelps and P. Raines (eds) *The Competition for Inward Investment*, Aldershot: Ashgate Publishing.

McGiffen, S. (2005) *The European Union: A Critical Guide*, London: Pluto Books.

Mandelson, P. (2005) *Challenges and Opportunities for EU and China in the Age of Globalisation*, Lecture to Central Party School, Beijing, Brussels: European Commission.

Munday, M. and Roberts, A. (2006) 'Developing Approaches to Measuring and Monitoring Sustainable Development in Wales: A Review', *Regional Studies* 40: 535–54.

Murphy, R. (2006) 'East Asia's Dollars', *New Left Review* 40: 39–64.

Parkinson, M. (2005) *Compete and competitive city regions*, Dortmund presentation, available at www.wirtschaftsfoerderung-dortmund.de/downloads/internationalitaet/Prof_Michael_Parkinson_COMPETE_and_competitive_city_regions.pdf (accessed 3 July 2008).

Prodi, R. (2004) *Economic Relations between EU and China*, Brussels: European Commission.

Reich, R. K. (1991) *The Work of Nations: Preparing Ourselves for 21st-century Capitalism*, New York: Vintage Books.

Samuelson, P. (2004) 'Where Ricardo and Mill rebut and Confirm Arguments of Mainstream Economists Supporting Globalization', *Journal of Economic Perspectives* 18: 135–46.

Sassen, S. (1991) *The Global City*, Princeton, NJ: Princeton University Press.

Schmitt, J. (2005) *How Good Is the Economy at Providing Good Jobs?*, Washington, DC: Centre for Economic and Policy Research.

Wolf, A. (2002) *Does Education Matter? Myths about Education and Economic Growth*, New York: Penguin Books.

Woodin, M. and Lucas, C. (2004) *Green Alternatives to Globalisation: A Manifesto*, London: Pluto Press.

5 China and the future of European cities

Ivan Turok

Introduction

Media coverage of China's rising global power has been less fearful in Britain than in Germany, the United States or some other countries. There are various reasons why China tends to be seen as less of an economic threat. One is that Britain has experienced an unusually long period of uninterrupted employment growth since the early 1990s. Most manufacturing jobs had already disappeared before China's rise to prominence, so British livelihoods are now perceived to be less directly dependent on this sector than they were two or three decades ago. Services have become a much larger part of Britain's labour market and many are 'high-touch' activities dependent on proximity between service providers and business clients or individual consumers. Service jobs that appear most vulnerable to movement offshore, such as routine information processing and call centres, seem more likely to go to India than China.

There are other reasons why 'China fever' may not have been contagious in Britain. Households have enjoyed the benefits of abundant consumer goods produced more cheaply in China than elsewhere. This has stimulated strong growth in retailing and distribution, and the resulting demand for consumer credit has spawned many new jobs in financial services as well. Chinese competition and cheap imports have also helped to keep overall inflation down and contributed to rising house prices, making homeowners feel better off and encouraging them to borrow more for higher spending on leisure, entertainment, restaurants, holidays and other personal services.

Higher education is another sector that has benefited directly from China's economic boom – there are currently more Chinese students attending British universities than from any other foreign country. The UK is one of the most important destinations for Chinese students going abroad, partly because of the English language. Less well known is the fact that China's burgeoning foreign-exchange reserves are an important source of investment in many Western economies. Besides these economic linkages, growing cultural curiosity and popular engagement through television and tourism may have moderated wider British anxieties about China's growing economic strength.

This is not to say that there are no concerns about the potential of China's resurgence to undermine the quality of life of ordinary people. The British government has repeatedly stressed the need for workers and their children to invest more time and money in boosting their education and skills in order to safeguard their employability and living standards, with China explicitly mentioned as a threat. A flexible labour market with less job security than in the past for less-skilled workers is also alleged to be important to enable Britain to remain competitive under globalization. Rising domestic prices of fuel, minerals, steel, cement and other basic resources and commodities are often attributed in the media to an insatiable demand stemming from China's rapid industrialization and urbanization. And looming environmental concerns such as global warming are increasingly linked to China's prolific use of non-renewable resources, its inefficient methods of energy production and its neglect of air and water pollution (Hutton 2007).

Emerging themes in urban policy

Beyond these general observations, there are a range of more specific arguments emerging within the academic and policy communities to suggest that cities in Britain and some other parts of Europe may be less vulnerable economically to the continuing growth of China and other emerging nations than commonly supposed. The core idea is that these cities are privileged locations well placed to maintain competitive advantage in the twenty-first century through their unique capacity to foster innovation and productivity growth (Hall and Pain 2006; OECD 2001, 2006; Parkinson *et al.* 2006). In an information-rich economy, they function as nodes of intense business interaction and sharing of ideas and insights, leading to mutual learning and creativity. Cities have a range of institutions and other assets that encourage enterprise and initiative, attract mobile investment and talent, enable continued adaptation to changing economic conditions, and thereby generate increased prosperity and employment over time.

Put simply, cities are the 'engines' of knowledge-based economies because they provide a source of dynamic competitive advantage that will not become obsolete. They are conducive environments offering scope for people and ideas to mix and mingle – places where knowledge is created, tested, adapted and disseminated, and where human capital is developed to best effect. Knowledge-intensive products and services incorporate considerable individual skill and creativity, and are continually being upgraded, and are therefore difficult for low-cost producers abroad to imitate. According to one of the first UK government reports to reflect this new thinking: 'The factors of productivity in advanced knowledge-based economies are concentrated in cities' (ODPM 2003: 1).

The purpose of this chapter is to elaborate these ideas and to consider some of their strengths and limitations. It is important to stress that these are provisional and largely theoretical notions rather than well-established conclusions, although they are sometimes presented by their proponents as if they are incontrovertible facts. They originate in particular cities and institutions and are spread across others through the influence of prominent urban theorists, international organizations, policy networks and think-tanks (Buck *et al.* 2005; Boland 2007; Cheshire 2006; Cochrane 2007). For example, Michael Porter was an early and highly influential advocate of the idea that place matters to national competitiveness because firms benefit from their local environment through cooperation and competition with other enterprises and related institutions.

> The drivers of prosperity are increasingly subnational, based in cities and regions… Many of the most important levers for competitiveness arise at the regional level, and reside in clusters that are geographically concentrated.
>
> (Porter 2001: 141, 156)

An attractive feature of the various propositions outlined here is that they offer some reassurance to the wider population that cities in advanced economies can survive and indeed prosper alongside the rise of China and other global economic powers. However, to avoid false promises and expectations, it is clearly important to encourage critical and constructive analysis and debate about the validity of these ideas. For example, an obvious question is whether the city is really the pre-eminent spatial unit for economic development, and what the 'city' actually means. Is it the continuous built-up urban area, the functional local labour market or the wider city-region based on trade flows and the catchment areas of high-order services? And, do these arguments apply equally to all cities and all social groups within cities? More generally, do innovation and productivity growth provide a sufficient and sustainable basis for all-round prosperity?

These ideas now appear in a wide range of local, regional, national and European policy statements expounding the case for cities as drivers of growth (van den Berg *et al.* 2004). It is not surprising that city authorities should make this case for obvious reasons of self-interest, but the fact that national and supranational organizations are also saying so is novel. For example, a strong emphasis on growth through innovation and productivity characterized the European Council's Lisbon Agenda aimed at transforming Europe into 'the most competitive and dynamic knowledge-based economy in the world'. There was no explicit urban dimension originally, but cities have since become a major component. The longest section of a recent Commission report called *Cities and the Lisbon Agenda* was titled 'Cities as Engines of Regional Development' (European Commission 2006a: 5). In another recent report for the European Council and Parliament, the Commission reiterated:

> The European Union will pursue its objectives of growth and jobs more successfully if all regions are able to play their part. Cities are particularly important in this context. Cities are home to most jobs, firms and institutes of higher education and their action is decisive in bringing about social cohesion. Cities are home to change based on innovation, spirit of enterprise and economic growth.
>
> (European Commission 2006b: 6)

In the UK, there has been an even bigger shift in government policy towards cities (Boddy and Parkinson 2004). Until quite recently, cities were typically seen as remnants of an industrial era replete with social and environmental problems. They were perceived to have become uncompetitive places for business and for people to live in a world of low communication costs where locations with less congestion, higher-quality environments and cheaper property were generally preferred. However, after a period of some debate and lobbying within and beyond government, the all-powerful UK Treasury has come to accept the arguments for supporting cities as sites of renewed economic dynamism and drivers of growth and development within their regions. In an important report published to coincide with the 2006 budget, it stated:

> Cities matter because the productivity benefits they provide to knowledge-intensive businesses are important for regional and national prosperity. Cities provide an opportunity to narrow the gap between our regions and to tackle deprivation at the local and neighbourhood levels.
>
> (HM Treasury 2006: i)

This report and that of the European Commission quoted earlier are important not simply because they argue that cities are engines of growth in a knowledge economy, but also because cities are portrayed as mechanisms to tackle spatial and social inequalities. This echoes the 'new conventional wisdom' in urban policy that cities have become the key spatial unit for combining the development of a more productive economy with the pursuit of social justice and equality (Buck *et al.* 2005; OECD 2006; Turok 2007). This is clearly an important claim.

Important supporting conditions

There are several important developments in the global economy that are believed to offer European cities new sources of competitive advantage, now and into the future (Turok 2005).

First, the emergence of new economic powers, not simply in China and India, but also Brazil and Russia, coupled with increasing international price pressures, encourage more advanced economies to place increasing emphasis on 'quality-based' competition, that is, higher-value, differentiated products and services with enhanced features and consumer loyalty. This makes these firms more reliant on proximity to market intelligence, technical knowledge and highly skilled workers than cheap routine inputs, natural resources and greenfield sites with space for expansion – the traditional factor endowments. Knowledge 'spills over' between firms and thereby improves productivity and technical progress across the local economy. There is co-evolution of human capital, business capabilities and other local organizations in a mutually reinforcing process.

There are major benefits to be gained for firms whose competitive strategies are based on continuing design improvements and rapid responses to market trends to be located in places where they can gain ready access to the knowledge, information and skills required to remain at the leading edge of developments in the economy. Their reputations are also built to a greater extent on customer responsiveness than on low price, so staying close to customers and being familiar with their requirements is crucial. Moving to lower-cost, more remote locations leads to a loss of managerial control and increases all sorts of political and business risks.

Second, in response to more unstable international markets and the speculative activities of global financial institutions and private equity groups, there is a trend in business towards vertical disintegration or fragmentation, that is, externalization and out-sourcing of non-strategic functions. This gives firms greater focus and flexibility to adjust their spending on labour and services more closely to their current needs and thereby return a regular profit to shareholders. To perform well requires closer communication, cooperation and trust between separate specialized enterprises to develop effective and efficient service and supply linkages.

In some circumstances, there is greater emphasis on re-consolidation, mergers and alliances in order to provide a seamless service and extend market reach. Ambitious companies have to be flexible and cannot afford to decouple themselves from their intricate business networks and shared support services by relocating key functions to lower-cost nations. Electronic communication cannot replace the multiple advantages of proximity. It is also much easier and less damaging to themselves and their workforces if they have access to deep labour pools if and when required to expand and contract in response to volatile demand for their products and services.

Third, falling trade barriers, improved transport links and more mobile capital are constantly increasing competitive pressures from abroad. However, globalization and improved international connectivity are also extending firms' access to new markets and financial resources, thereby creating opportunities among the most entrepreneurial and best-managed businesses for rapid growth. To take advantage, they need access to international gateways, such as airports with frequent flights to far-flung destinations and places of sufficient economic scale to justify an advanced telecommunications infrastructure. A number of British companies and entrepreneurs are in the process of building and acquiring successful firms in China or selling their products and services into rapidly expanding Chinese consumer and business markets.

Finally, breakthroughs in science and technology are giving rise to a whole new set of innovative industries, such as biotechnology, information and communications technologies (ICT) and various creative industries, such as digital media. Their innovative character requires proximity to advanced research facilities and scientific and technical expertise, and frequent exchange of all kinds of tacit and codified knowledge and ideas through close personal communication. It also requires access to specialized skills and business services such as patent offices, commercial lawyers, venture capital, marketing agents and other business intermediaries and advisors.

It is extremely difficult for emerging economies such as China to replicate the thick, dynamic web of personal and business relationships, institutional assets and stream of creative ideas that develop in successful industrial clusters. These places build reputations, encourage a sense of common interest and gain people's commitment and motivation. The aura of success also lures clever young adults, budding entrepreneurs and far-sighted investors. These distinctive, subtle and cumulative advantages mean they are likely to continue prospering well into the future, unless prosperity creates its own problems, such as complacency or congestion.

The essential economic arguments for cities

By re-establishing the importance of high-level information exchange through face-to-face contact between businesses and between service providers and their clients, these developments reinforce the significance of urban 'externalities' or spillovers. They also make it particularly advantageous for firms to have good access to a critical mass of suppliers, subcontractors, collaborators, 'thick' labour markets with diverse skill sets and good international connectivity. It is beneficial too for highly skilled workers and organizations providing specialized services to have access to a bigger choice of potential employers and customers. Young mobile professionals are likely to be drawn to the wider range of entertainment and retail facilities, the greater 'buzz' and excitement, in leading metropolitan areas. There may be a more interesting and tolerant social environment because of greater cultural diversity and a much bigger choice of quality residential environments available than in smaller settlements.

Changing demographics and patterns of household consumption may also reinforce the position of cities (Storper and Manville 2006; Turok and Mykhnenko 2007). An increase in single adults, couples with no children and families with two or more people who work means a stronger demand for living closer to city-centre employment and amenities. Rising incomes and more leisure time also mean higher levels of household spending on shopping, recreation, eating out and short breaks. Cities contain a much better choice of social infrastructure, cultural amenities and career options than other places, and are therefore better positioned to attract and retain affluent visitors and people with the education and creative abilities required to generate and exploit knowledge (Florida 2004). These points may apply even more strongly to foreign nationals than to local residents because cities conventionally function as gateways for international migrants.

These arguments relate particularly to industries in which knowledge is a high component of their value and frequent personal communication is important in generating and disseminating that knowledge. Advanced producer services are good examples, including activities supplying professional expertise and the processing of specialized and scarce information for which virtual communication is inadequate because it is too 'hard' or one-dimensional. They include banking and finance, insurance, legal services, accountancy, management consultancy, advertising, design consulting and logistical services (Hall and Pain 2006).

Other high-order business services include civil engineering, surveying and planning consultancy, elements of the media, computer software, architecture and fashion. There is significant joint working, business alliances and other forms of interaction across, as well as within, many of these sectors. Cooperation is often geared to providing an integrated service to meet the diverse needs of specialized multinational companies that have a presence in that city. And geographical concentration is important for the intense interaction and cross-fertilization that helps to generate and disseminate new ideas, products and processes – through inter-firm competition as well as collaboration.

There are believed to be important parallels too with the cultural or creative industries (Leadbeater and Oakley 1999; Turok 2003). They involve the supply of goods and services that contain a substantial element of artistic or imaginative and intellectual effort, or that are associated with and play a vital role in sustaining cultural activities. They typically include film, television, video, music, the visual and performing arts, publishing, games software and new digital media. There are growing business alliances and acquisitions across these sectors as technologies overlap and consumer markets become more sophisticated. High-value manufacturing is also relevant, as well as emerging industries such as genetics, diagnostic medicines, 'modern' pharmaceuticals and other life sciences and new energy-generation technologies.

Spatial proximity among enterprises is believed to foster social interaction and trust, particularly in cities with the organizations and infrastructure for firms to learn, compare, compete and collaborate. Companies work together and indeed consolidate for certain purposes, but may subsequently compete and break up again in an ongoing struggle for business and market share. Dense local networks create a dynamic atmosphere, new business alliances and specializations that spur creativity and innovation, attract resourceful people and generate growth through a self-reinforcing, endogenous process. Meanwhile, global markets for consumer products are expanding as a result of rising incomes and falling trade barriers, and China is the supreme example. Information and communications technologies such as the Internet are also opening up new marketing and distribution channels to local producers:

> the cultural industries based on local know-how and skills show how cities can negotiate a new accommodation with the global market, in which cultural producers sell into much larger markets but rely upon a distinctive and defensible local base.
>
> (Leadbeater and Oakley 1999: 14)

Policy implications

These arguments do not necessarily assume that cities will automatically be able to maintain a competitive position in global markets. In fact, they indicate renewed scope for a variety of local policy actions that can make a genuine difference in helping places to stay ahead. For instance, they suggest that important benefits may be derived from relatively straightforward enhancement and upgrading of their 'quality' assets. These include advanced skills, research and technology facilities, specialized services such as venture capital and international connectivity.

They are also used to justify public investment in cultural amenities, social infrastructure and public spaces in order to create or safeguard high-quality urban 'milieu' and lifestyles. Cities need nice living and working environments, reputable universities and diverse social facilities to attract and hold onto talented individuals in the new 'creative class' who have a choice about where to study, invest and settle down. 'The attractiveness of our cities as places to live, learn, work and visit is crucial to their economic and social prospects' (Scottish Executive 2004a: 29). A well-designed and secure public realm, distinctive cultural heritage, and a lively arts and music scene are all believed to add to the vitality and authenticity of the urban experience.

It is particularly important for city and regional authorities to limit the harmful effects of concentrated economic growth within cities in the form of congestion, high property prices and potential labour shortages. Without an effective land supply for housing and business development, an efficient, integrated metropolitan transport system and a high-quality, responsive education and training system, these dis-economies of scale can add substantially to business costs and undermine city competitiveness and long-term job creation. Urban labour and property markets need to become more flexible and adaptable to encourage investment and other mobile resources in a more dynamic and competitive economy.

These arguments also suggest a role for public policy in bringing together different firms and other actors in industry networks, sponsoring trade associations, stimulating business collaboration and supporting the transmission of knowledge and expertise across organizational boundaries for mutual support, learning and innovation. Some argue that strong social relationships and trust reduce opportunistic business practices and selfish workplace behaviour, and encourage long-term investment decisions. It is also suggested that these kinds of activities promote successful and sustainable economic growth with less need for traditional urban and regional policies based on moving jobs and investments between different locations.

Positive features of the new thinking

There are many positive features in the new thinking around urban policy. Recognition of the significance of cities to the economy and society is important. Europe is more urbanized than other continents, so its prosperity is bound up with the performance and perceptions of its cities. The efficient functioning of European nations depends on a coherent sense of how its cities relate to each other and to the wider world. European cities face exceptional challenges of

poverty and dereliction, as well as unique opportunities for growth and investment. Sustainable regeneration of the poorest neighbourhoods will not be
achieved without city-wide economic development.

The new cities agenda is also more integrated in that importance is attached
to the role of the physical and social infrastructure in conditioning economic
success. In a more mobile, service-oriented economy, the quality of places and
their connectivity are likely to exert a bigger influence on their prosperity, justi-
fying public investment in the physical environment and essential infrastructure.
On the social side, there is also growing awareness of the economic value of
European societies being open to new people and perspectives, and of tolerating
diverse lifestyles and identities.

Although there are some inherent tensions and dilemmas, this is not a narrow
agenda driven by immediate business needs without regard for people and place.
It signals a shift from the exclusive focus on skills and business development
exercised by many regional economic development agencies during the 1980s
and 1990s.

Sources of uncertainty and concern

Despite the positives, there are also many questions and uncertainties surrounding the new urban thinking. At the outset, one is struck by the generality of many
of the arguments. While fuzzy ideas may be helpful in building support across
government and civil society, there is a danger of ambiguity and a risk that strategic choices may be avoided. There is vagueness even in the way the 'city' is
identified as a driver of growth. In many cases, the revitalized commercial
centres are clearly the objects of attention, rather than the wider built-up areas,
including run-down inner areas and peripheral estates. Elsewhere, the term city-
region is used, implying the functional area including surrounding towns and
rural areas that interact with the core city and that benefit from the dispersal of
business activity. This is a much larger territory potentially covering most of the
area of most European countries. To say that such city-regions are the engines of
growth is fairly meaningless since almost nowhere is actually excluded.

The new thinking offers somewhat contradictory signals about the key determinants of prosperity in cities, particularly the economic advantage derived from
concentration, density and proximity between firms and people. Is this fundamentally an issue of urban *scale* (critical mass) resulting in higher-capacity
transport connections, a larger labour pool and greater choice of suppliers and
shared services? Or is it more an issue of the *quality* of urban assets, associated
with higher built-environment standards, unique cultural amenities, intense business collaboration in specialized clusters, and a strong place identity? Quite different policy implications flow from these two propositions.

The emphasis in some versions of current thinking is on building scale
because many European cities are quite small by international standards. This
requires boosting the population and strengthening the connections between
cities and towns, through high-speed rail, for example. Seductive mega-projects

of this kind risk skewing investment priorities away from other, potentially more valuable schemes to tackle infrastructure bottlenecks within each city. Elsewhere, the focus is on creating highly functional, rewarding and distinctive places to live and work, with their own special cultural and recreational facilities, that is, aspects of urban quality that have little to do with scale and mobility. Explicit choices are also sometimes required at the local level between the desire to retain and attract population through new housing development and the need to retain and increase employment, simply because well-located sites are often in short supply. This dilemma periodically provokes bitter arguments between the advocates of different interests within localities.

There are mixed messages about the importance of 'hard' infrastructure (such as an effective land supply and transport system) versus 'soft' assets (such as innovation and skills). A strategy focused on knowledge-intensive industries is bound to have more uneven spatial consequences than a broader and more diversified approach. Research and Development (R&D) spending is considered a key driver of the knowledge economy, but is skewed towards particular cities. National economic policies that simply respond to and build upon the inherited innovation strengths of places will widen the prosperity gap across their territories.

This bears upon another important distinction between education and cultural diversity. The current attention paid by policy-makers to attracting creative talent and developing cultural amenities can be traced partly to Florida's focus on the dynamic role of the creative class. However, other academics replicating his analysis have found that many of the differences in performance between US cities can be explained simply in terms of education without resorting to the more esoteric themes of creativity and diversity (Glaeser and Gottlieb 2006). Glaeser's own three Ss – skills, sun and sprawl – are much more straightforward than Florida's three Ts of technology, talent and tolerance. The implication for economic policy is that investment in human capital should dominate spending on urban amenities. But once again, some cities are much better placed than others in this respect, with a relatively high proportion of the population qualified to degree level (Parkinson *et al.* 2004).

The new conventional wisdom and social inclusion

One of the greatest sources of concern is whether this approach will deliver opportunities of sufficient scale and relevance to benefit all sections of urban society and all cities. The focus on high-value jobs and top-quality living environments for highly skilled and resourceful people is a narrow basis for urban revitalization and growth. It will do little directly to improve the life chances of people outside the creative class, that is, poor, low-skilled and unemployed groups, and it may even cause harm through gentrification of inner urban areas and displacement of low-income households. The theorists of the new urban economics have weak prescriptions for the large group of less-qualified losers from deindustrialization. Florida, for instance, suggests rather evasively that policy should seek to release their creativity (Peck 2005). The 'new conventional wisdom' (NCW) also risks favouring some cities over others because of their differential endowments of physical, economic and human assets and institutions.

This raises a further question about whether cities really are the drivers of regional and national growth, and whether this applies to all cities. The assumption that cities are growth engines has been accepted surprisingly uncritically. Just a few years ago, the received wisdom was that cities lagged behind the rest of the economy and that some of them were bound to continue declining through out-dated industrial structures, location disadvantages or congestion. Recent studies of European cities raise doubts about a general connection between cities and strong growth (Turok and Mykhnenko 2007).

The clear message is that economic and population growth is very uneven across countries. It is too simple to say categorically that cities are the drivers of regional and national economic development. Cities may well have the potential to be such if the reasoning behind the new approach is correct, but this is bound to vary between cities. They also face a variety of practical obstacles in the process, including relatively mundane but important deficiencies in transport and other basic infrastructure and the supply of development land. Many cities also face organizational difficulties arising from fragmentation and lack of strategic leadership. Local conflicts of interest and disagreements about strategic priorities hinder sound long-term decision-making.

Conclusion

There has been a shift in urban policy thinking and language across Europe recently. It stems from a growing recognition that cities constitute important economic, social and cultural assets, with a major influence on national economic and demographic success. There has also been more explicit acknowledgement that some towns and cities face much bigger problems of deprivation and dereliction than others, and require more deliberate targeting of investment. This is a much healthier situation than when the tendency was to play down Europe's diverse economic geography and to treat cities as largely problematic.

Yet there is much to be done in practical terms to move beyond the broad narrative and to equip cities better to deliver their potential as drivers of prosperity and social inclusion. Part of the challenge lies in the realm of ideas – thinking through the relationship between economic development and social equality more carefully at the level of both the city and nation in order to formulate strategies that support both objectives. This requires more openness about situations where there are tensions and trade-offs requiring choices to be made, as well as greater imagination to identify policies that can deliver cohesion and prosperity hand in hand. The new thinking is still vague in many respects and it risks targeting excessively narrow economic and social bases for urban revitalization. A focus on knowledge-based services and creative talent may skew the benefits to people and places already endowed with high-level skills and strong research and cultural institutions, thereby widening social and spatial disparities. Europe needs a broader, more fully developed version of the new thinking that does not involve sacrificing particular groups of people or writing off particular places on the basis of an incomplete or imbalanced assessment of their future prospects and potential.

One element of such a vision is bound to include a commitment to tackle economic inactivity. Unemployment is Europe's biggest social-inclusion challenge because of its scale and wide-ranging costs and consequences. Raising the employment rate is probably, therefore, the single most effective way of pursuing the goals of social equality and economic prosperity together. The challenge needs to be addressed with greater vigour at European, national and city levels, partly by linking policies to strengthen labour demand and job creation with suitably targeted supply-side measures to increase employability and skills. Britain has not traditionally been very successful at ensuring an inclusive labour market with equal opportunities for people from different places and backgrounds, partly because of the centralized nature of many strands of economic and employment policy. There is an argument for strengthening the capacity of cities to pursue joined-up economic and employment strategies with greater powers of policy coordination and more control over resources.

References

van den Berg, L., Braun, E. and van der Meer, J. (2004) *National Urban Policies in the European Union*, Rotterdam: EURICUR Erasmus University.

Boddy, M. and Parkinson, M. (eds) (2004) *City Matters: Competitiveness, Cohesion and Urban Governance*, Bristol: Policy Press.

Boland, P. (2007) 'Unpacking the Theory–Policy Interface of Local Economic Development', *Urban Studies* 44(5): 1019–40.

Buck, N., Gordon, I., Harding, A. and Turok, I. (eds) (2005) *Changing Cities: Rethinking Urban Competitiveness, Cohesion and Governance*, London: Palgrave.

Cheshire, P. (2006) 'Resurgent Cities, Urban Myths and Policy Hubris: What We Need to Know', *Urban Studies* 43(8): 1231–46.

Cochrane, A. (2007) *Understanding Urban Policy: A Critical Approach*, Oxford: Blackwell.

European Commission (2006a) *Cities and the Lisbon Agenda: Assessing the Performance of Cities*, Brussels: Directorate-General Regional Policy.

European Commission (2006b) 'Cohesion Policy and Cities: The Urban Contribution to Growth and Jobs in the Regions', Communication from the Commission to the Council and Parliament, Luxembourg: Office for Official Publications of the European Communities.

Florida, R. (2004) *The Rise of the Creative Class*, New York: Basic Books.

Glaeser, E. and Gottlieb, J. (2006) 'Urban Resurgence and the Consumer City', *Urban Studies* 43(8): 1275–99.

Hall, P. and Pain, K. (2006) *The Polycentric Metropolis*, London: Earthscan.

HM Treasury (2006) *Devolving Decision Making: 3 – Meeting the Regional Economic Challenge: The Importance of Cities to Regional Growth*, London: HM Treasury.

Hutton, W. (2007) *The Writing on the Wall: China and the West in the 21st Century*, London: Little, Brown.

Leadbeater, C. and Oakley, K. (1999) *The Independents: Britain's New Cultural Entrepreneurs*, London: Demos.

ODPM (2003) *Cities, Regions and Competitiveness*, London: Office of the Deputy Prime Minister.

OECD (2001) *Devolution and Globalisation: Implications for Local Decision-makers*, Paris: OECD.

OECD (2006) *Competitive Cities in the Global Economy*, Paris: OECD.

Parkinson, M. *et al.* (2004) *Competitive European Cities: Where Do the Core Cities Stand?*, London: ODPM.

Parkinson, M. *et al.* (2006) *State of the English Cities*, London: ODPM.

Peck, J. (2005) 'Struggling with the Creative Class', *International Journal of Urban and Regional Research* 29(4): 740–70.

Porter, M. (2001) 'Regions and the New Economics of Competition', in A. J. Scott (ed.) *Global City Regions: Trends, Theory, Policy*, Oxford: Oxford University Press: 139–57.

Storper, M. and Manville, M. (2006) 'Behaviour, Preferences and Cities: Urban Theory and Urban Resurgence', *Urban Studies* 43(8): 1247–74.

Turok, I. (2003) 'Cities, Clusters and Creative Industries: The Case of Film and Television in Scotland', *European Planning Studies* 11(5): 549–65.

Turok, I. (2005) 'Cities, Competition and Competitiveness: Identifying New Connections', in I. Buck, I. Gordon, A. Harding and I. Turok (eds) *Changing Cities*, London: Palgrave: 25–43.

Turok, I. (2007) 'Urban Policy in Scotland: New Conventional Wisdom, Old Problem?', in M. Keating (ed.) *Social Democracy in Scotland*, Brussels: Peter Lang: 141–68.

Turok, I. and Mykhnenko, V. (2007) 'The Trajectories of European Cities, 1960–2005', *Cities* 24(3): 165–82.

6 China Inc. and the future of European cities

Theatres or theme parks?

Tridib Banerjee

Contemporary globalization has many faces, images, and imperatives. In the next twenty-five years, the agencies of globalization – capital, culture, information, people, etc. (see Pizarro *et al.* 2004) – are likely to become more active and more pervasive. While the effect of globalization so far has been primarily a one-way process, from the north to the south, this will certainly change as the flow is reversed. The theme of this book – 'China and Europe' – is an appropriate metaphor that captures this scenario, although the reverse flow may not necessarily originate from China only, it may include other parts of the developing south. To a large extent, this flow will be manifested in the flow of labour, as we already see in many cities of Europe where the influx of foreign labour has led to segregated enclaves and ghettoes, contested places, and spaces of insurgent citizenship (Holston 1995). Inexorably, this will be followed by bourgeois tourists from emerging economies of the developing world, and we are likely to see unprecedented growth in tourism as the ranks of the middle class continue to increase in many parts of the world, China and India being the notable cases in point. According to one report, some 8.3 million Indians travelled abroad in 2006 spending $7.5 billion or $903 per person on average. The Chinese tourists spent $100 more on average (Indian Tribune 2007). Although only a fifth of the Indian travellers came to Europe, this number will surely grow in the years to come.

In this chapter, I will examine the implications of the inexorable growth in tourism and its associated consumption industry and the future choices for the conservation, design, and development of European cities. The central concept to be explored in this chapter is the concept of flânerie as it may apply to studying the prospects for the urbanism of entertainment. The act of flânerie involves looking, strolling, experiencing the urban sensorium (see Goonewardena 2005) and spectacles. There is a considerable body of literature on flânerie going back to the unfinished work of Walter Benjamin on the passages of Paris (Benjamin 1999). Susan Buck-Morss's (1991) use of Benjamin's project as an example of 'dialectics of seeing' provides an important theoretical referent for understanding how urban form and space can be suffused with the material culture of capitalist consumption. Benjamin (1999: 422) wrote:

> The flâneur is the observer of the marketplace... He is a spy for the capitalists, on assignment in the realm of consumers.

It can be argued that tourists today are the new flâneurs of the global economy, except that their flânerie might be more purposeful, focused, scripted, enlightened, and, indeed, shaped by various cultural filters and expectations.

In pursuing this objective, I will consider several theoretical concepts that are relevant to this scenario. First, there is the notion of contamination, which addresses the issue of authenticity and identity in a multicultural context, and presents the arguments of Anthony Appiah and other authors. The second concept is that of hybridity, which defines the cultural outcomes that result from this inevitable culture contact. Although written from the postcolonial subaltern perspective, both present optimistic views. The question is whether Europe will be ready to cope with the challenges of contamination and hybridity, or will it face a crisis of identity?

The spaces, places, and landscapes that service the tourism and leisure classes will require more systematic planning and design, and, indeed, more strategic thinking about the future urbanism of tourism. This chapter will discuss how the different images and demands of tourism may transform traditional urban form and create new urban spaces of consumption and production. But first, some notes about the rise of China and the effects of globalization on contemporary European cities.

The rise of China Inc.

According to a recent forecast by *The Economist*, in 2040, China will catch up with the United States as one of the two biggest economies in the world. Even today, China's GDP, when adjusted for purchasing power parity (PPP), is about four-fifths of the US GDP. One other sobering thought: In 2005, five European Union countries, Germany, Britain, France, Italy, and Spain, were among the top ten economies in the world. In the 2040 forecast only three, Germany, Britain, and France, will be in the top ten list, occupying eighth, ninth and tenth place, respectively, while the economies of India, Mexico, and Brazil will rank higher. Although this book focuses on China's impact on Europe, the spectre of the emerging economic power of the 'southern' economies and their impact on Europe must not be ignored. The subject of this chapter will be developed with this 'China plus' scenario of the future. But first, let us consider the coming dynasty of China Inc. and its corporate hegemony.

In the planning-theory literature today, we see references to the nature of planning in the time of the empire (for example, see Roy 2006) the reference here is to the seemingly hegemonic influence of the cultural, economic, military, and political power of the contemporary United States. Will we be seeing a similar analysis of China's expanding grasp on the global economy and primary resource-producing countries of the developing world? China's voracious appetite for energy and other primary resources is already having a palpable effect on the global economy and power alignment. Stories about China's expansion abound in the popular press: aluminium sidings are stripped from foreclosed houses in Ohio to be sold to China, a big importer of scrap metal; abandoned industrial plants in the Ruhr region are disassembled, packaged, and shipped to China to be reused in their new industrial infrastructure; energy deals are made between China and countries in Africa and Latin America (Sudan and Venezuela being cases in point) in exchange for infrastructure development; multi-purpose deals are closed with poorer countries like Cambodia for access to mineral resources and cheap labour, and so on. China has faced criticism for ignoring issues about human rights and other abuses in such client countries, and for its alliance with such large corporations as Walmart that had a devastating impact on small businesses in local communities in the US. China is now considered a major polluter, and a major contributor to global warming. Such scrutiny will no doubt increase as the rise of China Inc. continues at a fast pace.

Will China emerge as a neo-colonial power replacing the European countries of yesteryears and the contemporary US in expanding its hegemony to many developing countries in Africa, Asia, and Latin America? Will China colonize Europe in a role reversal or become the new global empire where the sun will never set? These are all engaging, if not entertaining, thoughts and largely a matter of speculation. There is little doubt that many in Europe may already empathize with the subalternity of colonized people of previous centuries as China becomes the 'global factory' and just about most products sold in the West, and globally, bear a 'Made in China' stamp. Klaus R. Kunzmann voices the poignant question reflecting the feelings of the European Union: If everything is made in China, what will Europe have to sell or export to the world, especially to China?

Chances are that China will not become an imperial power in the old sense with colonies in Africa, Asia, Europe (Eastern especially), and Latin America. Rather, the Chinese state will emerge as a transnational corporation – China Inc., so to speak – that will include and incorporate not only many of its state agencies such as the China Energy Corporation, but also primary resource-producing dependent states (e.g. Cambodia, Myanmar, Sudan) and multinationals such as IBM, Walmart, General Motors, Mercedes Benz, and recently Intel. But in order for Europe to benefit from the rise of China Inc. and the growth of other developing economies, it must openly embrace the new global economy, as *The Economist* (2006): 30 argues referring to a recent European Commission study:

> So to reap the full gains, Europe must urgently push ahead with making its markets more flexible and open. A study by the European Commission concludes that, if the European Union were to fully embrace the rise of China and India, its GDP per person by 2050 could be up 8 per cent higher than it would otherwise have been, implying a boost to average annual growth of 0.2 per cent over the period. If, on the other hand, EU countries lurch towards more protectionist policies, GDP per head could be 5 per cent lower than in the base case.

It is possible that through unbridled integration with the global economy, Europe might still be a part of the global factory, making components and luxury consumption goods and run mainly by China Inc. But the ownership of many of the firms manufacturing products in Europe might be acquired and merged into the transnational corporate state of China Inc. This scenario will require a significant change in the traditional ideology of the European state, as the neoliberal position articulated by the European Commission suggests. The neoliberal view presages a decline of the welfare state and indeed a withdrawal or shrinkage of the state as European nations have known it previously. As this minimalist or 'hollow state' transforms its traditional social-centered policies to market-oriented development strategies, the public realm will no doubt languish and even atrophy. This transition may indeed be at an incipient stage and inexorable, following the lead of North American cities, as recent studies of the dynamics of urban development in European cities seem to suggest.

Urbanism of flânerie

One scenario of how Europe might benefit from the rise of China Inc. and other emerging consumer classes of the south is by selling its 'culture': the experience of architecture, arts, music, food, entertainment, and certainly urbanism. One might wonder if the Chinese will necessarily come to consume the European culture and civilization. As Arthur Miller (1979) wrote some years ago: 'Chinese, like the French, have little interest in traveling abroad since their country is the center of the world.' Indeed, the canonical cities of China had always aspired to emulate the cosmic model where the cardinal axes and the *axis mundi* represented the centre of the universe.

Also, it will be recalled that in the late eighteenth century when China was the largest economy in the world, King George III sent Lord George Macartney as his emissary to Beijing to establish a trading relationship with the East India Company. However, he was promptly informed by the Ming emperor Qianlong that the Chinese did not have any use for the manufactured products of Europe. Interested in the silk, tea, ivory, jade, and other such products of China, the British did not give up and would eventually take advantage of the illegally generated demand for opium to begin a trade relationship, which would ultimately lead to the Opium Wars of the early nineteenth century. The British victory paved the way for the establishment of treaty ports, the only concession China made to Europe's colonial ambition there.

So, the question remains whether prosperous Chinese tourists will necessarily flock to Europe to consume its culture or tradition, especially if China Inc. believes that the Chinese culture is superior to that of Europe and thus has very little use for it, or at best that it could 'manufacture' an ersatz European experience as a copy or simulacrum in the vicinity of Beijing, Shanghai, Guangzhou, or Qongqing to draw the new tourists from the developing world. Indeed, the "One City, Nine Town" project in Shanghai is entering nine new towns in the images of European cities. If the Chinese are so successful in manufacturing just about every aspect of the Western consumer products, why wouldn't they also succeed in manufacturing an ersatz urban experience? In Macao, the Chinese entrepreneurs have already created an alternative, and a grander one, to Las Vegas, accessible to the *nouveau riche* of the developing world. Even if the Chinese tourists come, it will be properly packaged, scripted, and programmed by some subsidiary of China Inc. and on their own terms. We might see a rise of Chinese restaurants in Europe, not so much for the local demand, but to feed the Chinese tourists.

Nevertheless, even if the Chinese tourists don't come, there are reasons to believe that a prosperous Third World bourgeois class would come to Europe, especially from the former colonies, to experience the originals of the copies they have grown up in or with. Global travel has been increasing at a steady pace and the tourism industry has experienced a major boom in recent years. According to Alsayyad (2001: 1):

> Several world travel organizations predict that world tourism will grow at a rate of 4 per cent per annum, reaching a level of more than 700 million international arrivals and more than US$600 billion in revenue in the year 2000. And by 2010, it is predicted that arrivals will reach one billion and revenues will mount to nearly four times the current level. In the late 1970s less than one one-hundredth of a per cent of the world's population took an international trip in any given year. But by the end of the twentieth century this percentage had increased a hundred fold. As the twenty-first century unfolds, people of every class and from every country will be wandering to every part of the planet. This is indeed an age of voyaging on a global scale. Meanwhile, tourist destinations throughout the world find themselves in ever more fierce competition for tourist dollars.

Alsayyad and others have discussed what this culture of tourism might mean for the developing world, and how tradition will be consumed, and whether, or how, the heritage will be manufactured. Indeed, this is a narrative of commoditization, that of culture for the purposes of mass consumption. However, what this would mean for Europe, especially in the scenario of tourism from the south, remains to be explored.

One outcome is certain. The growth of tourism would lead to displacement of the local residents, as in the case of Venice. As indigenous urbanism, such as the culture of flânerie, sidewalk cafes, street entertainment, gets commoditized for tourist consumption, authenticity will decline and the urban spaces will become programmed stage sets. Spaces of leisure and public life will have to be relinquished for the consumption of the tourist class. The quintessential European city and its 'pleasures of urbanity' (Walzer 1995) will be reduced to a theme park, at least seasonally. Indeed, during the peak tourist season, the Piazza San Marco in Venice or Piazza della Signoria in Florence take on a carnival-like atmosphere and the ambience of an amusement park. See Figure 6.1.

As demand for low-wage workers increases to service the tourist class (see Figure 6.2), the ranks of the immigrant labour class will swell, contaminating European culture (not unlike the way Europeans contaminated the endogenous culture of the colonized nations) despite local pressure to maintain purity. The emerging urbanism will be one of contamination and hybridity and of contested

Figure 6.1 Piazza della Signoria, Florence: theatre or theme park? (Photo: author, 2007)

spaces as the immigrant class, only tentatively absorbed in the mainstream economy, engage in an informal economy to supplement their income. Decanted of the original population, increasingly, European inner cities will be occupied by migrant workers from the former colonies, Indian 'subcontinentals' and West Indians in Britain; Moroccans and Maghrebis in France; Somalis, Libyans, and Ethiopians in Italy; Turks in Germany, and the like. There are also the Chinese, other Arabs, Africans, Iranians, and East Europeans who are seeking income niches ranging from service work to the informal economy.

Local urban spaces are now contested and cohabited by immigrants, students, and tourists. Some of the tourist-oriented Italian restaurants in Venice are now owned and run by Chinese or Indian families with an Italian *maître d'* maintaining a token of authenticity. New lifestyles and commercial uses are redefining these historic urban spaces, the San Lorenzo neighbourhood in Florence being a case in point (Perrone 2004). Muslims are seen facing Mecca performing collective prayers in the Duomo Square as there are no major mosques in Florence (see Perrone 2004). Yet, not too long ago the authorities posted 'Sitting Prohibited' signs 'in the square in front of the Florence Cathedral below Brunelleschi's dome and Giotto's bell tower,' writes an incredulous Paloscia (2004: 8), 'next to the steps perennially crowded with passers-by, students, vendors of all colours, street-artists, kids with guitars round their necks and the tourists from the campsites, youth hostels, and small hotels, with their sandwiches and drinks'. This is

Figure 6.2 An immigrant sandwich man selling another immigrant commodity. Staromestske Namesti, Prague. (Photo: author, 2005)

the ideal democratic public space that Sennett (1990) longs for in American cities, and these are also the spaces of contamination and hybridity that Appiah (2006) will be championing. Yet, as we see in this example, the interests of 'primitive globalization' represented by the local state might begin to impact the local public realm in a significant way.

As predicted by Sites (2003) in his characterization of 'primitive globalization', the local or national state will play an important role in facilitating the tourist economy through major infrastructure investments. A case in point is a proposed subway that will link the airport to the centre of Venice, which has created considerable dissent among long-term residents who are already feeling marginalized by the tourist economy.

Contamination and hybridity

Both of these concepts are constructs from the south that have grown out of the postcolonial reflections of the colonial past. It will be recalled that colonial urban development, despite Anthony King's (1976) claim about the emergence of a Third Culture, resisted both hybridity and contamination. The European city was set apart from the native city and in part this distancing, the *cordon sanitaire*, grew out of a sense of vulnerability, a fear of contamination, from being close to the native population and their 'dirt and disease'. The architecture and planning of the colonial European cities reinforced this difference and the alterity of the native, and the subaltern status of the native settlements. The segregation of the immigrant population, social exclusion, and absence of economic integration still continues in many European cities today through the lives of generations of immigrants, as the INURA (2004) project amply documents, and as recent street riots in France attest. Indeed the *cordons sanitaires* in some form, ring roads or industrial belts, now separate the inner-city immigrant population from the affluent suburbs of the native Europeans.

Going back to the later years of colonial rules, one should note that European powers did attempt to claim cultural elements of the colony as part of an expanded sense of identity. This was evident in the various pavilions of the Paris Exposition of 1931 and the Tripoli Trade Fair of 1927. But the claim of hybridity today is made by the postcolonial theorists as a measure of identity and creativity. Anthony Appiah (2006), a philosophy professor at Princeton, contesting the impulse of the cultural preservationists to construct and conserve identity and cultural purity, has argued that contamination should be accepted and indeed celebrated as an inevitable outcome of culture contact accelerated by contemporary globalization. He writes:

> The ideal of contamination has few exponents more eloquent than Salman Rushdie, who has insisted that the novel that occasioned his fatwa 'celebrates hybridity, impurity, intermingling, the transformation that comes of new and unexpected combinations of human beings, cultures, ideas, politics, movies, songs. It rejoices mongrelisation and fears the absolutism of the Pure. MŽlange, hotch-potch, a bit of this and a bit of that is how newness enters the world.' No doubt there can be an easy and spurious utopianism of 'mixture,' as there is of 'purity' or 'authenticity.' And yet the larger human truth is on the side of contamination – that endless process of imitation and revision.

As China, Inc. continues to incorporate Europe, and as tourist flânerie increases, we will no doubt see a new European urbanism that will be shaped by contamination and hybridity. In this scenario, tourists from the south, Brazil, Mexico, India, for example, will be celebrating Oktoberfest with their German hosts by swinging steins of imported beer, only it will be Qingtao beer on tap this time, in a wonderful twist of irony rooted in colonial history. Cosmopolitanists like Appiah or Rushdie will certainly celebrate that, and why not? After all, devoted Hindus in Kolkata do not seem to be bothered by the fact that the small brass replicas of gods and god-desses they are buying outside the main temples all bear a 'Made in China' stamp.

Concluding observations: theatres or theme parks?

I would like to conclude by proposing that the choices for European cities facing the coming onslaught of Chinese tourists, if they come, or for certain the surge of tourists from other parts of the world, can be captured by two metaphors: the-atres and theme parks. I use the term theatre advisedly in conceiving of cities not only as stages or arenas of performance, arts, or cultural tableaux of various sorts, but also as the locus of social change, political action, and civic and public life. Furthermore, urban spaces in the public realm have always served an important function by embedding collective memory (see Halbwachs 1980; Boyer 1996). Hebbert (2005) has argued that the street can be seen as the locus of collective memory. To quote Benjamin (1999: 416):

> The street conducts the flâneur into a vanished time. For him, every street is precipitous. It leads downward – if not to the mythical Mothers, then into a past that can be all the more spellbinding because it is not his own, not private. Nevertheless, it always remains the time of a childhood. But why that of the life he has lived? In the asphalt over which he passes, his steps awaken a surprising resonance. The gaslight that streams down on the paving stones throws an equivocal light on this double ground.

Beyond the equivocalness, the ambiguity, and the 'dialectics of seeing' (Buck-Morss 1991) in the 'the gaze of the alienated man' (Benjamin 1999: 10), the metaphor of city as theatre may also include the rituals and ephemera, like the *Palio* in Siena or the Love Parade in Berlin (which now moved on to the Ruhr area), or the Bastille Day celebrations in Paris. But the idea of the city as a theatre also includes opportunities for free expression, political protests, public debates, civic engagement, and longer-term social and cultural changes that chal-lenge and reconstitute the identity of the city in the time of globalization.

Yet, it is the same globalizing forces, the hegemony of the global capital and the inevitable tendency of the local state to collaborate with global capital, in an increasingly common phenomenon of what Sites (2003) refers to as 'primitive glo-balization', to undertake projects of demolition, reuse, and redevelopment of urban space devoted to consumption, entertainment, and shopping. In their comparative study of European cities, Savitch and Kantor (2002) refer to these tendencies as 'local sweep' of the 'global broom'. The local state becomes the agency of change and is actively involved in the packaging and 'selling' of the city to attract global capital. The outcome is sometimes not very different from the thinking that goes behind designing 'theme parks' or some variations thereof, as Sorkin has argued. The critical choice for European cities as they face the inexorable growth of global tourism from China or other lands is: Can they maintain their historic role as thea-tres, or must they all opt to become some type of a theme park?

References

Alsayyad, N. (ed.) (2001) *Consuming Tradition, Manufacturing Heritage*, London: Routledge.

Appiah, K. A. (2006) 'The Case for Contamination', *The New York Times*, available at www.nytimes.com/2006/01/01/magazine/01cosmopolitan.html?ex=1136264400&en=4 51c69f1781822c8&ei=5070 (accessed 18 September 2008).

Banerjee, T. (2008) 'Urban Outcomes of Globalization: Theory, Research and Practice', *Journal of Urban History* 34 (6): 1044–54.

Benjamin, W. (1999) *The Arcades Project*, Cambridge, MA: Belknap Press of the Harvard University Press.

Boyer, M. C. (1996) *The City of Collective Memory: Its Historical Imagery and Architectural Entertainments*, Cambridge, MA: MIT Press.

Buck-Morss, S. (1991) *The Dialectics of Seeing: Walter Benjamin and the Arcades Project*, Cambridge, MA: MIT Press.

The Economist (2006) *Playing Leapfrog*, Issue of 14 September.

Goonewardena, K. (2005) 'The Urban Sensorium: Space, Ideology, and the Aestheticization of Politics', *Antipode* 37(1): 46–71.

Gugler, J. (ed.) (2004) *World Cities beyond the West: Globalization, Development and Inequality*, New York: Cambridge University Press.

Halbwachs, M. (1980) *The Collective Memory* (trans. F.J. and V.Y. Ditter, with an introduction by Mary Douglas), New York: Harper Colophon.

Hebbert, M. (2005) 'The Street as Locus of Collective Memory', *Environment and Planning D: Society and Space* 23(4): 581–96.

Holston, J. (1995) 'Spaces of Insurgent Citizenship', *Planning Theory* 13: 35–51.

INURA (2004) *The Contested Metropolis*, Basel, Boston, Berlin: Birkhäuser.

King, A. (1976) *Colonial Urban Development: Culture, Social Power and Environment*, London and Boston: Routledge and Kegan Paul.

Miller, A. (1979) 'In China', *Atlantic Monthly* 243(3): 90–117.

Paloscia, R. (2004) 'Introduction', in *The Contested Metropolis*, Basel, Boston, Berlin: Birkhäuser: 8–13.

Perrone, C. (2004) 'Urban Geographies, Coloured Networks, New Social Practices', in INURA, *The Contested Metropolis*, Basel, Boston, Berlin: Birkhäuser: 139–44.

Pizarro, R., Wei, L. and Banerjee, T. (2003) 'Agencies of Globalization and Third World Urban Form: Toward a Critical Framework', *Journal of Planning Literature* 18(2): 111–30.

Roy, A. (2006) 'Practice in the Time of Empire', *Planning Theory* 5(1): 7–29.

Savtich, H. V. and Kantor, P. (2002) *Cities in the International Marketplace: The Political Economy of Urban Development in North America and Western Europe*, Princeton, NJ: Princeton University Press.

Sennett, R. (1990) *The Conscience of the Eye: The Design and Social Life of Cities*, New York: Knopf.

Simmonds, R. and Hack, G. (ed.) (2001) *Global City Regions: Their Emerging Forms*, New York: Taylor & Francis Publishing Inc.

Sites, W. (2003) *Remaking New York: Primitive Globalization and the Politics of Urban Community*, Minneapolis: University of Minnesota Press.

Walzer, M. (1995) 'Pleasures and Costs of Urbanity', in P. Kasinitz (ed.) *Metropolis: Center and Symbol of Our Times*, New York: New York University Press.

7 What will become of European regions?

Driving forces, emerging mega-city regions, options

Alain Thierstein

Introduction

It is no easy task to consider what will become of European regions at the backdrop of the ascent of China as an economic, cultural, technological or maybe even a political force. One has to look at underlying driving forces, especially their emanation as emerging mega-city regions. Even more ambitious, it would seem, is the business of developing options for policy-making in Europe, especially for the European Commission and its informal policy guidelines for urban and regional development.

At that point, one has to be fully aware of the fact that there are numerous disciplinary angles to look at in the overarching topic of this book: *China and Europe.*

As an economist, planner and consultant, I prefer to first look at the underlying functional drivers that eventually shape and influence spatial structures and institutional behaviour, forces that, of course, in turn influence directions and impact of these same development drivers.

One promising and valuable way to proceed and gather necessary insights is to review what scholars and knowledgeable observers of the Chinese dynamics in spatial development have come up with, and then draw analogies or conclusions for the European situation. Thus, some observers of Chinese urban development in the mid-1990s already pointed out that Shanghai stands at the interface of the world economy and the Chinese nation state as other regional and global cities have done in the past. Shanghai, and other large cities, are bound to make possible an evolution from the city's dominant role of gateway and manufacturing centre towards one in which the tertiary sector has a greater weight.

This statement assumes that Chinese cities and city regions will follow a certain trajectory of economic structural change that in its most advanced features are visible in the development of European and New World cities today. In return, such a perspective would signify that by knowing how urban structure in Europe will evolve quasi-automatically, of course with a time lag, Chinese cities would follow suit. Such a simplifying assumption fundamentally ignores the importance of socio-cultural forces that in Europe over the centuries have given way to a unique urban model of the European core city.

Nevertheless, I argue in line with Hall and Pain (2006) that despite basic variations in socio-cultural traditions, an overall economic driver overshadows these differences. The expanding knowledge economy and, above all, the multi-branch, multi-location firms of the knowledge-intensive business services produce a phenomenon that Hall and Pain (2006) term 'mega-city regions'. This emerging large-scale multi-polar urban configuration was first described for one of China's most dynamic urban regions, the Pearl River Delta, the archetypal mega-city region. 'Mega-city regions are a series of anything between ten and 50 cities and towns physically separated but functionally networked, clustered around one or more larger central cities, and drawing enormous economic strength from a new functional division of labour' (Hall and Pain 2006: 3). The emergence of these mega-city regions is by and large driven by the interlocking firm networks of advanced producer service firms (APS) and supported by the high accessibility that a high-performance gateway infrastructure provides.

Thus, learning from China means – in the context of the urban future – to learn from the effects that the expanding knowledge economy is having on our European urban structures and our urban systems.

Urban reconfiguration in Europe

One can outline different theories of future urban growth across Europe. An initial theory posits that economic globalization, new communication technologies and information flow will have a levelling effect on urban structures, causing a flattening and redistribution of growth away from major cores (Friedman 2005). A countervailing theory suggests that these cores will retain their importance as nodes and gateways within a globalizing knowledge-based economy (Florida 2005), that is knowledge-intensive business services, hi-tech production firms and higher-education and research institutions. The recent book *Raumentwicklung im Verborgenen*, translated into English as *Spatial Development on the Quiet* (Thierstein *et al.* 2006), illustrates the latter reading of spatial development and pinpoints the fact that inter-firm and intra-firm connectivities of multi-location firms have begun to reshape urban structures.

At a European level, there are new functional linkages between mega-city regions (MCRs). But at a regional level, for example, in southeast England, in the Paris metropolitan area or in the Greater Dublin area, there is a new functional polycentricity, which has the effect of eroding the historical dominance of core centres.

New MCR scale interactions point to a need to think about growth, urban structures, information flow and physical connectivity in new ways.

MCRs provide a framework for understanding the new economic landscape of regions and of Europe as a whole and suggest that existing frameworks for economic growth, competitiveness, cohesion and sustainable development are not always mutually reinforcing. Sometimes, they pull against a polycentric reality: hence a pressing need to more fully appreciate the new dynamics of polycentric mega-city regions.

The changing world of firms and locations

Many of the corporations that dominated the world map at the turn of the century have already vanished. Some firms have been bought up by others figuring on that map or by smaller incumbents, while some have restructured or have changed their corporate names but still exist by delivering services and products. A fine indication for the dynamics of the corporate world is a brief look at the member's list of the Dow Jones Industrial Average Index or the DAX in Germany. Many firms that were included in these indexes 15 years ago have in the meantime disappeared or have been replaced by new ones. Besides the restructuring of firms, these changes strongly reflect the structural changes of the economy as a whole. Knowledge-intensive business activities grow rapidly and contribute larger shares to overall value-added and gross domestic product.

One telling example is steel production, once the backbone of industrialization that was dominated by giants like Bethlehem Steel or US Steel. Now Mittal Steel, originating from India, has become the world's largest steel producer. Its strength has been fuelled by the ever-increasing demand for infrastructures in the regions that have entered the world markets, especially the BRIC states: Brazil, Russia, India, and China. Needs and demand are changing; new players have entered the playing field, which has been getting larger and tougher to compete on. The question thus arises: What is going to happen? What signs are on the horizon?

Spatial hierarchy of locations

Table 7.1 indicates what it will really take in the future to get to the top of such a comprehensive ranking of quality of living. The aim of the business consultancy Mercer Human Resources' survey is to provide an objective, consistent and comprehensive evaluation of the differences in quality of living in any two cities. Governments and major companies use the information worldwide to determine appropriate allowances, reflecting differences in the quality of living for personnel transferred abroad. The study is based on detailed assessments and evaluations of 39 key quality-of-living determinants, grouped in the following categories: political and social environment, economic environment, socio-cultural environment, medical and health considerations, schools and education, public services and transportation, recreation, consumer goods, housing, and natural environment.

Up until today, there is no Chinese city in the top-ranking positions – but maybe in five or in 50 years? Of course, the above ranking only tells a fraction of the whole story of urban competitiveness, the knowledge economy and spatial restructuring.

In order to better understand these interrelationships, let's take a closer look at what is described as the mega-city region hypothesis (Hall and Pain 2006). Thierstein *et al.* (2006), taking part in the cross-sectional analysis of eight MCR case studies by Hall and Pain (2006), compared these eight MCRs and illustrated

Table 7.1 Worldwide quality of living ranking

Mercer Human Resource Consulting Worldwide Quality of Living Survey 2007
Top 50

Base city: New York, US (=100)

Rank 2007	Rank 2006	City	Country	Index 2007	Index 2006
1	1	ZURICH	Switzerland	108.1	108.2
2	2	GENEVA	Switzerland	108.0	108.1
3	3	VANCOUVER	Canada	107.7	107.7
3	4	VIENNA	Austria	107.7	107.5
5	5	AUCKLAND	New Zealand	107.3	107.3
5	6	DUSSELDORF	Germany	107.3	107.2
7	7	FRANKFURT	Germany	107.1	107.0
8	8	MUNICH	Germany	106.9	106.8
9	9	BERN	Switzerland	106.5	106.5
9	9	SYDNEY	Australia	106.5	106.5
11	11	COPENHAGEN	Denmark	106.2	106.2
12	12	WELLINGTON	New Zealand	105.8	105.8
13	13	AMSTERDAM	The Netherlands	105.7	105.7
14	14	BRUSSELS	Belgium	105.6	105.6
15	15	TORONTO	Canada	105.4	105.4
16	16	BERLIN	Germany	105.2	105.1
17	17	MELBOURNE	Australia	105.0	105.0
18	18	LUXEMBOURG	Luxembourg	104.8	104.8
18	18	OTTAWA	Canada	104.8	104.8
20	20	STOCKHOLM	Sweden	104.7	104.7
21	21	PERTH	Australia	104.5	104.5
22	22	MONTREAL	Canada	104.3	104.3
23	23	NURNBERG	Germany	104.2	104.1
24	25	CALGARY	Canada	103.6	103.6

24	26	HAMBURG	Germany	103.6	103.4
26	31	OSLO	Norway	103.5	102.8
27	24	DUBLIN	Ireland	103.3	103.8
27	27	HONOLULU, HI	United States	103.3	103.3
29	28	SAN FRANCISCO, CA	United States	103.2	103.2
30	29	ADELAIDE	Australia	103.1	103.1
30	29	HELSINKI	Finland	103.1	103.1
32	31	BRISBANE	Australia	102.8	102.8
33	33	PARIS	France	102.7	102.7
34	34	SINGAPORE	Singapore	102.5	102.5
35	35	TOKYO	Japan	102.3	102.3
36	37	LYON	France	101.9	101.6
36	36	BOSTON, MA	United States	101.9	101.9
38	37	YOKOHAMA	Japan	101.7	101.6
39	39	LONDON	United Kingdom	101.2	101.2
40	40	KOBE	Japan	101.0	101.0
41	44	BARCELONA	Spain	100.6	100.2
42	45	MADRID	Spain	100.5	100.1
42	51	OSAKA	Japan	100.5	99.6
44	41	WASHINGTON, DC	United States	100.4	100.4
44	41	CHICAGO, IL	United States	100.4	100.4
46	43	PORTLAND, OR	United States	100.3	100.3
47	53	LISBON	Portugal	100.1	98.9
48	46	NEW YORK CITY, NY	United States	100.0	100.0
49	51	MILAN	Italy	99.9	99.6
49	47	SEATTLE, WA	United States	99.9	99.9

Source: Mercer 2007.

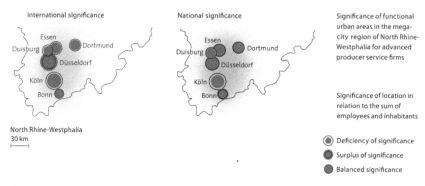

Figure 7.1 Non-physical interlocking firm networks produce mega-city regions – Rhine–Ruhr (source: Thierstein *et al.* 2006).

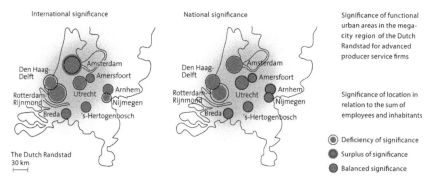

Figure 7.2 Non-physical interlocking firm networks produce mega-city regions – Dutch Randstad (source: Thierstein *et al.* 2006).

that some mega-city regions are self-evidently morphologically polycentric (see Figures 7.2 and 7.3) and thus follow a development form that is encouraged in EU spatial policy.

However, it is argued that inter-urban functional connections interlink the constituent cores of the MCRs in a common network. These inter-urban functional connections not only result from commuting but also from knowledge-intensive interactions within and between advanced business service firms. These interactions may be of a physical character such as business travel or of a non-physical quality such as virtual communications and information exchange. These intra-firm and inter-firm connections define a functional polycentric MCR that goes way beyond morphological polycentricity. We find internal MCR functional interaction to be well developed in southeast England (see Figure 7.3), given its apparent morphological monocentricity, and emergent also in Zurich (see Figure 7.4), with its backbone Zurich–Basel (Halbert *et al.* 2006).

Figures 7.1–7.4 indicate that within each MCR, there is only one 'knowledge hub' that connects the local with the global realm of the knowledge economy.

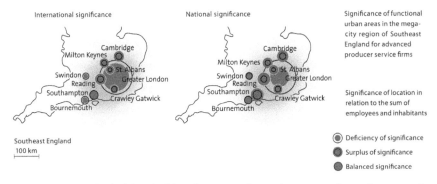

Figure 7.3 Non-physical interlocking firm networks produce mega-city regions – southeast England (source: Thierstein *et al.* 2006).

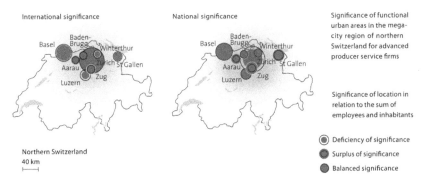

Figure 7.4 Non-physical interlocking firm networks produce mega-city regions – northern Switzerland (source: Thierstein *et al.* 2006).

Only one functional urban area (FUA) is able to assume the role of an international hub in the global space of knowledge flows (see Figure 7.5) (Thierstein *et al.* 2006). This, of course, could already be assumed from the sheer size of the primary city in each MCR, as for Greater London (see Figure 7.3) or Frankfurt Main (Thierstein *et al.* 2006). If one controls for size and compares the connectivity values to the sum of population and employment, then you get a picture that reveals how much an FUA is able to locate knowledge-intensive business service firms compared to its size. Figures 7.1–7.4 read as follows: If the shaded circle exceeds the black ring, we can regard this FUA as disproportionately important for the knowledge-based economy. If the black ring exceeds the shaded circle, then the significance of the FUA is below average. Figures 7.1–7.4 look at two spatial scales of the interlocking firm networks that have been analyzed. Most of the eight MCRs that were analyzed in an INTERREG IIIB study in northwestern Europe (Hall and Pain 2006; Thierstein *et al.* 2006) show on an international scale, a pattern where the core FUA accounts for a surplus of significance compared to its size. Exceptions are the MCRs of southeast England

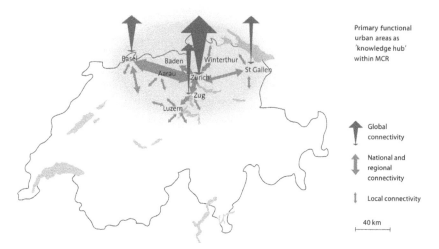

Figure 7.5 Primary functional urban area as a 'knowledge hub' within an MCR Ruhr (source: Thierstein *et al.* 2006).

and Île-de-France, Paris (Thierstein *et al.* 2006). In these large-scale polycentric MCRs, the core FUA of Greater London and of Île-de-France, Paris can no longer locate enough firms that are internationally interlinked compared to its potential by size. Reasons for this decreasing return on interlinked connectivity may be due to disadvantages of density such as traffic congestion and prices or availability of real estate. Other FUAs such as Cambridge have been able to attract some of these locations with international interlinkages.

Looking at these findings, one can easily imagine that emerging mega-city regions tend to become a basic challenge for large-scale strategic spatial planning. Both in terms of securing accessibility between MCRs as well as organizing increased business and leisure travel within the MCR that is between the constituent FUAs, in a more sustainable way. Thus, mega-city regions, to conclude, will increasingly shape the urban form and structure of tomorrow.

What is up in China?

A brief glance at some recent developments in China aims to inform us about the dynamics and future options of this vast country. Electronic and print media coverage of China's development represents a steady stream of information – most of the time we are taken aback by the sheer dimension of growth and change, without putting information into perspective. Even when talking to fellow architect and planner colleagues, they are mostly thrilled by opportunities but feel swamped by the sheer amount of diverse impressions. Thus, I will just list a number of recent information bytes that I hit upon while preparing this paper. Hardly a single day goes by without a serious piece in the newspapers on the rapid change in China, or elsewhere in the BRIC states:

- BRIC states combine 28 per cent of the global economic growth with 42 per cent of the global population.
- China of the two economies: the rural developing areas and the 'first-world' regions: Pearl River Delta, the Shanghai MCR and the southeast coast.
- Rising wage levels in first-world regions, shortage of qualified people (finance specialists as expensive as in Europe).
- Inefficient industrial production due to subsidized cheap energy input.
- Environmental damages in 2004 amount to 3.05 per cent of GDP (equals Maastricht criterion for EU budget deficit).
- Consumer spending projected to rise per annum with 10 per cent for recreation, education, 12 per cent for health care.
- BBC World News in 2006 advertising 'Beijing Shopping'.
- Net female imports: (number of males per 100 females): Europe 92.7; China 105.6; (number of male babies to 100 female babies: China 117).
- Net human-capital flow of Chinese engineers from US to China.
- The Shanghai Jiao Tong University Index ranks among the world's leading academic institutions; an effort not delivered by the Chinese government and not by Harvard University nor the Dow Jones stockmarket index.
- The (former) world track and field record holder for the 110 metre hurdle and 2004 Olympic Champion is Chinese.
- The Female Junior World Champion in Cross-Country Mountain Biking is Chinese – and mountain biking, by the way is no former socialist sport, but a brand-oriented lifestyle sport.
- Large-scale corruption and fraud cases in 2006 of social-security pension funds in Shanghai and other large cities.
- As well as constant violations of human rights, as reported by Amnesty International.

Of course, the globalized economy is a mixed blessing and no one-way endeavour: what goes around comes around. Look, for example, at the fact of consumption spending in China, projected to rise annually by 10 per cent for recreation and education and by 12 per cent for health care. One clearly gets an indication of the huge market potential for European firms and European 'regional production systems' (Maillat and Kebir 1999) that are capable of pulling together the necessary resources in order to market a value chain of hi-tech and high-touch services. Take, for example, the trend of tourists from BRIC states travelling to the mega-city region of Munich for a 'theme landscape' that consists of attractive wellness spas and health foods, plastic surgery and rehabilitation facilities combined with a hi-tech medical-devices industry, high-end as well as down-home cultural events, well-kept cultural landscapes and recreation.

The driving forces behind large-scale urban restructuring

Let us return for a moment to the basic question: What drives the process of urban polycentric restructuring? Quick replies and explanations offer the usual suspects: technological developments such as information and telecommunication technologies, nanotechnology, genetic engineering, demography with more elderly and fewer children, the knowledge economy and globalization, relative energy prices, urbanization and mega-cities, the skills divide that produces social exclusion, the systems stabilization effect of middle-class purchasing power, etcetera.

Each and every indicator has, of course, a strong case to make. But, behind each story and each key driving factor of the day, there is always another story behind the story.

A very basic concept for explaining long-term structural change, also in spatial terms, is what Immanuel Wallerstein laid down as an analysis of the emerging world system and the core mechanism of the European capitalist trade system (Wallerstein 1986). Thus, the world capitalist system is organized in three parts: (1) the core areas – European territorial entities or states have been the 'core' of the world economy for a long time; (2) the peripheral areas that have been exploited to supply cheap labour and natural resources and were markets for surpluses of the core area; (3) the semi-peripheral areas that always mediated, and still do so today, in the sense of transaction services between the former two areas. A key lesson to be learnt from Wallerstein's analysis is the constant change of power and spatial hierarchy over a long period of time. That means that core areas may lose their role and become semi-peripheral while peripheral areas may gain in importance and climb up the ladder of spatio-economic hierarchy.

A recent study by the EU Commission may illustrate the secular shift of economic power within the global hierarchy. The study states that the US enjoys a continuing increase in its share of world production, which contrasts sharply with the relative performance of the EU and Japan, both of which are expected to witness a significant decline in their relative economic importance in the world over the coming decades. The authors then continue by saying that in the case of the EU, its share of world output falls from 18 per cent at present to 10 per cent in 2050, compared with 23 per cent for the US. While the US has been able to retain its share over the last 30 years and is expected to continue to do so over the next 50 years, the EU has already witnessed steady erosion in its share of global output (McMorrow and Röger 2003). One trend thus becomes evident: the remaining and increasing share of world output will be realized by Asia. The consequence will be a shift of economic vitality to the Pacific Rim on its Asian and North/South American sides. Today, this region increases the mutual integration in trade, currency and policy.

To wrap it up, new regions on the globe are becoming powerful parts of the world economy. The strong European position as a core region will continue to dwindle unless states and firms put a much stronger effort into capitalizing on the potential of the expanding knowledge economy. Spatial development in general and urban large-scale restructuring in particular is very much challenged by that seemingly external push.

One key area of concern in Europe, of course, is the labour market and the availability of qualified craftsmen and highly qualified professionals. Looking at the aforementioned trends of urbanization and the knowledge economy, there will be impacts on the behaviour of young professionals throughout the countries. To them, it might be boring to live in Inverness, Auvergne, Rostock, Gallipoli or Estremadura – and in St. Gallen, just to mention the region where I grew up. The stiff competition for human capital or 'talents' (Florida 2002) implies a crucial issue of large-scale urban structures: Which region is attractive enough by not only offering dense, qualified labour markets but in addition the right amenities, habitat and leisure surroundings?

The answer may lie with the emerging mega-city regions that combine the following (Thierstein *et al.* 2003; Bonneville 1994; Blotevogel 2001):

- Innovative strength and competitiveness.
- High accessibility by road, high-speed train and intercontinental air transport.
- Density of regulative institutions, headquarters of private and public firms, public administrations, headquarters of international institutions in sports, culture, tourism and nongovernmental organizations.
- Symbolic qualities, such as attractiveness of public spaces, urban design, architectural icons and branding, internationally renowned events.

Since the phenomenon of emerging MCRs is rather new and it usually takes some time to get adequate attention from politicians and planners, some open questions arise to date:

- Economic development: What is the importance of the MCR for a more competitive European economy, which has to put much more emphasis on the issue of the expanding knowledge economy?
- Social inequities: Can functionally polycentric MCRs counter socio-spatial fragmentation, and eventually exclusion, and if yes, on what spatial scale with what impact?
- Environment sustainability: Are the overall consequences of MCR formation processes harming or protecting the environment? In Switzerland, commuters working for advanced producer service firms more frequently reside in core cities or FUA ring communities, but at the same time they have the longest average commuting time and tend to favour more centrally located employment than do other workers. Complex off-setting mechanisms are in place that do not help get the overall sustainability pattern straight easily (Thierstein *et al.* 2006).
- Territorial cohesion: To what extent do MCR processes contribute to or limit European territorial cohesion, since we witness simultaneous expanding and shrinking of spaces on different spatial scales (Hall and Pain 2006).

These are basic policy issues that will keep European policy-makers busy for the next two to three decades.

What lies ahead: them and us?

The future depends on a variety of factors that are partially in our own hands in Europe and partially at the disposition of other world regions. At the same time, development is always path-dependent: you do not break out easily or quickly from the road taken. Thus, the answers to the four policy questions above depend as much on us as on them, the BRIC states and China in particular.

Learning from Immanuel Wallerstein's analysis, one could guess that the answer to what will be happening with China is to be found in our own recent past. To know your own past is to understand the future. Europe in the nineteenth and twentieth centuries has experienced some growth phenomena that seem to be replicated in the China of today, although maybe in compressed time, with less violence, and less involvement of civil society. These growth phenomena were a deteriorating environment, social unrest and upheaval, rapid urban growth, technological progress and an innovation push. When looking at Europe's policy replies to these growth phenomena, one wonders whether China will not face similar upcoming needs and necessities and respond in the same ways:

- Unfolding of a welfare state with a social market economy, social-security legislation Bismarck-style, rapidly increasing wage levels for most qualifications.
- Regulations or liberalization and intelligent re-regulation.
- Battle against urban sprawl.
- Externalization of problems and use of 'grey resources', affluent Chinese recreating abroad in well kept European-style, semi-urban landscapes close to airports and heritage sites.
- Consuming more sustainable home-made Chinese facilities, thus simulating European recreation destinations, like the Entertainment Centre Rust in Southern Germany, or combining it with Chinese heritage sites, e.g. along the ancient Silk Route.

Coming to a tentative conclusion, it becomes clear that learning from China is above all learning from our own past, meaning to be much more aware of the already ongoing process of spatial restructuring, with new spatial hierarchies and emerging mega-city regions.

What about the future of Europe's regions in the light of the above-mentioned trends in China? What did Europe do wrong in the last ten years? Will the jobs lost abroad never come back? Do we all have to learn Chinese now as we had to learn Japanese in the 1980s and Russian in the 1990s? Or is it more like the French saying: 'reculer pour mieux sauter', but this time in the context of new opportunities of the knowledge economy?

The knowledge economy is changing its spatial structures almost on the quiet (Thierstein *et al.* 2006). Key factors for being competitive within the knowledge-intensive activities are produced and redesigned fully by us. Thus, it is to postulate that the future lies in our own hands, or else there is no future for Europe at all. Polycentric mega-city regions will play a master role for repositioning Europe in a multi-polar global network.

What is to be done? First of all, it will be innovative and socially responsible enterprises that are aware of their single most important production factor, their highly qualified and motivated human capital. Second, there will be less public policy able to solely change things around. Furthermore, there will be more public–private partnerships, some will thrive, and some will falter. Looking ahead, there will be two to three decades of structural transition from the still lingering old-style industrial world to the knowledge economy with its knowledge-intensive and comfort industries. There will be better-educated people who are more cosmopolitan and less nationalistic. And, there will be more precarious living conditions for the unqualified.

As nobody knows the future, we all have to guess, and while we are waiting, it was worthwhile to pose at least some interesting questions, while the answers are in the making, maybe elsewhere, anyway.

References

Blotevogel, H. (2001) 'Die Metropolregionen in der Raumordnungspolitik Deutschlands – ein neues strategisches Raumbild?', *Geographica Helvetica*, 56(3): 157–68.

Bonneville, M. (1994) 'Internationalization of Non-capital Cities in Europe: Aspects, Processes, and Prospects', *European Planning Studies*, 2(3): 267–85.

Florida, R. (2002) *The Rise of the Creative Class*, New York: Basic Books.

Florida, R. (2005) 'The World Is Spiky. The World in Numbers. Globalization Has Changed the Economic Playing Field, but Hasn't Leveled It', *Atlantic*, October 2005, 26: 48–51.

Friedman, T. (2005) *The World Is Flat. A Brief History of the Twenty-first Century*, New York: Farrar, Strauss and Giroux.

Halbert, L., Convery, F. J. and Thierstein, A. (2006) 'Reflecting on the Polycentric Metropolis', *Built Environment*, 32(2): 110–13.

Hall, P. and Pain, K. (2006) *The Polycentric Metropolis. Learning from Mega-City Regions in Europe*, London: Earthscan.

Ludovic, H., Pain, K. and Thierstein, A. (2006) 'European Polycentricity and E-merging Mega-city Regions: "One Size Fits All" Policy?', *Built Environment*, 32(2): 206–18.

Maillat, D. and Kebir, L. (1999) ' "Learning Region" et systèmes territoriaux de production', *Revue d'Economie régionale et urbaine (RERU)*, 3: 429–48.

McMorrow, K. and Röger, W. (2003) 'Economic and financial market consequences of ageing populations', EU Commission, Brussels.

Mercer (2007) 'Mercer Human Resource Consulting Worldwide Quality of Living Survey 2007', available www.mercer.com (accessed 9 November 2007).

Thierstein, A., Dümmler, P. and Kruse, C. (2003) 'Die europäische Metropolregion Zürich: zu gross um wahr zu sein?', *DISP* 152: 87–94.

Thierstein, A., Kruse, C., Glanzmann, L., Gabi, S. and Grillon, N. (2006) *Raumentwicklung im Verborgenen. Untersuchungen und Handlungsfelder für die Entwicklung der Metropolregion Nordschweiz*, Zürich: NZZ Buchverlag.

Wallerstein, I. (1986) *Das moderne Weltsystem – Die Anfänge kapitalistischer Landwirtschaft und die europäische Weltökonomie im 16. Jahrhundert*, Frankfurt am Main: Syndikat.

8 The implications of the rise of China for planning in urban Switzerland

Angelo Rossi

Introduction

In Lugano, a Swiss city of around 50,000 inhabitants, in the autumn of 2005, 40 people initiated a course in Chinese at the Adult Educational School of the Migros, the largest retail distribution chain in Switzerland. Most of these people were businessmen and women, who were either actually trading with China, or wanted to. In Lugano today, there are other groups of people learning Chinese. If we take all these people as a proportion of the managers' population in the Lugano region, they represent some 2 per cent of the total, a percentage which is surely significant. This new interest in the Chinese language in a medium-sized Swiss town like Lugano testifies to the increasing presence of China in one of the smallest European nations. The fact that the Swiss population takes a growing interest in Chinese and in some other aspects of the Chinese culture does not mean, however, that today's China is very well known in Switzerland (Hugger 2005). When one looks at publications on the development of the relationship between China and Switzerland, one still finds more historical than contemporary studies. The *chinoiserie* fashion waves of the eighteenth century or the selling success of the *montre chinoise* in the nineteenth century have certainly been better analyzed by Swiss students, than, for instance, the link between the present imports of goods from China and the foreign direct investments of Switzerland in that country (Boerlin-Brodbeck 2005; Voire 2005; Chapuis 1923). As far as the future development of these relationships is concerned, there are practically no analyses, with the exception of the increasingly frequent newspaper articles depicting the incredible economic and welfare targets that China could achieve if the average growth rates of the last decade should continue for another decade or two, or illustrating the devastating consequences that the rapid rise of China to the rank of global economic power could have for the European economies and, in particular, for that of Switzerland.

The Swiss urban system, as with most of the national urban systems of Middle Europe, has developed in three successive periods. The oldest towns have a Roman antecedent. Then there were the numerous city foundings of the Middle Ages. The third urbanization surge came with the industrialization of the nation and, above all, with the construction of the railway network between the middle of the nineteenth century and the First World War. It is not easy to anticipate whether a fourth urban development period will take place in the twenty-first century. However, if this were to happen, the major factors determining it will certainly be of an economic nature. The international flow of goods, services, capitals and manpower, as well as changes in the economic base, which are determined by the progression of the international division of labour (globalization), will certainly be among the most important determinants of the next urban development bounce. Contrary to the picture presently circulating, which shows Switzerland as a country with tendencies toward isolation, the small nation in the centre of the Alps mountain chain, has always been, at least from an economic point of view, a very open country. This is especially true of the period since 1975. As a matter of fact, with the onset of globalization tendencies, the share of exports in the Swiss GDP has constantly increased. From 24 per cent in 1975, this ratio has risen to 33 per cent in 2004. And, there is no reason why this share should not grow over the next two decades.

Taking this background into account, what are the implications of the rise of China as a global economic power for the urban regions of Switzerland? The diagram in Figure 8.1 tries to give an abridged answer to this question. The future economic growth of China will probably influence:

- The growth rate of aggregate demand and therefore also the speed with which the Swiss economy is going to develop.
- The way in which the urban hierarchy, as well as the economic and spatial structures of the urban centres, are going to change.
- The urban agglomeration policy, with the multiplication of efforts at local and regional levels to reinforce the international competitive capacity of the Swiss urban centres.

These repercussions will be dealt with in further sections of this chapter. But, before going on with the argument, it is useful to recall that the measurement of the possible influence of China on the development of Switzerland and its urban system is made difficult by, among others, an evident problem of scale. We have, as a matter of fact, on the one side, a nation that extends over 9.6 million square kilometres and counts around 1.3 billion inhabitants, i.e. more than one-fifth of the world population, and, on the other side, a country with an area of 41,000 square kilometres and 7.3 million inhabitants, which represents more or less 1/1,000 of the world population. Comparing China to Switzerland is therefore like comparing an elephant with an ant. However, one should keep in mind that Switzerland's GDP is still among the top 20 in the world. Through the export of high-technology investment goods, Switzerland is still among the ten leading countries of the world (Wachter 1995). Moreover, following a series of financial indicators, such as FDI, to mention only one, Switzerland also occupies one of the first places in the world list. Therefore, a comparison on economic terms makes much more sense than one on spatial or demographic terms. Even so,

China remains an elephant and Switzerland an ant. While there is probably no danger that China will stop the economic growth of Switzerland and her internationally oriented cities in the near future, the question of where the Chinese elephant, in moving forward, is going to put down its feet is surely an important one for the Swiss ant.

The importance of China for Switzerland today and some meaningful extrapolations

What is the economic importance of the People's Republic of China (PRC) for Switzerland at the beginning of the twenty-first century, when economic development is strongly influenced by the tendency towards globalization and globalization is increasingly taking on the features of Chinese businessmen? And, what are the developments going to be in the next decade or two in Switzerland and the PRC? One can begin to appreciate the present importance of China with the help of the indicators of Table 8.1. Further, one can attempt to forecast the future development of these indicators by using the present rates of growth for an extrapolation. This, however, leads to forecasted values that are difficult to interpret. The indicators in Table 8.1 concern imports, exports and the FDI export flows and stocks. Next to them, one finds data on the share of Chinese in the resident population of Switzerland, on the importance of overnight stays of Chinese tourists, on the share of Chinese restaurants and on the share of Swiss doctors with Traditional Chinese Medicine (TCM) certificates, because the activities of these people are concentrated in the urban centres and can therefore be considered to be direct indicators of the present degree of penetration of Chinese culture and economic interests in the urban centres of Switzerland.

Table 8.1 Quantification of the present importance of China for Switzerland

Flows and stocks	Percentage share in the total	Largest partner share in %
Imports 2005	2.3	33.3 Germany
Exports 2005	2.1	20.0 Germany
FDI exports 2004	0.6	10.4 Great Britain
Number of jobs created in China by Swiss firms until 2004 as percentage of total jobs created abroad	3.6	15.9 United States
Chinese tourists' overnight stays as a share of foreign tourists' overnight stays 2005	1.1	30.4 Germany
Chinese as a share of foreign resident population	0.5	18.7 Italy
Chinese restaurants	1.1	
Medical doctors with additional training in Traditional Chinese Medicine (TCM) or acupuncture	2.5	

- Import and export figures are derived from the *Swiss National Bank Bulletin.*
- FDI figures are derived from the specific annual publication by the Swiss National Bank.
- Foreign tourists' overnight stays are derived from the Federal Statistical Office's specific annual publication.
- Resident foreign population figures are derived from the Federal Statistical Office's specific annual publication.
- Restaurant figures are derived from the *Swiss Food Guide.*
- The number of doctors certified to practise TCM or acupuncture has been derived from the Swiss Medical Doctors Statistics of 2005 (see also Iten and Saller 2005).

The percentage values in the table show that the influence of the People's Republic of China is still small but beginning to become significant. To explain the modesty of these values, it is important to recall that the revival of economic relationships between Switzerland and the PRC only started in the middle of the 1980s (Straubhaar 1985). Further, it is important to stress that the Swiss official statistical sources still distinguish between Hong Kong and the People's Republic of China. For the time being, China is not in the list of the top ten economic partners of Switzerland. There is, however, an exception and this is represented by the number of jobs created abroad; in this ranking, China is already in sixth place. Although the economic influence of the People's Republic of China has only recently started to rise, it is growing very rapidly.

One of the main difficulties in interpreting data on Switzerland's economic relationship with the PRC is, as mentioned above, that the Swiss official statistics still distinguish between Hong Kong and the People's Republic. In the main, the export of goods and capital to Hong Kong are the same size as the export to the PRC. It is to be assumed that, for many transactions, in particular the financial ones, Hong Kong plays the role of entry door to the PRC, or at least to some of her southern regions (see also Roth 2005). The percentage shares in Table 8.1 are calculated with reference only to the values of the transactions with the People's Republic of China, because it is impossible to get an estimation of the net effect of those with Hong Kong.

If we now extrapolate the pattern of development realized in the period 2000 to 2005 for another 20 years, we notice that, as far as imports and exports are concerned, China could become as important a partner to Switzerland as Italy or France, countries occupying, at present, second and third place in the ranking for imports, or the United States, at second place in the ranking for exports. If this were to happen, then there is a serious possibility that, parallel to the mounting importance of the China shares, the shares of the European partners will decline. The weight of Swiss external relationships will therefore shift from the major European partners to China. This shift will concern, above all, the import trade. Most of this expected development will, of course, depend on the behaviour of the Chinese government towards opening the country.[1] From this point of view,

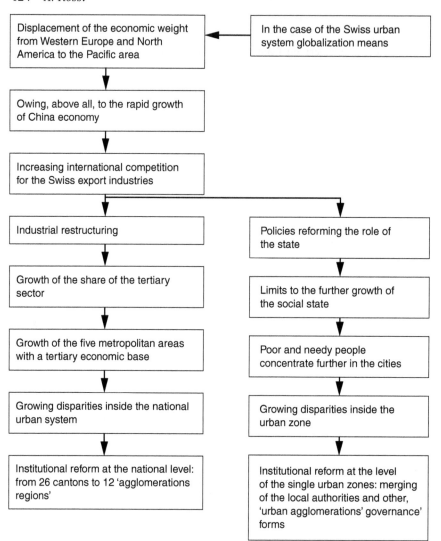

Figure 8.1 The relationship between globalization and urban development in Switzerland.

the future development of the tourist flow represents a very important issue for Switzerland and its cities. First of all, because China's tourism abroad is still in its infancy. Second, because, even though the largest share of Chinese tourists are visiting nearby Asian countries, a growing number are also touring Europe (Droz 2004). One speaks of the potential of between 11 and 80 million possible visitors to Europe over the next years. Third, because Switzerland has a good image in China (Pasquier and Weiss 2006). However, all these favourable premises would be of no consequence if tourists were not allowed to come to Switzerland. In this respect, the decision taken by the Chinese government in

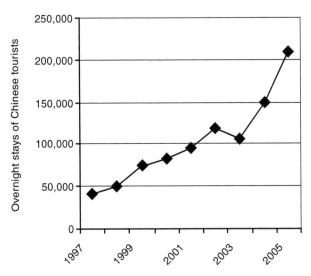

Figure 8.2 Time development of Chinese tourists' overnight stays in Switzerland (source: Droz (2004) for the data up until 2004; Federal Statistical Office for 2005).

2003 to grant Switzerland Approved Destination Status is therefore of great importance. As one can see in Figure 8.2, this decision promptly stimulated the number of overnight stays of Chinese tourists in Switzerland. At present, Swiss tourist operators estimate that the number of overnight stays from Chinese tourists should double every five years. Calculating from this growth rate, in 20 years Chinese tourists will represent the second-largest group of foreign tourists in Switzerland, after the Germans. As the Director of Zurich Tourism recently affirmed, soon one will meet Chinese tourists in the streets of Zurich every day of the year (Reuss and Kaminski 2006).

It is clear that the Swiss government will also play a role in the development of the relationship with China (especially with regard to the allotment of residence permits for students and Chinese employees). One can, however, affirm that the decisions of the Chinese government will be a lot more important than those of the Swiss government. Nevertheless, when interpreting the meaning of the extrapolations, it is important to recall that both governments could put some kind of brakes on development in the form of protectionist measures. Before closing this short presentation of the balance of trade between Switzerland and China, it is interesting to observe that the largest shares of import and export are in the same industries. Machinery, chemicals and watches make up 46 per cent of the imports from China and 70 per cent of the exports. The one specific import industry is textiles (17 per cent of the imports) and the one specific export industry is pharmaceuticals (8 per cent of the exports). This kind of exchange structure is typical of two countries which, for the moment, are exchanging investment goods and technology against goods of large consumption. It is, however, to be expected that in the future this kind of exchange could be modified as China climbs up the technological ladder. This will of course add a supplementary difficulty to the task of correctly forecasting the future development of the economic relationship between these two countries.[2]

The tendencies in the capital flow tell a somewhat different story. There is, at present, no significant flow of Chinese FDI into the Swiss economy. The largest Chinese firm in Switzerland, i.e. IBM PC which has been bought by Lenovo, is located in Zurich and employs 70 people. Instead, Switzerland is exporting capital to both the People's Republic of China and Hong Kong.[3] The share of the FDI of Switzerland to China is, however, less important than the shares of intertrade between the two countries. It is very difficult to argue the future development of the Swiss FDI on the basis of extrapolation of the capital flow figures, as they can vary considerably from year to year. A more interesting conclusion on the development of direct investment in China can be drawn from the consideration of the development of the stocks, for example, the number of jobs created by these investments. Recently, the Swiss National Bank published a diagram comparing the development of jobs created by Swiss direct investment in India and China, from 1995 to 2004 (see Figure 8.3).

It showed that while the stock of jobs created by FDI in India stagnates, the stock of jobs created in China is increasing very rapidly (17 per cent per year). With the average rate of yearly change in the period 1995–2004, one has extrapolated the development of these two variables from 2005 to 2020. The results, shown in Figure 8.3, indicate that while the two economies belong to those that

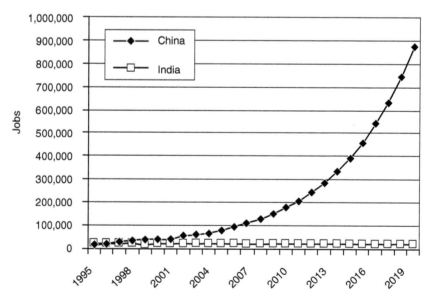

Figure 8.3 Time development of the number of jobs created by Swiss FDI in China and India (source: Swiss National Bank (2005) till 2004 and author's extrapolation since then).

are growing fast, the number of jobs created by Swiss firms in China will increase more rapidly than jobs created by Swiss firms in India. The different development pattern can probably be explained by differences in labour productivity between the two countries. The extrapolation for the year 2020 gives a number of Swiss firms' jobs in China, near 900,000. This figure represents around 50 per cent of the present stock of jobs relocated out of Switzerland. This implies that in order to reach this target, Swiss firms would be obliged to reorient their FDI from European markets to China.

Finally, one can conclude that the possible scenario of the future development of the international economic relationships of Switzerland, which anticipates a shift from Europe and North America towards Asia, is going to profit from the traditional orientation of Swiss foreign policy. However, as the influence of China is rapidly growing, Swiss foreign policy is also adjusting rapidly (at least for the speed at which political decisions are usually taken) to this global power shift. While researchers at the beginning of the 1990s were timidly asking whether Switzerland, given the impending incertitude over the future of her relationship to Europe, wasn't interested in putting two irons in the fire, namely, one for Europe and another for Asia (Etienne *et al.* 1992), the government was already working to intensify Swiss relationships with Asian countries through the signing of new agreements (Hirschi *et al.* 1999). In the future, the importance of the Asian countries in Swiss foreign-policy should further increase. As one can read in the 2005 report on the state and development of Swiss foreign policy, the importance of the EU foreign-policy agenda should not prevent Switzerland from putting more effort into relationships with the US and other important partners. In the list of emerging new partners of this report, India and China also figure. In conclusion, China is now visible on both the economic as well as on the foreign-policy agenda of Switzerland. The future will be probably see a shift of importance in the economic and political relationships of Switzerland, from Europe to the US and Asiatic countries, China in particular.[4]

What about the presence of China in Swiss cities? Since at least the middle of the last century, Chinese restaurants have developed in the main cities of Switzerland. As shown by the example of the Canton of Zurich, Chinese restaurants are concentrated in large towns (55 per cent of the 65 restaurants of the Canton) (Gyr and Unterweger 2005). In the City of Zurich, the Chinese restaurants are to be found in the central districts (Districts 1 and 4). There are no statistics available on the spatial distribution of Swiss medical doctors practising TCM. If, however, we restrict our inquiry to the centres for TCM that are operated by Chinese doctors, i.e. to the centres of the three organizations MediQi, Chinamed and Sinomed, we notice that one-third is located in the metropolitan areas of Zurich and nearly one-quarter in the large towns of Basel, Bern and Lausanne (Iten and Saller 2005). Chinese tourists also prefer urban destinations. In 2005, 15 per cent of the overnight stays of Chinese tourists were in Zurich. It is more difficult to inquire about the importance of other relationships, for instance, the importance of China as a possible destination for the capital that is accumulated in Zurich banks, although one knows that the Swiss banks are very much interested in the Chinese economy. It appears that while the larger banks are developing their own branches in China, either independently or through joint ventures, the medium-sized and smaller banks will go on doing business with China from the banking centres in Switzerland. It is finally interesting to recall the results of a recent empirical investigation on the communication networks of the firms located in the Zurich agglomeration area, according to which, the firms in the central city communicated mainly with capital cities situated in the rest of the world. The ranking of these capitals was led by London. After London, the largest share of communications was with Paris, New York and Milan, in that order. Then at fifth place, before any other European business centre, was Hong Kong (Thierstein *et al.* 2006). As the bulk of the communication in Zurich concerned firms in the service sector, and particularly firms offering financial services, one can maintain that, from the economic point of view, one of the sectors of the Swiss economy which is certainly going to be influenced by the rise of China to the rank of global power, will be the financial sector. This sector is concentrated in the three gateway towns of Geneva, Basel and Zurich, as well as in the medium-sized towns of Lugano and Zug.

Urban development in Switzerland and globalization

As has already been illustrated in Figure 8.1, the effects of the rise of China on the development of the Swiss urban system can only be appreciated in an indirect way, namely, in looking at the possible urban repercussions of globalization. This analysis can further be made only if one assumes that the future influence of globalization will not be very different from that in the past, i.e. by extrapolation of the present tendencies. Keeping this in mind, one can continue to examine the diagram of Figure 8.1. One notes that globalization has increased international competition and provoked, on one side, a process of structural change that has led to the emergence of metropolitan areas, and, on the other side, to the concentration of social problems in the central cities of the Swiss urban agglomerations. Through these two phenomena, recent urban development in Switzerland has been characterized by the concentration of population, jobs and other economic resources, as well as social problems, in the urban areas. In the year 2001, the federal government of Switzerland acknowledged the importance of this development by publishing a White Paper on what was called the 'agglomerations' policy' (Consiglio Federale 2001). One has to consider this publication as a major change in the orientation of planning at the national level because it put the urban areas at the centre of attention. The White Paper affirms that, in the present stage of development of the international economy, the urban areas have become the motors of economic activity.[5] As a matter of fact, more than 70 per cent of the population and more than three-quarters of the total employment of Switzerland are concentrated in these urban areas. When dealing with the characteristics of urban development, the White Paper insisted particularly on two points, namely:

1   the growing polarization of the urban system;
2   the continuing suburbanization tendencies and their consequences.

These characteristics testify to a tendency to territorial specialization both at the national level as well as at the level of the single urban area. At the national level, the structural change, with the tertiarization of the economy, as well as the important changes which showed up in transport and information technology, have favoured a spatial concentration of economic resources and power, and led to the emergence of metropolitan areas of national importance (Rossi 1995).[6] At the moment, there are five such agglomerations: Zurich, Basel, Geneva-Lausanne, Bern and the southern part of the Canton of Ticino (Schuler *et al.* 2005). Of these, the metropolitan areas of Zurich, Basel and Geneva-Lausanne are, in economic terms, the more dynamic ones. This is so, in particular, because, owing to the presence of international airports, these three metropolitan areas are also the international gateways of the Swiss economy. The White Paper of the federal government notes further that the agglomerations in the immediate prox-imity of the metropolitan areas are successively falling into their gravitational fields. The medium-sized and small cities and urban areas in peripheral locations are, on the contrary, not influenced by the polarized economic dynamism of the metropolitan areas. Consequently they do not grow.[7]

As far as suburbanization is concerned, the White Paper stresses two tenden-cies in particular, which it calls:

1   functional differentiation;
2   social differentiation (or social disaggregation).

With respect to functional differentiation, i.e. specialization at the level of the single urban zone, the White Paper observes that, over the last few decades, sub-urbanization in Switzerland has involved not only populations but also jobs. The share of the central city in the total population and in the total number of jobs of the urban zones has tended to decrease. The social differentiation tendency is characterized by the growing share of old people, poor people, people living alone, families with only one parent, drug addicts, unemployed, foreigners with scarce resources and, in general, people needing financial help in making a living in the central cities. This leads not only to the concentration of social problems in the cities but, owing as well to a significant spillover flow, to the deterioration of their financial situation. Consequently, governance of the agglomeration is to be considered one of the main problems that the 'agglomerations' policy has to deal with.

One important implication of the globalization process: institutional reforms

A federal system is, by definition, a system in which governmental power is decentralized. As Tocqueville, in his classic study on democracy in America,

stated, 'This brings with it, on the one side, the drawbacks of governmental fragmentation, but on the other side, the immense advantage of a larger political participation.'[8] As far as federal Switzerland is concerned, one has long considered
the last advantage, i.e. a larger involvement of the citizens in the government
and in the administration of their communes, as the most important one. Self-
government in small units was also seen as the most efficient solution, as it per-
mitted the users of the public services to decide on their extent and quality in the
perfect knowledge that they would have to pay for them. With the onset of globalization and the weakening of the competitive capacity and growth rates of the
Swiss economy, this position on the advantages of institutional fragmentation
has recently come under criticism. On the one side, it was found that the present
cantonal borders have become outdated and that it is time to redesign the cantonal tier of government with the aim of creating internationally visible and competitive regions. On the other, it was found that governance problems in the
agglomerations, created by suburbanization, were probably hindering their economic growth and therefore appeals were made for institutional reforms.

The regionalization of Switzerland

It seems that globalization, as well as international political and economic integration, have led to a decreasing importance of the central government in the
determination of economic-growth policies. The statement of this tendency has
given rise, in Switzerland, to a debate on the reforms that were necessary to reinforce the competitive position of the regions. As Ratti (1995), in a very early
stage of the debate, put it: 'The globalization processes were asking Switzerland
to regenerate her "territoriality", i.e. the existing system of managing her internal
and external relationships.' The most visible result of globalization was represented by the poor growth performance of the economy. But why should insufficient performance of the economy be countered with institutional reforms in the
public sector? The link between globalization and reforms in the public sector
was made clear by Borner and Bodmer (2004). In their empirical inquiry, in
which they compared Swiss growth performance with that of other European
countries, these two authors demonstrated that the poor performance of the
Swiss economy could not be attributed to variables such the investment ratio, or
the level of education of the working population, or the real exchange rate and
so on, but to two other groups of braking factors whose influence was very difficult to quantify. The first one was denominated, in a very general way, as
'economic-policy' causes. It included factors such as the growing presence of
the state, or the weakening degree of international competitive capacity. The
other one was called by these authors, 'the political system'. When speaking of
the reforms that were needed to improve the situation, they also distinguished
between reforms in the fields of economic policy and what they called 'institutional reforms'. The main target of the Borner and Bodmer reform proposals was
not the federal frame of government as such, but the so-called 'direct democracy', i.e. the possibility for the electorate to contest decisions that have been

taken by the parliaments, or to put forward proposals for changes in the constitution. They considered 'direct democracy' as a force hindering the possibility of introducing the drastic reforms which they regarded necessary to relaunch economic growth. In a publication that appeared in 2005, Blöchliger (2005) resumed this criticism and directly tackled the problem of institutional reform at the regional level. For this author, decentralized decision-making and working competition among the public institutions were, in principle, good things. But one should also consider the less ideal aspects of institutional fragmentation. Too much decision autonomy attributed to too-small governments produced at least three main problems:

1   hindering reforms;
2   increasing public expenditures;
3   braking growth, especially of the metropolitan regions.

Blöchliger (2005) proposed a new intermediate tier of government. The cantons should be substituted by large economic regions. He put forward two reform variants:

1   the reduction of the middle tier of government from 26 cantons to nine regions of whom six were 'metropolitan regions' and three 'countryside' regions, or
2   the reduction from 26 cantons to 12 so-called 'agglomeration' regions.

Finally, it is useful to observe that the constitution of large regions is not only an academic subject. In its last report on the state of spatial development, the federal office responsible for it presented four development scenarios, each of which was based on different patterns of urban development (Bundesamt für Raumentwicklung 2005). These are:

1   a metropolitan Switzerland;
2   a suburbanized Switzerland;
3   a Switzerland with urban networks;
4   a Switzerland of regions.

While in this report there is no hint about a need for institutional reforms, one suggests at least, as was already done in the 2001 'agglomerations' policy White Paper, that the large regions should be considered as the territorial units of reference in the formulation of the planning policy at the national level.

Governance problems in the agglomerations

Turning now to the agglomerations, one can specify that here there is a governance problem, given by the fact that, as Kübler recently put it: 'The contemporary city extends its influence to an area in which there is mainly an integration of a functional nature, while the institutional landscape remains highly fragmented' (Kübler 2005; translated by the author). The attempts to solve this problem are always, according to this author, of two kinds:

1   The classic position that consists in the promotion of merging the local authorities in the ring with the central city.
2   Alternative, more flexible solutions, based on the creation of cooperation networks of local authorities, which has been put forward in recent times by the so-called 'new regionalism' authors (see, e.g. Frisken and Norris 2001).

Switzerland is at present experimenting with both types of solutions. While the consolidation of local power, through merging, is a solution which has been applied, mainly by middle-sized agglomeration centres (the cases of the Nuova Lugano and of Rapperswil-Jona can be quoted as the most important projects of this kind recently realized), the flexible network solutions are used both in greater agglomerations as well as in middle-sized ones to try to reinforce the inter-communal cooperation in such policy fields as economic development, planning or transport, whose strategy visions, or projects, extend over the territory of a single local authority. Sometimes, as in the so-called GLOW association in the Glattal region, in the eastern part of the Zurich agglomeration, the network among the local authorities seems to have been created not only to improve the cooperation at the regional level and to shape an attractive, liveable region, but also to learn from the project how to improve cooperation among local institutions and local economic interests, while realizing it (Thierstein and Gabi 2004). Some of these urban networks have been started as local contributions to the 'Best Practice Models', a programme promoted by the federal government in the framework of its agglomeration policy (Thierstein *et al.* 2004). The central idea of the urban network is that in order to improve cooperation among the local authorities of the agglomeration, it is not necessary to integrate these local authorities in a new institution by merging or creating a new intermediate government tier. Instead, one tries to deal with the governance problem by promoting inter-communal cooperation in the agglomeration, by applying soft instruments, such as contracts or projects, which can also have, as shown by the GLOW association project, an important learning-by-doing content.

Conclusions

What are the implications of the rise of China to the rank of global economic power for urban Switzerland? In the former sections of this chapter, indirect answers to this question have been presented. In a nutshell, these are the most important points of the arguments:

•   About the development of China's influence on Switzerland
    Today, the shares of China or of the Chinese in a series of economic and cultural indicators like imports and exports of goods, FDI flow and stocks,

tourist overnight stays, resident population, restaurants and medical doctors practising TCM are modest but already significant.

China's influence is however increasing very rapidly. Most of the indicators are developing in an exponential way. If their growth should continue for the next 15 to 20 years it is possible that (1) China will become a major economic partner for Switzerland and (2) the importance of present major European and American partners will diminish.

This emergence of China as a possible important partner has led the Swiss government to revise the orientation of its foreign policy. With this revision more room will be given to the foreign policy for North America and Asia (India and China, in particular).

But the pace and nature of the future relationships with China will also depend on the decisions the Chinese government may take with respect to the opening of its country to foreign trade and foreign relationships.

- About the impact of globalization on urban development

The impact of globalization on the urbanization tendencies in Switzerland is at best illustrated by the structural change and its consequences.

At the level of the national urban system, one can consider structural change as a process that has led, and is still leading, to significant changes in the economic base of Swiss cities. Some of them have managed to substitute the suppressed industrial jobs with jobs in the tertiary sector, experiencing a new growth wave. Others, instead, whose economy was largely based on the manufacturing sector, did not manage to find new economic impulses and have stagnated. Consequently, the urban hierarchy has grown steeper with the emergence of 'metropolitan areas'. This movement will go on over the next few decades.

At the level of the single urban agglomeration, the structural change stimulated the suburbanization of jobs and the concentration of poorer classes of population in the central city. Governance of the agglomeration has become more difficult.

Two debates have followed. The first concerns the necessity to reinforce the position of the intermediate tier of government, by substituting the cantons with a reduced number of regional governments, some of which would be based in the emerging five or six metropolitan areas. The second one considers the governance problem inside the urban agglomeration. In this case, one is searching for 'best practice models' to improve cooperation between the central city and the surrounding local authorities. The available solutions vary between the merging of local authorities, which is considered an efficient, but hardly innovative, solution and networking with these in different types of associations, which is considered a more flexible and educational solution. While the debates are developing in a very intensive way, the practical experience in restructuring agglomeration governance is still scanty. This will certainly change over the next decade or two.

If China continues its present high rate of growth in the future, and if its government continues to follow a policy of cautious opening of the country, there is no doubt that over the next 15 to 20 years, China is going to become one of the most important economic partners of Switzerland, as far as international trade, foreign direct investment and tourism are concerned. It is also possible that the growing Chinese influence on the Swiss economy could change the structure of foreign relationships of its economy. China could, in this respect, take the place of some European countries. This should lead to a growing importance of Chinese economy and Chinese culture for the development of the Swiss urban system, in particular, for the growth of the three metropolitan areas that are considered the gateways of Switzerland, namely Zurich, Geneva and Basel. The presence of Chinese people (businessmen as well as students), Chinese tourists, TCM centres and general practitioners practising TCM as well as Chinese restaurants will certainly increase in Swiss cities. Soon one will also have a growing number of Chinese firms moving into Switzerland. The language and culture of China will therefore become more important, in an urban context, than they already are.[9] A growing number of mayors and councillors of Swiss cities are going to visit Chinese cities, trying to negotiate cooperation agreements. There will certainly be mounting attention in Chinese culture, arts, philosophy, history and way of life as is, among other instances, testified by the growing number of newspaper articles on Chinese subjects. Soon a large share of the Swiss population will know that 'Sulishi' is Zurich in Chinese.

Notes

1 Just to mention a recent example, we recall that the introduction of a luxury tax on Swiss watches by the Chinese government immediately had a negative impact on the export of Swiss watches to China.

2 Specialists of the international investment flow are at present anticipating a rapid increase of China's FDI. One of the main reasons for China to invest abroad seems actually to be the wish to have a better mastery of the development of its firms' technology (*Neue Zürcher Zeitung* 2006).

3 In absolute terms, the figures for Hong Kong and those for the People's Republic of China are the same size.

4 This shift concerns not only the international trade flow, but also the financial transactions. In the words of a bank manager, 'Asia will be in the future what London and New York were in the eighties and nineties of the past century' (Vetterli 2006).

5 With the term 'agglomeration', Swiss statistics define a polarized region composed of a central city of at least 10,000 inhabitants and a ring of local authorities which are connected in different ways with the central city. There are around 50 such agglomerations with more than 900 local authorities. The term urban zones, or urban regions, in Switzerland indicates the set composed by the agglomerations and by the so-called 'isolated' cities, i.e. cities without a ring. In the year 2000, according to the last population census, there were five isolated cities (Schuler *et al.* 2005).

6 In fact, tertiarization is only one aspect of the development incurred by the economic base of the urban areas. The other one has been the disappearance of the manufacturing sector, especially from the central cities. It is only because the development of the tertiary sector more than compensated for the de-industrialization that some of these areas could develop further. A major reason for the de-industrialization, at least in industries with lower productivity levels, was the shift of jobs and firms abroad, especially to countries with lower labour costs.

7 It is interesting to observe that this subdivision of the urban system into dynamic and

stagnating urban zones is matched by the subdivision that some Swiss economists make between a dynamic group of firms (the multinationals which are, as a rule, located in the metropolitan areas) and the group of firms which are either producing for the multinationals or for the internal market and whose location is more homogenously distributed in space. (See also Thierstein *et al.* 2006.)

8 To mention de Tocqueville:

> J'admettrai, du reste, si l'on veut que les villages et les comtés des Etats-Unis seraient plus utilement administrés par une autorité centrale placée loin d'eux, et qui leur resterait étrangère, que par des fonctionnaires pris dans leur sein. Je reconnaîtrai, si on l'exige, qu'il régnerait plus de sécurité en Amérique, qu'on y ferait un emploi plus sage et plus judicieux des ressources sociales, si l'administration de tout le pays était concentrée dans une seule main. Les avantages que les Américains retirent du système de la décentralisation me le feraient encore préférer au système contraire.
>
> (de Tocqueville 1968)

9 In this respect it is interesting to quote the opinion of a Swiss sinologist who believes that the Chinese presence in Zurich can already no longer be considered exceptional. She reports that she recently helped a group of Chinese tourists to find the correct way to the Zurich zoo. While in the past, the fact that she was speaking Chinese had raised astonishment on the part of the visitors, this time the tourists did not show any particular reaction. For them it was normal, probably, that in a town with international ambitions like Zurich, one spoke fluent Chinese (Hool Twerenbold 2006).

References

Blöchliger, H. (2005) 'Baustelle Föderalismus', in Avenir Suisse (ed.) *Baustelle Föderalismus*, Zurich: Verlag Neue Zürcher Zeitung.

Boerlin-Brodbeck, Y. (2005) 'Chinoiserien in der Deutschsprachigen Schweiz', in P. Hugger (ed.) *China in der Schweiz*, Zürich: Offizin Verlag: 27–40.

Borner, S. and Bodmer, F. (2004) *Wohlstand ohne Wachstum, Eine Schweizer Illusion*, Zurich: Orell Füssli.

Bundesamt für Raumentwicklung (2005) *Raumentwicklungsbericht 2005*, Berne: Bundesamt für Raumentwicklung.

Chapuis, A. (1923) *La montre chinoise*, Neuchâtel: Attinger Frères.

Consiglio Federale (2001) *Politica degli agglomerati della Confederazione*, Berne: Consiglio Federale.

De Tocqueville, A. (1968) *De la démocratie en Amérique, les grands thèmes, idées*, Paris: Gallimard.

Droz, P. (2004) *Erwartungen und Potentiale für den Schweizer Tourismus aufgezeigt am neuen Markt China*, Diplomarbeit, Siders: Schweizerische Tourismusfachschule.

Etienne, G., Maurer, J.-L. and Renaudin, Ch. (1992) *Suisse-Asie – Pour un Nouveau Partenariat*, Einsiedeln: SNF.

Frisken, F. and Norris, D. F. (2001) 'Regionalism Reconsidered', *Journal of Urban Affairs* 23(5): 467–78.

Gyr, U. and Unterweger, G. (2005) 'Chinesisch essen, zwischen urbaner Weltküche und vertrauter Exotik', in P. Hugger (ed.) *China in der Schweiz*, Zurich: Offizin Verlag: 161–76.

Hirschi, Ch., Serdült, U. and Widmer, Th. (1999) 'Schweizerische Aussenpolitik im Wandel: Internationalisierung, Globalisierung und Multilateralisierung', *Swiss Political Science Review* 5(1): 31–56.

Hool Twerenbold, Ch. (2006) Declaration reported in the article by M. Reuss and R. Kaminski, 'Sulishi hat einen guten Klang', *Tages Anzeiger* 17 February, Zurich: Tamedia.

Hugger, P. (2005) 'Wenn fernstes näher wird', in P. Hugger (ed.) *China in der Schweiz*, Zurich: Offizin Verlag: 7–10.

Iten, F. and Saller, R. (2005) 'Traditionelle chinesische Medizin in der Schweiz', in P. Hugger. (ed.) *China in der Schweiz*, Zurich: Offizin Verlag: 177–200.

Kübler, D. (2005) 'Démocratie et gouvernance d'agglomération. Quelques leçons européennes', in *Pouvoirs locaux* 65 (II/2005): 85–91.

Landes, D.S. (1999) *The Wealth and Poverty of Nations*, New York: W.W. Norton and Company Inc.

Neue Zürcher Zeitung (2006) 'China investiert vermehrt im Ausland', *Neue Zürcher Zeitung* 24 July: 13

Pasquier, M. and Weiss, R. M. (2006) *The Swiss Image in China*, Bern/Chavannes-près-Renens: Präsenz Schweiz/IDHEAP.

Ratti, R. (1995) *Leggere la Svizzera*, Lugano: G. Casagrande editore.

Reuss, M. and Kaminski, R. (2006) 'Sulishi hat einen guten Klang', *Tages Anzeiger* 17 February, Zurich: Tamedia.

Rossi, A. (1995) *Concurrence territoriale et réseaux urbains: l'armature urbaine de la Suisse en transition*, Zurich: vdf Verlag.

Roth, J. (2005) 'Die gegenseitigen Wirtschaftsbeziehungen im geschichtlichen Abriss', in P. Hugger (ed.) *China in der Schweiz*, Zurich: Offizin Verlag: 205–14.

Schuler, M., Dessemontet, P. and Joye, D. (2005) *Les niveaux géographiques de la Suisse*, Neuchâtel: Swiss Federal Statistical Office.

Straubhaar, Th. (1985) *Die Wirtschaftsbeziehungen der Schweiz mit China*, Zurich: Zürich Wirtschaftsförderung.

Swiss National Bank (2005) *Die Entwicklung der Direktinvestitionen im Jahr 2004*, Zurich: Swiss National Bank.

Thierstein, A. and Gabi, S. (2004) 'When Creativity Meets Metropolitan Governance', *DISP* 158, Zurich: Netzwerk Stadt und Landschaft, ETH Zürich: 34–40.

Thierstein, A., Boulianne, L., Gabi, S. and Reinhard, M. (2004) *Die Modellvorhaben der Agglomerationspolitik: Auswirkungen auf die wirtschaftliche Entwicklung. Wirkungsabschätzung von neun Agglomerationen*, Zurich, Lausanne.

Thierstein, A., Kruse, Ch., Glanzmann, L., Gabi, S. and Grillon, N. (2006) *Raumentwicklung im Verborgenen. Die Entwicklung der Metropolregion Nordschweiz*, Zurich: Verlag Neue Zürcher Zeitung.

Vetterli, M. (2006) 'Der Ferne Osten liegt den Bankern am Herzen', *Tages Anzeiger* 13 July, Zurich: Tamedia: 25.

Voire, J.-P. (2005) 'Genf und die Verbreitung der Chinoiserien in der Schweiz', in P. Hugger (ed.) *China in der Schweiz*, Zurich: Offizin Verlag: 13–26.

Wachter, D. (1995) *Schweiz, eine moderne Geographie*, Zurich: Verlag NZZ.

Part II

Scenarios and strategies for Europe to address the challenges from the East

9 A sustainable quality of life for Europeans in 2031

A framework for shaping policies to address major changes in the global operating environment

Simon Miles

1 Introduction

The purpose of this chapter is to assist European public policy-makers, especially those with a particular interest in the role of the settlement system and the biophysical environment in providing for a sustainable quality of life, to shape public policy in response to continuing change in their operating context. That operating context is global. The rise of China as a global economic power, although a key reference point for this book, is only one of many factors to be considered in that global context. Thus, in considering the implications of the rise of China for the form and functioning of Europe's settlement system and biophysical environment 25 years from now, we require a conceptual framework within which to organize our analysis and shape possible policy responses.

Such an organizing framework is elaborated in Section 2 of this chapter in the form of a schema conceptualizing the process of human and societal development, that is, the process that public policy has to sustain.

One key component of this framework is the developmental setting within which individuals and groups live out their lives. Conceptually, it can be broken down into any number of developmental environments, the precise breakdown depending on one's particular focus for analysis. Each one is the product of the interactions of forces at work globally and within any one country (or group of countries, such as Europe). The biophysical environment and the built environment are two such environments. In the interest of brevity, most references are to the biophysical environment. In Section 3, key considerations relative to the nature of each force of change are identified. The rise of China is not seen as one such force; rather, it is part of the change taking place in several such forces. Likewise, climate change, which I see as being far more significant a development than the rise of China (but one which is also linked, in part, to the rise of China) is not treated as one such force but, again, is considered within the context of several of the key forces. Similarly, the important advances with respect to connectivity that are in process are seen as part of several such forces of change, most obviously that of technological developments but also, notably, that of the explosion of information and the growth of understanding.

For each one of the nine forces of change, following the discussion of key considerations, there is a discussion of the needed response. While very tentative, given the further research required, this first proposes a broad statement of national interest and then suggests broad, supportive policy positions and the supportive strategic initiatives to realize those interests.

The chapter's treatment of these issues is necessarily brief, given the scope of what has to be considered. The intent is to convey that scope and how further research can be organized with a view to identifying connections between policy initiatives proposed in response to different forces at work in the current developmental setting in Europe. The chapter presents the case for a more integrated approach to research and policy-making. The 'why' and the 'what' are conveyed with the model of the human and societal development process. The 'what' is further elaborated in the discussion of key considerations relating to each force and the 'how' is answered in large part by the articulation of national interests and supportive policies. Not discussed, but implicit, and possibly of significance for the 'how', is the strengthening of institutional capacities to conduct the research, to shape integrated policy responses and to implement them.

2   A conceptual framework for shaping policies supportive of sustainable development

The Brundtland Commission gave the world a popular definition of sustainable development as 'development that meets the needs of the present without compromising the ability of future generations to meet their needs' (World Commission on Environment and Development 1987). However, precisely what has to be done in order to ensure that the approach to sustainability will be adjusted on an ongoing basis as we learn more about the threats to sustainability? Before we can address this, there is another more fundamental question.

What do we mean by development? The Brundtland Commission put the emphasis on economic development. It is suggested here that we should focus on human and societal development. I suggest that we look upon human development as a continuing process that people undergo in relation to their developmental setting. It is a process of continuing enrichment of experience and improvement in the quality of our associations and ties (i.e. our ligatures) and thus our ability, not only to survive, but also to respond to new situations in spontaneous and creative ways. This enrichment of experience is seen to derive from the continuing interaction with one's surrounding developmental environments (or components, whether economic, social, technological, political, biophysical or whatever, of one's developmental setting).[1] The opportunities to interact are dependent on the options open. The quality of the ligatures with people, places and things is also dependent upon the options open for interaction, but at the same time upon an ability to be selective in spending time with those people, places and things which provide the greatest satisfaction.[2] Thus, the quality of the resultant human development is directly related to the quality of the links or associations that individuals and groups enjoy with those environments and the options those environments create or hold open for them.

In essence, societal development can be seen as human development writ large, with considerable emphasis placed on the strength of the linkages between its members. This notion of interaction is as fundamental to societal development as it is to human development. This is well illustrated by the importance we place on the participation of individuals in societal activities (i.e. interaction) for their development and that of society. Equally, however, it applies to any interaction with the natural environment. And, it is not too difficult to see how this concept of development applies to other species (i.e. wildlife), something very significant given our increased understanding of the importance of biodiversity for human survival and well-being.

This suggests that the ultimate purpose to be served by European policy-makers and planners as they contemplate the future shape and functioning of Europe's settlement system and biophysical environment is to help ensure that these developmental interactions between people and their developmental environments can take place on a sustainable basis and, over time, can lead to an enrichment of those people's lives.

Of these various developmental environments, it is the productive capacities of the natural environment that are most vulnerable to destruction. All other environments have been created by humans. These are constantly being refitted, reshaped, rebuilt or rehabilitated by people. In many instances, and especially so with the economic environment, this is done largely at the expense of the biophysical environment. Man has tended to take the biophysical environment for granted in large part because certain elements are self-renewing if they are not subjected to undue stress. While our understanding of what constitutes undue stress is still appallingly limited, it is becoming apparent that both in individual countries and globally, large parts of the biophysical environment are beyond rehabilitation.

However, while this vulnerability of the biophysical environment to pressures arising largely in other environments may constitute our central interest relative to the unsustainability of human and societal development in most parts of the world today, our central concern has to be with the behaviour of people as it affects that environment, whether directly or indirectly. And to make matters more complex, as factors like climate change illustrate, in many instances, it is the behaviour of people globally that has to be addressed.

Thus, if European policy-makers are to facilitate human and societal development by improving the condition of the biophysical environment as a resource base, as an amenity, as a sink for our wastes and as a habitat for wildlife, then they will have to concern themselves with the nature of human interactions in other developmental environments, as they bear upon the conditions of the biophysical environment. In short, this means that strategies have to influence critical choices guiding those interactions. To determine more precisely what this calls for by way of action, policy-makers require a framework for assessing the

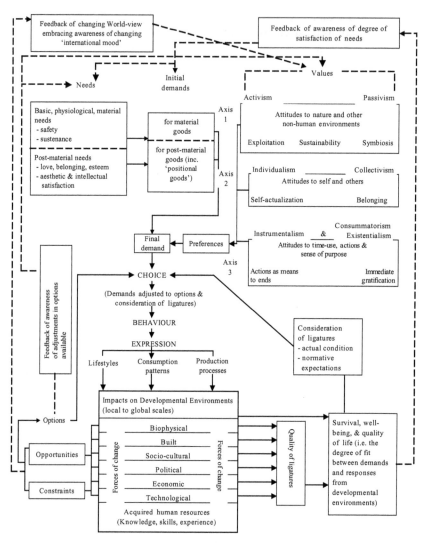

Figure 9.1 Schema of relations between various components involved in the process of human and societal development.

strategic importance of proposals for addressing the forces of change influencing human behaviour and, thus, the condition of our developmental environments.

What the above suggests is that if European policy-makers are to facilitate human and societal development through interventions that are to promote sustainability, they will need to have a conceptual model of that development process. Such a model can be helpful in understanding how interactions that make unsustainable demands on any one developmental environment can be modified.

Figure 9.1 presents the development process in schematic form. The intent is to understand how the development process works and how policy goals and objectives can be realized through appropriate strategic policy interventions by national governments. These strategic policy interventions are expected to influence major forces bearing on the central concern. Although our central interest is the condition of, say, the biophysical environment, our central concern is the behaviour of people as it affects the biophysical environment.

The forces bearing on their behaviour emanate from the developmental setting. This setting has been broken down conceptually into the 'developmental environments'. They have local and global dimensions and are listed in the lower part of the schema. They include *human resources*, which, in turn, include motivating forces, although these have been separated out as needs, values and demands because of their importance to the development process. Also separated out, because of its importance to us here and because it has not had sufficient attention in the past, is the *consideration of ligatures*. For example, the attachment to land felt by farmers is a major factor in their remaining in farming even though it may have a bearing on the economic viability of the farms in question.

The central point in the schema is making a choice. Here, demands are adjusted to options perceived to be open while consideration is given to the quality of one's ligatures or associations and ties with people, places and things that might be affected by the choice of behaviour. The intent of any choice made is to improve the fit between demands and the actual responses from the surrounding developmental environments. However, this intent is difficult to realize since the information on the options is likely to be far from perfect. Thus, the fit that is eventually realized is not necessarily to be equated with the adjustment or fit initially perceived to be realizable between the demands and the options at the time of making the choice. The reasons for any difference go beyond the quality of the information to the quality of the judgements made and the degree of realism in the expectations. Thus, in exercising the choice, there may well be adverse effects on one or more of the developmental environments (such as the biophysical environment) and, to the extent that this is obvious to the individual or group in question, some dissatisfaction may be registered.

This would affect the quality of life. Indeed, this is exactly what has happened with the demands made on the biophysical environment as a resource base. Aware people feel that the quality of life has been adversely affected because of the qualitative and quantitative losses they have observed.

Information on the actual response of the developmental environments and the ways they are changing often takes time to be registered and contribute to our sense of our quality of life. This registering of our quality of life is shown on the right lower corner of the scheme. This register is important because it incorporates values (in the context of demands). Those who are concerned about sustainability register their perceptions about sustainability here. Feedback about the degree of satisfaction with life may result in new priorities accorded to certain needs. This feedback loop is shown on the right side. This is to be distinguished from the more specific information on the actual condition of the developmental environments and the constraints and opportunities open that will become part of the feedback shown on the left side of the schema.

This more specific feedback is of two types. The feedback based on an awareness of adjustments in options begins to affect both the priorities accorded to needs (e.g. with water pollution or the loss of the best agricultural soils, the message is eventually received that basic survival may be at stake) and values (e.g. regarding attitudes to the biophysical environment).

There is also feedback on what is happening in the world around us, whether we are talking only of our neighbours or the world at large. This information will also affect our values and our preferences for the way in which we satisfy our needs, but it will not affect the priorities we accord our needs until it has worked its way through our value system.

What the schema does offer is a checklist of strategically important activities that can be undertaken to influence choices made by various key actors relative to the maintenance and enhancement of conditions in the various developmental environments.

The model supports the previous statement that the central concern of policy-makers has to be with the behaviour of people as it affects any one developmental environment. It also makes clear that because this behaviour is a product of the forces emanating from the various developmental environments, one has to comprehend what is going on in these developmental environments if, say, the biophysical environment is to be successfully managed. What the model provides, visually in a schema, is an aid in compiling a checklist of strategically important activities that can be undertaken in order to influence the critical choices made by key decision-makers directly or indirectly affecting the biophysical environment.[3] And, of course, the same can be said of any other developmental environment with which one is concerned, such as the economic, socio-cultural and politico-administrative environments.

The key decision-makers referred to above fall into three groups: persons directly affecting the biophysical environment; central government policy-makers; and intermediaries, both in and outside of government.

The strategically important activities can be identified by tracing back from the desired choice of action to those variables that are manoeuvrable. In essence, there are three broad strategic thrusts through which behaviour, and thus the condition of the biophysical environment, can be modified. One can modify the demands that various groups place on the natural environment; one can modify the options arising from the combination of political, economic, social, technological and other constraints and opportunities; and one can improve the ability of the individual or group in question to manage or cope with the forces bearing on the biophysical environment.

This suggests that European policy-makers should be interested in activities that are supportive of one or more of the above strategic thrusts. The pursuit of these thrusts will involve, among other things, more attention to four initial areas of activity:

- Improved information on and analysis of factors relating to the selection of the appropriate strategic thrust or thrusts and supportive instruments, which implies improvements in capabilities for research and information management for strategic planning and policy-making purposes.
- Improved systems for communicating this and other information and intelligence to the relevant key decision-makers, which implies improvements in extension services, improved professional media channels, workshops, etc.
- Clearer statements of collective interest (either locally, nationally, or regionally) to guide the strategic choices by government and avoid different agencies or levels of government working at cross-purposes, which also implies improvements to the functioning of cross-sectoral decision-making bodies from cabinets on down.
- Continuing improvements to the development of human resources, which implies more attention to education and training, whether of farmer, consumer, senior civil servant, or whomever, with special attention to shifting the development paradigm or perspective to one that embraces environmental and social considerations along with the economic and technological.

Hopefully, this conceptual model, and the notes on how to use it as a checklist to identify some of the more important activities to be undertaken, should assist European policy-makers in, first, identifying the nature of the pressure from international forces and their implications for the developmental environments of interest and, second, planning strategic responses.

3 Global forces of change: key considerations and needed responses

To summarize the argument thus far: the conditions prevailing in any one of the developmental environments are the product of the behaviour of countless players in the public, private and popular sectors all over the world. That behaviour is a product of choices being made that are designed to satisfy demands in light of the options available. Those options are a product of forces of change that emanate from and contribute to the shaping of (but are not necessarily aligned with) various developmental environments. If the conditions in any one developmental environment for Europeans (e.g. the biophysical environment) are to change for the better, behaviour has to change, which requires that the forces (including 'needs, values and demands') have to be changed.

Thus, just as the economic environment has changed in Europe, in part because of the choices and behaviour of China (and countless others linked by their economic production processes), so will Europeans have to manipulate the forces of change or accommodate them. Acceptance of a changed condition is easier when dealing with the economic environment than, say, the biophysical, if one has a truly sustainable concept of development in mind. Obviously, a good understanding of these forces of change will reveal the extent to which they can be manipulated or must be accommodated.

While thorough studies of these forces are required relative to each country in Europe, many of the manifestations of the forces will be similar in different countries. What's not being conducted now are holistic studies that look at all forces on a global scale. We have countless unisectoral studies (e.g. the economic or social or political) that do not take into consideration the findings of studies of other sectors in any systematic way. This is due largely to the structure and operation of government departments. Thus, it can be fairly concluded that enhanced capacity to conduct such integrated studies is a basic need in most, if not all, countries.

What follows here is a brief analysis of each of nine major forces of change. For each one, some key considerations are identified (to suggest further direction for research and to give a sense of what one may expect) and then some suggestions are made as to the needed response. This response is first given direction by suggesting a likely statement of national interest on the part of a European country and, second, by articulating some supportive policy positions, designed to realize that national interest.

Since the improvement of conditions in the developmental environments of Europeans may require considerable change in conditions in other countries, foreign policy, trade policy and international developmental assistance policy have a significant role to play. This, in turn, implies that for diplomacy, trade and international development assistance to be effective, one needs to have thorough studies on the likely effects of these same global forces on the countries which one is negotiating with or assisting.

3.1 The exacerbation of poverty

Although there is continuing debate over whether the gaps between the rich and poor within countries and between countries are growing or shrinking, my assessment is that while the poor are becoming better off on average in absolute terms, they are not closing the gap between themselves and the rich. This growing poverty gap in most developing countries and in some of the industrialized countries (as measured by purchasing power parity (PPP) dollars) is likely to drive more poor people to externalize their production and consumption costs as environmental costs. This will further erode the value of the natural capital on which one-third of the world's population is directly dependent for their livelihood. This is likely to exacerbate poverty for future generations. For example, the poorest 50 per cent of Brazil's population received 18 per cent of national income in 1960 and 11.5 per cent in 1995 (UNDP 1998: 29). Brazil's take-off preceded China's. It appears that a similar gap is developing in China's income structure. There, however, the value of the natural capital is being eroded largely by the pollution from dirty production processes and using productive agricultural land for industrial expansion (generally without compensation).

The gap between poor and rich countries is also growing. This results in a lack of international purchasing power (as measured in constant dollar price per capita incomes) for developing countries, which helps explain: the lack of funding for research into solving problems of third-world environmental management (e.g. improved food crops); the inability of developing countries to import new, environmentally sound technologies; and, the often inadequate (or missing) representation of developing countries at the negotiating tables on global agreements on the environment.

Trade and investment flows are not always helpful for the poorest countries. Commodity prices in late 2006 have been at their highest levels in 25 years. Yet, in 2002, these prices were at their lowest in 150 years. And 80 per cent of foreign direct investments to the developing countries flows to just 12 of those countries (Jolly 1999: 7). China receives the largest share. This, combined with the growing inequality, is making many developing countries more vulnerable to economic crises. Such crises are known to have an irreversible and negative effect on health, education and nutrition and thus reduce the human capital (work-related knowledge, information and skills) of the poor and their ability to escape from poverty (Lustig and Arias 2000: 31). The relative wealth of the industrialized countries makes possible consumption patterns that are arguably doing even more damage to the biophysical environment in terms of per capita impact. Climate change is the most worrisome longer-term change in this regard. Climate change (see later discussion in Section 3.8) will have major implications for biodiversity and for food production worldwide, including Europe.

The above does not bode well for the environmental health of the planet. That will, in time, put increased pressure on Europe's biophysical environment, especially as a resource base for food production (including fisheries) and forest products. The lack of purchasing power in many developing countries means that, without a concentrated effort to develop their economies, the growth in export markets for Europe's increasing knowledge-based services will be confined largely to the fast-growing middle-income countries and especially the 'big four' (China, Russia, India and Brazil), also known as the BRIC countries.

The needed response. The national interest of the typical European country would appear to be to minimize the pressures arising from poverty on the biophysical (as well as the social, cultural, economic and political) environments in developing countries. Supportive, broad policy initiatives will be required to:

- Promote and support efforts by all countries to place a renewed emphasis on equity in the operations of the global economy.
- Assist developing countries to introduce social safety nets to smooth the consumption and protect the human capital of the poor in times of crisis.

As China and its counterparts develop economically, there will be a tendency for them to develop their 'trading empires' and to exploit the poorer countries. Not only should this be discouraged, more importantly, they should be encouraged to assume a much bigger role in assisting the poorest countries. Bringing this about will require a concerted effort on the part of European and OECD member countries.

3.2 Population growth

Earth is a finite space with finite resources. The continuing growth of the population globally should be of concern to all countries. This suggests that multilateral collaboration is the likely preferred approach to action. There has been a slight drop in the rate of growth of the global population to about 76 million pa. But the 6.5 billion of 2005 is expected to reach 8.2 billion by 2031 and 9.1 billion by 2050 according to the UN's medium variant projection (UN Department of Economic and Social Affairs 2005: xiv). The high variant projection would produce a global population of 10.6 billion by 2050 (ibid.). Some 95 per cent of this growth is expected in the developing countries, with the fastest growth in the poorest of these.

China is expected to contribute significantly to global population growth with its 1.315 billion (2005) becoming 1.441 billion (2025) before dropping back to 1.392 billion (2050). The UN estimates that nine countries are expected to account for half of the projected population growth between 2005 and 2050. They are, in order of the size of their contribution in that period: India, Pakistan, Nigeria, the Democratic Republic of Congo, Bangladesh, Uganda, the US, Ethiopia and China (ibid.: xv). This is despite the fact that China's fertility rate is currently 1.7 children per woman (ibid.: xvii).

Europe (east and west) currently has the lowest fertility rates (1.4) of all continental regions. And according to the UN's medium variant, it would still have the lowest rate in 2050 (1.83) (ibid.). Not surprisingly, therefore, Europe is expected to be the first global region to experience a decline in total population. By 2050, this decline may average 0.24 per cent pa (medium variant) (ibid.: xvi).

Although Europe's population will age rapidly, the developing countries' share of the global population aged 60 or more will move even more rapidly from 60 per cent today to 80 per cent in 2050. In developed countries today, 20 per cent of the population is aged 60 or over. By 2050 this will have grown to 32 per cent (ibid.: xix). Physical safety and social security for the ageing, backed by 'grey power' will become more important everywhere.

International migration, according to UN estimates, is expected to result in an average of 2.2 million migrating annually from less-developed to more-developed regions of the world between 2005 and 2050. This should largely offset the loss of 73 million arising from the excess of deaths over births in the same period in developed regions. For the developing world, however, the 98 million emigrants over this period represent less than 4 per cent of the expected population growth. China is expected to be the source of most emigrants annually, at 327,000, followed by Mexico (293,000) and India (241,000) (ibid.). Within the industrialized countries, the integration of immigrants has been achieved with varying degrees of success. The greatest challenges have been experienced by visible minorities from developing countries when seeking employment that makes full use of their skills.

The population dynamics are putting direct and indirect pressures on Europe's biophysical environment as a resource base and as an amenity. Direct pressures are also being put on its social, cultural and politico-administrative environments. Its economic environment has enjoyed benefits, but has also carried the costs of absorbing immigrants and losing emigrants (especially to North America and Australia). The Chinese have tended to favour North America when emigrating. There has been no significant immigrant population in China but its population is still growing. Given its fertility rate of 1.7, its one-child policy, which is applicable only in urban areas, while admirable, is clearly under pressure.

The needed response. The national interest of the typical European country would appear to be to minimize the pressures arising from the future global population on the global and national biophysical environments as a resource base, a sink for wastes, an amenity, and a habitat for wildlife. Supportive, broad policy initiatives will be required to:

- Promote and support efforts by all countries with growing populations to stabilize their population levels in ways acceptable to their societies, as well as taking action nationally.
- Promote management practices domestically and for all other countries, especially resource-importing countries, which will enable people possibly to enhance but certainly to maintain the sustainable productive capacities of their renewable resources base and to extend the life of their non-renewables through careful husbandry.
- Adopt an international development assistance policy and an immigration policy that together will provide improved assistance, at short notice, to an expected increase in the number of refugees in turbulent times.

3.3 Changing needs, values and demands

Key considerations relative to changing needs, values and demands in industrialized and developing countries, as they bear upon the condition of the biophysical environment, are as follows (Inglehart and Baker 2000):[4]

- Economic development brings changes in values, but these changes are 'path-dependent' (i.e. they are influenced by the history of the culture of which they are a part). Not surprisingly, a combination of economic and cultural indicators explains more about variances in economic development than do economic indicators alone.
- The value shifts in a period of industrialization (mainly from traditional values to secular-rational values) are very distinct from those in the post-industrialization period (mainly from absolute norms to greater self-expression). Thus, developing countries undergoing industrialization (such as China) tend to be preoccupied with overcoming nature and tend to regard environmental problems as being fixable without international collaboration. This does not mean that countries like China will not seek advice on how Europeans have 'fixed' their environmental problems; they will. But it does

mean that international collaboration on, say, climate change is of less interest to them.

• Only among those in a society for whom survival is assured will there be a great interest in the environment and therefore in environmental activism.

Efforts to encourage people in both developing and industrialized countries to attach greater value to the environment will have to make clear its importance for their survival as individuals, groups and society, and such efforts will have to reflect recognition of the differences between the general population and the relatively few who are not preoccupied with their economic survival and meeting basic needs. Although improved communications are not homogenizing values, the explosion of knowledge has affected the perceptions of people everywhere and the secure groups in any society are more likely to recognize the implications of the explosions of population and technology for the environment.

The needed response. The national interest of the typical European country would appear to be to respond to and take advantage of changing needs, values and demands internationally and domestically in ways that will continue to maintain or improve the quality of life for people today and for future generations both in Europe and worldwide. Supportive, broad policy initiatives will be required to:

• Promote recognition of the importance of healthy ecosystems and a productive resources base as being integral to the economic survival (and, more broadly, the human security) of the local communities and the country.
• Foster social networks to build commitment to act in the long-term and collective interest of society.
• Support and facilitate the enrichment and diversification of everyday living environments.

3.4 Urbanization trends

Globally, the percentage of the population living in urban areas worldwide has grown from 33 per cent in 1960, to 47 per cent in 1999 (at 2.8 billion), and is expected to reach 61 per cent (or 4.9 billion) in 2030 (UNFPA 1999: 25). The rate of growth is about 60 million pa. The developing countries will account for about 90 per cent of this increase. Some of their cities are growing at 10 per cent pa and squatter communities within those cities are often growing at 20 per cent pa. Their big cities are growing faster than the smaller ones. This rapid rate of urbanization in developing countries is creating three major problems: the threat to the carrying capacity of the biophysical environment, inadequate urban management and a growing rural–urban divide. China is no exception: from 1995 to 2005 the population had moved from being 30 per cent (ibid.: 70) to 40 per cent (UNFPA 2006: 99) urban.

In Europe and other industrialized regions of the world, for the most part, the pace of urbanization is much slower. The addition of numbers to older, built-up areas is putting further pressure on ageing infrastructure, but much of this (e.g.

water and sewage systems, transportation systems) has been in need of renewal for a long time.

A much neglected link between the fate of the urban areas in developing and industrialized countries is the risk of a global pandemic affecting human health. The combination of the extremely unhealthy living conditions in large tracts of many of the cities in developing countries and the increasing movement of goods and travellers between these areas and the industrialized world is a problem waiting to happen. On top of the diseases that may originate from a simple lack of sewers, one has to consider the threats from what one analyst calls the 'biological bombs', 'the hidden micro-terrorists on our global doorstep', such as avian flu, anthrax, mad-cow disease, severe acute respiratory syndrome (SARS) and the methicillin-resistant Staphylococcus aureus (MRSA) that is making many hospitals unhealthy places to be (Nikiforuk 2006).

The needed response. The quality of life for those living in European cities will be influenced by the conditions prevailing in cities in the developing world. This suggests that the national interest of the typical European country would appear to be to enhance the management of urban growth, both domestically and internationally, in ways that minimize its adverse effects on the biophysical and other environments. Supportive, broad policy initiatives will be required both domestically and internationally to:

- Improve urban planning and the financing of urban infrastructure and services.
- Facilitate the enrichment and diversification of everyday living environments.
- Foster social networks to build commitment to act in the long-term and collective interest of society.
- Optimize opportunities for employment in the context of a globally viable international division of labour.
- Promote an ecosystems view of the world aimed at the preservation of the human species and its life-support systems.

3.5 Technological developments

Globally, new techniques and products are constantly being sought to enhance economic, social or environmental productivity in ways that reflect the demands of their users. Differing demands obviously lead to differing technologies. It is this link between demand and technology that contributes one key component in identifying the nature of future technological developments. The other is an understanding of the major constraints that are likely to emerge, creating a need to open new options through new technologies.

Today, relative to the possible move towards sustainable development, there are two broad categories of technological development of interest. The new-generation technologies (the term is applied here to describe those that have been designed to be ecologically sound) are to be encouraged. They internalize environmental and social costs. In time, they could prove valuable in reducing waste, limiting environmental degradation, improving food production, health and education. The old-generation technologies are a mixed bag. Some are environmentally benign. But we can expect continued use and development of many that externalize costs. The pressures from international competition tend to intensify this. Side-effects, especially on the global commons, can be expected. It is in this context that further action is needed on those technologies that are contributing to climate change.

While all of the above applies globally, we can expect that old-generation technologies will be more dominant in the developing countries. This is because environmental and social costs do not rank very highly as concerns (see Section 3.3). Partly, however, it is because new ideas take a long time to spread. Determining which new technologies really qualify as new-generation technologies, which will not create unanticipated side-effects, may prove an enormous challenge (e.g. the biofuels debate), even given the political commitment to conducting strategic impact assessments and verification procedures ahead of the technologies being launched.

China is no exception: old- and new-generation technologies are being adopted simultaneously. Chinese satellites, which make modern communications possible, are found alongside highly polluting production processes. As noted in Section 3.3, the prevailing values lead to a preoccupation with overcoming nature and seeking a quick fix for environmental problems. Closing down all polluting industry for the Olympics is a simple expression of those values.

Thus, globally, we can expect a continuing build-up of the already well-known environmental challenges of our time, ranging from those that are already acknowledged as being of global consequence (such as climate change, stratospheric ozone depletion and nitrogen loading), to those that are slowly gaining such acknowledgement (pesticide and herbicide overuse, toxic and hazardous wastes, chemical warfare, genetic modification, and further 'Bhopals').

To illustrate the complexity of managing technological change, a further look at climate change is helpful. Climate change has been gaining recognition among scientists worldwide and more governments in the industrialized world see it as one of the world's most serious problems.[5] Although there is still much uncertainty about the rate and the extent of global warming, mid-range scenarios, until recently, have projected an increase in global mean temperature of 2°C (within a range of 1.0 to 3.5°C) by the year 2100. This would be the most significant warming over the last 10,000 years. Under such a scenario, there would be:

- An average rise in sea level of about 50 centimetres, which would submerge some island states and displace millions of coastal dwellers, many living in big cities in Europe.
- Some increased food production in higher latitudes (though soil conditions would limit this increase) and reduced production in tropical areas.
- A loss of forests and major changes to other habitats, causing a reduction in numbers of many species.

- Increased variability in water flow, with implications for potable water supply, agriculture, and power generation.
- Increased susceptibility to ill health arising from such varied factors as heat-waves and the increased incidence of vector-borne diseases (e.g. malaria reappearing in Europe).
- Increased damage to property and crops from violent storms.

The cause of this seemingly inevitable change in climate and living conditions is the rapid growth of greenhouse gases (GHG) since the time of the industrial revolution, but especially since the Second World War. (The annual global emissions of CO_2 of 1950 had almost quadrupled by 1996.) Future GHG emissions will be a function of global energy demand and the technologies employed to generate that energy. Clearly, major political commitments are needed to support the introduction of carbon-free and low-carbon energy-production processes. The inability of most developed countries to meet their commitments to the Kyoto Protocol is tragic; it is scandalous when one acknowledges that much more will have to be done, beyond Kyoto, in order to assure future generations a reasonably liveable climate.

One area of technological development that has enormous potential to reduce human adverse impact on the biophysical environment is that of connectivity. To date, it has been disappointing. Electronic communication of the written word is not saving nearly as much paper as had been anticipated. The ability to print out working documents and record the new-found replacement for so many phone calls has often added to the demand for paper. Yet the potential to reduce air and road transportation movements is very real. It would require major changes in production, consumption and lifestyles, but this is probably going to be inevitable, especially with respect to air travel and airborne trade. It could also have major implications for mobility in the city and for urban form.

Dematerialization (or miniaturization) of goods production is another area of technological development that has great potential for a more environmentally sustainable way of life. Continuing advances are demonstrating that there can be reductions in demand for natural resources relative to the performance of human activities. Yet these advances are also making the cost of the goods (such as computers and telephones) much cheaper and therefore the number of such goods is multiplying.

The needed response. The national interest of the typical European country would appear to be to effect a transition from old-generation to new-generation technologies as swiftly as can be borne by society, while minimizing the impact of any future developments of the old-generation technologies on the productive capacities of the global commons or on the biophysical and social environments of the country. To this end, supportive, broad policy initiatives will be required to:

- Promote the development of new-generation technologies that respect the sustainable productive capacities of natural systems and social systems by avoiding the creation of social and environmental costs.

- Foster more meaningful international cooperation on the protection of the commons.

Additional policy initiatives that will be needed are mentioned in association with other national interests. See especially:

- In Section 3.6, re. political developments, the first and second initiatives.
- In Section 3.3, re. needs, values and demands, all three initiatives.
- In Section 3.2, re. population growth, all three initiatives.

3.6 Political developments

It has become increasingly important to be able to negotiate effectively in international arenas to ensure that other countries play their part on what should be a level playing field and that international collaboration can work to the advantage of all countries involved. To that end, all countries could benefit from improved analysis of geopolitical developments that may be of consequence for the ways in which they manage their biophysical environment. However, what any one country should already be aware of is that there are a large number of international agreements that already make demands on that country to live up to certain specific commitments. Beyond those that have been signed or endorsed by the country in question, there may be some still awaiting such consideration. There are also non-binding instruments. (There were some 230 such agreements and instruments pertaining to Canada as of 1998 (Commissioner for Environment and Sustainable Development 1998: 2–32).)

Whether a country is operating within or outside of those agreements, that country is likely to be interested in the way in which other countries are attempting to satisfy four demands:

1   Maximize the benefits to be derived from their own resources (e.g. it is to be expected that, as big countries, such as China, India and Brazil, become more active as trading partners with much smaller countries, they may tend to use their political power to exploit the resources of those smaller countries).
2   Minimize their vulnerability to the vagaries of the external market.
3   Minimize internal discontent arising from shortages of natural resources (or, more positively, to ensure environmental security).[6]
4   Acknowledge the interest of other countries, and especially the interest of one's own country (e.g. the growing pressure by consumers in export markets for the labelling of natural-resource products to certify that production/harvesting was ecologically sound).

The ways in which these demands will be pursued by the various countries around the world will affect other nations in different ways. But, the net result is likely to be that one's own country will be facing environmental policy issues relating to: the rate and manner of extraction of its own non-renewable resources; its response to the variable demands for its exports of natural-resource products; and, the maintenance of the sustainable productive capacities of the global economy. The articulation of national interests in response to these and other issues is likely to be influenced to some degree (although less so in developing than industrialized countries) by two other considerations: (1) as the cumulative effects of economic developments on the biophysical environment become better understood, longer-term planning will become more acceptable; (2) the tendency for 'science to get ahead of the ethics of an issue' is likely to be questioned with greater frequency, thus creating added dilemmas for decision-makers, on which they will seek guidance.

The needed response. The national interest of the typical European country would appear to be fourfold. The first of these interests is to regulate the extraction of non-renewable resources in the country at a rate and in a manner that minimizes any undesirable side-effects on the social and biophysical environments. The second is to regulate the extraction of non-renewable resources in the country at a rate and in a manner that maximizes their value as natural capital to be used in maintaining sustainable societal development for current and future generations. A third national interest is to optimize the global production and consumption patterns, for those products of renewable resources that constitute a significant export for the country, in a manner that respects the sustainable productive capacities of each country's resource base and especially that of one's own country. Finally, a fourth national interest is to minimize future pressures on the global commons due to any lack of understanding by any country or group as to the collective interest of all states in the commons. Supportive, broad policy initiatives will be required to:

- Ensure that production processes internalize all costs of maintaining stable social and biophysical environments.
- Ensure that production processes internalize all costs of effecting the switch, by the current or future workforce, to new employment upon termination of extraction operations.
- Promote recognition of the importance of healthy ecosystems and a productive resources base as being integral to economic survival.
- Promote management practices on the part of all countries, but especially major importers of the products in question, which enable them possibly to enhance but certainly to maintain the sustainable productive capacities of the resource base.
- Promote international understanding as to what constitutes the collective interest in the sound management of the commons.

3.7 Changes in the distribution and structure of economic activity

Key considerations relative to global changes in the distribution and structure of economic activity and their implications for various groupings of countries include, among others, international competitiveness, factors affecting continued economic expansion, the vulnerability of the biophysical environment, the lack of effective demand for environmental clean-up and protection, and the costs of sustainable development. These are elaborated briefly here.

The quality of life of people everywhere is becoming increasingly dependent on the international competitiveness of their production processes. This competition is being affected, first, by attitudes to employment and productivity on the part of the state, the employers and the employees, second, by the deployment of key inputs into production processes, human capital (knowledge and skills), financial capital, technology, energy and other resources; and third, by the ways in which production takes place.

In 1998, the OECD's Forum for the Future anticipated the possibility of a surprisingly long-term (20-year) boom for the global economy (of 3 per cent pa per capita on average). Since then, the global economy has been expanding and, although it shows some signs of faltering now, the long-term prospects still appear good. What is of particular interest, however, is that the OECD saw such continuing expansion as being very dependent upon three factors: improved productivity from the shift to the knowledge-based economy; globally, more integrated markets, for labour, capital and products; and, a redirection of humanity's relationship with the biophysical environment (OECD Secretariat 1999: 1)

However, the much-expected gains in productivity from a knowledge-based economy have been slow to appear. Greater productivity gains are being achieved in places like China. The markets are not becoming much more integrated. There is no one market for labour, or for capital, or for products. Globalization, as a prevailing condition, is a long way off. (Even the so-called globalization of electronic communications, which has made possible the very rapid transfer of financial capital, has to be qualified by the recognition that 75 per cent of the world's population has yet to make a telephone call.) This is not to say that globalization, as a process, is not underway; it is. But the critical questions here are whether many developing countries will be part of any boom and whether the environment will be managed sustainably.

Whether or not a boom continues over the next decade or two, the biophysical environment is vulnerable in several respects. Although the developing countries are particularly vulnerable, the more industrialized countries are far from immune. And the linkages between the two groupings take on quite distinct and varied forms. For example, one has the relocation of dirty production processes to developing countries, the clearance of hedgerows in Europe to facilitate the production of subsidized agricultural exports, the invoking of free trade as a reason for not protecting the global commons from exploitation, and the inadvertent introduction, through trade, of invasive species.

The shift in the distribution and structure of economic activity has not brought great wealth to the public sector in either the industrialized or the developing countries. Thus, there is a distinct lack of funds for environmental protection and clean-up. In both industrialized and developing countries, this lack of money for environmental clean-up and protection is largely a product of the attempt to reduce taxes, especially on corporations that may flee the tax jurisdiction. Thus, although there has been a rapid growth in environmental technologies and services globally, the lack of effective demand from developing countries has meant that most of that growth has been in the industrialized countries. Further, that effective demand is falling far short of what is really required to: clean up decades of pollution; rectify the extensive degradation; and, take advantage of the best available technologies for today's production processes.

In sum, if the developing countries are to participate actively in any ongoing economic boom, then they will have to be ready to participate in a much more intensive form of international collaboration on economic, social and environmental policy matters. If the development is to be sustainable, they will have to undergo a further conscious adjustment of their economic and social structures to broaden their economic base, while reducing their social and environmental costs. This may be quite painful.

For their part, European and other industrialized countries will have to do more to encourage and facilitate this changed behaviour on the part of the developing countries (and especially major players like China, India, Russia and Brazil). And similarly, the Europeans and other industrialized countries will have to do much more to reduce their environmental costs, most notably with respect to the generation of GHGs. This may also be quite painful. Remarkably, albeit somewhat surprisingly, Ben Bernanke was arguing at the 2006 annual meeting of central bankers at Jackson Hole (which focused on the implications of the rise of China, India and other countries for the reshaping of the global economy) that the industrialized countries should be doing more to ensure that the benefits of global economic integration are sufficiently widely shared (*The Economist* 2006a: 66). Although his interest was to maintain support for free trade throughout both industrialized and developing-country economies, he recognized that the current winners from the changing economy had an obligation to help the losers.

The needed response. The national interest of the typical European country would appear to be twofold. The first of these interests is to facilitate the adjustment of the country's economy and social structures to the world's economic system in ways that respect the tolerances of the biophysical and social systems. The second interest is to minimize the undesirable impact of future developments in the world's economic system on the sustainable and globally viable productive capacities of the commons. Supportive, broad policy initiatives will be required to:

- Promote productive processes that exhibit global viability, offer human fulfilment, internalize the costs of maintaining international competitiveness, and render possible the distribution of the net benefits of participation and wealth generation more equitably throughout society.
- Strengthen local social systems to withstand the localized impact of changes in the global distribution and structure of employment.

Additional policy initiatives that will be needed are mentioned in association with other national interests. See especially:

*   In Section 3.6, re. political developments, the fifth initiative.
*   In Section 3.5, re. technological developments, the second initiative.
*   In Section 3.2, re. population growth, the first and second initiatives.

3.8 Changes in resource management and the availability of global goods

The ways in which the rest of the world manages its natural resources has an enormous impact on the ways in which any one country manages its own resources. There are widening gaps between supply and demand and, distinct from this, between supply and need as a result of increasing population and poor resource management. Priority concerns for any one country would emerge from an in-depth analysis of each of its major natural resources and the availability of the globally traded goods they yield. This would have to be done in a global context.

Overall, the implications for Europeans are that, if they wish to maintain the health of their biophysical environment and, more generally, their standard of living, they will have to be more mindful not only of how they manage their own resources, but how other countries manage theirs. It is reasonable to expect that statements of national interest are likely to be very similar relative to each of these resources and goods. However, first it is worth looking at some broad trends and the issues they raise.

Agricultural lands and food production. Between 1960 and 2000, the world population doubled and yet food production per capita increased 25 per cent while food prices dropped 40 per cent in real terms (*The Economist* 2000: 3). Despite this impressive achievement, the FAO estimates that, globally, 1.2 billion (790 million in developing countries) are still chronically hungry because the global (and indeed, intra-national) food distribution problem has not been solved.[7] And, the environmental costs are unsustainable. This pressure has meant: more irrigation (40 per cent of the world's food now comes from that 5 per cent of land that is under irrigation) which means more salinization and increased water scarcity; increased use of nitrogen and disruptions to the nitrogen cycle; more soil degradation (65 per cent of the world's agricultural land is already degraded (ibid.: 11)); more pesticides contaminating drinking water sources; and another 13.7 million hectares of cleared forest each year in the developing countries (FAO 1999).

By 2050, with another 50 per cent increase in population (almost all in developing countries) and the same pressure to reduce hunger, food production will have to double. This will require, *inter alia*, improvements in: purchasing power on the part of the poor; trade in agricultural goods; water resources management; ways of 'getting off chemicals' (e.g. with integrated pest management, and traditional mixed farming and crop rotations); and, managing the potential and the risks of the genetic modification of plants and animals.

Forests. Over 80 per cent of the planet's original forest cover has been removed. Of that remaining, about 50 per cent is in tropical developing countries (UNEP 1999: 38). And this is being cleared at the rate of about 13.7 million hectares pa. (The developed countries are actually adding to their forest cover, thus reducing the net global loss to about 11.2 million hectares pa.). About two-thirds of the clearance is for agricultural purposes and much of this is through burning. Most of the rest is cut for timber. Globally, the demand for wood products (including fuel wood and charcoal for energy) has not grown as rapidly as has population growth. However, this masks local pressures where firewood consumption has grown with the very rapid rate of population growth, especially in poorer regions where it is the only source of energy. And again, the environmental and social costs have been high. The uncontrolled burning to clear land leads to uncontrolled runoff, floods, loss of life and property and increased prevalence of waterborne diseases. And, it should be noted that deforestation is now recognized as the second largest contributor to global emissions of CO_2 (at 18 per cent of the total) (*The Economist* 2006b: 24).

By 2050, another 17 per cent (net) of the world's forest cover will have been removed, all in the developing countries, if business continues as usual (UNEP 1999: 342). Fortunately, there are signs that concern is growing. Following the UN Conference on the Environment in Rio in 1992, the UN established the Intergovernmental Panel on Forests, which later became the Intergovernmental Forum on Forests. This has made some real progress in identifying what is required and the essential challenges. In essence, if national governments are to work together to address the big issues (such as the role of the forests in local economies, as reservoirs for biodiversity, as carbon sinks regulating climate change, and as symbols central to the spiritual life of forest dwellers), then there will need to be much more attention to: strengthened capacity building; more partnerships between governments and the private sector and NGOs; improved mobilization of financial and other resources; and, above all, greater political commitment to action. (Economic and Social Council of the UN *et al.* 2000: 14–16)

Energy resources. Here, again, the expanding economies of China and other developing countries are very significant for the global situation. Power generation is the largest contributor to CO_2 emissions globally, accounting for 24.5 per cent (*The Economist* 2006b: 23). Most of that power comes from coal. And China, which is expanding its power-generating capacity by 60 gigawatts pa (which is almost equivalent to Britain's existing capacity), is relying on coal for 80 per cent of this new power. Not surprisingly, China is expected to be the world's largest source of CO_2 emissions by 2015 (ibid.: 18). The ways in which the developing countries continue to try to satisfy their increased demands for power is of great consequence for Europe. China, not surprisingly, found that its initial quadrupling of its GDP, from 1980 to 2000, could be accomplished with a mere doubling of its energy consumption. But from 2000 to 2004 the energy elasticity of GDP (the relationship between changes in energy consumption and changes in GDP) moved from 0.5 to 1.5. The Chinese government has stated in its 11th five-year plan (2006) that it will aim for 20 per cent more energy efficiency by 2010 (ibid.). Whether this will be achieved is another matter.

While both developed and developing countries share the challenge of obtaining cheap, reliable energy from renewable resources, with minimal environmental impact, the developing countries have the added challenge of a lack of distribution infrastructure. However, this lack of infrastructure offers great opportunities to put in place small-scale, decentralized, environmentally sound power-generating systems that could make a major contribution to meeting Kyoto Protocol targets. These systems range from fuel-efficient engines to photovoltaic cells, with fuel cells of various kinds in between. It is noteworthy that China's richest man, Shi Zhengrong, with a net worth of US$2.2 billion, has made his fortune through solar power (*Globe and Mail* 2006: B9).

And yet, to date, these opportunities are far from being fully realized and a price is being paid in economic terms. China, for example, is now suffering an annual loss to its crops and forests of over US$5 billion from acid rain. Yet sulphur dioxide emissions can be reduced relatively easily: west, central and east European states reduced theirs by 50 per cent from 1985 to 1994 (UNEP 1999: 46). Fortunately, there are enough exceptions to show that developing countries can make changes. Some are working on improving demandside management (ibid.: 243), others on energy-generation technologies (Brown *et al.* 2000: 159).

The Europeans appear to be taking the right approach to the above challenges. In Helsinki, in September 2006, at the sixth summit in the last decade between 25 European and 13 Asian leaders (including China), the leaders pledged to continue reductions in GHG emissions after the Kyoto Protocol expires in 2012. They will share appropriate technologies to improve energy efficiency and reduce environmental impacts. They will work with international financing and development institutions to encourage investments in clean energy (Wielaard 2006).

The other interest that the Europeans have in collaborating closely with Asia is that they need carbon credits from investments in clean energy projects in developing countries in order to meet their Kyoto targets. The Europeans, in contrast to the US and Canada, have been making good progress in meeting these targets. This is, in part, assisted by the establishment of the EU's Emissions-Trading System (ETS) in 2005, which is aimed at reducing emissions of the five dirtiest European industries. The ETS has led to a rapid expansion in the monetary value of carbon credits being traded. Globally (i.e. including but beyond ETS) in the first half of 2006, about US$15 billion of carbon was traded. This represents a fivefold increase over the same period in 2005 (*The Economist* 2006b: 17). However, there appears to be a lot of scope for improving the effectiveness of both the Clean Development Mechanism (for trading emissions credits with the developing countries), and Joint Implementation, which allows 'donor' countries to invest in pollution-abatement measures in 'host' countries in return for credits to be used to meet the donor countries' pollution-abatement targets. Most obviously, the caps on allowances have to be progressively reduced. More effective, in my view, would be a carbon tax.[8]

Freshwater supplies. Between 1900 and 1995 global freshwater consumption grew about sixfold, more than twice the rate of population growth (UNEP 1999: 41). Today, from 10 per cent to 30 per cent of the global population lives in areas with moderate to high water stress[9] (i.e. essentially unsustainable in that more than 10 per cent of the renewable water supply is being used each year (ibid.)). In parts of West Asia, withdrawal rates are already exceeding recharge rates. Globally, 70 per cent to 95 per cent of freshwater consumption is for agricultural purposes.[10] The lowering of the water tables increases the cost of sinking wells and thus increases social inequity. At the same time, the quality of the supplies is being degraded from: pollution arising from increased industrial effluent; flooding and waterborne diseases; and, in coastal cities, from saline intrusion. Thus, today 20 per cent of the world's population lacks access to safe drinking water (and about 50 per cent lacks adequate sanitation (ibid.: 42)).

By 2025, the global demand for water for household consumption is expected to increase by 70 per cent (*The Economist* 2000: 20) and that for industrial use to double. (Agricultural usage could double by 2050, recognizing that the population is growing and people are trying, not always successfully, to eat more.) This may mean that up to 66 per cent of all people will live in water-stressed areas (UNEP 1999: 41). Water security is thus becoming a critical issue for developing countries. India, for example, with a population of 1 billion, expanding at 18 million pa, is already withdrawing water at twice the recharge rate. Already, 53 per cent of its children are malnourished (UNFPA 1999: 28) and the likelihood of India improving food production without concerted efforts to improve water management is negligible. Thus, there are very real possibilities of wars and even more so of internal feuding over water resources. Water supplies in most of Europe are unlikely to be under anything like the same pressure as that expected in the developing countries. However, precisely for that reason, though among others, Europe will become increasingly attractive to would-be immigrants from water-stressed developing countries.

Fisheries. The world's fisheries are in trouble. Since the rapid growth of fishing fleets in the 1950s, pressure has been increasing. Today, 60 per cent of the world's fish stocks are either overfished (25 per cent) or on the verge of being so (35 per cent) (WRI 1998: 95). In both the developing and industrialized countries, there is a growing gap between sustainable catch and both the effective, market-based demand and need (or 'normative demand'). The larger these gaps, the greater the likelihood of overfishing. Unfortunately, overfishing can only be established several years after it has occurred. And it can arise from factors other than harvesting, such as slight changes in ocean currents and water temperatures, and changing populations of predator species. For the most part, however, the overfishing reflects the importance of fish and fisheries: as a source of protein (about 20 per cent of animal protein for human intake (ibid.: 196), up from 14 per cent in 1980);[11] as a source of employment, especially for many small-scale operators; and, as the prime source of food supply for one billion people (ibid.).

Between 1975 and 1995, the global marine fish catch (by traditional means) had expanded from 50 million metric tonnes (mmt) to 91 mmt. One-third of this went to fishmeal or oil, the rest for human consumption. In addition, production of fish and shellfish from aquaculture had more than doubled between 1984 and 1995 to reach 21 mmt, almost all being for human consumption. Thus, of the 81 mmt for human consumption, about 25 per cent came from aquaculture (ibid.: 158).

By 2010, FAO anticipates a growth in demand for human consumption to about 110 or 120 mmt (ibid.: 196). This is assumed to be 'normative demand', since it is unlikely to be realized without enormous effort and expenditure – which may put the market price beyond the reach of poorer consumers. Until recently, there was a generally accepted assumption that aquaculture would meet all additional demands, even as traditional fish catches stabilized or declined. Certainly, it plays a very important role in supplying much of the market in Canada, a country which has been grossly overfishing its fisheries. (Some 95 per cent of fish sold in Toronto is from aquaculture sources.) However, if there is to be any increase in production on a sustainable basis and in ways that will not further reduce the number of jobs for artisanal fishers (from the advent of large trawlers), then there will have to be a number of major improvements in fisheries management in both European and other industrialized countries as well as in the developing countries. Most developing countries require assistance, but particular attention should be given to those where aquaculture and or landings have been growing rapidly (e.g. China and Chile).

Non-fuel minerals. The production (and thus the associated environmental impact) of non-fuel minerals is expected to continue to be largely a product of the interplay of three forces already discussed: political developments; technological developments, and, changes in the distribution and structure of economic activity. Both the industrialized and the developing countries are interested in security of supply. Also, to minimize processing costs, international companies often opt for processing in developing countries where environmental regulations are less demanding. International bankers, interested in seeing a return on their investments in developing countries, encourage such exports. Until 2002, commodity prices were continuing their long-term decline. Indeed, *The Economist* industrial commodity price index, measured in constant dollar terms, has seen a decline from 100 in 1845 to 20 in 2002 (*The Economist* 2006c: 18). This was due to a variety of factors, including product miniaturization, material substitution and dematerialization. This had made it difficult for producers to afford clean production processes. Small producers in developing countries were particularly hard hit.

In 2002, the effects of the increasing demand, from China in particular, began to be reflected in a sharp turnaround in the commodity price index. Today, it is slightly over 50. *The Economist*'s recent survey of the world economy reviews a range of analyses and comes up with no definitive conclusion other than that the era of cheap materials is over (ibid.: 20). In part, this conclusion is arrived at because, although China's demands are likely to grow at a slower rate over the next 15 years, India's demands will likely grow at a faster rate. Some developing-country producers could get hurt in the ups and downs of the next

20 years. This could mean a continuation of their dirty production processes. The European interest, in this instance, is likely to focus primarily on stability of supply at stable prices. However, pressure can be expected from the European body politic for cleaner production processes, especially by international companies.

The needed response. As suggested above, the statements of national interest of the typical European country relative to each of the above resources and goods are very similar. In essence, the national interest would appear to be twofold. The first of these interests is to optimize the global production and consumption patterns for renewable and non-renewable resources in a manner that protects the sustainable productive capacities of the commons and of each country's renewable resources base and that husbands the non-renewables until such time as the renewables can provide substitutes for the global goods currently available. Supportive, broad policy initiatives will be required. The key ones have already been mentioned in association with other national interests. See especially:

- In Section 3.2, re. population growth, the first and second initiatives.
- In Section 3.6, re. political developments, the fifth initiative.
- In Section 3.5, re. technological developments, the first and second initiatives.

A second national interest is to regulate the exploitation of the country's resources (that are either non-renewable or renewable only through conscious effort) at a rate and in a manner that: minimizes any undesirable side-effects on the social and biophysical environments; and, maximizes their value as natural capital to be used in maintaining sustainable societal development for current and future generations. Supportive, broad policy initiatives will be required. Again, the key ones have already been mentioned in association with other national interests. See especially:

- In Section 3.6, re. political developments, the first and second initiatives.
- In Section 3.1, re. the exacerbation of poverty, the second policy initiative.

3.9   The explosion of information and the growth of understanding

This force of change is often referred to as 'the explosion of knowledge'. However, this masks an important distinction between two different interpretations of knowledge: information and understanding. It is arguable as to what constitutes the fundamental force of change: the explosion in the availability of information, or the growth of understanding on the part of individuals. The position taken here is that it is the growth in understanding that is the more potent force of change. Information does not, in itself, bring about change unless there is a growth in understanding. However, growth in understanding may constitute a better understanding of what is not known (or how little we know), which may lead to greater uncertainty about the nature of a problem and the most appropriate solution. Worse still, the explosion of information may result in 'infoglut', which only serves to confuse. This growing uncertainty has been very significant in dealing with the biophysical environment and in attempts to move global and national societies towards a sustainable form of development.

Any one country must have a minimum critical mass of people who are able to understand the nature of a broad array of forces and their interplay and be in a position to contribute to steering their society towards a form of development that is sustainable biophysically, socially, culturally and politically, as well as economically. This is a tall order for any country. Thus, whether the environmental issue is something as broad as climate change or as focused as water pollution, there is a need to understand the forces that lie behind that particular outcome of human behaviour.

What is obvious everywhere is that there is a growing understanding that understanding is important. But it is only a growing understanding. Some have confused the acquisition of access to information as being synonymous with the development of understanding. They may then become overwhelmed with information, explain it away as rapid change and be deterred from making any commitment to long-term planning. Thus, if the potential of the explosion of information from the information revolution is to be realized, it will require far more attention, not just to information management, but also to the more basic capacities that are developed through education, most obviously, the ability to think about complex issues. These considerations pertain to all countries. However, the developing countries face greater challenges in that so few of their people receive an excellent education and many of those who do then leave the country.

The needed response. In light of the above, the national interest of the typical European country would appear to be to take advantage of the explosion in information and the growth in understanding on the part of individuals in other countries relative to the management of the forces of change in support of the realization of sustainable societal development. Supportive, broad policy initiatives will be required to:

- Develop the capacities on the part of individuals (and thus institutions) to grasp, retain and focus on the essentials in a decision-making environment of increasing uncertainty.
- Promote the development of information technologies appropriate to the capabilities and resources of the users in the various sectors of society.
- Foster networks to facilitate collaboration between institutions of learning and other key groups of players (governments, NGOs, business and professional consultants) with the intention of improving understandings of the biophysical environment.

4 Conclusion

Futures studies can make valuable contributions to shaping public policy. However, they need to be well financed in order to produce credible and thus useful scenarios of the future for any one region or field of public policy. This chapter has not attempted to present a precise portrait of Europe and its life 25 years from now. Instead, it offers some guidance on undertaking such futures studies. It has suggested why one should be concerned about the conditions facing Europeans in the future. In that regard, it has provided a conceptual model of the process of human and societal development to help explain the rationale for the approach to the futures studies on this subject. It has also suggested how one should be looking at Europe's future. And it has offered guidance on what one should be thinking about and researching. It has then given an indication as to what one is likely to find relative to each of the nine forces of change shaping the developmental environments of Europeans and, on the basis of this tentative indication of the evolution of conditions, it has suggested national interests and supportive policies in order to realize those interests. Two major messages emerge from this overall analysis:

1   The discussion of the overall quality of life of Europeans, or of the conditions in any one of the developmental environments of Europeans, cannot be confined to what is going on within the political boundaries of Europe. Such discussion has to be conducted in a global context. Thus, in asking ourselves what will be the condition of the biophysical environment that Europeans will enjoy, we have to consider the biophysical environment globally. And to do that, we must look at all nine major forces at work on that biophysical environment.

2   The developing countries as a whole are becoming increasingly significant players. There are, however, very different types of developing countries, ranging from the BRIC countries to the failed states, and those struggling in between. (This was also a major message of the September 2006 survey of the world economy by *The Economist*.)

With respect to China, I have to conclude that the speculation over China's rise now seems similar to the speculation over Japan's rise in the 1960s. At that time, it was anticipated that if things continued as they were, Japan's economy would overtake America's before the end of that century. As we know, it did not. Japan was very protectionist and closed to immigration. It also suffered from the corruption prevalent in an increasingly complacent Liberal Party that has dominated Japan's post-war politics.

It will not be hard for China to falter. The costs of rapid growth are everywhere more evident. The latest is the rapidly rising number of babies born with birth defects. This is hardly surprisingly, given the deteriorating condition of the biophysical environment.

Nevertheless, the BRIC countries, and a small group of other developing countries, can be expected to expand and thus influence conditions in Europe in the ways that have been hinted at in the elaboration of key considerations relative to the major forces to be considered. While these key considerations are articulated primarily as pointers to needed research, they give some indication of what we can expect in Europe and elsewhere.

What, then, are some of the more dominant features of Europe 25 years from now? Of course, it depends on the policies acted upon. However, my (highly speculative) guess, is that the Europe of 2031 is likely:

- Along with other parts of the industrialized world, to still be much richer than the developing world.
- To have an ageing population that is only holding its overall numbers steady through increasing immigration, much more of which will be accounted for by environmental refugees from the developing countries.
- To have health budgets that continue to consume much of the tax revenues. This will be for both the conventional afflictions of ageing and because the health of Europeans will be increasingly susceptible to the diseases of the developing countries, especially of their cities. It is unlikely that the expenditures will be sufficient to prevent a pandemic, given the atrocious conditions in most cities in developing countries.
- To be even more conscious of how the future of the countries of the industrialized world is becoming ever more linked to the fate of the rest of the world. This is likely to have been reinforced by the Europeans recognizing that their stable, and later shrinking, population, is part of a shrinking developed world relative to today's developing world. Thus the Europeans will likely recognize that their values of liberty, democracy, tolerance, justice and, hopefully, ecosystem integrity, must become more widely accepted and promoted; but, again, hopefully, in peaceful ways.
- To be living in a warmer world and constantly reminded that global warming is still a problem that needs more attention. In looking for technological fixes to this problem (and others) Europe will be turning to new-generation technologies that are more sound, both socially and environmentally. But these will take time to spread both within the industrialized and the developing world. With respect to climate change, this can be said of the technologies that have already been applied, such as wind power, and some of the more challenging proposals in the field of geo-engineering that focus on adaptation (such as the deployment of albedo spray vessels to create whiter clouds, an idea being explored at the University of Edinburgh).[12]
- To be living in a world in which the health of the global commons is given much more value, in large part because the health of those commons will have deteriorated further in the intervening 25 years. Thus, political interests are likely to be articulated in ways that align them more with the interests of other nations, including those in the developing world.
- To be giving more assistance to people who are losing out as a result of the continuing restructuring of the global economy.
- With respect to the role of the biophysical environment as a resource base,

to be taking a far keener interest in how other countries are managing their natural resources.

• To be giving a little more, but still far from sufficient, attention to fostering an in-depth understanding of the major public-policy issues confronting Europe and the rest of the world and how to get effective action on those issues that serve the interests of Europeans and the majority of other peoples in the world. With respect to climate change, the next small but doubtless very valuable contribution to advancing understanding and action is expected within weeks from Sir Nicholas Stern in the UK.[13]

This short list of pointers suggests that the quality of life of Europeans is very vulnerable to major changes in the global operating environment. It also suggests that, if the key considerations on which it is based were indeed to be subjected to further rigorous and systematic study in order to arrive at the types of policy initiatives tentatively proposed here, and if these policy initiatives were indeed to be acted upon, Europe, and indeed the rest of the world, can continue to be a liveable place.

Notes

1 This concept of developmental environments was first elaborated in Miles 1979.
2 For an elaboration of the significance of the quality of ligatures, in combination with the availability of options for societal development see Dahrendorf 1979.
3 This conceptual model was first tested on the analysis of global developments in a study for Environment Canada. See Miles 1981. It was used to brief the Canadian Prime Minister prior to hosting the G-7 Summit of 1981, hosted by Canada. More recently the model served as a guide for shaping the programming of international assistance in the environmental field. See Miles 2000. This latter report, for the Canadian International Development Agency, was drawn upon for Section 3 of this chapter.
4 Ronald Inglehart and Wayne Baker (2000) 'Modernization, Cultural Change, and the Persistence of Traditional Values', *American Sociological Review* 65: 19–51.
5 This discussion on climate change is based largely on: UNEP 1999: 24–8.
6 Thomas Homer-Dixon, of the University of Toronto, is a leading authority on the factors that lead to environmental insecurity and the tensions to which it can give rise. Most of these are internal to states though some are international in nature. See, for example, Homer-Dixon 1999.
7 For a useful discussion of hunger and types of malnutrition, including a discussion of FAO data, see Brown *et al.* 2000, Ch. 4.
8 For two helpful discussions on improving the control of carbon emissions, see Greenspan-Bell 2006: 105ff; and, a series of four articles by Martin Wolf in the *Financial Times* (London), published on 27 June, 4, 11 and 18 July 2006.
9 Ibid., for the 30 per cent figure. The 10 per cent figure, included to illustrate the variations in estimates, is from UNFPA 1999: 28.
10 Ibid., for the 70 per cent figure. The 95 per cent figure appeared in *The Economist* (2006a: 64), in a story reporting on the preliminary findings of the 'Comprehensive Assessment' undertaken by the Consultative Group on International Agricultural Research, which was released in November 2006.
11 Estimate by the author.

12 See Canadian Broadcasting Corporation Radio (2006). For further information contact Dr Stephen Salter, email S.Salter@ed.ac.uk.
13 This is a reference to Sir Nicholas Stern's report on the economics of climate change that was released by the UK Treasury in late October 2006.

References

Brown, L. R. *et al.* (2000) *State of the World 2000*, New York: W. W. Norton.

Canadian Broadcasting Corporation Radio (2006) *The Current* 25 September, Toronto: CBC.

Commissioner for Environment and Sustainable Development (1998) *Report of the Commissioner of the Environment and Sustainable Development to the House of Commons*, Ottawa: Public Works on Government Services.

Dahrendorf, R. (1979) *Life Chances*, Chicago, IL: Chicago University Press.

Economic and Social Council of the UN, Commission on Sustainable Development, Intergovernmental Forum on Forests (eds.) (2000) *Category III: International Arrangements and Mechanisms to Promote the Management, Conservation and Sustainable Development of All Types of Forests: Priority Forest Policy Issues – Note from the Secretariat #1(ref # E/CN.17/IFF/2000)*, New York: UN.

The Economist (2000) 'A Survey of Agriculture and Technology' 25 March, London: The Economist Newspaper Ltd.

The Economist (2006a) 2 September, London: The Economist Newspaper Ltd.

The Economist (2006b) 'The Heat Is On: A Survey of Climate Change', 9 September, London: The Economist Newspaper Ltd.

The Economist (2006c) 'The New Titans: A Survey of the Global Economy', 16 September, London: The Economist Newspaper Ltd.

FAO (1999) *State of the World's Forests 1999*, FAO: Rome.

Globe and Mail (2006) 19 April, Toronto.

Greenspan-Bell, R. (2006) 'What To Do About Climate Change', *Foreign Affairs* 85 (3): 105–13.

Homer-Dixon, T. (1999) *Environment, Scarcity and Violence*, Princeton, NJ: Princeton University Press.

Inglehart, R. and Baker, W. (2000) 'Modernization, Cultural Change, and the Persistence of Traditional Values', *American Sociological Review* 65: 19–51.

Jolly, R. (1999) *Global Inequality, Human Rights and the Challenge of the 21st Century*, paper for an OECD Forum in December on the Future, Berlin.

Lustig, N. and Arias, O. (2000) 'Poverty Reduction', *Finance and Development* March, Washington, DC: IMF.

Miles, S. (1979) *Ecodevelopment and Third World Urban Regions: A Prospective for International Development Cooperation Policy*, Ottawa: Supply and Services.

Miles, S. (1981) *The Changing World: Implications for Canada in the Eighties*, unpublished.

Miles, S. (2000) *Future Challenges for Environment Programming*, unpublished.

Nikiforuk, A. (2006) *Pandemonium: Bird Flu, Mad Cow Disease, and other Biological Plagues of the 21st Century*, Toronto: Viking.

OECD Secretariat (Advisory Unit to the Secretary-General) (1999) *Key Points of the Discussions of Conference 2 on '21st Century Economic Dynamics: Anatomy of a Long Boom'*, 2–3 December 1998, Paris: OECD.

UN, Population Division, Department of Economic and Social Affairs (2005) *World Population Prospects: The 2004 Revision – Executive Summary*, New York: UN.

UNDP (1998) *Human Development Report 1998*, New York: Oxford University Press.

UNEP (1999) *GEO-2000 Global Environment Outlook 2000*, Nairobi: UNEP.

UNFPA (1999) *6 Billion: A Time for Choices*, *The State of the World Population 1999*, New York: UNFPA.

UNFPA (2006) *A Passage to Hope: Women and International Migration, State of the World Population 2006*, New York: UNFPA.

Wielaard, R. (2006) *Europe, Asia Pledge to Cut Emissions*, ENN, Environmental News Network, 12 September, Associated Press.

World Commission on Environment and Development (1987) *Our Common Future*, Oxford: Oxford University Press.

WRI (1998) *World Resources 1998–1999*, Oxford: Oxford University Press.

10 The rise of China and the need for cross-border governance in Europe's borderlands

Robert Knippschild

The rise of China and East Asia

With its Lisbon Strategy from the year 2000, the European Union aimed to become the world's most competitive and dynamic economic area. Between 1995 and 2004, economic growth in the EU 27 was 2.4 per cent (European Commission 2007: 178; European Communities 2007). Although China's GDP is only about one-quarter of the European average, in recent years it has enjoyed an average annual growth of about 10 per cent, accompanied by massive industrialization and creation of jobs. Regional disparities are significant in both Europe and China. While the GDP of Europe's strongest region is eight times that of the weakest region, in China the disparity is a factor of seven. In contrast, regional disparities in the US are far less significant: there the factor is 2.5 (Deutsche Botschaft Peking 2006; European Commission 2007: 5; Pilny 2005). China and East Asia are still big markets for European exports of technology and know-how – but for how long?

Furthermore, a rail connection between East Asia and Europe might provide quicker and cheaper transportation than today's sea link. It is possible that in the near future trains will cover the distance between China and Europe in 12 days, while the sea link currently takes 40. This will boost the exchange of goods and accelerate the process of globalization (Indo-Burma News 2007; MacWilliam 2004).

Instead of achieving the aims of the Lisbon Strategy, Europe's economic growth continues to disappoint, while at the same time East Asia, in particular, has developed massively to become one of the most prosperous economic areas in the world.

Consequences for Europe and Europe's borderlands

There is no unity of opinion regarding the macro-economic consequences of the rise of China and East Asia for European cities and regions. Will Europe fail to meet the challenges of globalization, thereby suffering deindustrialization and reacting with protectionism? Or will it benefit from the Asian boom, participating in worldwide growth (Berger and Stein 2005)? In view of the significant

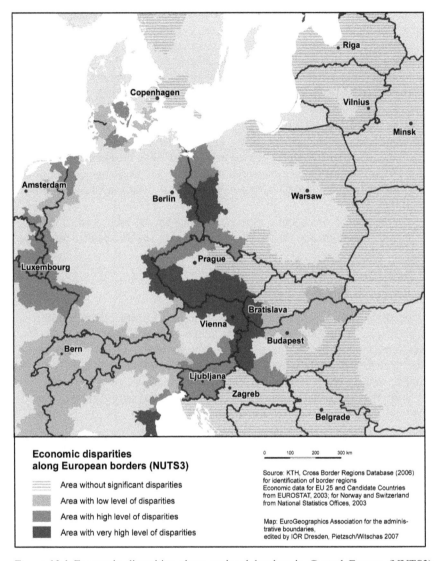

Figure 10.1 Economic disparities along national borders in Central Europe (NUTS3) (source: ESPON 2007: 27, cartography: Pietzsch, Witschas, IÖR).

regional economic disparities between western and eastern Europe, that is weak and strong regions (particularly visible along European borders, see Figure 10.1) and between metropolitan and peripheral regions, the answer will probably be 'both'. Due to a lack of infrastructure, weak soft-location factors and out-migration of high-skilled young people, Europe's peripheral regions may be hit hard by the Asian boom.

Another important question is the impact which the main east–west transport corridors will have on the development of Europe's peripheral regions, in particular, the borderlands. Again, opinions vary. Possible developments such as added value from additional transport infrastructure are weighed against negative transit effects such as pollution, or an acceleration of out-migration. Peripheral regions could thereby become transit regions, leap-frogged, so to speak, by economic development and human capital (Müller *et al.* 2002; Neumann and Steinacker 2005: 18f.).

Furthermore, Europe suffers from a diversion of interests concerning economic and spatial development owing to its numerous (and in comparison to Asia, rather small) nation states. Between 2004 and 2007, the number of member states of the European Union increased from 15 to 27. This fragmented Europe faces a strongly centralized Chinese government with clear spatial and economic policies.

After these macro-economic aspects, the chapter will now turn to the role of spatial development and spatial planning in enhancing European competitiveness.

Challenges in Europe's periphery

Europe faces some severe challenges in its desire to maintain competitiveness and participate in the Asian boom. As part of the Territorial Agenda, EU member states agreed to mobilize the potential of European cities and regions in order to foster growth and create jobs. The aim of the Territorial Agenda is to better utilize spatial diversity to enhance Europe's international competitiveness. To this end, the Territorial Agenda describes the reciprocity between macro-economic requirements and the role of spatial development in Europe (Federal Ministry of Transport, Building and Urban Affairs 2007).

Disadvantaged regions must receive support to prevent them being leap-frogged by other more nimble regions. Also, the process of European integration has to be accelerated by further deepening and extending a joint European economic area and joint labour market (Pilny 2005: 5).

Borderlands are the interfaces of European integration. They are the places where different economic and administrative systems, languages and cultures clash. The enlargements of 2004 and 2007, which more than tripled the length of land borders in the European Union, also greatly increased the significance of borderlands (Royal Institute of Technology 2003: 77).

The 'new' EU borderlands

The 'new' borderlands along the former external border of the European Union are lagging behind other areas. Their limited experience in self-determination and regional cooperation after the political changes in 1989/1990 must now be remedied. The development of borderlands requires a joint understanding of regional strengths and weaknesses, with joint cross-border strategies and a possible division of functions. Furthermore, the severe structural problems of borderlands (particularly in central Europe) must also be addressed.

The borderlands in central Europe have been widely affected by economic and demographic change. Former socialist countries have suffered badly from deindustrialization, with eastern Germany one of the worst affected examples. The repercussions are high unemployment, massive decreases in population and out-migration (reducing a highly skilled labour force), overcapacity in social and technical infrastructure and vacancies in housing stock (see Table 10.1).

A closer look at the German-Polish-Czech borderland highlights the structural problems of these regions. Growth domestic products are low and unemployment rates are high in comparison to national averages (see Table 10.2).

These dramatic changes have weakened the technical and social infrastructure, and thereby the quality of life. For example, the closure of schools presents a serious problem. The resulting lengthening of school journeys for pupils causes costs to rise and decreases the quality of life. Finally, as infrastructure and amenities are reduced to a minimum, the borderlands become less attractive to new citizens and investors. Furthermore, labour markets in central Europe are still separated by legal barriers. For example, an interim regulation currently limits the number of workers from the new member states who may enter the German labour market. This regulation will probably remain in force until 2011, even though local entrepreneurs are already suffering from a lack of skilled labour (Killisch *et al.* 2004: 68f). The current situation leads one to conclude that borderlands are in danger of losing their function as the interfaces of European integration and convergence. See Figure 10.2.

Table 10.1 Development of population in the German-Polish borderland

	City of Görlitz (Germany)	District of Zgorzelec (Poland)
1991	74,000	101,000
2003	58,000	96,000

Source: Statistisches Landesamt des Freistaates Sachsen (ed.) 2005.

Table 10.2 Characteristic data on German, Polish and Czech borderlands (NUTS2) in national comparison

	GDP per capita EU25 = 100 (2001)	Unemployment rate (2002) (%)
Administrative districts		
Dresden and Chemnitz	73	20.7
Germany	110	9.4
Voivodship Lower Silesia	47	26.1
Poland	45	19.9
Southwest and southeast	54	8.4
Czech Republic	67	7.3

Source: European Commission 2004: 188–200.

Figure 10.2 The demographic change becomes evident – deconstruction of housing stock in Eisenhüttenstadt, in the German–Polish borderland.

Beside these structural considerations, eastern German borderlands and their inhabitants also face cultural and mental challenges. Central European borderlands are characterized by differences in the mentality of the cooperating actors, as well as methodological differences and institutional asymmetries concerning spatial planning. In particular, cross-border cooperation is hindered by language barriers: on the German side, locals have only limited knowledge of the Polish and Czech languages. In most cases, face-to-face communication is impossible without an interpreter, while non-professional translators and interpreters often cause information to be lost.

Strengthening cross-border potentials

It is with these rather depressing framework conditions in mind that one turns to the question of the development alternatives which exist for central European peripheries and borderlands. One alternative could be to strengthen cross-border potential. The main objectives in borderlands should be to improve the quality of life and the attractiveness for investors and human capital. This requires a stabilization in population trends, development of the technical and social infrastructure, and improvements in skills and the knowledge base (in particular, education). In borderlands, these objectives can only be achieved by exploiting cross-border potential.

This potential can be found in transboundary qualification measures, transboundary complementarities and functions, transboundary housing markets, as well as infrastructures and regional images. The following cross-border solutions and potential have been mentioned by local stakeholders in the German-Polish-

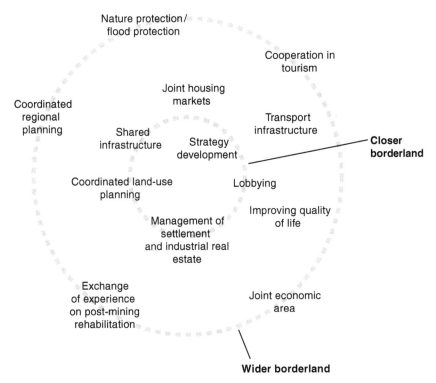

Figure 10.3 Scope of cross-border potential and solutions in the spatial dimension (source: Knippschild 2007: 132).

Czech borderland (Knippschild 2008). In cities and regions located close to the border, cross-border solutions are identified in the joint development of strategies, in the sharing of infrastructure, in coordinated land-use planning, joint housing markets and the joint management of settlements and industrial real estate. In wider borderland issues such as tourism, solutions and potential were identified in the creation of a joint economic area and in political lobbying.

One can see that ideas on cross-border potential and solutions are rather vague in the wider borderland (e.g. joint economic area, improving quality of life), whereas closer to the border they become more and more precise (e.g. management of settlement and industrial real estate, development of strategy, shared infrastructure).

The role of cross-border governance

If Europe wants to take advantage of its numerous borderlands and the clash of different cultures and potentials, then it must ensure that actions and strategies for spatial development are coordinated in such areas. But how is this coordination to be achieved? A basis for cross-border coordination is difficult to

identify, particularly across the 'new' European borders. Cross-border cooperation here suffers from the following deficits:

- Lack of transboundary institutions.[1]
- No legal framework or experience with new legal instruments (e.g. with European Groupings for Territorial Cooperation – EGTC).
- Administrative asymmetries (depending on the administrative structure, Germany has up to six administrative levels in the states, while there are only four in Poland and three/four in the Czech Republic (see Figure 10.4).
- Significant differences in the resources of public administrations (see Table 10.3).
- Language barriers, mentioned above, cultural differences and differences in mentality (see Figure 10.3).

In view of these framework conditions, the main mode of interaction is negotiation. Furthermore, legal execution and institutional control in these borderlands
are limited due to the lack of a cross-border legal framework and institutions. An
alternative to hierarchic control is cross-border governance characterized by the
ability to cope with multi-level constellations of institutions and asymmetries
(Scott 2002; Gualini 2003).

At the same time, cooperation in cross-border spatial development between
the 'old' and 'new' member states is facing a dilemma. The framework con-

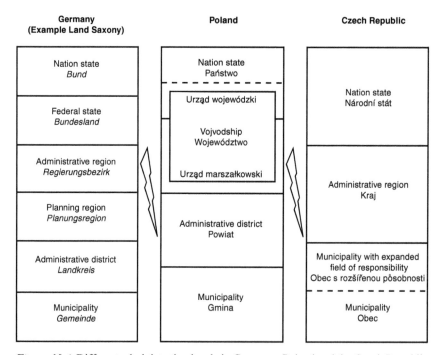

Figure 10.4 Different administrative levels in Germany, Poland and the Czech Republic.

Table 10.3 Different resources available to municipalities in the German-Polish-Czech borderland

	Number of staff in municipalities*	Inhabitants per employee
Germany		
Dresden	6,250	80
Chemnitz	3,950	62
Görlitz	880	65
Poland		
Wrocław	1,400	453
Zgorzelec	95	350
Bogatynia	120	213
Czech Republic		
Ústí nad Labem	350	266
Hrádek nad Nisou	27	271

Source: oral information, own calculation.

Note
*Concerns only the core administration without municipal enterprises and employment programmes.

ditions for cooperation are better than ever, and cross-border coordination is urgently needed; however cross-border cooperation is often patchy and many actors are 'tired of cooperation'.

In the new period for EU Structural Funds from 2007–13, enormous sums have been earmarked for territorial cooperation. A new legal instrument (European Grouping for Territorial Cooperation) serves to provide a legal framework. European integration is proceeding apace. The Schengen Treaty came into force in Poland and the Czech Republic in December 2007. European and national spatial development policy increasingly requires cross-border coordination to deal with demographic change, to establish polycentric spatial structures and avoid undesirable spatial development. However, much cooperation has proved sporadic or has failed to meet expectations. This is a discouragement to the actors involved.

One can conclude that there still remain numerous obstacles before 'good governance' is established in cross-border cooperation between central European regions. According to the White Paper on European Governance, this would comprise better involvement of local and regional governments and more openness towards civil society, more flexible administration concerning cross-border cooperation, as well as better policies and regulations to simplify and foster cross-border cooperation (European Commission 2001).

How to promote cross-border governance? Five factors for success

An in-depth study carried out in the German-Polish-Czech borderland has helped identify some influencing factors on good-practice cooperation in spatial development (Knippschild 2008). The five most important factors are presented below.

Continuity is important for successful cooperation in spatial development. Joint action will only be achieved as part of long-term cooperation. On the one hand, the process of getting to know one another, of building trust and exchanging experiences about challenges and priorities of spatial development is time-consuming. On the other hand, actors will be motivated to take part in cooperative action when they see the long-term benefits ('Shadow of future', Scott 2002). Continuity does not emerge of its own accord, but can be enabled and supported. A continuous process of communication, ensuring regular contacts between the involved actors and cross-border organizational and institutional structures, supports continuity in cooperation. Continuity can be further assured by securing political support for cross-border cooperation. Agreements and commitments achieved in communication processes have to be recognized and implemented in political decision-making.

Inadequate or unclear objectives can significantly hinder cross-border cooperation. However, adequate objectives and joint strategies provide the guidelines for cooperation, assuring joint and purposive action in cities and regions in borderlands. Even in small cooperation areas where the challenges of spatial development are clear, the objectives of cross-border cooperation are often vague or may even diverge. Therefore, an intensive process of goal definition and agenda-setting, as well as the involvement of political actors, is crucial when cross-border cooperation is at the initial stage. However, unrealistic objectives and too high expectations can lead to frustration among the actors and even misunderstandings that can block cooperation.

Cross-border cooperation is never an automatic success. Key actors and their individual motivations in the cooperating administrations are necessary, even in well-institutionalized cooperation processes, and especially at the beginning of the cooperation process. These key actors have to be committed to cross-border cooperation, and can support cooperation by supplying ideas and activities. Early and constant involvement by political decision-makers has also shown to be of equal importance.

An independent mediator is helpful to ensure a continuous process of communication. Such mediation can support cooperation when it is well staffed with experienced, independent and professional collaborators, who are recognized by the cooperating municipal and regional administrations. Negative experiences have occurred when mediation staff are predominately made up of workers from one of the cooperation partners, or where collaborators are excessively controlled by public administrations.

External funding and the investment of own resources are still important pre-conditions for the start of cross-border cooperation. None of the cooperating administrations in the case studies were able to bear the emerging transaction costs of cross-border cooperation (for translating, interpreting and travelling) alone, and cooperation would have been impossible without external funding. However, it is still essential that some of the administrations' own resources be invested to ensure that cooperation is wholehearted and binding. One of the case studies showed that administrations are capable and willing to cover the transactions costs associated with ongoing cooperation when the results and benefit of cooperation become more tangible and transaction costs decrease with improved cooperation.

Conclusions: enhancing cross-border governance in Europe

This chapter aimed to highlight cross-border governance as one precondition for integration and cohesion in Europe, and a factor to help enhance competitiveness at a time when strong pressures are felt from the Chinese and East Asian economies.

Cross-border governance is a precondition for a joint understanding of problems, priorities and strategies in European borderlands. It forms a basis for the joint cross-border utilization of infrastructure, to realize complementarities and foster a division of functions across borders, and for transboundary regional profiling. With these, it becomes possible to stabilize social, cultural and technical infrastructure, and enhance the quality of life in Europe's numerous borderlands. This increasingly attracts new inhabitants. Hence, cross-border governance can help to utilize integrated borderlands as a European factor of high value, comprising a diversity of different regional profiles, cultures and languages.

Subsidies for cross-border cooperation are of little help when there is no foundation of 'good cross-border governance' in the borderlands. At the same time, it became clear from studies that cross-border cooperation (particularly in an early phase of cooperation) brings transaction costs that require compensation by external funding. In this respect, European funding offers a great chance to support cross-border governance. At the same time, own resources from cooperating cities and regions are crucial to ensure real commitment to cooperation.

Following the enlargements of 2004 and 2007, Europe is now an economic zone significantly characterized by borderlands. Therefore, the aspects considered here are crucial in creating a clear European profile to counterbalance a rising China and East Asia. If Europe succeeds in promoting cross-border governance in all its borderlands, in order to harmonize interests, priorities and strategies, then this will be an important milestone in overcoming regional disparities. The EU will then be on the way to becoming one of the world's most competitive areas, with good long-term perspectives.

Note

1 The Euroregions have restricted human resources and competences, and cannot be compared with their counterparts along western European borders.

References

Berger, U. and Stein, C. (2005) *Der Aufstieg Chinas zur politischen und wirtschaftlichen Weltmacht* [*The Rise of China towards a Political and Economic Global Power*], available at www.heise.de/tp/r4/artikel/19/19949/1.html (accessed 25 July 2007).

Deutsche Botschaft Peking (2006) *Wirtschaftsdaten kompakt – Daten zur chinesischen Wirtschaft* [*Economic data compact – Data of the Chinese Economy*], available at www.auswaertiges-amt.de/diplo/de/Laenderinformationen/China/Wirtschaftsdaten-blattChina.pdf (accessed 1 August 2007).

European Commission (2001) *European Governance. A White Paper*, Brussels, available at http://eur-lex.europa.eu/LexUriServ/site/en/com/2001/com2001_0428en01.pdf (accessed 12 August 2007).

European Commission (2007) *Growing Regions, Growing Europe. Fourth Report on Economic and Social Cohesion*, Luxembourg, available at http://ec.europa.eu/regional_policy/sources/docoffic/official/reports/cohesion4/pdf/4cr_en.pdf (accessed 1 August 2007).

European Communities (2007) *Europa Glossary*, available at http://europa.eu/scadplus/glossary/lisbon_strategy_en.htm (accessed 25 July 2007).

Federal Ministry of Transport, Building and Urban Affairs (2007) *Territorial Agenda of the European Union. Towards a More Competitive and Sustainable Europe of Diverse Regions*, available at www.bmvbs.de/Anlage/original_1005295/Territorial-Agenda-of-the-European-Union-Agreed-on-25-May-2007-accessible.pdf (accessed 12 August 2007).

Gualini, E. (2003) 'Cross-border Governance: Inventing Regions in a Trans-national Multi-level policy', *DISP* 152: 43–52.

Indo-Burma News (2007) *Rail Link with Southeast Asia, Turkey and Europe Soon*, available at www.indoburmanews.net/archives-1/2007/july/rail-link-with-southeast-asia-turkey-and-europe-soon (accessed 1 August 2007).

Killisch, W., Oertel, H., and Siedhoff, M. (2004) *Die Zukunft des Humankapitals in Sachsen* [*The Future of Human Capital in Saxony*], Dresden: Tu Dresden.

Knippschild, R. (2008) *Grenzüberschreitende Kooperation: Gestaltung und Management grenzüberschreitender Kooperationsprozesse in der Raumentwicklung im Deutsch-Polnisch-Tschechischen Grenzraum* [*Cross-border Cooperation: Design and Management of Cooperation Processes in Spatial Development in the German–Polish–Czech Borderland*], Dresden: IOER, available at www.ioer.de/index.php?id=664.

MacWilliam, I. (2004) 'China to Europe Rail-link Planned', *BBC News*, available at http://news.bbc.co.uk/2/hi/asia-pacific/3671105.stm (accessed 1 August 2007).

Müller, B., Leibenath, M., Pallagst, K. M., Knippschild, R., Kopietz-Unger, J. and Hess, J. (2002) *Konzept zur Nutzung der Entwicklungsimpulse der Paneuropäischen Verkehrskorridore in den Beitrittsstaaten und den zukünftigen Nachbarstaaten der EU – das Beispiel des deutsch-polnischen Grenzraums* [*Concept for Utilizing Development Incentives of Pan-European Transport Corridors in Accession Countries And Future Neighbour States in the EU – The Example of the German–Polish Borderland*], Dresden, Cologne, Poznan: IOER (www.ioer.de/ptc/PDF/Endbericht-04.pdf).

Neumann, I. and Steinacker, U. (2005) 'Die Zukunft der Europastadt Görlitz/Zgorzelec bis zum Jahre 2030 [The Future of the Europe City Görlitz/Zgorzelec till the Year 2030]', in I. Neumann (ed.) *Die Zukunft des deutsch-polnischen Grenzraums gestalten* [*Designing the Future of the German–Polish Borderland*], Dresden Thelem Universitätsverlag.

Pilny, K. H. (2005) 'Weltmacht des Asiatischen Jahrhunderts [Global Power of the Asian Century]', *Eurasisches Magazin*, available at www.karlpilny.com/pdfs/eurasisch0705.pdf#search=%22Europa%20und%20der%20Aufstieg%20Chinas%20Zeit%22 (accessed 25 July 2007).

Royal Institute of Technology (2003) *ESPON action 1.1.3 – Particular Effects of Enlarge-*

ment of the EU and Beyond on the Polycentric Spatial Tissue with Special Attention on Discontinuities and Barriers. Second Interim Report Part II 'Options for Spatially Balanced Developments in the Enlargement of the European Union', Stockholm, available at   www.espon.eu/mmp/online/website/content/projects/259/650/file_1194/2.ir_1.1.3-full.pdf (accessed 17 April 2007).

Scott, J. W. (2002) 'Cross-border Governance in the Baltic Sea Region', *Regional and Federal Studies* 12(4): 135–53.

Statistisches Landesamt des Freistaates Sachsen (ed.) (2005) *Statistisches Jahrbuch der Euroregion Neisse–Nisa–Nysa* [*Statistical Office of the Land Saxony: Statistical Yearbook of the Euroregion Neisse-Nisa-Nysa*], Kamenz, Wrocław, Liberec.

11   What kind of spatial planning do we need?

An approach based on visioning, action and co-production!

Jef van den Broeck

The current evolution in Asia, not only in China but also in Vietnam, South Korea, Thailand, Malaysia and other Asian countries, indicates that the already huge and vast population is growing at a rapid pace. This also applies to economic growth and the continent's impressive technological advancement. The dynamism and energy of the (largely young) population is quite invigorating: it seems that in Seoul people (officially) work 2,088 hours a year. In Paris, the average is 1,480 hours per year. Asians are generally optimistic and eager to create 'a better life' for themselves. Asian societies are in motion, even literally so: in Ho Chi Minh City 500 new motorbikes and 100 new cars a day require more space and infrastructure. The atmosphere in the region reminds us a bit of the 1950s and 1960s in the Western industrial countries. But the scale and the pace of these developments are different.

But the coin also has a reverse side. The gap between rich and poor is growing rapidly. So is the tension between governmental systems and their form, on the one hand, and individual and human rights and the demands of the civil society on the other. The education level remains low, especially in rural areas. Sustainable development doesn't seem to be an objective, which will have a direct impact on the quality of life and health conditions in the long term. According to the Chinese state media, environmental pollution cost the Chinese economy approximately €50 billion in 2004 or 3.1 per cent of the GDP. Between 2000 and 2004, air pollution due to SO_2 from coal-fired power plants rose by 27 per cent. The fast development and the investors behind the scenes are not interested in traditional values and culture. From discussions with responsible politicians, officials, academics and students it becomes clear that the majority of the population and the authorities do not really care about these issues.

And what about 'old' Europe? Each day there are stories in the papers about the ageing of the European population, the growing inactivity rate, the pension issue and more. All these issues create a kind of pessimism, negativism and even nationalism. Sociologists and politicians refer to Europe as a 'soured society'. The industry is migrating its activities to Asia and Eastern Europe, while the Antwerp diamond sector is dominated by Indians and Singapore and Shanghai are investing in terminals in the ports of Antwerp and Zeebrugge. On the other hand, the average hourly wage in Europe (€15 before tax) is much higher than in

Asia (€3–4) and studies about the 'feelgood rate' of people, based upon housing and environmental conditions, welfare, health care, public services, educational and cultural equipment and opportunities result in a positive image.

The trend is set to continue in Asia, and this will have consequences for Europe. How can Europe and European cities react to this new context? Do we have to compete with the 'new' world? What does it mean? Is it possible and how can we do this? What kind of (strategic) planning is needed and what is possible?

We can try to think about possible strategies in order to deal with the effects, the situation and trends in Europe. I assume that such strategies should be based upon endogenous capacities and assets as well on intellectual, social, cultural, economic and spatial potential. What are our strengths and what should we focus on in planning? What is the role of space and place in the search for opportunities and a future?

Specifically, I want to argue that 'space and place' have to be considered an important resource and a main asset for creating a better quality of life. Space is considered to be an integrating framework for sustainable ecological and economic development. I also want to stress the importance of 'visioning and design', in a broad sense, as tools to further creativity and innovation and for research purposes (Loeckx and Shannon 2004: 164; Schreurs 2006). They are also tools with which to explore the assets and the potential of a place and its possible future, and even the potential of a society. Last but not least, visioning and design can be tools in a process to negotiate agreements (Van den Broeck 2006).

There are two assumptions underlying this statement. The first is that visioning enables long-term planning and serves to motivate and encourage people who definitely need a perspective. The second assumption is that design, in contrast to verbal communication, can reveal another kind of knowledge about spaces and has the power to integrate different (sectoral and fragmented) aspects in one image. As I have already stated, visioning and design have to be interpreted in a broad sense. They can be defined as a way to engage and develop our creative capacities (Albrechts 2005) in order to look for innovative possibilities to transform the present situation. In this sense, visioning and design are not (static) products, but tools that generate creativity and innovation.

In this chapter I want to argue that space, as I have already stated, has to be considered a main resource and asset and that design can function as a strategy to explore assets and opportunities. To argue this statement, I will cite an example from Africa. Second, I want to focus on two kinds of spaces, which for different reasons have been of strategic importance to date: the 'urban/city-region or network' and the 'locus'. Both are keys to a better quality of life and sustainable development. Third, I would like to suggest a strategy for planning: a 'trialogue' between visioning, action and the co-production of policy and implementation. There is another important trialogue: it covers the relationship between local authorities, civil society and the private sector, but that falls outside the purview of this chapter.

Space as a resource and a basic asset, design as a strategy

In his paper for the UN-Habitat World Urban Forum in Vancouver in June 2006, John Friedmann (2006) proposed seven clusters of regional tangible assets for consideration 'that will generate the true wealth of city regions': human, social, cultural, intellectual, natural, environmental and urban assets. I certainly agree with these clusters and with his arguments in favour of each of them. But in my mind, one essential asset is missing: space.

By and large, sectoral issues are used as the entry point for planning. This is understandable as the need for basic services: water, sewage, flood protection, housing, road infrastructure, business and industrial areas, and the quality of air and water, remains a primary concern for most people and authorities. It is an issue that people are very willing to talk about, which is why participatory processes often start with discussions about sectoral needs and their related priorities. It is also the reason why assets are discussed in the same way. This is understandable as most governments are organized in a hierarchical sectoral way: it is the ministries and their departments that deal with the development and realization of sectoral programmes. In the minds of many people, even of spatial planners, a spatial plan is the (coordinated) sum of all these needs translated into land use. Quite often, such a plan is a grey compromise between various interests. Even most research is oriented towards the deduction and programming of sectoral needs.

In most UN publications and other literature, the sustainability of space is primarily addressed through two biases: land itself as a neutral entity, an unqualified surface versus environmental quality (Loeckx and Shannon 2004: 160). Research and policy proposals normally deal with land (re-)distribution, the reduction of pollution and sometimes with ecological concerns and nature protection.

However, while spatial planning has to deal with the spatial needs of a society and their programmatic realization, the pursuit of spatial quality involves much more and should remain the main objective of planners. Housing, infrastructure, business areas, etc., are located somewhere in a space with its own identity, name, specific characteristics (e.g. topography, soil), structure, fabric and form, which are the endogenous assets of the place. Space is always an integrative framework for social, cultural, economic and ecological artefacts and activities, wherein the relationships between them will be materialized.

For spatial planners, space should be the entry point, the focus, because of its integrative relational potentialities. This means that the structure of space, seen here as the expression of relationships, and the design of space as their form, is a key medium for spatial quality and for sustainable development. It is thus much more than the 'protection of the rights' of the next generation as it also requires investment for future generations (Loeckx and Shannon 2004: 160).

Design can function as a medium in the exploration of possible investments. Design proposals, when considered as a research activity, can frame different fragmented opinions, can reveal (win-win) opportunities and open the mind of actors with their different interests, values, visions and power. 'The implicit power of images marks them as uniquely placed to convince various stakeholders. They come into a process in a threefold manner: to read the characteristics of spaces, as a tool for negotiation and as a concrete frame for agreements' (de Meulder *et al.* 2004). Design has to be interpreted in two ways. At a conceptual level, images, possibly combined with metaphors, can represent, eventually in a schematic way, the vision and the intended structure (the set of relationships between physical components) of a space. At the project level, programmes, fabric and form can be researched and discussed. To illustrate this, I will present an example from a project in Africa.

Nakuru, Kenya is seeking to create a sustainable relationship between city and nature by protecting and emphasizing natural assets connected by a green urban fabric. The image and the metaphor (Nakuru, an eco and green city) (see Figure 11.1) served to launch the discussions between the national park management and the city about their social and physical relationship, as well as discussions about a dangerous fault area in the city and about the use of assets for tourism. The (in-depth) discussion led to an agreement between both actors about the accessibility of the park for inhabitants, measures concerning the pollution of the park's lake caused by industry and about the future of the 'twilight zone' between park and city.

Another design (see Figure 11.2) became the focus for a discussion regarding the assets of the park edge as an attractive interface between both areas. The present dumping of garbage by the inhabitants, the opportunities for tourism and the security of the area were issues on the agenda.

A focus for planning: urban region and place

City-regions and the core cities that are part of them are a extremely important assets for Europe. These concentrations of knowledge, culture and energy have a strong and organized civil society. The multiplicity and proximity of settlements and nodes and the relationships between them, the structure of the area, the connecting physical networks (road, rail, air, ICT, etc.) and the expanding

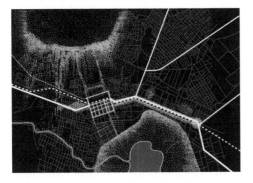

Figure 11.1 Nakuru: an eco and green city.

Figure 11.2 The park edge: a 'communicative' space.

collaboration between actors means that borders are disappearing, resulting in a new type of entity with considerable potential power.

Policy concepts have already been developed for some of these regions. The Second Benelux Structural Outline (Benelux Economische Unie 1996) recognized the existence and the potential power of such networks, as did the European Spatial Development Perspective. LIKOTO (Lille–Kortrijk–Tournay), Randstad Holland, the Flemish Diamond are a few examples of this.

Some regions have already made considerable progress and are searching for strategies to develop their potential. Others have already developed it, Emscherpark (Rhein/Ruhr) and Bilbao are well-known examples. The origin of these regions are determined by different factors.

According to Mitchell (2001) '[t]he emerging trend of urban evolution is leading to a nomadic lifestyle and new urban patterns: more flexible work patterns, greater fluidity, adjacency matters less than connectivity, dispersal and fragmentation'. The city and its surrounding region are becoming a new kind of settlement: the city-region with many and diverse nodes and dwelling environments, a dense infrastructural and service network, many nodes offering different functions all accessible within a limited time. In some countries with a dense fabric of independent but neighbouring cities, a polycentric city, a conglomerate of different bigger and smaller cities, each with a specific character and profile, is growing. In Europe, among others, there's Paris and London, but also polycentric types like the Rhein/Ruhr area (Germany), the Randstad in the Netherlands and the Belgian Central Conglomeration, which is called 'The Flemish Diamond' in the Flemish Spatial Structure Plan (1998, 2004).

We can define such urban regions as densely urbanized areas with strategic economic activities, headquarters of multinationals, important governmental services and institutions, universities, research centres, high-level cultural and recreational activities, attractive surroundings and many diverse 'housing habitats', and, of course, different infrastructures. It is no longer a hypothesis that these regions are steering and managing worldwide economic processes and that they are important motors for (economic) development (Leitner *et al.* 2002; Massey 1993; Scott *et al.* 2001).

Within Europe, but also elsewhere, competition between such regions is growing. Each is trying to attract public and private world actors, activities and money from national and supranational governments and organizations. But as Friedmann (2006) points out '[t]he competition is not for the attention of consumers but for outside investors. [...] Capital will go wherever the prospects of growing capital are the most promising. Global capital is footloose. It has no loyalty to place, and its horizon of expectation is short.'

I fully agree with Friedmann's statement that we should first count on our own endogenous and tangible assets, which are always unique when it comes to place (and space)-specific qualities. In autumn 2006, a deputy mayor of the city of Ghent (Belgium) stated that the city (which has an important port) should not only strive to retain Volvo, Toyota and SIDMAR with their decision-making headquarters in Sweden, Japan and India respectively, but above all it should try to support local, small and bigger, industries and businesses with social and cultural roots in the region. He also mentioned the importance of a sound cooperation between these companies, the city and the university.

In fact, the basic idea of the concept is cooperation and networking. Networking between the different actors within urban regions and alliances can be seen as an answer to the sharp competition and aims to combine forces and power. Such a cooperation does not mean that competition between the actors is completely excluded. On the contrary (D'Hondt *et al.* 2002), cooperation will always focus on specific issues with an interest for all actors.

An urban network can be considered an urban region where different actors are working together in an informal or formal cooperation focusing on chosen key issues in order to develop a common vision for the area and a concrete action plan concerning some common key issues. An agreement about a limited number of aspects can be the result of this cooperation.

Mitchell (2001) refers to another 'revenge of place' in the information age. It occurs at the regional and local level and is based upon individual and collective values, interests and priorities related to specific places: social proximity, liveability, security, natural values, existing (historic) fabrics, etc. In his mind, 'a smart region is a highly differentiated microstructure, with local advantages and subcultures. It offers a great variety and diversity, together with specialization sustained through global connections'.

But what is happening at this level? The suburbanization of typical urban functions and activities, sprawl and spatial fragmentation. Certainly the dichotomy between urban and rural is disappearing in urban regions as well as the traditional hierarchical structure of settlements: former central places lose their importance and new nodes appear, planned and spontaneous, near main roads and railway infrastructures. The huge increase in individual mobility is undoubtedly an important reason for this evolution. Nevertheless, flexibility and a 'nomadic or hybrid' lifestyle did not lead to a complete homogeneous space where any location is possible everywhere. Enterprises and people have their own logic and strategy when looking for a proper location: urban, when they are searching for a representative or creative environment; rural or peripheral if the cost of land or accessibility is a criterion. In a specialized network economy, every activity has specific location conditions. Households too, even when they are very mobile, are looking for specific microcosms. Analysis proves that the demand for housing and environments, depending on social-demographic characteristics, relationships, but also on emotional aspects and tradition, is extremely diverse. This is not only the case in Belgium, but also in many other countries.

Challenges for spatial planning in Flanders

What are the challenges for planning in such a dynamic environment?

For Flanders, the recommendations of a study concerning networking and urban networks (Albrechts *et al.* 2003) are:

- Stimulation of the competitive capacities of the urban networks/regions through networking and by creating strategic alliances between different public and private actors in the area and by focusing on key issues and opportunities; a key issue in Flanders is definitely the accessibility of central places and business areas and the creation of top locations for investors.
- A permanent concern for the liveability of a very dense area that is already congested and overcharged; creating a diverse environment, a diverse housing market and qualitative public transport can be the main objective as well as the concern for nature, landscape and open space.
- Selective and strategic use of means as well as finances as human resources; networking as a necessary tool for planning is very time- and means-consuming and is only possible in circumstances where actors are willing to contribute.

Apparently, these challenges, which occur mostly in dense urban networks, seem to be contradictory. Only an integrated, non-sectoral approach can handle these conflicting visions, opinions, values and interests. The role of public authorities and planners as facilitators and negotiators will be considerable in negotiation processes.

According to Mitchell's message for planning and urban design, a 'smart' region will 'focus on the organization of land-use patterns and new building types, transportation and telecommunication networks and above all control systems to support communities and their new systems of production, exchange and consumption'.

What does 'smart' mean in the Flemish Diamond (or Belgian Central urban network) (Van den Broeck 2005)? Employing in-depth interviews, the authors of the aforementioned study researched key issues and key actors willing to initiate a territorial-focused integrated process within a network organization. Common key issues mentioned by different actors were:

- Improved accessibility, internal and external, by connecting the public transport networks of the different main cities in the area, Brussels, Antwerp, Ghent and Leuven, and the coordination of their management.
- The development of strategic internationally oriented (endogenous) industrial zones in suitable locations.
- The development of mixed housing projects linked with public transport nodes; thus, a settlement structure will be created based upon these nodes.
- The protection of valuable natural areas to strengthen the natural structure based on the river valleys.
- Landscaping as a means to create a new coherent image for the urban network and as a way to strengthen its viability.
- Joint international promotion of the network.
- Joint proposals for European programmes.

A trialogue

A strategy for planning can be a continuous, permanent and dynamic 'trialogue': the relationship between 'visioning' as a framework for the development of a sustainable future, 'strategic actions and projects' as a tool and medium for realization and 'co-production' as a way to involve and engage different actors in the planning and decision-making process.

This relationship is represented in the following diagram referring to the three-track approach (see Figure 11.3) that we developed and have been practising already for some years in Belgium and elsewhere (Van den Broeck 1987, 1995a, 1995b, 2001a, 2001b, 2004; Albrechts 1999, 2004; Albrechts and van den Broeck 2004; de Meulder *et al.* 2004: 187).

The three-track approach, as a strategic planning process, can be defined as 'a social process aimed at designing and realizing an intended spatial development of a given area'. Within this process, three sub-processes can be distinguished: one leading to the design of a dynamic and sustainable long-term perspective or vision, a second dealing with daily policy, trouble-shooting, process-supporting actions and the realization of strategic projects, and a third track dealing with the involvement of actors in the co-production of visioning and decision-making.

Of course, this is not a linear process and it goes without saying that it has to be designed as a function of the specific context in the different cities. The three tracks are continuously interrelated. At regular meeting points, policy decisions are formalized through 'urban pacts', consisting of results-oriented, negotiated agreements between all the actors involved. Such pacts should be integrated in the institutional framework of the local authorities. At a certain point in time such a process can lead to a strategic plan (see Figure 11.4), which is in fact a selective commitment regarding a (dynamic and adaptive) long-term perspective

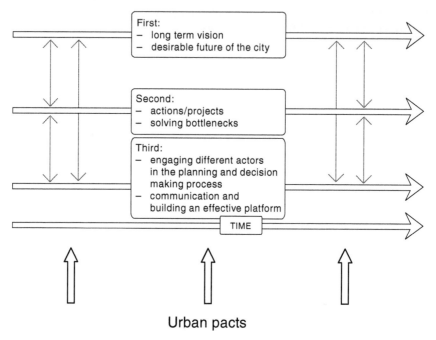

Figure 11.3 Working along three tracks.

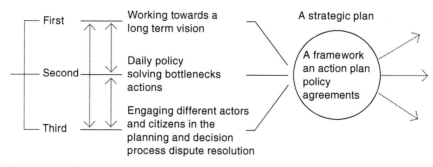

Figure 11.4 The three-track or strategic process.

or framework and a short-term action plan (related to different budgets), stipulating a concrete policy for a specific period.

Visioning

According to Zonneveld and Faludi (1997: 7), visioning or framing is 'a way of selecting, organizing, interpreting and making sense of a complex reality so as to provide guideposts for knowing, analyzing, persuading and acting. It is a perspective from which an amorphous, ill-defined problematic situation can be made sense of and acted upon.' The use of appealing frameworks enables long-term planning and it serves to motivate and encourage people who definitely need a perspective. Visions and concepts create an image of a dynamic future and are aimed at the realization of fundamental goals (sustainable development, spatial quality, coherence, diversity, equity, solidarity and democracy). Visioning tries to create an insight into a dynamic uncertain evolution and into possible futures and to give meaning to isolated issues, measures and projects (Van den Broeck 2006).

In practice, we often see that the need for a vision can originate from a problem situation, a sudden opportunity or a combination of both. In St Etienne, Bilbao, the Ruhr region and in the Rupel region in Belgium, the discussion about a desired future was fuelled as a result of years of degradation of the city and region, high unemployment figures, environmental pollution and a very uncertain future (Charbonneau 2006: 240). Elsewhere, cities or regions took advantage of opportunities or political situations. In Barcelona, nation-building was an important motivation for urban renewal, with the aim of shaping greater independence for Catalonia and forging the region's own identity.

We feel that the design of a vision is a co-productive design process, during which, if necessary, one needs to consciously abandon well-trodden paths in search of new opportunities and quality. Quality is not considered as a concept that needs to be determined objectively, but rather as the result of a process aimed at creating it (Schreurs 2006: 118). Hence, the formulation of a vision will shape the debate and provide content, thus making quality a subject of discussion and putting it on the (political) agenda. It is also a communications tool between the different actors about the desired future of a region, its realization and the framework in which a project is developed.

Finally, visioning enables agreements during the different project development phases between the various parties involved, with public and private actors, investors, project developers, the population and with users. At a certain point, a decision needs to be made, not only about which direction needs to be followed but also about the consequences of certain choices in the long and short term. Actors want immediate results, meaning that many partners, whether social or financial, require guarantees. This paves the way for a discourse about the degree of abstraction of visions. We will discuss this later as this is a fundamental discourse. At any rate, all types of commitments will have to be made not only by public institutions but also by different actors who stand to reap the material benefits of decisions when developing an urban project.

Some authors, politicians, developers and planners deny the value of visions and the shaping of a vision. They say that it is impossible. A waste of time, a restriction, often a grey compromise and one that infringes on active interventions. It is easy to argue in favour of this. Lindblom, for instance (1959), states that a consensus about visions and perspectives is impossible because the value systems of all parties involved are too diverse, because there is not enough knowledge available to design a well-founded vision and because decision-making will always be determined by power structures and concrete representation of interests.

According to Lindblom and other critics, visioning will always require a lot of time and will lead to discussions with no perspective as well as conflicts which politicians prefer to avoid. Next to this, visions, once accepted, limit your freedom to adapt the project to suit new situations, needs and even new knowledge. Proponents of this approach are in favour of immediately taking the bull by the horns and 'doing something', seeing how things work out en route or *post factum*. Or as Achiel van Acker (a former Belgian prime minister) put it succinctly: '*J'agis, puis je réfléchis.*'

Without wanting to be blind to obstacles, we defend the premise that the dynamic and phased shaping of a vision is essential to achieve spatial and social quality and a means of renovating and innovating space. We believe in the necessity and the importance of a vision as a starting point for quality, good governance and even democracy. We think it is necessary to consciously raise issues like values and interests so that the underlying motives of actors become clear, are featured and up for discussion. In a distant future, they will maybe even give rise to a fundamental change of direction. We are not talking about blueprints here or about an all-encompassing consensus about everything. Rather, this should be a dynamic vision that can be adjusted in time, linked to (policy) agreements in which a limited number of specific and concrete agreements are made between all parties involved.

Action/projects

There are different types of actions: studies, programmes, ad hoc projects that supply an answer to specific and sometimes isolated problems and also strategic projects aimed at a sustainable development that influence the structure and the fundamental characteristics of the city as a result of their multiplying capacity. Strategic projects have an integrating capacity: they link spaces and (sectoral) actions and projects. They can also link actors and stakeholders because the realization of such projects requires their involvement.

Strategic urban projects can be defined as spatial projects with a (mostly) medium-term perspective of an intermediate scale, coordinated by public actors in close cooperation with the private sector, and other semi-public actors. Strategic projects are considered necessary to achieve normative policy objectives and goals (such as sustainable development and spatial quality, security) embedded in strategic planning processes. They have an impact on a larger area, and aim to transform the spatial, economic and socio-cultural development of this larger area through a punctual intervention. Strategic projects aim to integrate the different goals and objectives of different policy sectors, ambitions and goals from the private sector, inhabitants and users of the area.

Strategic urban projects should consolidate, transform, restructure or reuse the urban areas/places for new and emerging demands of public and private (individuals, economic and cultural) actors in society. They play a key role in the regeneration and transformation of cities and embody an important paradigmatic shift in urban planning from master planning and regulations to urban development and regeneration based upon active intervention.

Finally, their realization should engage inhabitants in the improvement of their own living conditions by involving them in project definition, development, decision-making and the implementation process.

Co-production

The debate on participation has been on the agenda worldwide since the end of the 1960s (Arnstein 1969). Today it is considered an important issue in spatial planning theory (Healey 1997) and practice, certainly at the local level where people are asking for attention for local ambitions in urban projects. Of course, the notion of participation has changed fundamentally, in definition, content and practice, due to changing circumstances. Often top-down participation procedures were, and still are, in most cases, only paying lip service to information and consultation and act as a lubricant to smoothe over the authorities' decision-making procedures. At its worst, such participation functioned as an instrument to manipulate citizens. Real involvement is based on the co-production of visions, concepts, policy and decision-making and on implementation. It is based on the acceptance of the specific and relative autonomy of the different actors with regard to the sharing of responsibility and delegation of power. Of course, there is a strong opposition to collaboration and certainly co-production, which argues that it is against human nature, given its often relentless pursuit of power and the furthering of its interests. Hence, cooperation is not the driving force, as competition may prove to be stronger or even the motor of development. But competition and cooperation are not necessarily contradictory and can be combined when a win-win situation can be created. The belief in the possibility of building agreements between different actors is the starting point of co-production (Van den Broeck 1995a; Albrechts and van den Broeck 2004). Overall agreements on all issues are, of course, impossible. So they always will be selective and limited to the means available and to a set of issues for which a win-win situation for the majority of actors is possible. Of course, many questions remain: Is real collaboration and co-production of policy possible? How can we deal with the many obstacles that limit people's involvement? Are policy agreements between actors a suitable instrument? How can we deal with a multicultural and diverse population, etc.?

Conclusion

At the WPSC-Congress in Mexico (2006), Shipra Narang (UN Habitat) stated that in her mind 'the urbanization of poverty and disaster prevention and management' are the main key issues for planning and planners in the next decades at global level. Poverty is not only an issue in developing countries where we can see the explosion of slums, but also in developed countries: unemployment, segregation and disintegration, etc., often localized in specific deteriorated city quarters where people live with a limited access to education and social and cultural networks. These are not the issues of our present, increasingly market-driven society.

In Europe as well as China, and much more than to date, (spatial) planning should be oriented not only towards 'hard development' (Moulaert 2006) as such, but towards sustainable social innovation through cooperative interventions and initiatives in order to create contextual urban quality, to optimize endogenous local and specific tangible space/place-specific assets, to localize global currents and to involve people and local communities in policy-making and development.

Traditional plans, as a rule, are no longer the answer to spatial and social transformations and context. The design and management of specific processes and the realization of projects will be the new components of policy, strategy and the tasks of public-planning organizations. Plans will only be instruments for the implementation of a policy resulting from the agreement between actors. The notion of a plan should refer to a dynamic vision for the long term, a set of (win-win) actions for the short term and concrete policy agreements that specify the partners' commitment concerning the realization of actions.

And what is the role of the planner in this? Maybe it is also ambiguous: is he a designer of visions, concepts and solutions, a designer of processes, a facilitator, a process manager, etc.? In my mind, quality awareness, visioning and design as defined above, should remain the planner's first concern and tasks.

References

Albrechts, L. (1999) *In Pursuit of New Approaches to Strategic Spatial Planning*, paper presented at the ACSP Annual Conference 'Rebuilding Nature's Metropolis, Growth and Sustainability in the 21st century', Chicago.

Albrechts, L. (2004) 'Strategic (Spatial) Planning Re-examined', *Environment and Planning B: Planning and Design* 31: 743–58.

Albrechts, L. (2005) 'Creativity as a Driving Force', *Planning Theory* 4(3): 247–69.

Albrechts, L. and van den Broeck, J. (2004) 'From Discourse to Facts: The Case of the ROM-project in Ghent, Belgium', *Town Planning Review* 75(2): 127–50.

Albrechts, L., Schreurs, J. and van den Broeck, J. (2003) 'In Search of Indicators and Processes for Strengthening Spatial Quality: The Case of Belgium', *Built Environment* 29(4): 288–95.

Arnstein, A. (1969) 'A Ladder of Citizen Participation', *Journal of the American Planning Association* 35(4): 216–24.

Benelux Economische Unie (1996) *Ruimte voor samenwerking*, Brussels: Tweede Benelux Structuurschets.

Charbonneau, J. (2006) 'Tussenkomen in de gedaanteverandering van steden', in L. Boudry, A. Loeckx and J. van den Broeck (eds) *Inzet/Opzet/Voorzet: Stadsprojecten in Vlaanderen*, Antwerp/Apeldoorn: Garant.

De Meulder, B., Loeckx, A. and Shannon, K. (2004) 'A Project of Projects', in A. Loeckx, K. Shannon, R. Tuts and H. Verschure (eds) *Urban Trialogues: visions_projects_co-productions*, Nairobi: UN-Habitat, KULeuven.

D'Hondt, F., Janssens, P. and van den Broeck, J. (2002) *Com-cooperation in Transnational Planning, Experience-based Strategy for transnational and cross-border Planning*, paper presented at the XVIth AESOP Congress, 'Planning and Regional Development in Border Regions', Volos, July.

Friedmann, J. (2006) *The Wealth of Cities: Towards an Asset-based Development of Newly Urbanised Regions*, paper presented at the UN-Habitat World Urban Forum, Vancouver.

Healey, P. (1997) *Collaborative Planning: Shaping Places in Fragmented Societies*, London: Macmillan.

Leitner, H., Pavlik, C. and Sheppard, E. (2002) 'Networks, Governance and the Politics of Scale: Inter-urban networks and the European Union', in A. Herod and M. Wright (eds) *Geographies of Power*, Oxford: Blackwell Publishing: 274–303.

Lindblom, C. (1959) 'The Science of Muddling Through', *Public Administration Review* 19: 79–88.

Loeckx, A. and Shannon, K. (2004) 'Qualifying Urban Space', in A. Loeckx, K. Shannon, R. Tuts and H. Verschure (eds) *Urban Trialogues: visions_projects_co-productions*, Nairobi: UN-Habitat-KULeuven.

Massey, D. (1993) 'Power Geometry and a Progressive Sense of Place', in J. Bird, T. Curtis, T. Putnam, G. Robertson and L. Tickner (eds) *Mapping the Future: Local Cultures, Global Change*, London: Routledge: 59–69.

Mitchell, W. (2001) *Planning and Design for the Information Age*, paper presented at the 37th IsoCaRP Congress on Planning in the Information Age, Utrecht.

Moulaert, F. (2006) *Social Innovation and Urban Development: The Role of Public Policy*, paper presented at the 42nd ISoCaRP Congress, Istanbul.

Narang, S. (2006) *A New Agenda for Planning and Planning Education: WUF, WPC and the Way Forward*, paper presented at the World Planning Schools Congress, Mexico City.

Schreurs, J. (2006) 'Ontwerpend Onderzoek: een constante zorg', in L. Boudry, A. Loeckx and J. van den Broeck (eds) *Inzet, Opzet, Voorzet, Stadsprojecten in Vlaanderen*, Antwerp/Apeldoorn.

Scott, A. (ed.) (2001) *Global City-regions: Trends, Theory, Policy*, Oxford: Oxford University Press.

Van den Broeck, J. (1987) 'Structuurplanning in de praktijk: werken op drie sporen', *Ruimtelijke Planning* Afl. 19, II.A.2.c, Antwerp: Van Loghum Slaterus: 53–119.

Van den Broeck, J. (1995a) *Pursuit of a Collective Urban Pact between Partners*, paper presented at the 31st IsoCaRP International Congress, Sydney.

Van den Broeck, J. (1995b) 'Sustainable Strategic Planning: A Way to Localise Agenda 21', *Proceedings of the Nakuru Consultative Workshop*, Nakuru, Kenya.

Van den Broeck, J. (2001a) *Central Belgium, a Park City?: A Policy Based on Deconcentrated Clustering*, paper for the International Workshop 'New Approaches to Land Management for Sustainable Urban Regions', University of Tokyo.

Van den Broeck, J. (2001b) *Informal Arenas and Policy Agreements Changing Institutional Capacities*, paper presented at the First World Planning Schools Congress, Shanghai.

Van den Broeck, J. (2004) 'Strategic Structure Planning', in A. Loeckx, K. Shannon, R. Tuts and H. Verschure (eds) *Urban Trialogues: visions_projects_co-productions*, Nairobi: UN-Habitat, KULeuven.

Van den Broeck, J. (2005) 'Networking and Urban Networks: A Challenge for Spatial Planning: The Case of the Flemish Diamond', in P. La Greca (ed.) *Planning in a More Globalised and Competitive World*, Proceedings of the XXXIX International ISoCaRP Congress.

Van den Broeck, J. (2006) 'Visievorming in co-productie: dynamisch en trapsgewijs', in L. Boudry, A. Loeckx and J. van den Broeck (eds) *Inzet/Voorzet/Inzet, Stadsprojecten in Vlaanderen*, Antwerp/Apeldoorn: Garant.

Van den Broeck, J., Verschure, H. and Esho, L. (2004) 'Urban Development by Co-production', in A. Loeckx, K. Shannon, R. Tuts and H. Verschure (eds) *Urban Trialogues: visions_projects_co-productions.* Nairobi: UN-Habitat-KULeuven.

Zonneveld, W. and Faludi, A. (1997) 'Vanishing Borders: The Second Benelux Structural Outline', *Built Environment* 23: 5–13.

12 Is the 'new' strategic planning suited to coping with the issues of globalization?

Louis Albrechts

The autobiography *My Art, My Life* is a richly revealing document by the painter Diego Rivera, who revolutionized modern mural painting and was the principal figure in launching the Mexican Renaissance. It is one of the frankest confessions I have ever read. The breadth of his sympathies, his vitality and his love for life run through his prose as it does through his paintings. It is Rivera's apologia: a self-portrait of a complex and controversial personality. Perhaps the greatest artist the Americas have ever produced, Rivera tells the story of his intellectual and artistic journey. He introduces us to the masters and the ideology to which he was most drawn, his warm friendships and his bitter fights.

What is the link here with globalization? Well, Rivera reveals that his real coming to maturity, to his own identity and style, coincided with his second return from Europe to his homeland in 1921. He stresses (p. 31) that 'he who hopes to be universal in his art must plant in his own soil' and 'the more native the art is, the more it belongs to the entire world'. I would like to take these sentences as a starting point for my article. Only I won't be talking about paintings and painters, but rather about planning approaches and the way they respond to the challenges and developments (also of globalization) faced by our cities and city-regions.

My argument has five parts. First, I want to focus on the developments and challenges that our cities and city-regions are facing. Second, I will argue that a planning approach, in a sense like Rivera's position, should be centred on the elaboration of a mutually beneficial dialectic between a response to globalization and local uniqueness. Third, I would like to consider an alternative planning approach that combines vision and action, the global and the local, diversity and specificity. Fourth, I want to reflect on what kind of governance is needed for such an approach. And finally, I will close with some comments on the contribution that planning and planners can make, along with a few remarks on growth fetishism.

1 Challenges and developments

Western society, but also that of a number of rapidly developing countries like China, is finding itself confronted with major developments and challenges: the growing complexity of global issues (the rise of new technologies, changes in production processes, the crisis of representative democracy, diversity, migration, and the globalization of culture and the economy), increasing concern about the rapid and apparently random course of (uneven) development, the problems of fragmentation, the ageing of the population (in Western society as well as in China), the increasing awareness (on all scales, from local to global) of environmental issues, the growing strength of the environmental movement, the long-standing quest for better coordination (both horizontal and vertical), and the reemphasis on the need for long-term thinking. Moreover, the need felt by many governments to adopt a more entrepreneurial style of planning in order to enhance city competitiveness, the growing awareness that a number of planning concepts (compact cities, liveable cities, creative cities, multicultural cities, fair cities) cannot be achieved solely through physical hard planning, and the fact that (in addition to traditional land-use regulation, urban maintenance, production and management of services) city governments are being called upon to respond to new demands that imply the abandonment of bureaucratic approaches and the involvement of skills and resources that are external to the traditional administrative apparatus, all serve to expand the agenda.

Some of these developments and challenges could be brought under the heading of globalization. Without entering into the academic discussion as to whether globalization is a real phenomenon or only a myth, there is a common understanding that all the regions of the world are increasingly sharing problems and challenges that have no regard for nation-state borders. These include the growth of international trade and the international flow of capital; the international division of labour, i.e. the shift of labour-intensive production processes to China; pollution, i.e. the impact of the growth in China and India on global warming; access to cultural diversity; and immigration. The anti-globalist movement, ironically itself an exponent of globalization, opposes certain aspects or forms of globalization (globalization of money and corporations), but is in favour of others (globalization of people and unions).

The challenge for each region and interest group seems to be to develop its own assets (cultural, intellectual, natural, etc.) while developing an ability to think critically, to transcend local loyalties and to approach global issues as 'citizens of the world' (Nussbaum 1998).

2   What kind of planning approach is suited to meeting these challenges?

We may consider four different types of reaction to these developments and challenges: reactive (the rear-view mirror), inactive (going with the flow), preactive (preparing for the future) and proactive (designing the future and making it happen) (see Ackoff 1981). My thesis is that only the 'proactive' reaction is appropriate, as it calls for the transformative practices that are needed to cope with the continuing and unabated pace of change driven by the (structural) developments and challenges. Transformative practices focus on the structural problems in society; they construct images/visions of a preferred outcome and they strive to implement them (see Friedmann 1987). Transformative practices without creativity, without new ideas about how to tackle the developments and challenges seem futile.

2.1 Traditional and positivist views of planning

Traditional spatial planning is basically concerned with the location, intensity, form, amount and harmonization of land development required for the various space-using functions. In a number of Western countries, spatial planning evolved in the 1960s and 1970s towards a system of comprehensive planning, the integration of nearly everything, at different administrative levels. In the 1980s, when the neo-liberal paradigm replaced the Keynesian–Fordist paradigm and when public intervention retrenched in all domains, Europe witnessed a retreat from planning fuelled not only by the neo-conservative disdain for planning, but also by postmodernist scepticism, both of which tend to view progress as something which, if it happens, cannot be planned. Accordingly, the focus of urban and regional planning practices shifted to projects (Secchi 1986), especially those involving the revival of rundown sections of cities and regions, and to the development of land-use regulations.

A positivist view of planning assumes that the one best future follows automatically if the analytical and forecasting techniques are rigorously applied. The same reasoning made modernist planners believe that the future could be predicted and controlled (see Ogilvy 2002). There is ample evidence, however, that the problems and challenges that places are confronted with cannot be tackled and managed adequately with this old intellectual apparatus and mindset. Consequently, we have to reflect creatively and innovatively on the approaches (both in terms of process and substance), the concepts and the techniques that we engage and the logic that we apply in tackling these problems and challenges. We have to think afresh and, as it were, reinvent our places in order to secure a better future and to improve the quality of life for all citizens. Therefore, planning must involve a creative effort to imagine (structurally) different futures, and to bring this creative imagination to bear on political decisions and the implementation of these decisions. The challenge is to find a systematic approach that provides a critical interpretation of existing reality and that thinks creatively about possible futures and how to get there.

2.2 'New' strategic spatial planning

The motivations for constructing a 'new' type of strategic spatial planning vary, but the objectives have typically been to construct a challenging, coherent and coordinated vision, to frame an integrated long-term spatial logic (for land-use regulation, for resource protection, for sustainable development, etc.), and to enhance action orientation and a more open multi-level type of governance.

My definition of 'new' strategic planning contains three components: a what, a how and a why.

2.2.1 What?

'New' strategic spatial planning is a transformative, integrative and (preferably) public sector-led socio-spatial process through which visions/frames of reference, justification for coherent actions and means for implementation are produced that shape and frame what a place is and what it might become (see Albrechts 2004, 2006).

The term 'spatial' brings into focus the 'where of things', whether static or dynamic; the creation and management of special 'places' and sites; the interrelations between different activities and networks in an area; and significant intersections and nodes in an area which are physically co-located (Healey 2004: 46). Amin (2004: 43) argues that cities and regions possess a distinctive spatiality as agglomerations of heterogeneity locked into a multitude of relational networks of varying geographical reach. Strategic spatial planning processes with an appreciation of 'relational complexity' demand a capacity to 'hear', 'see', 'feel' and 'read' the multiple dynamics of a place in a way that can identify just those key issues that require collective attention through a focus on place qualities (see Healey 2005, 2006).

The focus on the spatial relations of territories allows for a more effective way of integrating different agendas (economic, environmental, cultural, social and policy agendas) as these agendas affect places. It also carries a potential for a 'rescaling' of issue agendas down from the national or state level and up from the municipal level. The search for new scales of policy articulation and new policy concepts is also linked to attempts to widen the range of actors involved in policy processes, new alliances, actor partnerships and consultative processes (Albrechts *et al.* 2003). Moreover, a territorial focus seems to provide a promising basis for encouraging levels of government to work together (multi-level governance) and in partnership with actors in diverse positions in the economy and civil society.

2.2.2 How?

'New' strategic spatial planning focuses on a limited number of strategic key issues, and it takes a critical view of the environment in terms of determining strengths and weaknesses in the context of opportunities and threats (see China's policy to secure access to basic resources). Strategic spatial planning focuses on place-specific qualities and assets, social, cultural and intellectual, including the physical and social qualities of the urban tissue, within a global context. It studies the external trends, forces and resources available. Strategic spatial planning identifies and gathers major actors (public and private: see Chinese investors in Europe), it allows for a broad (multi-level governance) and diverse (public, economic, civil society) involvement during the planning process, it creates solid, workable long-term visions/perspectives (a geography of the unknown) and strategies at different levels, taking into account the power structures (political, economic, gender, cultural: see the growing influence of China in worldwide organizations), uncertainties and competing values. Strategic spatial planning designs plan-making structures and develops content, images and decision frameworks for influencing and managing spatial change. It is about building new ideas and processes that can carry them (ideas and process) forward, thus generating ways of understanding, ways of building agreements, and ways of organizing and mobilizing for the purpose of exerting influence in different arenas. Finally, strategic spatial planning, both in the short and the long term, focuses on framing decisions, actions, projects, results and implementation, for which purpose it incorporates monitoring, feedback, adjustment and revision.

2.2.3 Why?

The why question deals with values and meaning: 'what ought to be'. Without the normative, we risk adopting a pernicious relativism where anything goes (see Ogilvy 2002). In a conscious, purposive, contextual, creative and continuous process, new strategic planning is aimed at enabling a transformative shift, where necessary, to develop openness to new ideas, and to understand and accept the need and opportunity for change. Transformative practices oppose a blind operation of the market forces and involve constructing 'desired' answers to the structural problems of our society. Normativeness indicates the relations with place-specific values, desires, wishes or needs for the future that transcend mere feasibility and that result from judgements and choices formed, in the first place, with reference to the idea of 'desirability', to the idea of 'betterment' and to the practice of the good society (Friedmann 1982). To 'will' particular future states is an act of choice involving valuation, judgement and the making of decisions that relate to human-determined ends and to the selection of the most appropriate means for coping with such ends. This is contrary to futures as extensions of the here and now. 'Futures' must symbolize some good, some qualities and some virtues that the present lacks. Speaking of quality, virtues and values is a way of describing the sort of place we want to live in, or think we should live in.

2.3 Differences from traditional planning

This strategic spatial planning is presented not as a new ideology preaching a new world order but as a method for creating and steering a (range of) better future(s) for a place based on shared values (see also Ogilvy 2002). Its normative viewpoint produces quite a different picture from traditional planning in terms of plans (strategic plans versus master plans or land-use plans), types of planning (providing a framework versus technical/legal regulation), types of governance (government-led versus government-led but negotiated forms of governance) and content (vision and concrete actions that accept the full diversity of a place while focusing on local assets and networks in a global context), social-spatial quality, a fair distribution of the joys and burdens. The normative point of view may seem to some people (see Mintzberg 1994) too broad a view of strategic spatial planning; however, the many experiences documented in the planning literature (Healey *et al.* 1997; Pascual Esteve 1997; Hamnett and Free-stone 2000; Albrechts *et al.* 2001, 2003; Pugliese and Spaziante 2003; Martinelli 2005) back up (parts of) this broader view. This view also implies that strategic spatial planning is not a single concept, procedure or tool. In fact, it is a set of concepts, procedures and tools that must be tailored carefully to whatever situation is at hand if desirable outcomes are to be achieved. Strategic spatial planning is as much about process, institutional design and mobilization as it is about the development of substantive theories. The many Chinese students at my institute are challenged to adapt this strategic planning to the Chinese context, culture and legal setting. Content relates to the strategic issues selected in the process. The capacity of a strategic spatial planning system to deliver the desired outcomes is dependent not only on the system itself, but also on the conditions underlying it. These conditions, including political, cultural and professional attitudes towards spatial planning (in terms of planning content and process) and the political will on the part of the institutions involved in setting the process in motion, affect the ability of the planning systems to implement the chosen strategies.

2.4   *Four-track approach*

The 'new' strategic (spatial) planning approach is operationalized in a four-track approach. The four tracks (Albrechts 1999; see also Van den Broeck 1987, 2001) can be seen as working tracks: one for the vision, one for the short-term and long-term actions, a third for the involvement of the key actors and, finally, a fourth track for a more permanent process (mainly at the local level) involving the broader public in major decisions. The proposed tracks may not be viewed in a purely linear way. The context forms the setting of the planning process but also takes form and undergoes changes in the process (see Dyrberg 1997).

In the first track, the emphasis is on the long-term vision. In this sense, the long term constitutes the time span one needs to construct/realize the vision. The envisioning process translates complex interrelations between place qualities and multiple space-time relational dynamics into multiplex, relational spatial imaginations (see also Healey 2006). The vision (the product of envisioning) is constructed in relation to the social values to which a particular environment is historically committed (see Ozbekhan 1969). By introducing envisioning, 'new' strategic planning transcends mere contingency planning.

In track 2, the focus is on solving problems through short-term actions. It concerns acting in such a way as to make the future conform to the vision constructed in track 1 and to tackle problems in view of this vision. Tackling concrete problems during the planning process is a means of creating trust between the actors.

Spatial planning has almost no potential for concretizing strategies, so track 3 involves relevant actors who are needed for their substantive contribution, their procedural competence and the role they might play in acceptance, in getting basic support and in vouchsafing legitimacy. Both the technical skills and the power to allocate sufficient means to implement proposed actions are usually spread over a number of diverse sectors, actors, policy levels and departments. Integration in its three dimensions, substantive, organizational and instrumental (legal, budget), is at stake here.

The fourth track is about an inclusive and more permanent empowerment process (Forester 1989; Friedmann 1992) involving citizens in major decisions. In this process, citizens learn about one another and about different points of view, and they come to reflect on their own points of view. In this way, a store of mutual understanding can be built up, a sort of 'social and intellectual capital' (see Innes 1996; but see also the more critical view of Mayer 2003).

The end product consists of an analysis of the main processes shaping our environment, which amounts to a dynamic, integrated and indicative long-term vision (frame), a plan for short-term and long-term actions, a budget, and a strategy for implementation. It constitutes a consensus or (partial) (dis-)agreement between the key actors. For the implementation, credible commitments to action engagement (commitment package), and a clear and explicit link to the budget are needed where citizens, the private sector, different levels of governance and planners enter into moral, administrative and financial agreements to realize these actions (collective spatial agreement).

3 Governance

The values and images of what a society wants to achieve must be discussed in the planning process (value rationality). Values and images are not generated in isolation, but are socially constructed and given meaning and validated by the traditions of belief and practice; they are reviewed, reconstructed and invented through collective experience (see Ozbekhan 1969, but also Foucault 1980: 11; Hillier 1999; Elchardus *et al.* 2000: 24). We must be aware of the impact on the social and psychological milieu of consumer society, rapidly growing in China, that teaches citizens how to think about themselves and their goals. Citizens' tastes, priorities and value systems are, to a large degree, manipulated by the very markets that are supposed to serve them (Hamilton 2004: 66). Within (and constrained by) this established framework of the market society, places and communities face the challenge to construct (or reject) and implement the discourses of cultural diversity (a major issue in China), sustainability and place quality and, subsequently, to creatively transform their own functioning and practice. In the context of this article, this creative transformation refers to changes in governance relating to current and historical relations of dominance and oppression (Young 1990). Planning and governance cannot be looked upon as separate, autonomous spheres within society, so we have to look for a type of governance that interlinks with the planning approach outlined above.

In the field of governance, there is a pervasive struggle among a variety of pluralistic democratic tendencies, each of which seeks to acknowledge a wide range of actors in policy-making and techno-corporate tendencies. This is a struggle to maintain control over the management of a place using the tools of technical analysis and management, and following the standardized rulebooks or recipes of conventional collaboration between government, major business organizations and trade unions (see Healey 1997; Albrechts 1999).

I argue that a feasible and efficient planning process should be centred on the elaboration of a mutually beneficial dialectic between top-down structural policies and bottom-up local uniqueness. Both a bottom-up approach rooted in the conditions and potentialities of local assets (interpreted in their broadest sense) and a complementary multi-level, top-down approach aimed at introducing fundamental and structural changes, are indispensable. Indeed, a mere top-down and centrally organized approach runs the danger of overshooting the local, historically evolved and accumulated knowledge and qualification potential, while a one-dimensional emphasis on a bottom-up approach tends to deny, or at least to underestimate, the importance of linking local differences to structural global tendencies (Albrechts and Swyngedouw 1989). This dialectic constitutes the bare essence of multi-level governance.

3.1 Pluralist and interculturalist places

Some politicians are reluctant to involve the public in decision-making, because it involves giving up some control, and people who hold power are generally not inclined either to give it up or to share it. In other places, there is a tendency to involve major actors in the process. As spatial planning has almost no potential for concretizing strategies, the relevant actors are getting involved. These actors are needed for their substantive contribution, their procedural competences and the role they might play in acceptance, in getting basic support and in providing (a kind of) legitimacy. However, planning potentially has an impact on and links to a very wide range of issues (from citizens with interests in specific places to nature in general). These interests can be very diverse and conflicting. Some citizens have the knowledge, the skills, the power and the networks through which they are able to influence or even steer planning proposals and policy decisions. Others lack the means and the cultural codes to participate in the system. Their voice has hardly any impact on decisions. Class, gender, race and religion do matter in terms of whether citizens are included in the process (Young 1990). The future must be created under conditions of inequality and diversity. Any change must deal with issues of power and resistance, and the irreconcilability of certain forms of interests. This requires a democratic polity that can encompass the realities of difference, inequality, etc. (Huxley 2000). The core is a democratic struggle for inclusiveness in democratic procedures, for transparency in government transactions, for accountability of the state and planners to the citizens for whom they work, for the right of citizens to be heard and to have a creative input in matters affecting their interests and concerns at different scale levels, and for reducing or eliminating unequal power structures between social groups and classes (see also Friedmann and Douglas 1998). Pluralist democratic tendencies are developing in the wake of a crisis of representative democracy and a demand to transform the state in ways that will serve all of its citizens, especially the least powerful. This type of approach uses public involvement to present real political opportunities, learning from action, not only what works but also what matters. The involvement of citizens (and especially of weak groups) in socially and politically relevant actions is intended to achieve some degree of empowerment, ownership and acceptance for these citizen groups (see Friedmann 1992).

Increased personal mobility has made places more mixed. This can be seen either as a threat or as an opportunity. On one hand, it can destabilize a place as migrants bring in habits, attitudes and skills alien to the original society; while on the other, it can enrich and stimulate the potential of a place by creating hybrids, crossovers and boundary blurring (Landry 2000: 264). Places must be creative, with mutual understanding between cultures based on the ideal of equity (this is nothing less than a claim to full citizenship, see Sandercock 2003: 98). Interculturalism builds bridges, helps foster cohesion and conciliation, and produces something new out of the multicultural patchwork of places (Landry 2000), so that the views of a place held by minorities or otherwise socially excluded groups are taken into account and their ideas are brought to bear on the planning, political decision-making and implementation process.

3.2 Learning processes

Society as a whole (both citizens and politicians) feels uncomfortable when challenged to think beyond the short term and to reflect on multiple futures, and consequently, it takes an unconsciously deterministic view of events. How can citizens, politicians and planners be convinced that they can have meaningful choices and will not be complete prisoners of circumstances? How can different groups in a place be made aware that they are interdependent, that they share the same physical space and may therefore face similar problems, and that there are some problems that they cannot solve on their own? How can they be made aware that they may lose if they do not cooperate? How can they be persuaded to consider the alternative to what they feel in their hearts? Yet, when the sustainability, local assets, quality and equity of places are at stake, then this is exactly what we may need to do: to imagine alternative futures in order to master change.

The building of scenarios can become a learning process if it looks in an open way to the future, if it integrates the knowledge of what might happen with an understanding of the driving forces and a sense of what it means to a place and its citizens. The active participation in a collective action of scenario building may generate trust as participants in the process are likely to find that – and to understand why – some scenarios present a future that certain people would like to inhabit, while other possible futures are considered highly undesirable. The process helps the participants to think more broadly about the future and its driving forces and to realize that their own actions may move a place towards a particular kind of future. The process allows participants to step away from entrenched positions and identify positive futures that they can work at creating. It allows for a high degree of ownership of the final product and illustrates that citizens do have a responsibility for the(ir) future. So the real test is not whether one has fully achieved the 'conceived' future, but rather whether anyone has changed their behaviour because they saw the future differently (see also Schwartz 1991).

4 Some reflections

What can planning and planners contribute in this respect? Many of the ideas I have formulated already exist in the dispersed experience of global best practice (see Landry 2000; Healey 2004). Planners have to grasp the momentum. They need to lure citizens and politicians outside the comfort and familiarity of their traditional mindsets, concepts and modes of operation. They need to explore with them a set of distinctive, plausible and sustainable (in the broadest sense) futures that could unfold. This demands creativity and a thorough understanding and analysis of the driving forces of change and of what might be. Hence, the need for a type of planning that embraces creativity and critical analysis. This kind of planning is very much concerned with 'possibilities' and 'what ought to be'. In creativity, there is the dimension of the 'new', the dimension of bringing something into being and the dimension of values.

So what kinds of 'powers' need to be addressed? Anxiety about the 'other' strengthens right-wing, anti-immigrant parties in most European cities (see Albrechts 2003; Sandercock 2003). But places must also avoid turning themselves into pure commodities for the capital market. They are not just containers for inbound investments. There is growing evidence that the current pattern of material consumption is environmentally unsustainable and that more economic growth and more technology will not solve this problem (see Mishan 1967; Sachs and Esteva 2003; Hamilton 2004). For Hamilton (2004), growth fetishism and the predominantly market-led society lie at the heart of these ills. The concepts of sustainability and multicultural society applauded in many government reports cannot be achieved with more market (Sachs and Esteva 2003; Hamilton 2004). Neither can they be achieved by extrapolating from the past and the present, by simply relying on economic growth (Mishan 1967; Hamilton 2004), or by keeping to vested interests (Europe vs China), concepts, discourses and practices. Because society is not a prisoner of its past and because it has a responsibility for the future, it is fated to find alternatives. It must study the forces of change and look for means and instruments to make this change happen. This means that we need creativity (in planning, in governance, in implementation) to structurally transform our attitudes to places, to the natural environment, to our relationships with others (especially 'the other') and our modes of governance. Such transformation requires structural reforms in power relationships to tackle the overpowering dominance of the market and it requires institutional reform. A number of strong manifestos for change have been drawn up: for reconsidering the absolute faith in economic growth (Mishan 1967; Hamilton 2004), for living interculturally (Landry 2000; Sandercock 1998, 2003), and for creating a more sustainable society (Sachs and Esteva 2003). Like Rivera, these manifestos stress that our 'art' of planning and policy-making must be strongly locally embedded to make full use of the global context.

References

Ackoff, R. (1981) *Creating the Corporate Future*, New York: John Wiley.

Albrechts, L. (1999) 'Planners as Catalysts and Initiators of Change. The new Structure Plan for Flanders', *European Planning Studies* 7(5): 587–603.

Albrechts, L. (2003) 'Planning and Power: Towards an Emancipatory Approach', *Environment and Planning C* 21(6): 905–24.

Albrechts, L. (2004) 'Strategic (Spatial) Planning Re-examined', *Environment and Planning B: Planning and Design* 31: 743–58.

Albrechts, L. (2006) 'Shifts in Strategic Spatial Planning? Some Evidence from Europe and Australia', *Environment and Planning A* 38(6): 1149–70.

Albrechts, L. and Swyngedouw, E. (1989) 'The Challenges for a Regional Policy under a Flexible Regime of Accumulation', in L. Albrechts, F. Moulaert, P. Roberts and E. Swyngedouw (eds) *Regional Policy at the Crossroads*, London: Jessica Kingsley: 67–89.

Albrechts, L., Alden, J. and da Rosa Pires, A. (2001) (eds) *The Changing Institutional Landscape of Planning*, Aldershot: Ashgate.

Albrechts, L., Healey, P. and Kunzmann, K. (2003) 'Strategic Spatial Planning and Regional Governance in Europe', *Journal of the American Planning Association* 69: 113–29.

Amin, A. (2004) 'Regions Unbound: Towards a New Politics of Place', *Geografisker Annaler* 86B: 33–44.

Dyrberg, T. B. (1997) *The Circular Structure of Power*, London: Verso.

Elchardus, M., Hooghe, M. and Smits, W. (2000) 'De vormen van middenveld participatie', in M. Elchardus, L. Huyse and M. Hooghe (eds) *Het maatschappelijk middenveld in Vlaanderen*, Brussels: VUB Press: 15–46.

Forester, J. (1989) *Planning in the Face of Power*, Berkeley: University of California Press.

Foucault, M. (1980) *The History of Sexuality*, New York: Vintage.

Friedmann, J. (1982) *The Good Society*, Cambridge, MA: MIT Press.

Friedmann, J. (1987) *Planning in the Public Domain: From Knowledge to Action*, Princeton, NJ: Princeton University Press.

Friedmann, J. (1992) *Empowerment. The Politics of Alternative Development*, Oxford: Blackwell.

Friedmann, J. and Douglas, M. (1998) 'Editor's Introduction', in M. Douglas and J. Friedmann (eds) *Cities for Citizens*, Chichester: John Wiley & Sons.

Hamilton, C. (2004) *Growth Fetish*, London: Pluto Press.

Hamnett, S. and Freestone, R. (eds) (2000) *The Australian Metropolis*, Sydney: Allen & Unwin.

Healey, P. (1997) *Collaborative Planning: Shaping Places in Fragmented Societies*, London: Macmillan.

Healey, P. (2004) 'The Treatment of Space and Place in the New Strategic Spatial Planning in Europe', *International Journal of Urban and Regional Research* 28(1): 45–67.

Healey, P. (2005) 'Network Complexity and the Imaginative Power of Strategic Spatial Planning', in L. Albrechts and S. Mandelbaum. (eds) *The Network Society: A New Context for Planning?*, New York: Routledge: 146–60.

Healey, P. (2006) 'Relational Complexity and the Imaginative Power of Strategic Spatial Planning', *European Planning Studies* 14(4): 525–46.

Healey, P., Cameron, S., Davoudi, S., Graham, S. and Mandanipour, A. (1995) *Managing Cities: The New Urban Context*, Chichester: Wiley.

Healey, P., Khakee, A., Motte, A. and Needham, B. (1997) *Making Strategic Spatial Plans. Innovation in Europe*, London: UCL Press.

Hillier, J. (1999) 'What Values? Whose Values?', *Ethics, Place and Environment* 2(2): 179–99.

Huxley, M. (2000) 'The Limits of Communicative Planning', *Journal of Planning Education and Research* 19 (4): 369–77.

Innes, J. (1996) 'Planning through Consensus-building: A New View of the Comprehensive Planning Ideal', *Journal of the American Institute of Planners* 62(4): 460–72.

Landry, Ch. (2000) *The Creative City: A Toolkit for Urban Innovators*, London: Earthscan.

Martinelli, F. (2005) 'Introduzione', in F. Martinelli (ed.) *La pianificazione strategica in Italia e in Europa: Methodologie ed esiti a confronto*, Milan: Franco Angeli.

Mayer, M. (2003) 'The Onward Sweep of Social Capital: Causes and Consequences for Understanding Cities, Communities and Urban Movements', *International Journal of Urban and Regional Research* 27(1): 110–32.

Mintzberg, H. (1994) *The Rise and Fall of Strategic Spatial Planning*, New York: Free Press.

Mishan, E. (1967) *The Costs of Economic Growth*, London: Staple Press.

Nussbaum, M. C. (1998) *Cultivating Humanity: A Classical Defense of Reform in Liberal Education*, Cambridge, MA: Harvard University Press.

Ogilvy, J. (2002) *Creating Better Futures*, Oxford: Oxford University Press.

Ozbekhan, H. (1969) Towards a General Theory of Planning, in E. Jantsch (ed.) *Perspective of Planning*, Paris: OECD: 45–155.

Pascual Esteve, J. M. (1997) *La estrategia de las ciudades: Los planes estratégicos como instrumento: métodos, téchnicias y buenas practices*, Barcelona: Diputacion de Barcelona.

Pugliese, T. and Spaziante, A. (eds) (2003) *Pianificazione strategica per le città: riflessioni dale pratiche*, Milan: F. Angeli.

Rivera, D. (1991) *My Art, My Life. An Autobiography*. New York: Dover Publications, originally published in 1960 by Citadel Press.

Sachs, W. and Esteva, G. (2003) *Des ruines du développement*, Paris: Le Serpent à Plumes.

Sandercock, L. (1998) *Towards Cosmopolis. Planning for Multicultural Cities*, Chichester: John Wiley & Sons.

Sandercock, L. (2003) *Cosmopolis II. Mongrel Cities in the 21st Century*, London: Continuum.

Schwartz, P. (1991) *The Art of the Long View*, New York: Doubleday Currency.

Secchi, B. (1986) 'Una nuova forma di piano [A new form of play]', *Urbanistica* 82: 6–13.

Van den Broeck, J. (1987) 'Structuurplanning in praktijk: werken op drie sporen', *Ruimtelijke Planning* ll.A.2.C: 53–119.

Van den Broeck, J. (2001) *Informal Arenas and Policy Agreements Changing Institutional Capacity*, Shanghai: Paper First World Planning School Congress.

Young, I. (1990) *Justice and the Politics of Difference*, Princeton, NJ: Princeton University Press.

13 The European house

Museum and supermarket

Achim Prossek

In 2004 a conference was held in Berlin entitled 'A Soul for Europe', taking a quotation from Jaques Delors as its motto. A soul for Europe is necessary, Delors once argued, because 'no one falls in love with a single market'. Politicians, artists, academics and journalists discussed the presence and possible future of the European Union at a time of huge development: the enlargement of the EU by ten countries. It was assumed that the new phase of development of the European Union would be attractive for investors and inhabitants, but might be considered critically at the same time. The main criticism: The EU is still an economic and political project, rather than a cultural one. Therefore, culture became the focal point of the discussion. José Manuel Barroso, president of the EU Commission, said in his opening speech:

> We need common ground and common reflection about what the EU can be, and what it will be cannot succeed without a proper look at Europe's cultural dimension. [...] Europe's true 'cultural identity' is made of its different heritages, of its multiplicity of histories and of languages, of its diverse literary, artistic and popular traditions. [...] The EU has reached a stage of its history where its cultural dimension can no longer be ignored.
>
> (Barroso 2004)

The cultural differences of the EU have been incorporated in the Preamble of the Constitutional Treaty. It states that Europe is 'united in its diversity', and that diversity is a structural element of European unity.

If it is true that the cultural dimension of the European Union can no longer be neglected, this provides a good reason to look at how some artists see Europe and the development of European cities, regions and countrysides. I will present two statements from Eastern Europe for the inner continental perspective, and two global perspectives on Europe. This is to discuss possible futures and the role culture will play.

First, I would like to show the contrast between the situation today and that at the time of the foundation of the EU. This gives us an explanation of the reasons why the cultural aspects of Europe have been less important in the development of the Union than other aspects. According to Jean Monnet, the first president of the European Coal and Steel Community (ECSC), there was the need for economic development and also the need to establish institutions. I quote from two speeches, held in 1952 and 1953:

> The unification cannot sustain on goodwill. Uniform appointments are necessary. Men die away and others will come in our place. What we devise for them is not our personal experience. [...] What we are able to devise are institutions. Institutions live longer than men, and therefore they are able, if solidly built, to store the wisdom of consecutive generations. [...] It is our duty to develop and strengthen them to become independent from our affinity for temporary compromises.
>
> (Monnet 1952: 3f., translated by author)

> The European Community is the beginning of Europe. It not only consists of coal and steel, but also includes committees authorized for acting under the authority of the parliaments of the six countries. It creates common norms, or, in other words: it causes European civilization to come into being.
>
> (Monnet 1953: 18, translated by author)

This short retrospection highlights the difference between the situation at the beginning and that of today. From our perspective, the belief in institutions may be hard to understand. We all know some excesses of regulation produced in the name of the EU. But Monnet was influenced by the experience of the Second World War, so for him an impersonal, inter-, even supranational institution seemed to be a guarantee for a peaceful development of the continent. The development of the European Coal and Steel Community into the Common Market, the European Community and then the European Union in a six-decade period of peace (at least in Western Europe) represents a historical singularity for this continent and is predominantly regarded as a success story. And, for Monnet, it was more than a project of political unification: He saw it as the rebirth of European civilization, which means it is most of all a cultural concern.

In the opinion of Thomas Meyer, this 'Monnet method' (as he calls it) caused the current problem of low voter participation in elections for the European Parliament, in comparison to national elections. The author states that the 'systematic depoliticization of the political process was regarded as the ideal way in the beginning'. Now, 'the depoliticization proves to be the main hindrance for European civil consciousness. Anything else would be a miracle' (Meyer 2004: 43, translated by author). Barroso, in contrast, puts a positive value on this 'method':

> You know as well as I do that the famous 'bon mot' attributed to Jean Monnet – that if he was going to start again, he would start with culture – is spurious, as he knew that European integration would have failed if it had not started with the economies and the markets.
>
> (Barroso 2004)

The quoted statements of Monnet himself already lead one to believe that Barroso's estimation is true. But now, after the failing of the draft for a European Treaty, political and, in particular, cultural aspects become more important. They, more than politics, are able to form a European identity, which is necessary for a stronger sense of community. For Ole B. Jensen, a European identity 'could work as a stimulus to the new real or imagined geographies of Europe' (Jensen 2002: 118). This process should not be underestimated, especially for the integration of new member states in the Union. And, if the result is a 'kind of postmodern equivalent of medievalism, a neo-medieval empire' (Zielonka 2006: 11), the enlarged EU has a character shaped by its variety and diversity of cultures. Territorial cohesion, therefore, is an object demanding attention in European spatial planning policy. I present different perspectives of Europe, which, altogether, give an impression of the contrary developments the continent is undergoing.

Europe as a museum: the global perspective

The new world order for the twenty-first century: For an unnamed former Brazilian minister of finance, it is clear what it will look like: China will be the factory, India the office. The United States will be the shopping mall, Latin America the circus – and Europe's role is to become the museum of the world (Frankenberger 2006). One cannot claim that this is a differentiated, legitimate perspective. But nonetheless, there is some truth in these sentences. We all know about the background of demographic and economic aspects that are probably the most decisive factors for this change. Curious: Where is Africa? Still not on the map, not even at the beginning of the twenty-first century? The article discussing the minister's thesis does not mention Africa, because it localizes the important processes somewhere else: Therefore, it is about the rise of China, India and other Asian states. And, it is about the little role left over for Europe. It seems that it is only a little bit more important than the black continent. So it is an incomplete image of the world, but a complete description of the world order.

A museum is an archive of cultural and collective memories. But who is interested in this cultural richness in an ever-faster high-, micro- and biotechnological world? Economic development brings a display of political power for China. Globalization changed the country; now, and even more in the future, the country will influence globalization. It is a challenge for European countries and the European Union. Even if they keep up, they have to find solutions for the demographic problems, for the shrinking and ageing of their societies. Another factor is the rise of migration, not only from outer Europe, but also intracontinental. For example, several hundred thousand young Polish people work in the UK. And, more than 600,000 inhabitants of Moldova work in Russia or in countries of the EU. This is job migration, which means earning money is the main intention, but all these people also experience the European space and culture. The question is: What they will learn? As we will see below, the answer to this is not as clear as we might think.

One of Klaus Kunzmann's scenarios is 'Europe, a culture park'; Europe as 'Historywood'. Well, this vision of Europe is probably less far away than we think. Some of the so-called Bollywood movies, Indian productions, are filmed in Germany because the landscape gives the right setting for stories full of love and opportunities to sing. It is true: If Europe erects more leisure paradises and tourist circuits, it may garner international success. Klaus Kunzmann said: 'Cultural tradition and urban heritage will gain further importance as economic assets' (see also Kunzmann 2006: 22). Yes, this is true, too. Integrated in festivals and efforts for cultural capital festivalization, with historical locations combined with routes of industrial heritage (regional, national, even international), Europe displays enormous potential.

A scenario for Europe in 2030 could be to dramatize the continent as a museum of the nineteenth and twentieth centuries. If the future is to be in China, India and other emerging markets, why not try to earn from the past and its rich history?

One consequence could be that Europe becomes the charming region of the world, which is not as fast as the boomtowns of the East, where some things are allowed to be old, where the past can be seen – all reasons, by the way, why Berlin is so attractive to many foreign tourists. Berlin is in some way a theme park of the twentieth century. It is nice that it has Potsdamer Platz, but the density of historic sites is more important. It is a city where remembrance of the past and the present live side by side.

Europe as a museum: the inner-continental perspective

The inner-continental perspective is highly influenced by the transformation process in Eastern Europe since the mid-1980s and the enlargement of the EU in 2004. Some fear the consequences, some are euphoric. The historian Karl Schlögel describes the changes vividly, and it seems that, for him, it is all positive. His euphoria is about a rebirth, a reincarnation not only of cities, but of a European habitus. It is about 'the reincarnation of Europe out of the cities' spirit'. His 'Archipelago Europe' consists not only of cities, but of a variety of places, events and things: Europort Rotterdam, Heathrow, Ikea, high-speed train routes, golden domes in Kiev, high-quality newspapers, Easyjet and Ryanair, holiday mobility, mobile phones in trains, the bridge over the Belt, security, cash machines at the University of Sofia, Kanaksprak, plastic rubbish, Eurolille, Love Parade, the skyline of Tallin (Schlögel 2005: 67). With this kind of reading of the space, he draws a cartography of a new Europe. It's a cartography of the changes in everyday life, bathed in an optimistic perspective of European development.

But this is only one side of the coin of transformation in Eastern Europe, and not everyone is as optimistic. There are places remaining that have fallen out of economic interest, lost all their inhabitants and have no perspective for future development. The Polish writer Andrzej Stasiuk often writes about the geography of Europe, about the transformation process his country is undergoing.

Sometimes he reaches places on his journeys where he feels as if he were the last human – No wonder he writes about a 'melancholic geography of Europe':

> There are places where we suspect that what we are seeing is what will happen only in the future. Rudňany took the shape of a ruin, past and gone, that reminds us, however, of a prophecy that will come true. Rudňany is the story of a world where a growing number of geographic, historic and human places are becoming unnecessary. The rich and self-sufficient part will take off from the rest of the world at a certain moment and start into the future like a paradise island. The leftover is stuck in a present that changes mercilessly into a deeper and deeper past, until we lose sight of it and it dissolves into emptiness.
>
> (Stasiuk 2006: 323, translated by author)

Middle Europe or the Balkan states are probably the best regions for melancholic geography. The head of Middle Europe, Stasiuk suggests with bitter irony, should consist of two parts: semidarkness and emptiness. It is a melancholy born in the twentieth century, being deeply rooted in history. It is a melancholy based on the certainty that the number of those places is increasing. It would be easy to neglect this topographic mood, even if it is typically European, a deep romantic feeling. But, is there a chance to accept these feelings as part of present European life, to value them as richness, as potential, something that could be arranged and shaped? Or are spaces just waiting for investors to erect theme parks or the state to declare national parks? Stasiuk's essay is not only about a melancholic geography of Europe, but in favour of it. The slight difference is important, because it shows the author's wish not to overlook these regions and their decline.

Europe from its edge: a supermarket

Despite the geography, the Cold War told us something different: Poland is not Eastern Europe, but right in the middle, even though clear demarcations were never set. Because we still have the tendency to overlook those countries that belong to Europe, but not (yet) to the European Union, an additional view from the very eastern edge will be presented.

It is not easy to find Moldova. I consulted my *Diercke World-Atlas*, the atlas almost every German pupil owns. On the map entitled Middle Europe, I found the European continent from Den Hague to Minsk, from Geneve to Bečau in Romania. But where is Moldova? There is only a part of it to be seen on the right side of the Middle-Europe map, only the northwestern part of the country. No city can be seen. To get a look at the nation as a whole, I have to flip through the atlas. Almost 100 pages later, on the Balkan peninsula map, east of the Carpathian mountains, Moldova lies, home of Bessarabia, a landscape which my old geographic encyclopaedia describes as one of the old European areas with a relatively high population density. (The name is misleading: It has nothing to do with Arabia. It's named after a prince). It is not part of the European Union and is not due to become a member in the near future. But, it is part of Europe (in a geographical sense) and since 2007, when Romania became a member state of the EU, it is a direct neighbour of the political construct of Europe, the Union. Since then, the country is of much more importance for Europe than it used to be. Although Moldova has undergone the same transformation processes since 1989 as the countries of the former Eastern Bloc, it has remained the poorest European country. It is a country that is still not on the map, neither the printed nor the mental one.

Nicoleta Esinencu, a young dramatist, gives us an impression – or shall I say: a lesson – of city life in Chişinău in Moldova and the people's relationship to Europe. It appears in a book entitled *Leap into the City*, published as part of the cultural-project relations funded by the German Federal Cultural Foundation. The essay starts with the remembrance of the situation in the USSR (the country it used to belong to): Not Europe, but Eurasia was the preferred name. But what happened? 'EURASIA has transformed over time into EUROPE and ASIA, with the emphasis naturally on EUROPE' (Esinencu 2006: 37). For the historian Tony Judt, the Moldovans' confession of European affiliation is not based on historic or geographic reasons. It is a rejection of both history and geography, with the potential increase of EU membership being less important than the loss in case of denied affiliation (Judt 2006: 874). Esinencu realizes the situation nowadays: 'The Chişinău of today gives you the impression of an increasingly European city. New buildings, neon advertisements, designer shops, supermarkets, shopping malls, cinemas…' (Esinencu 2006: 37). She wonders what makes a place European. It is not only the architecture, the shopping facilities and the advertisements. The people are responsible for the feeling of being in a European city. Remember Karl Schlögel speaking of the cities' spirits, not the city, which can only come to fruition through people's lives. Having this in mind, Esinencu comes to the result: Chişinău is not a European city. It gives the impression of being one, but this is just on a superficial level. And, what is underneath? 'There is one thing that has not changed at all and that I do not believe will change in the near future and that is our way of thinking' (ibid.). Esinencu, reporting people's attitudes:

> We want the EU! We can get jobs from the EU without even asking! But what do we give? "These Germans are just a bunch of idiots and country bumpkins, just as well that we came along to wake them up!" says a young man recently back from Germany where he was working illegally. [...] Moldovans really want to be part of Europe! In their imagination, Europe is one enormous supermarket with everything you could possibly want.
>
> (ibid.: 42)

Esinencu seems to be suffering from this double life in Chişinău: 'What does a city have to do to be European? First of all, sort out its inhabitants! The inhabitants of Chişinău produce nothing apart from headaches. They give each other headaches. Chişinău – a city of headaches' (ibid.: 43).

It seems Chişinău might be a city that gives us headaches as well; far away from it, but not unconcerned. We as Germans and old Europeans are the mentioned others, the bunch of idiots who need lessons from people who know how to get what they want. The planners know about work migration, about push-and-pull factors of regions. We discuss the competition between cities and regions to benefit from globalization. But we are hardly aware of what lies behind the metropolitan regions and growth corridors. And we barely think about how strenuous this life is there, how inconsistent.

Given that economic growth needs some time (if there is any development at all), it is unlikely that external borders can stop people from working abroad. They will be seen as aggravating circumstances rather than an insurmountable hindrance. At the external EU borders, people can be seen day after day risking their lives to get to the other side. The report about Chişinău clearly pictured the condition of the civil society and the public life in cities at the edge of Europe. Even within the EU, there are different values and habits, but there is no chance to escape from these conflicts. The members decide which type of frontier they think necessary, whom they want to stay on the other side. The societies themselves are responsible for the way they separate from others, how they defend themselves at their borders and how they handle illegal immigrants. This is indeed not only a question of political action, but of the ways people arrange their lives.

The disappearance of industries, cities, landscapes, and the uselessness of the facilities of a forgotten history are all a result of the same dynamics that led to the rise of some cities, to the growth of transit corridors, the appearance of so-called non-spaces of transportation. The perspective of the writer and dramatist I have presented tells a sad story. The melancholic geography is a geography, a cartography of a not-yet-recognized, partly vanishing Europe, of places that will not even be integrated into heritage routes at some future time.

China in Europe: losers and winners in a land of milk and honey

A city of the former industrial heart of Germany provides the setting for a film that focuses on one aspect of globalization and the economic growth and technological make-up of China. The documentary *Losers and Winners* is a film about Chinese workers dismantling a huge coking plant in the city of Dortmund over 2003 and 2004. It was one of the largest industrial relocations so far and the first ever instance of a coking plant being dismantled and reconstructed. It had only been working for eight years, so the plant was still the most modern in the world. Of course, the Chinese not only bought the plant but the construction plans as well. The last German workers supervising the Chinese at the beginning were melancholic: They defined themselves mainly through their work and were now facing the dismantling of their former workplace. In comparison, the Asian workers were rather unsentimental and disciplined, working 60 hours a week in the hope for a better future and in the consciousness of the importance of their work for the Republic of China. (And, in contrast to the safety-oriented Germans, the Chinese company doesn't care about a few badly injured workers; it has fixed an allowed rate.)

Its director Mo Lishi looks upon Germany as a country where no one really works, for him Germans always have a rest. He admires and desires the newest Mercedes cars, and he has a clear vision about the future of China and Europe. He, who has experience in dismantling industries for more than two decades, is working in Germany for the third time. His dream is to come back in 20 years to dismantle the Airbus production plants. But, his wish is not to deindustrialize Germany, but to profit from German technological knowledge. In 20 years, he fantasizes about a Germany where everybody will drive his own spacecraft. This is why airplanes will no longer be needed in Germany. But he also has a realistic view on the economic power of Germany: He attests to a weakness that could have influence on Germany's position as one of the leading (technological, industrial) countries in the world. Just like the Moldovans, he classifies Europe as a supermarket, but one of an enormous, unique dimension.

Although the film shows an aspect of globalization of increasing significance by describing the rise of China as a global player, it is not a film about globalization in the first place. Its main emphasis is on the people, picturing the workers, how they perceive the transformation process, their hopes and their worries. Beside this, it shows the different habitus of the workers from the two nations. Ulrike Franke and Michael Loeken, the directors, describe their experience in relation to their own work: The Chinese workers had been faster in dismantling the coking plant than they had been with the financing of the film project. And, the reconstruction in China again had been faster than the editing of the film (see the website for *Losers and Winners*). The German workers couldn't believe that, and they were not prepared for transformations and competitors such as these. But for the filmmakers, they were not the only losers: The Chinese workers have the vision of a better future, but in the case of an accident they are just one more victim of the revolution or the company's goals.

The film conveys a clear sense that this is only the beginning of a process that will be repeated in the future. With hundreds of thousands of highly educated Chinese students, the pressure on Europe will actually increase. Mo Lishi and his colleagues had been working in Dortmund for one and a half years, but with no time or money to visit the city or the country. European culture has for them the face of technology, symbolized mainly by the best cars in the world. There is a chance that in a few years, China will be interested in things and issues that Germans are wondering about today: technologies for environmental protection of natural resources, solutions for sustainable public-transport systems, eco-friendly car technologies (even the Japanese were number one), solutions for an ageing society. With growing differences between regions in China, with the highest number of accidents in the industry, mainly the coal-mining industry with 5,493 accidents of a total of 6,476 worldwide (in comparison, France: 40; see Hui 2007: 59), with the shortage of drinking water – just to name a few problems which already cause political trouble – China will have to react in the near future. And, for a while it may be easier (and faster) to copy from Europeans than to invent everything themselves.

The end of the film confronts us with the coach ready to leave to transport the workers back to the airport. For a moment, we can read big letters on its side – showing the name of the company: Euro Star Touristik. We do not know if this is coincidence or intention. But it brings us back to the issue of culture.

Europe's star, concludes Jürgen Mittelstrass in his reflections about inventing Europe, is its culture. But not its culture in terms of a museum or a tourist event, but in terms of explaining ideas and values. Values born in the past (such as freedom, justice, equality, human dignity and human rights), which can serve as a guiding star for the future (Mittelstraß 2005: 36). Europe has to reinvent itself to find its role in the globalized world. Is there a chance to reconcile the melancholic geography, the loser feeling with the idea of the European (guiding) star? When Peter Sloterdijk was talking to Rem Koolhaas about European identities and myths, he denoted Europe as a semi-depressive large construct, a vast coat not yet fitting most Europeans, confirming the melancholic view we have become acquainted with already. His way out stands not in opposition to this; instead he uses it as the foundation for the future. The consequence: It is time to think about the first European legends, the Aeneas myth from Virgil.

Aeneus is a loser who gets a second chance. This legend has been transferred to the US, but now it is necessary to bring it back, to adopt it once more. Without the legend of the second chance, it is, according to Sloterdijk, impossible to regenerate Europe (Allianz 2006). This regeneration, one has to accept, will never lead to a homogenous space, but this is inherent in the process and an advantage rather than a risk. The effect could be that the European star will shine over the twenty-first century, because, as Tony Judt thinks, neither the US nor China can play the role of a model for the world (Judt 2006: 930). And Mark Leonard even argues that China could adopt the EU as a model for its own territory (Leonard 2007: 149). So what's called the 'star' here could be the thing people are looking for when searching for the soul of Europe. Do we believe in an immortal soul? The Latin word for soul, *anima*, also means breath and wind. Europe has different climatic zones, but the winds do not stop at the borders.

References

Allianz (2006) *Europäische Identitäten und Mythen*, Allianz Lecture: Munich, 17 May, available at www.allianz.com/azcom/dp/cda/0,,1145532–49,00.html (accessed 29 September 2006).

Barroso, J. M. D. (2004) 'Opening Speech', in Bundeszentrale für politische Bildung (ed.) 'Europa eine Seele geben/A Soul for Europe', *Dokumentation der Konferenz vom 26. und 27. November 2004*, Bonn.

Esinencu, N. (2006) 'Chişinău – A City of Headaches', in K. Klingan and I. Kappert (eds): *Leap into the City*, Chişinău, Sofia, Pristina, Sarajevo, Warsaw, Zagreb, Ljubljana. Cologne: 32–43.

Frankenberger, K. D. (2006) 'Europa als Museum der Welt?', *Frankfurter Allgemeine Zeitung* 24 May, Frankfurt: FAZ.

Hui, W. (2007) 'Postmaoistischer Staat und Neoliberalismus in China', in 'China: Verord-nete Harmonie, entfesselter Kapitalismus', *Edition Le Monde diplomatique* 1, Berlin: 56–60.

Jensen, O. B. (2002) 'Imagining European Identity: Discourses Underlying the ESDP', in A. Faludi (ed.) *European Spatial Planning*, Cambridge, MA: Lincoln Institute of Land Policy: 105–20.

Judt, T. (2006) *Geschichte Europas von 1945 bis zur Gegenwart*, Munich: Hanser.

Kunzmann, K. R. (2006) 'Spatial Development and Territorial Cohesion in Europe', in U. Altrock S. and Güntner *et al.* (eds) *Spatial Planning and Urban Development in the new EU Member States: From Adjustment to Reinvention*, Burlington, VT and Alder-shot: Ashgate: 19–30.

Leonard, M. (2007) *Warum Europa die Zukunft gehört*, Munich: dtv.

Losers and Winners website (2007) available at www.losers-andwinners. net/sites_en/ filmmakers/interview.htm (accessed 18 June 2007).

Meyer, T. (2004) *Die Identität Europa*, Frankfurt/Main: Suhrkamp.

Mittelstraß, J. (2005) 'Europa erfinden. Über die europäische Idee, die europäische Kultur und die Geisteswissenschaften', *Merkur, Deutsche Zeitschrift für europäisches Denken* 59. Jg., Heft 1: 28–37.

Monnet, J. (1952) 'Ansprache des Herrn Jean Monnet, Präsident der Hohen Behörde', anläßlich der ersten Tagung der Gemeinsamen Versammlung (Strassburg am 11. Sep-tember 1952), in Europäische Gemeinschaft für Kohle und Stahl (Hrsg.): *Ansprachen des Herrn Jean Monnet, Präsident der Hohen Behörde, anläßlich der ersten Sitzung der Hohen Behörde am 10. August 1952 in Luxemburg und der ersten Tagung der Gemeinsamen Versammlung am 11. September 1952 in Strassburg*: 17–31.

Monnet, J. (1953) 'Europa ist im Entstehen', in Europäische Gemeinschaft für Kohle und Stahl (Hrsg.): *Europa ist im Entstehen. Ansprache des Präsidenten der Hohen Behörde der Europäischen Gemeinschaft für Kohle und Stahl, Jean Monnet, vor der Societe d'Economie Politique de Belgique in Brüssel, am 30. Juni 1953*.

Schlögel, K. (2005) *Marjampole oder Europas Wiederkehr aus dem Geist der Städte*, Munich: Hanser.

Stasiuk, A. (2006) 'Für eine melancholische Geographie unsere Kontinents', in K. Raabe and M. Sznaiderman (eds) *Last&Lost. Ein Atlas des verschwindenden Europas*, Frank-furt/Main: Suhrkamp, 316–29.

Zielonka, J. (2006) *Europe as Empire: The Nature of the Enlarged European Union*, Oxford: Oxford University Press.

14 PEACE at Odessa

Andreas Faludi

The Odessa **P**an**E**ur**A**sian **C**ouncil for the **E**conomy (PEACE) of 29–30 September 2031 can congratulate itself. Even after the near-demise of the EU, the ESDP continues, and to remarkably good effect. Before elaborating, I'll report on the award, which took place in the margins of the meeting, of a prize to a young academic from the Azerbaijan branch of the European School of Planning (A-ESOP). There was a small fracas over his impetuous suggestion in his word of thanks that the issues on the table of PEACE needed to be considered against the backdrop of an overall spatial framework for the balanced development of the EurAsian continent.

The occasion for the award was the discovery by the laureate of a dusty document in the archives. With Azerbaijan owing so much to the ESDP, he was interested to learn that there had once before been an ESDP in the 1990s, called the European Spatial Development Perspective. It is hard for us to imagine conditions in the late twentieth century. The breakthrough in nanotechnology achieved at the Delft University of Technology in 2006[1] gave us the quantum computer and real-time Translation and Contextual Interpretation (TCI), but the creators of the ESDP confronted language divides with their bare hands, so to speak. The DMR (distorted meanings rate) must have been awesome – and we are only too well aware that noise is still a problem, as in the case of the blind woman from Samoa being fined for illegally visiting the pay-as-you-see virtual Louvre.

Our Azerbaijani got curious about the ESDP Mark 1. His father had spoken Russian, so he could at least appreciate what the Slovene version was about. What had once been the EU Documentation Services, still headquartered in Brussels, but in fact one of many cottage industries in rural areas where former EU interpreters eke out a living, were of inestimable assistance. The young man delivered a report, self-evidently, in Azerbaijani. The Baku ESDP anchor informed his Odessa counterpart on secondment from the private security and risk management conglomerate GLOBSTRAG, successor to the UK private military company, AEGIS[2] of Iraq fame. Having been involved in the Strategic Plan for Barcelona, the anchor made a casual mention of the report to the PEACE President. The President decided to award the young Azerbaijani the prize mentioned above. The occasion was to be the informal dinner, always sure to hit the newscasts, on the evening before the delegates would retire to the decision room, to remain there in conclave until at least two-thirds of the agenda was dealt with. (The President may have wanted to distract from the appearance of Lord Tony Blair of Basra, still looking young, and still controversial, as honorary guest of the Ukrainian hosts.)

The prize is in convertible euros, the internal euro being of little value since a succession of pension crises forced the European Central Bank to devalue it.[3] The convertible euro, of course, alongside the yuan and the dinar, is public tender in Azerbaijan. The laureate was allowed to address the meeting. My trusted Babel Fish, being the nickname of our earplugs laden with nanotechnology,[4] rendered this account:

> Madame President, Distinguished Delegates,
> I wish to thank you for this award. Your generosity will allow me to go more deeply into the pre-history of the ESDP. There are still people around who were involved, and there should be secondary literature, not the least because in those days academics were expected to generate as many papers as possible. (One is alleged to have done 27 papers on the ESDP.) As you are aware, I am not talking about the ESDP as we know it. I am talking about the puny efforts of the member states of the EU of old to formulate a spatial framework, an effort that floundered, ultimately because they could not square the circle of wanting a common framework, but not wanting to relinquish control. So they could not make sense of the projects and policies of the EU of old. As a result, infrastructures cut landscapes into ribbons, destroying, to name but one example, one of the last remaining bear habitats in the process; grants went to places where business was already good and people were drifting like flotsam after jobs in iterant industries, leaving desolate regions behind them. One Dr Kunzmann seems to have been particularly critical of all this, but I still need to verify this.
> We may ask ourselves whether the troubles of the past decades have at least partially been the result of not heeding the message of the ESDP Mark 1. More to the point, the 10,000 Friends of EurAsia,[5] of whom I am a member, humbly submit that you are in danger of going down the same path. In deciding on the issues before you, you should rather avail yourselves of a framework, a EurAsian Spatial Development Perspective (EASDP)....

At this point, a defect caused Babel Fish to switch to English, and so the French got up to leave. This was fortuitous. Our young fellow had overstayed his welcome. The President made good use of the ensuing commotion. Being of a generation with now defunct language skills, she thanked him in French. Fine-tuned to input from native speakers, Babel Fish had problems in coping, but the French appreciated her gesture. The leader of the delegation kissed her hand, a time-honoured French tradition at international gatherings. The Azerbaijani was hustled out of the room, and the delegates settled down to eating caviar smuggled from Iran, which came from the one and only sturgeon harvested in years.

The incident was a mere flash on the newscasts, but one may ask why there is no institution, indeed nobody, except perhaps the 10,000 Friends of EurAsia, taking an overall view? We have broken up the Holy Trinity of Nation-State-Territory. We have undermined the state monopoly on the legitimate use of force. The Chinese extraterritorial colonies and markets dotting the landscape make sovereignty seem a hollow concept. The huge theme parks,[6] festivals and games, the bread and butter of our event-economy, require supraterritorial[7] consortia in order to operate. However, does this mean that there can be no overall view, no common spatial development perspective?

Before discussing this issue, recall how all this came about, starting with the Chinese colonial cities, a new phenomenon, but the Budapest China Town was the handwriting on the wall. Going by educational achievement and occupational position, highly skilled multilingual immigrants, especially those from India and China, and in particular the women, had already been successful. (Other immigrants, about whom more below, had slipped into public housing estates.) However, the new immigration into China Towns was different. Being self-contained and closed, they had no need for services, social, educational, health, police or otherwise. Although they were, of course, open to business contacts, they kept a lid on integration. In practice, they were extra-territorial.

Was this to be allowed? How about public-service obligations, or control over educational curricula? Where does this leave sovereignty? National governments had no answers. Being left to deal with the China Towns as well as they could, city governments started to address the situation. It transpired that the business communities often came from one and the same town or city and kept their family, economic and political roots there. Some experts assumed that, rather like the cities of classical Greece spawning colonies, Chinese cities were in fact sending business leaders out in groups, providing them with support, including cheap labour drawn from the seemingly inexhaustible pool of peasants looking for work. (There were rumours about labour conditions flying in the face of EU occupational health standards, but it was difficult to get to the bottom of this.)

City governments decided to engage directly with the social, political and business networks in the donor cities, entering into all sorts of alliances. Some were about delegating service obligations. This is how, for instance, Chinese police, nominally in the service of the European host cities, started patrolling the streets of China Towns. (Magnanimously, Chinese authorities accepted internal euros for these services.)

Not that there was much crime. Social control was strong, making China Towns safe places. The role of the Chinese police seemed to be to contain malcontents among the workforce. Anyhow, in return for such mutually beneficial arrangements, city governments agreed to share in the management of 'responsible migration', thereby acquiescing to a limited but steady trickle of more Chinese coming in.

This became a model for dealing with immigrant communities, but not all were as well organized or enjoyed the support of their home-base. However, by the time it was realized that the recipe only worked for the Chinese, worldwide city-to-city diplomacy had become common. Cities entering into foreign-policy agreements, traditionally a preserve of national governments, weakened the position of the nation-states.

Cities happily entered the fray. The elites already had a taste of foreign travel from the many partnership agreements. Cities even had their embryonic diplomatic services: European sections that had previously been busily engaged in organizing exchange networks, particularly, the consortia needed to obtain EU funding. Such networks carried on even after the funds dried up. As indicated, events on a scale necessary to compete in a global entertainment market require cooperation, which is why Territorial Cooperation was the only remaining objective under the Financial Perspective 2014–23.

This brings us to the event economy, in which there has been much innovation. Montenegro was the first to call its king back, mounting a colourful coronation and repeating it each year. Baden followed suit and emulated the example of the hourly Changing of the Guards at Buckingham Palace, a great success with Chinese and Vietnamese tourists. (There are, most likely unfounded, rumours that *The Last Emperor* will be re-enacted in the Forbidden City.) Macedonia claimed to have discovered the DNA of Alexander the Great, holding great pageants to celebrate its national heritage.

This was just the beginning. At present, major events are global in scale and demand huge support networks. This has been the lesson of the unsuccessful bid for the 2024 European Delta Games. Originally, these were conceived as the Dutch Delta Games.[8] However, the Dutch Olympic Committee decided to invite Flanders to participate, hence European Delta Games, but France, still reeling under the shock of the rejection of the Parisian bid for 2012, gave only token support to this, the only European bid. In the end, the 2024 games went to a combination of Francophone states in Africa, but not before a pledge to deploy the Foreign Legion in a huge security operation. The lesson has sunk in. We are now looking forward to the 2032 EurOlympics, sometimes called, to avoid association with the hapless euro, the Polycentric Games.

Behind these games is a network of Mega-City Regions. The works involved, including the building of dedicated lines for magnetic levitation trains to move visitors around, require massive compensation for the sensitive areas affected. It was decided to search for compensation areas in so-called Stabilization Zones. The re-naturalization of industrial, commercial and housing areas standing empty was seen as a substantial contribution to the main purpose behind this policy: to stabilize the decline to a steady 1 per cent per annum, until the optimum was reached. To retain at least some of the workforce, the policy allowed for the creation of fairs with walk-in computer games, but also urban warfare parks where visitors could hone their survival skills in the original settings. (However, a Partisan Park in the marshes of Eastern Europe never got off the ground.) The Stabilization Zones are also where so-called Sun Cities have been developed for the elderly, for instance, in Bavaria, Sachsen-Anhalt, Brandenburg, Mecklenburg-Vorpommern and the Black Forest, but the better-known examples are, of course, in Spain and Italy.[9] As far as compensation is concerned, the far more significant projects are the Alpine Capricorn Environment, the German-Polish Wolf Habitat and the Bison Habitat on the East Polish Border.

Policing game parks and nature reserves in the huge areas vacated by most of their inhabitants, except the newcomers in the Sun Cities, of course, as well as stage-managing festivals and multi-arena shows, sporting events and a World Exhibition, requires multinational forces. This once again undermines the state monopoly on the use of legitimate force. In this respect though, what finally did it were the Asymmetric Wars. What this title denoted were turf battles and outright rebellions in public-housing estates, as well as the protracted struggle to strangle the trade in drugs, arms and women, including the raid in the Netherlands Antilles against smugglers of near-extinct plants from the Amazon Basin used for cancer treatment. The large-scale humanitarian interventions in the Transnistria[10] and Donjets Republics and in Kurdistan were also described with this, perhaps unfortunate,[11] term as the Asymmetric Wars.

The engagements had in common the fact that they required new types of forces, not less well trained than existing ones, but with different skills, including multicultural intelligence and communication (no need to remind the reader that the Babel Fish was developed for the use of these forces), medical and other emergency-service skills and, last but not least, training in urban warfare. Special forces might have been up to it,[12] but they were too expensive. Anyhow, there were not enough volunteers, especially not after the troops of a warlord massacred a group of Turkish volunteers from the Federal Republic, the only ones from Germany willing to go to the Caucasus.

Now, the German-Turkish volunteers were not European citizens, yet they had given their lives under the 12 golden stars of Europe! What did this mean? Surely, it was to have an effect on citizenship as conceived in the late eighteenth century in revolutionary France, where '300,000 men were called for, to be conscripted if they would not volunteer, and in August the decree of the *levé en masse*, putting all fit males at the disposal of the Republic, was promulgated'.[13] Since then, conscript armies had been the most pronounced manifestation of the Holy Trinity Nation-State-Territory. By implication, once armies ceased to be national and citizens no longer served in them, something was bound to happen to the concept of citizenship.

This was not immediately realized, nor was the deeper meaning of the emergence of security companies providing 'innovative, flexible training and operational solutions to support security and peace, and freedom and democracy everywhere',[14] naturally for a price. Rather, the immediate effect was the recruitment of volunteers from outside Europe. This only served to widen the gap between traditional and new-style security forces.

Before elaborating, we need to discuss the immediate effect of the tragic events in the Caucasus. It was that the EU had lamely offered membership to Turkey, whose citizens had given their lives for Europe, but it did so only to its European part! Anatolia was given the prospect of full membership in 2040. Meanwhile, it was to become part of the European Economic Area, together with Iceland and Liechtenstein, the only two countries remaining in the EEA after

Norway joined the EU. The result was that the Turks had had enough and withdrew from the association agreement, strangled the EU's lucrative export business and virtually ordered Turkish immigrants back home. Attracted by glowing offers, Turks complied, especially the young and highly educated, thus exacerbating labour shortages in Europe, resulting in our now compulsory 48-hour working week.

Taking advantage of the confusion, disgruntled Ireland left the EU (invoking articles in the Treaty of Lisbon of 2007 vintage which Ireland, as the only member state, had steadfastly refused to ratify). So it was Ireland rather than Turkey that joined the EEA, sending delegates to headquarters in Vaduz in Liechtenstein. Various other member states and, most significantly, regions like Padania and Catalonia followed suit, but whether this was constitutionally possible was hotly debated. Be that as it may, things became messy. In the end, 28 EU members remained, some of them de facto truncated. (This did not apply to Belgium where all three regions remained in the EU, but insisting that, if Padania and Catalonia could do what they wanted, then so could they, each sent its own representative to meetings of the Council of Ministers.)

The UK took an altogether different course. During the commotion, it joined NAFTA, claiming that it was the sovereign right of Parliament in Westminster to do so. Already traumatized, the EU acquiesced and the UK remained a member.

The other effect of the massacre in the Caucasus was even more unexpected, and here we return to the citizenship issue. Posthumously, the Turkish volunteers were declared to have been Europeans. However, to become European citizens, they needed to be German citizens. For Germany, with its large number of Turkish immigrants, this would have created an unwelcome precedent. Leaving for the bathroom in the early hours of the morning, an extremely irate German Chancellor is reputed to have shouted: 'If you want them, why don't you take them?' On the spur of the moment, the heads of state and government created a European citizenship and awarded a hastily prepared certificate to the bedazzled next of kin of the youngest of the seven Turks, who were present, or so they thought, merely to receive the condolences of the Croatian President of the EU.

While they were at it, the heads of state and government reckoned they might just as well solve another, even more burning humanitarian issue. Thousands of unaccompanied and undocumented immigrant children were stuck on Malta, the Canary Islands, Madeira and Lampedusa and the Spanish enclaves on African soil, Ceuta and Mellila. They had arrived by the boatload and, in the case of Ceuta and Mellila, through a network of tunnels during one dramatic night when the Spanish police were busy repulsing a diversionary attempt by hundreds of immigrants to scale the border fence.

The responses of the authorities varied. On Madeira, there were relatively few, and the children were absorbed. In Malta, too, the numbers were manageable thanks to the rapid reaction boat squad of the European joint border guards.[15] Authorities on the Canary Islands corralled the children on one of the smaller islands. To their credit, they looked after them well, putting them up in dysfunctional tourist accommodation.[16] The authorities in Ceuta and Melilla were unable to cope. In all cases, national authorities tried to prevent the children from slipping through to the mainland.

Now, there had been much debate about these children, and so, in an effort at burden-sharing, the heads of state and government (declaring that they were meeting, not as the European Council, but as the representatives of the member states) decided to treat the stranded young people as Children of Europe. After completing their education, for which the EU would share the costs, they would become European citizens.

In this way, the concept of European citizenship became soft. This made it possible to solve an altogether different problem, recruitment for the all-European voluntary force to equip the ESDP with teeth. As the reader is aware, ESDP stands for European Security and Defence Policy. The solution has already been touched upon: recruits from all over the world, male and female, are now accepted. They have the prospect of receiving one of the new European passports after three years of service and the certainty that their dependants would be granted such a passport in the event that they become casualties.[17] Recruiting agencies worked overtime to screen applicants, less than 5 per cent of whom were admitted, but under the rigorous control of the Antidiscrimination League, the composition of the force was such that not even the Cosmopolitan Party could complain. The reverse side of the coin is that many parts of the world are now deprived of the most enterprising and physically and mentally fit doctors, computer scientists, civil engineers, nurses and midwives, as well as professional officers. Even the National Health Service in the UK, recruiting personnel worldwide as it does, feels the pinch. Once a citizen, the recruits may sign on for another term, with some of them becoming officers, a rank reserved for bearers of European passports.

Having thus been stripped of their most important function, supplying troops for ESDP actions, national armies have become part-time national guards or auxiliary policy forces. Some demobilized soldiers are joining the ESDP force, but without obtaining preferential treatment. The only exception has been for general officers. A small group of them has been taken on board to work out the military doctrine of 'war among the people'.[18]

The build-up of the force is still going on, but within 18 months, the first contingent of all-European volunteers (AEVs, pronounce like in aaivees) joined in battle with the warlord whose troops had butchered the Turkish volunteers, delivering him to the European Court in chains, thus proving that a well-trained and well-led multinational force can give an account of itself.[19] After three years, the first AEVs from outside Europe duly received European passports. This was the first such occasion after the posthumous award of improvised documents to the Turkish volunteers and the award of several dozen passports to the first classes of graduates from the schools set up for the Children of Europe. The effect of this widely publicized event, with a military parade and the singing of the European anthem, was unexpected: European civil servants, the offspring of the numerous mixed marriages,[20] Dutch *pensionados* around the Mediterranean who under Dutch law had to pay Dutch health insurance without receiving Dutch benefits, as well as thousands of other migrants decided that a European passport proper was for them.

While politicians were still considering the implications, northern Cyprus became a hotspot.[21] Turkey reimposed its ban on Cypriot ships calling at Turkish ports. Now, it had taken much arm-twisting for the Greek Cypriots to effectuate EU membership in northern Cyprus. No sooner was the embargo announced, than Greek Cypriots vented their anger on Turkish families occupying premises that their forebears had been forced to vacate in 1974. ESDP forces were sent in to try to restore peace. They painted the contested properties blue and put them under their protection. However, their inhabitants were constrained to stay in their homes. Their Cypriot identity cards gave them away as Turks. The Macedonian Human Rights Commissioner came up with the idea of giving them European passports. However, there were not enough of the expensive documents laden with computer chips available, so European driving licences were accepted as proof of European citizenship.

Ethnic Russians discriminated against in the Baltic States quickly latched on to this. Padanians wanting to leave Italy started burning their Italian passports and waving their driving licences as proof of European identity. An unforeseen effect of driving licences being accepted in lieu of passports was that immigrants with driving licences were all of a sudden on *a par* with European citizens. In this haphazard manner, millions of functional Europeans were created. Various NGOs pointed out quickly that persons less than 18 years old did not have driving licences. A non-driving version of the driving licence was produced. It became known as the 'Blue Card'.[22]

The final act was when the population of Kaliningrad Oblast were issued the Blue Card as proof of identity.[23] There had been Russian hints that unless travel from Kaliningrad to Russia were to be finally freed from restrictions, gas deliveries might be diverted. What the Russian authorities did not foresee was that issuing Blue Cards to Kaliningrad residents virtually amounted to their absorption in the EU. There were even Russians moving to Kaliningrad to obtain them. By the time the Russian authorities realized that citizens were voting for Europe with their feet, it was too late. There were presidential elections in the offing, and the incumbent did not want to jeopardize her chances.

The softening of European citizenship, or, as the Cosmopolitan Party was quick to point out, the creation of a new type of inclusive citizenship, triggered a wide-ranging discussion about the meaning of the nation-state and its sovereign control over its citizens and territory. A case brought before the European Court of Justice by a Irish citizen added fuel to the debate. Her lawyers argued that, although citizenship may be granted at the pleasure of state authorities, in renouncing her European citizenship without her consent the Irish government had violated her human rights. European law takes precedence over national law, and, indeed, the European Court of Justice is the highest court in the land, so this is fair and proper. However, where does this leave nation-states? The same may be asked about cosmopolitan AEVs rather than European citizens serving in the forces protecting them. Control over territory, too, is in fact exercised on various levels above and below that of the nation-states of old, and labour markets and schools and universities and theatres and orchestras and, above all, football teams are self-evidently trans-territorial.

In the past, the conventional wisdom has been that in the fullness of time the EU would fill the position of the nation-states, but in the meantime the EU has become weaker. Surprisingly, this does not seem to make much difference. For certain purposes, the EEA suffices. The UK is content with dual membership in the EU and NAFTA, providing interesting business openings for other European countries as well. There are other arrangements, such as the Mediterranean Union, also called the Barcelona Space, after the Barcelona Process,[24] under which citizens from around the Mediterranean enjoy controlled access to the European labour market, starved as it is of fresh blood. As if this still mattered in the age of Babel Fish, France is delighted that this makes French into the first language of the wider integrated market.

There are also downsides. There is much anxiety, in particular amongst the older generation and/or the less well-educated classes possessing only the dysfunctional skills of an industrial age, an anxiety exacerbated by the complexity of governance and administration and life in general. Finding out where to turn in obtaining benefits, registering complaints, voicing opinions and, more generally, participating in decision-making can sometimes be a nightmare. The EurAsian Federalists (EAF) know the solution: a EurAsian Government, but with neither Russia nor China likely to join, they cannot say where their EurAsia ends. The UK does not even bother to denounce the idea as implying a superstate.

Regular meetings, such as the one covered in this report, of PEACE, the **P**an-**E**ur**A**sian **C**ouncil for the **E**conomy, act as an expedient in coping with this confusion. Membership is open. Not only nation-states, but also networks of regions and non-state actors can join. Nor are any geographic boundaries drawn. The whole of the Barcelona Space including its North African members participates, and so does Greenland, without bothering to reverse its decision of many decades ago to leave the European Community. (With global warming, Greenland has become a favourite tourist destination, but is still far from green.) South Africa has observer status, although, since no binding votes are taken, there is little difference between observer status and the status of members. City regions, especially those with a cross-border character, like Basel-Mulhouse, the Øresund Region and Helsinki-Tallinn-Petersburg send delegations, as well as regions with an axe to grind with one or more nation-states, like Catalonia, North and South Tyrol and Padania.

As indicated, the only obligation, and this is an obligation of delegates, not of whoever sends them, is to come to a resolution on at least two-thirds of the issues on the table of the meetings in which they participate. If they fail to do so, cuts to their rations have been suggested, but this has not so far been necessary.

For the purpose of preparing delegates, ad hoc coalitions are formed. Consultants make good business in producing briefing notes. All this material provides a great deal of intelligence and is in the public domain.

Open membership seems natural, the more so since PEACE resolutions are not binding. The force they only carry in moral. Whether PEACE will ever go beyond deliberation and become formalized, and if so how, is the subject of debate among scholars, but the EurAsian Federalists aside, there has so far been little interest in the matter. (The campaign by the 10,000 Friends of EurAsia, about which more below, may change this.)

This brings us back to Odessa. Having awarded the prize to our young Azerbaijani and eaten their dinner, there were many toasts, among others to the birthday of Confucius so as to please the Chinese guests, and delegates settled down the next day to discuss items of great importance. The dealings in the decision room are not public. Calls for transparency have long been silenced by the realization that to let delegates debate in public increases the chances of a stalemate.[25] So the rules of the conclave are strict and leaks lead to ostracism.

The proposal to upgrade energy networks to Trans EurAsian Corridors (TEACs) figured on the agenda.[26] Rival proposals are an Arctic Motorway of the Sea (AMS) and the Northwest Passage. All have in common the fact that they provide an answer to the menace to shipping of state-sponsored piracy between East Asia and Europe. Also on the agenda is the proposal for a welfare-and-work programme to avoid repetition of uprisings in public-housing estates.

Of course, the proposal of upgrading the energy and transportation networks spanning the Eurasian continent draws on the successful example of the Trans-Texas Corridor Network.[27] The idea is to combine dedicated highways, both for passenger vehicles and trucks, in particular, with high-speed passenger and freight rail. The corridors will also have utility zones. To give added benefit to the infrastructure, there will be brain ports with clusters of institutes of techno-logy, turning the TEACs into veritable Corridors of Innovation and Cooperation (COINCOs).[28]

As the briefing notes point out, there are plenty of things to consider. Action groups have argued that the last remaining herds of the Bakhtrian camel in the Gobi Desert would become extinct, and this has become an emblematic issue, with the public still smarting from the extinction of the Siberian tiger. Nor is it clear whether the water resources of Central Asia could sustain the effort. Would huge desalination plants on the shores of the Black Sea and pipelines taking the water across the expanses of Central Asia be enough? (There is very little chance that the Soviet-era plan of reversing the flow of Siberian rivers will be revived. Russia would never contemplate this, pointing to the huge ecological con-sequences.) To sort out water management, cooperation would be essential. The same is true for the planning, development and operation of the TEACs.

What the briefing notes do not tell you, but what is certain to be on the mind of European delegates, is that Central Asia lacks a tradition of cooperation. Also, the TEACs would strengthen still further the Central Asian republics, immensely rich as they are, with the notable exception of Kyrgyzstan. Unfortunately, these republics seem to be genetically unfit to form a common position. Thus, in exchange for the use of air bases, US forces are allowed into Uzbekistan. Tajikistan has been drawn into the Pakistan-Afghan orbit. In Turkmenistan, there is a European presence, with projects and programmes shining like beacons across the Iranian border. Kazakhstan alone has been able to stave off any foreign interference. Las Vegas East, fittingly located in the desert – with a 'Love City' as a unique selling point – forms the core of a casino economy run by the third-generation descendants of the nomenclatura of old.

The former Soviet republics have played off their major customers for oil and gas against each other: China, Vietnam, the Indian subcontinent, the US and Europe, while also succeeding in keeping Russia at bay, but none of this augurs particularly well for the TEACs. Nevertheless, a forceful position paper claims that there is no alternative. The emergence of state-sponsored piracy, involving old and new, large and small island states, some of them in an apocalyptic mood as a result of the acute threat from rising sea levels, has virtually strangled maritime trade via the usual route from Southeast Asia to Europe. The United States Pacific Command (USPACOM)[29] and the Chinese People's Liberation Army Navy (PLAN)[30] are too busy shadowing each other to be able to confront this menace, and, although the protection of maritime trade is one of their agreed tasks, the Japanese Maritime Self-Defence Forces (MSDF)[31] are reluctant to return to areas where they were during the Second World War. More to the point, neither aircraft-carrier groups nor nuclear submarine fleets have been designed to deal with bazookas being fired from nimble sailing vessels, dugout canoes, or fibreglass speedboats for that matter, yet such bazookas have sunk container ships! Re-routing convoys to the Roaring Forties along the Clipper Route[32] has been the, exceedingly costly, alternative to the direct route via the US, utilizing transcontinental corridors that are getting, however, increasingly clogged.

The alternative is the Arctic Motorway of the Sea.[33] Navigation of the short northern route from Europe to East Asia is now within reach. However, this would imply reliance on a fleet of Russian nuclear icebreakers, the only ones up to the job of keeping the AMS open in the winter. The PEACE meeting might disregard massive protest from environmentalists against the comeback of nuclear technology, but there are other concerns. Naturally, quite apart from the service that its icebreakers would render, Russia would be a major player. It would have to provide logistic support and standby rescue services. Also, there is the uncomfortable truth that at the drop of a hat Russia could strangle traffic on the AMS. There is not the slightest indication that the President, another honoured guest at Odessa, is contemplating such a move. However, she has been asking, not only for the logistic infrastructure to be financed out of a toll to be levied on the use of what she describes as Russian waters, but also for massive investment in the building of port facilities along the Siberian coast. The future of Russia is in Siberia, an immense, resource-rich expanse. With global warming, Siberia is ripe for development, or at least this is what her electoral and foreign-policy plank says. (She has never answered the question of where the people should come from. Russia's population is still in decline, and to make things worse, Russia still operates a strict anti-immigration policy.)

As if two alternatives, the TEACs and the AMS, were not enough, NATO has tabled another, the Northwest Passage, also called the Amundsen Option in honour of another epic voyage of the first man to reach the South Pole in 1903–6 proving that this extremely important geostrategic maritime route is feasible.[34] There is the problem of the shortage of icebreakers, but a crash-building pro-gramme (taking advantage of spare capacity in the US industrial-military complex) could solve this issue. The Atlanticists are enthusiastic, seeing oppor-tunities for a revival of the almost defunct alliance with the US. To make this seem even more attractive, upon taking office President Clinton has vowed to reopen the US to the world.

Needless to say, the Amundsen Option has its opponents. Since they are always talking about the Eurasian heartland, they are called 'Heartlanders'. Their arguments are the mirror-image of those of the Atlanticists. They point out that diminishing American commitment in Europe has been a blessing in disguise in that it has forced Europe to look, not just to East, South East and South, but also to Central Asia. They will tell you that US and Canadian (Canada is of course in on this) strategic leverage over trade between Europe and East Asia is fraught with as much danger as Russian leverage is. Behind closed doors, they will tell you that Europe's huge debt to Russia for natural gas and oil deliveries is making Russia far too concerned with European economic growth to allow for any adventurism. No such 'symbiotic' relation exists with the US.

Nobody expects Odessa to come to a definite conclusion. (Remember that delegates are only obliged to come to a resolution, not a solution to the problem.) Nor, once again, does it have the power to make decisions. And, even if it had that power, PEACE has no means to implement decisions. Instead, there are always international energy consortia, logistics conglomerates and huge engin-eering firms backed by venture capitalists as well as governments willing to work out the plans.

In this respect, the Amundsen Option looks distinctly the weakest of the three, but Chelsea Clinton's representative may still give it a boost. He may promise that she will put before Congress a law giving a tax break to investors in Arctic technology, a measure that is sure to raise interest among US venture capitalists. Be that as it may, the advisors of the PEACE Presidency with their penchant for compromise, deeply engrained in their culture from the days when they were still serving at Brussels, may suggest a scaled down version of the TEACs in combination with the AMS as the most robust strategy.

This is not where the worries of the delegates end. There is another serious matter on the table. A consortium of NGOs and some national and subnational gov-ernments in cahoots with the ESDP general staff have drawn attention to the danger of another eruption of the Asymmetric Wars. Some of the warlords have, of course, been brought to justice and others have become part of the establishment. Flash-points in the Western Balkans, the Caucasus and around the Mediterranean have been eliminated. However, there are persistent pockets of unrest in many impover-ished areas in industrial decline. In these pockets, the dysfunctional working class of an industrial past mingles with an even more frustrated lower-middle class in decline, both in competition with immigrants. Many, but not all immigrant com-munities have done remarkably well, in particular the better educated for whom management and administration have furnished avenues of upward social mobility. Even the less well-educated are benefiting from persistent labour shortages in the service industry, including the event economy with its extreme fluctuations in demand for labour. Still, immigrants often continue to be constrained to living in dilapidated public housing disparagingly called WELSTAT.[35]

We now know that the troubles of the 2000s in the French *banlieves*, with hundreds of cars going up in flames, were child's play in comparison with the *Plattenbauten* Wars in the former German Democratic Republic, which in turn triggered the rebellion in the factory workers' new town Nova Hutta, with large-scale unrest in housing estates all over Central and Eastern Europe in its wake. (Glasgow congratulated itself for having demolished the poorly designed Queen Elizabeth Square flats in the Gorbals in 1993, a process of restructuring that continued into the 2000s.)

ESDP forces have been able to cope with any outbreak of new unrest so far, but there has been very little social and economic follow-up. The millions still living in WELSTAT, especially in Central and Eastern Europe, continue to form an explosive mixture. The ESDP general staff argue that, unless urgent action is taken, another urban guerrilla war looms on the horizon. They are reluctant to see ESDP units face European Supremacists, Urban Survivalists, Yellow Foxes and Underground Rogues operating behind the shield of disenchanted masses going on the rampage. They add force to their argument, saying that, if there were attacks on one or more China Towns, a renewal of the Asymmetric Wars could take on geo-strategic proportions.

The proposal is to start social and educational and, in particular, work programmes, but nobody really knows how. Experience in administering such programmes has been allowed to dissipate. Anyhow, the Liberal Party (also called the Thatcher Guys and Gals, after the legendary Mrs Thatcher) is massively opposed. Pointing, among other examples, to the Structural Funds of the EU, they argue that such programmes have been tried before, but without success. In fact, they have been counterproductive, making whole groups, towns, cities and even regions dependent on handouts. They add, in no uncertain terms, pointing to the fact that the source of trouble was the former public-housing estates, that WELSTAT represents the problem rather than the solution. Rather than promoting a dependence culture, the solution is more economic growth until even the last remaining pockets of poverty have been drowned in the wealth trickling down onto them. However, even if a WELSTAT-type programme were appropriate, PEACE is about the economy and has no business in redistributive policies.

Realistically speaking, there is little chance of a welfare programme on the requisite scale becoming reality. Huge sums of money would be needed, which PEACE does not have. And, operating a welfare-and-works programme would require an apparatus, which PEACE does not have either. Nor is there anybody who wants a return to bureaucratic rule. In fact, as the Thatcher Guys and Gals rightly point out, the programme would require PEACE to change into something like a state, an unlikely scenario. Unfortunately, it is also inconceivable that a private consortium will come forward to do the job.

Maybe, though, an ad hoc coalition of existing states will pick up the gauntlet. States are on the defensive. As emphasized before, states have lost their exclusive control over their people, their territories and armies. Maybe by combining their forces, and their taxes, states can regain the moral high ground by engaging in forward-looking social and territorial policies. Maybe they will also regain some of the loyalty and commitment, never completely lost, of their citizens. Maybe, saying that we need to return to something like the ESDP of the 1990s, an argument that he was prevented from delivering to the PEACE delegates, the young Azerbaijani has a point. Maybe we need to reevaluate the EU of old.

Clearly, there are too many 'ifs' and 'buts' to make this into a realistic prospect, but this is what yours truly discovered when he talked to the young Azerbaijani: the 10,000 Friends of EurAsia argue that states need to be brought back into the equation, that government needs to be factored into governance. I doubt whether they understand all the implications, but I would finally like to share with the reader my sense that our 10,000 Friends are on to something.

At least our Azerbaijani made some sense. He was well aware that the Holy Trinity will never come back, that it was the product of specific historic circumstances with its apotheosis, and its undoing, in the twentieth century. So he distanced himself from the daydreams of the EurAsian Federalists, pointing out at the same time though that some distribution was necessary, and that there needed to be something like a framework, if for no other reason than for giving policymakers a sense of direction. He agreed with me that such a framework could never be legislated. In fact, he seemed to think that the framework would be of the nature of a fleeting agreement, the temporal outcome of many inputs, and subject to many interpretations.

I was confused, but quizzed him further, asking what kind of arrangement the 10,000 had in mind. He was saying something about an inclusive Union of EurAsian Unions. I also asked about the proposed EurAsian Spatial Development Perspective. He became very enthusiastic, saying that the EASDP would not be a document but rather an arena for discussing many alternative visions of the spatial or territorial main structure of EurAsia, as well as the spatial or territorial policies proposed by the actors involved and whether they would have a positive or negative, as the case may be, impact on each other and on any of the prevailing visions. He claimed that this was the only way in which responsible decisions, such as decisions on the weighty issues before the PEACE meeting, could be taken.

Sufficiently impressed, I asked for the actual number of members of the 10,000 Friends. With a twinkle in his eye, he said that the name was programmatic and that there was room for me to join. I was taken by surprise and paid my lifelong membership in dinars, which I still had from when World Wide Newscast (whisper W-W-N into your Babel Fish, and you are connected to the world) was still reporting from the Gulf. I hope my employer will reimburse me in convertible euros.

Sunday 092831 2300 Zulu Time[36] (Monday 092931 0100 in Odessa – time to sign off).

Postscript

With his promise that over the next 25 years he will comment on developments since his retirement, Klaus Kunzmann has dictated the date of PEACE: 29–30 September 2031. The venue, Odessa, should encourage the reader to ask whether the Ukraine will be a member of the EU. However, this assumption is immediately thrown into doubt: PEACE is not an EU formation.

PEACE itself is, of course, a teaser. It is not about peace nor about Europe but about the economy and EurAsia. (The capitalization of Asia is meant to take away the condescending element in the usual spelling of Eurasia.)

Initially, there is ambiguity over whether there is still an EU, but the reader learns later that there is, albeit with a reduced membership: after several member states have left, an EU 28 remain. The reader may of course guess which these are, but neither Turkey nor, indeed, Ireland belong to the EU.

The other teaser is the ESDP. The reader learns that the acronym stands for something very dear to Azerbaijanis, and at the same time something that collects dust on the shelves. Only later does the reader learn that ESDP also stands for European Security and Defence Policy.

The concerns that I wanted to express throughout are those on the nature of the EU, conventionally discussed in terms of federalism/supranationalism or intergovernmentalism. Occasionally, there is talk about the EU being a formation *sui generis*, and one for which we still lack the categories in which to think about it. Related issues are the future of the nation-state and of citizenship, with side glances at the 'Europe of the regions'.

What also feeds into the scenario is an abiding interest in military history and geo-strategic thinking. One need not be militaristic to agree that the privatization and/or cosmopolitanization of the military (both responses to the difficulties of recruitment from the standard sources of military capacity, the citizenry of nation-states that the military is called upon to defend) has repercussions for the Holy Trinity Nation-State-Territory.

In writing the scenario, a decision had to be made on whether to address issues in the news, such as the war on terror and the 'clash of civilizations', Iraq, the Middle East conflict in general and the Israeli situation in particular. The conclusion was negative. The scenario simply assumes that the 'Barcelona Space', embracing all countries around the Mediterranean, had been pacified.

This chapter does not represent the outcome of any type of systematic scenario building. A literary form, the well-trodden path of writing about a fictitious future event and its context, was chosen instead. The informal dinner before the PEACE meeting, and a handful of actors involved: the reporter, the Azerbaijani planning academic and the President of PEACE, provided the occasion. The chapter conveys a sense also of the role of incidents and random elements in policy-making, so the reader is treated to an array of more or less likely, but nevertheless believable events that turn out to be decisive, like the coming of Lord Blair of Basra to attend the dinner, the slaughter of Turkish volunteers in the Caucasus, the Turkish anger about admission being offered only to its European part and its ripple effects from northern Cyprus to Kaliningrad.

Another problem was not to give offence. There is no 'axis of evil', and where the state-sponsored piracy comes from is left to the reader's imagination. Russia is not aggressive, and China is nothing like a menace. Extra-territorial China Towns just happen, simply because of the well-known fact that Chinese communities abroad are self-reliant.

Writing scenarios is certainly no sinecure. At the same time, it is a process in which your boyhood dreams, your abiding interests and your predilections play a role, as much as the latest news, at that time, from the Canary Islands about refugees stranded there.

Oh, yes, writing 'PEACE at Odessa' has been fun: It was fun to think about teasers, and it was tantalizing to be able to play God: the story could be given any twist that the author wanted.

During the discussion, John Friedmann commented on the sense of doom about Europe, not only in this scenario, but in other papers as well, including the brilliant one by Philippe Doucet (see Chapter 17 in this volume). Maybe this is a true reflection of the situation of Europe, but it is quite unlike the present author to be pessimistic! Most of the time he operates as a one-man pressure group for European spatial planning, pointing out signs of progress and of learning wherever he can find them. Indeed, the reader may have expected quite a different scenario, which is why the story of PEACE at Odessa is on this count ambiguous, to say the least, but note that the 10,000 Friends of EurAsia are optimists.

Delft, 30 March 2007

Acknowledgement

Thanks are due to Klaus Kunzmann for challenging me to go beyond my usual limits, and to Vincent Nadin, at the time my roommate, for encouraging me to go down the path that I have chosen. Raya, my wife, and Daan van Eijck, my son-in-law, have lent a sympathetic ear to urgent requests for attention to the latest ideas coming into my mind.

Notes

1 See www.tudelft.nl/live/pagina.jsp?id=4b3e55d0–1a34–4388-b3ca-acbe48c87696& lang=en. (accessed 23 September 2008).
2 A glimpse at the role of private security firms in Iraq is given by Collins (2005). See also www.aegisworld.com. Another example is Blackwater, claiming to be the most comprehensive professional military, law enforcement, security, peacekeeping, and stability operations company in the world. 'We have established a global presence and provide training and operational solutions for the twenty-first century in support of security and peace, and freedom and democracy everywhere,' says their website (www.blackwaterusa.com).
3 Simon Tilford (2006), head of the business unit at the Centre for European Reform, argues that unless the members rapidly boost their reform efforts, and unless

economic growth across the eurozone accelerates, EMU faces a bleak future. What happens in Italy will be critical.

4 'The Babel fish', said the Hitch Hiker's Guide to the Galaxy quietly,

> is small, yellow and leech-like, and probably the oddest thing in the Universe. It feeds on brainwave energy received not from its own carrier but from those around it. It absorbs all unconscious mental frequencies from this brainwave energy to nourish itself with. It then excretes into the mind of its carrier a tele-pathic matrix formed by combining the conscious through frequencies with nerve signals picked up from the speech centres of the brain which has supplied them. The practical upshot of all this is that if you stick a Babel fish in your ear you can instantly understand anything said to you in any form of language....
>
> (Adams 1979: 49f.)

This must have inspired Altavista to name their translation tool Babel Fish. See http://babelfish.altavista.com/tr (accessed 23 September 2008).

5 1,000 Friends of Oregon is a non-profit advocacy, education and research organization involved in issues of land use and planning. See www.friends.org (accessed 23 September 2008).

6 On theme parks as a perspective for Europe see Kunzmann (1996).

7 On the concept of supraterritoriality see Scholte 2000: 48ff.

8 Readers familiar with Dutch can consult number 3 of volume 2006 of *Ruimte in Debat* (Debating Space), the two-monthly periodical of the Netherlands Institute for Spatial Research (Ruimtelijk Planbureau, RPB). See www.ruimtemonitor.nl/upload/documenten/RID_2006_03_kleur.pdf (accessed 23 September 2008).

9 On Sun Cities, in particular in Germany, see Einzenhöfer and Link (2005).

10 On 17 September 2006, the people of this unrecognized Moldavian Republic that is mainly inhabited by Ukrainians and Russians voted in a referendum in favour of independence – with the aim of subsequently joining the Russian Federation.

11 Introducing the concept of 'war amongst the people', Smith (2005: 4) points out that labelling wars as asymmetric is a euphemism 'to avoid acknowledging that my opponent is not playing to my strengths and I am not winning. In which case, perhaps the model of war rather than its name is no longer relevant: the paradigm has changed.'

12 For American forces in general and Special Operations Forces around the world in particular see Kaplan (2005).

13 See Keegan (1993: 350).

14 See the Website of Blackwater: www.blackwaterusa.com/about/ (accessed 23 September 2008).

15 The EU has launched its first joint border patrol aimed at stopping illegal immigrants coming to the Canary Islands from Africa in 2006. According to the *Malta Times*, there was a prospect of a similar operation being launched from Malta. See www.timesofmalta.com/core/article.php?id=233645 (accessed 30 March 2007).

16 On 10 September 2006, the BBC reported that there are already fears that immigration will negatively affect the vast tourist trade on the Canary Islands. See http://news.bbc.co.uk/2/hi/europe/5332162.stm (accessed 23 September 2008).

17 A documentary shown on the third Dutch TV channel on 24 August 2006 was about the first US soldier to die in Iraq, José Antonio Gutierrez from Guatemala, one of 40,000 'green card soldiers'. CNN put a different spin on this, but the facts of the matter remain:

> Lance Cpl. Jose Antonio Gutierrez, 22, an orphan who grew up on the streets of Guatemala City, made the perilous border crossing through Mexico and entered the U.S. illegally when he was 14, his family said. He was later granted legal resident status and went to high school and college in California before joining the

Marines in March 2002. Only a year in the service, Gutierrez died March 21 in a firefight near the Iraqi port city of Umm Qasr. 'He has been given many opportunities since coming here and he wanted to give back a little bit to his adopted country,' said Nora Mosquera, Gutierrez's foster mother. The lanky youth dreamed of becoming an architect and bringing his sister, Engracia Sirin Gutierrez, from Guatemala. The sister visited Southern California in time to meet Gutierrez's flag-draped casket at the entrance of St. Margaret Mary Catholic Church April 7. Now she's hoping for permission to live in the United States. 'I do feel proud, because not just anyone gives up their life for another country,' she told reporters at a news conference recently. 'But at the same time it makes me sad because he fought for something that wasn't his.' Cardinal Roger Mahony told the standing-room-only crowd at Gutierrez's mass that they were honoring 'a great man' and an American citizen. Gutierrez was awarded his U.S. citizenship posthumously.

> (www.cnn.com/SPECIALS/2003/iraq/heroes/jose.gutierrez.html (accessed 23 September 2008))

18 The basic point is that

> the people are not the enemy. The enemy is amongst the people, and the purpose of any use of military force and other power is to differentiate between the enemy and the people, and to win the latter over to you, which leads to a further point about the approach. In deciding the method of operation, once one has gained initial entry, the primary purpose must be the acquisition of information so as to identify the true target from amongst the people, to understand the context in which the target is operating, and to be able to exploit a successful attack upon that target. This means that in all but a few cases the deployment of forces ... is to result in the collection of information and in support of the other levers of power: it is they that can exploit the successful tactical action.
>
> (Smith 2005: 397)

19 When Tim Collins, author of *Rules of Engagement: A Life in Conflict* took over as commanding officer of his regime – a position that he would also occupy when in 2003 his UK troops went into Iraq – there were no less than 19 nationalities present, including an Iranian:

> Muslims and a Jewish officer serving in the same company, and one of my South African lads, brought up in the Orange Free State and speaking English as a second language, shared a room with three Fijians. We even had two Gypsies from families at daggers drawn, and that rivalry too was left at home.
>
> (Collins 2005: 26)

20 Approximately 16 per cent of the 2.2 million marriages and 875,000 divorces per year in the EU are of international character; see www.euractiv.com/en/justice/ commission-looks-halt-divorce-shopping/article-156838 (accessed 23 September 2008).

21 For an analysis of the Cyprus conundrum and the obvious link with Turkish accession see Hannay (2006).

22 A proposal to introduce a Blue Card for immigrants with specific skills selected on the basis of a points system and to give these immigrants access to the whole European market has been made by Jakob von Weizsäcker: 'A European blue card proposal'. See www.strategie.gouv.fr/revue/article.php3?id_article=52 (accessed 23 September 2008).

23 On the complex situation in and around Kaliningrad see http://ec.europa.eu/comm/ external_relations/north_dim/kalin/index.htm (accessed 23 September 2008).

24 Since 1 May 2004, the Euro-Mediterranean Partnership comprises 35 members, 25 EU member states and 10 Mediterranean partners (Algeria, Egypt, Israel, Jordan, Lebanon, Morocco, Palestinian Authority, Syria, Tunisia and Turkey). Libya has had observer status since 1999. (http://ec.europa.eu/comm/external_relations/euromed/index.htm; accessed 23 September 2008).

25 'If negotiators are subject to control by external institutions ... they tend to rely on bargaining instead of arguing, and they fight harder for their constituents than for a joint policy...' (Benz 2002: 146).

26 A meeting of ASEAN and EU representatives at Helsinki discussed reviving the Silk Route on 10 September 2006. For further details see www.cafebabel.com/en/article. asp?T=A&Id=2004 (accessed 23 September 2008).

27 See www.keeptexasmoving.com/index.php/ttc (accessed 8 October 2007).

28 The term has been used by Per Horman Jespersen reporting on an INTERREG Project. See http://sally.ruc.dk/site/research/jespersen_per_homann(5256)|publications (accessed 23 September 2008).

29 See www.pacom.mil/ (accessed 23 September 2008).

30 See www.sinodefence.com/navy/default.asp (accessed 23 September 2008).

31 See www.jda.go.jp/e/index_.htm (accessed 30 March 2007).

32 See www.pizzacomodor.plus.com/pages/PAGE2.HTM (accessed 23 September 2008).

33 For the concept of Motorways of the Sea as adopted in the Transport White Paper of 2001 and developed at a ministerial conference in January 2006, see http://ec.europa. eu/transport/intermodality/motorways_sea/index_en.htm (accessed 23 September 2008).

34 See www.babouche-expe.eu/enwp.html (accessed 23 September 2008).

35 Professor Tom Blair coined the term in the early 1970s, when he divided the British housing market into three separate categories: the POD (Property-Owning Democracy), WELSTAT (the public-housing estates), and the PITs (Poor Insecure Tenants).

36 American military at major air bases around the world use Zulu time so as to facilitate the coordination of air assets. See Kaplan 2005: 197. For practical purposes, it is the same as Greenwich Mean Time. See also http://en.wikipedia.org/wiki/Zulu_time (accessed 23 September 2008).

References

Adams, D. (1979) *The Hitch Hiker's Guide to the Galaxy*, London: Pan Books.

Benz, A. (2002) 'How to Reduce the Burden of Coordination in European Spatial Planning', in A. Faludi (ed.) *European Spatial Planning*, Cambridge, MA: Lincoln Institute of Land Policy.

Collins, T. (2005) *Rules of Engagement: A Life in Conflict*, London: Headline Book Publishing.

Einzenhöfer, R. and Link, A. (2005) 'Sun City in Deutschland – ein seniorenspezifisches Wohnmodell mit Zukunft', *Materialen zur Regionalentwicklung und Raumordnung* Band 14, Kaiserslautern: Selbstverlag Regionalentwicklung und Raumordnung, Technische Universität Kaiserslautern.

Hannay, D. (2006) *Cyprus, Turkey and the EU: Time for a Sense of Proportion and Compromise*, London: Centre for European Reform Policy Brief, available at www.cer.org. uk/pdf/policybrief_cyprus_hannay_july06.pdf (accessed 23 September 2008).

Kaplan, R. A. (2005) *Imperial Grunts: The American Military on the Ground*, New York: Random House.

Keegan, J. (1993) *A History of Warfare*, New York: Alfred A. Knopf.

Kunzmann, K. R. (1996) 'Euro-megalopolis or Theme Park Europe? – Scenarios for European Spatial Development', *International Planning Studies* 1(2): 143–63.

Scholte, J. A. (2000) *Globalization: A Critical Introduction*, London: Macmillan Press.

Smith, Sir R. (2005) *The Utility of Force: The Art of War in the Modern World*, London: Allen Lane.

Tilford, S. (2006) *Will the Eurozone Crack?*, available at www.cer.org.uk/publications_new/688.html (accessed 23 September 2008).

15 China's ascension and European cities in 2040

A scenario

Marco Keiner

Introduction

The tremendous transitions going on in China since the Deng reforms in the 1980s are not only fundamentally changing the country itself, but will also have a global impact. Today, despite the price of oil and the scarcity of other raw materials, there is no clear sign that the rise of China as an economic superpower will come to any halt in the near future.

In this chapter, we sketch a gloomy 'doom' scenario on how cities in Europe can benefit in the short term, but may in the long term suffer tremendously from China's current and future economic success story. The time horizon for our adventurous projection is the year 2040. Our hypothesis for the following scenario is that over the next several decades economic growth in China will continue, thus affecting European cities much more and in different ways than today. Scenarios do not predict what will be. They mainly serve as models for thinking about possible futures. Therefore, scenarios may be extreme. To build an extreme scenario, we did not take possible discontinuities, such as war, heavy pandemics, etc., into account. Also, we did not consider economic reactions when the balance of trade changes, such as increased tariffs and barriers for trade. In our simplified scenario, the national frontiers for imports and exports are as open as they are today, and moreover, we did not consider the impact of changing currency-exchange rates between the yuan and the euro.

The scenario is narrative, looking back from a 2040 perspective, the Chinese year of the monkey, the 100th anniversary of the birth of John Lennon, the year when royalty was finally abolished in Great Britain, and the first evacuations of Pacific Islands due to rising sea levels started.

First, we try to sketch out China's increasingly important role in the world of tomorrow and then show possible reasons for its ascension. Second, we imagine the impact on European cities in 2040. Finally, we conclude that in addition to our doom scenario, positive scenarios and related actions are needed in order to maintain the quality of life in Europe's cities.

China's role in 2040

During the last few decades, the influence of China on the global economy has grown rapidly, and in 2040, China finally surpassed the US as the largest economy in the world. In the 2010s, the Chinese economic area, comprising China, Hong Kong and Taiwan, had become the economic hub for the entire Yellow Sea region with real GDP growth rates of 6–10 per cent per annum. The ideal combination of China's still cheap labour and rich natural resources, Hong Kong's intermediation services and Taiwan's capital and managerial know-how have proven to be the key to success. In 2030, after the peaceful unification of these countries, China's share of the world GDP accounted for 12 per cent and has continued to grow since then. Now, in 2040, it stands at 15 per cent. Compared to the year 2000, industrial production in China has more than tripled. Industry's share of the GDP has climbed from 58 per cent in 2000 to almost 70 per cent in 2040, and the GDP ratio of goods exports has increased from 15 per cent in 2000 to 25 per cent in 2040.

What are the reasons for China's growth since 2000? The economic reforms implemented since the 1980s and the opening of trade with foreign investors have led to a huge wave of direct investments and joint ventures. With the ascension of China to the WTO in late 2001, the country has gained full access to the world market. The World Urban Forum in Nanjing, the Olympic Games in Beijing, both in 2008, the World Expo 2010 in Shanghai, the Soccer World Cup in 2022 and many other events have underlined not only the economic but the overall opening of China. More than 50,000 firms in China have been equipped with money and technological and managerial know-how from Europe. Transnational enterprises have relocated enormous numbers of manufacturing jobs to Southeast Asia's low-wage countries. From 2010 to 2030, over 50 per cent of the jobs moving away from Europe went to China. Most of all, highly profitable and well-known companies moved many jobs out of Europe to the frustration of workers' unions.

The country's economy has risen faster than the objectives set by the Chinese leadership. A large number of state-owned enterprises have been privatized or closed as a measure to combat the inflation caused by former massive financial support from the state. Privatization in industrial and service sectors has gained momentum, and the efficiency of state-owned enterprises has largely improved due to better management. The Communist ideology has been overcome by the pragmatic pursuit of economic development, but the rule of the Party has not. An obvious sign for the transition from a largely command economy to a more liberal, market-based regime occurred in 2025 when a proposition was made in a special session in the Standing Committee of the Communist Party to rename the party the Capitalist Party, but was rejected in a 5:4 vote. However, economic liberalism and the obsolete Maoist Marxism–Leninism have not led to more individual freedom. An authoritarian one-party system with a strict control over opposition and the media continues to exist. As long as people are able to earn more money and freely consume goods, the Party's role is not really in danger. Being a member of the Party is necessary in order to advance and join or remain in the oligarchy.

Economic growth has concentrated in the urban agglomerations in the east and south: Hong Kong/Shenzen/Guangzhou, Shanghai/Pearl River Delta, Beijing, Beihai, but also Chongqing. Since 2000, following rapid industrialization, more than 750 million people have moved from rural areas to cities. The number of rural dwellers has decreased to less than 100 million. Today, there are more than 20 agglomerations with more than ten million inhabitants. Beijing and Shanghai are still the largest cities with over 30 million inhabitants each, followed by Chongqing, which has been the fastest growing mega-city over the last three decades worldwide, attracting 20 million new residents. Thus, China's urbanization rate stands at 65 per cent in 2040, compared to only 47 per cent in 2000.

Health conditions in the urban areas have massively deteriorated, and air quality has severely suffered from coal burning, industrial emissions, and gas emissions from the steadily growing number of private cars (over 800 million in 2040). Since 2030, China has become the world's largest CO_2 emitter. The environment has suffered a similar fate: sustainable (environmental) development has been a main target for 35 years but environmental depletion has continued. Many rivers and lakes are dead and large surfaces formerly earmarked for agricultural production have been taken from farmers and transformed into industrial sites.

Since the 2010s, China has seen important social changes. With rapid urbanization and economic growth, the middle class has grown substantially. A large number of young people have been educated at foreign universities. These people are called the 'lucky generation', because they never experienced the strict socialist model of the pre-1978 type. They have grown up with cell phones, computers, McDonald's, Starbucks and the Rolling Stones, and with their competitive salaries, they have been able to afford air conditioners, refrigerators, washing machines, luxury products and cars. They have benefited most from the 'Second Great Leap Forward', which started in 2015. There is also a very wealthy class of private entrepreneurs, with close relations to Party leaders, who have only grown wealthier from China's economic success.

In the rural areas, however, there is still widespread poverty, and the inequality between rich and poor has become wider than ever before. The slogan 'one country, two systems', used to describe China's unique blend of Communism and capitalism, has ironically been changed into 'one country, two classes'. The backwardness of rural areas has persisted, although all the five-year plans since 2005 have proclaimed the improvement of rural living conditions to be a top priority. There are still no property rights for farmers. Due to the broader gap between rural and urban areas and the fact that centralized planning could not maintain its guidance function for economic activity, there have been calls for more autonomy and even political unrest in some of the western provinces, municipalities and autonomous regions, leading to more instability. As regional disparities have increased, maintaining national cohesion has become a problem. From 2015 to 2020, the Army and Secret Intelligence Service successfully suppressed minor uprisings, but massacres like the one in 1989 in Tiananmen Square have not been repeated.

The problems for further economic growth are scarce natural resources, bottlenecks in road-transport infrastructure, and the limited capacity of European and American ports to discharge cargo ships from China. Since the beginning of the twenty-first millennium, the prices for oil, copper, platinum and other raw materials have risen sharply with the growing demand from China. The consumption of oil has more than tripled during the past four decades, from 300 million tons per annum to almost one billion, thus topping the US in 2035. This was possible through the signing of exclusive oil and gas supply deals with Arab, African and Russian companies. However, the price of oil has also led to the development of alternative energy sources, rather than to a more efficient use of energy. The country has begun to exploit its own reserves: ten billion tons of oil have been pumped from the Tarim basin, and, whereas the national coal reserves were around 170 billion tons in 2000, annually increasing energy demand has reduced the number to 90 billion tons in 2040.

Due to the rural exodus in China, and the concentration on manufacturing based on unskilled labour, the country's agricultural production has dropped sharply. In addition, global climate change has increased the temperature in most parts of China by up to 3°C, leading to droughts, stronger erosion and soil depletion fuelled by irregular precipitation and heavy storms, which have destroyed harvests. By 2040, when the first taikonaut set foot on Mars, China has become dependent on food imports. European farmers, mainly in Central and Eastern Europe, but also in Russia behind the Ural Mountains and Kazakhstan, have become important agricultural producers for the Chinese market, along with US farmers. However, although they have increased the productivity and are employing the most sophisticated hi-tech methods and machines, they have not been able to deliver the required quantities, which has led to recurrent food crises felt mainly in the less accessible rural areas of the western part of China. Agricultural structural change in Europe has slowed down considerably: very large farms (500 ha +) still offer employment opportunities, and the share of the primary sector in total GDP has increased. In addition to grains, the Chinese market has experienced an increased demand for tasty, fresh and attractive fruit, even if these are genetically modified. In this context, European fruit farmers have been able to share the market seasonally with their competitors from Latin America and southern Africa.

European economy and cities in 2040

China's leaps in industrialization, its membership in the WTO, along with more available money for the individual, have led to a big demand for technology. European countries and cities have benefited from increased Chinese demand for capital goods and technology-intensive products. To meet increasing energy demands, China has imported hi-tech equipment to increase energy efficiency. Many of these products and technologies have been developed in Europe, such as highly efficient photovoltaic, wind-energy and geothermal installations, as well as fuel-cell cars. In a first phase, from 2005 to 2020, Europe's economy benefited from increased exports of hi-tech machines, coal-loading systems, construction cranes, airplanes and luxury cars to China. Private enterprises engaged in trade with China were able to create more than 100,000 new jobs. Higher sales and income taxes led to increased internal revenues in the cities hosting the enterprises. Smaller cities flourished as well. The European economy recovered from the long economic slump of the 1990s and early 2000s. Up until 2020, China's increasing imports had led to a balance of trade. European cities were able to achieve the targets of the Lisbon Agenda, and cities were able to cover the high costs of unemployment and social care for the long-term unemployed, the elderly and children.

However, from 2020 on, the China boom burst all over Europe as the Chinese economy caught up in terms of producing quality products. Moreover, Chinese firms have continued to copy Western products, thus being able to reproduce the results without paying for the development costs, paying licences or respecting patents. On the other hand, the ageing European population has not been able to maintain its leading role for innovative products. Chinese researchers and developers have gradually taken over. This has resulted in fewer exports from Europe to China. The European products exported to China in 2040 range from pharmaceuticals, food products (grains), (Swiss) watches, chemical products, precious stones, and precious metals (mainly platinum and gold) to optic and medical instruments. In this context, there are some regions still benefiting from exports to China, such as Munich, Stuttgart, Nürnberg, Göttingen, Braunschweig, Berlin, Hamburg (optic and medical instruments), Pforzheim (precious stones), Dresden/Glashütte, Biel, Black Forest (watches), Ruhr area, Frankfurt, Mannheim/Ludwigshafen, Basel, Ingolstadt and Halle/Leipzig (chemical products), to name just a few in Germany and Switzerland.

In 2000, China was already the world's Number-one producer of iron and steel, coal, cement, fertilizer and televisions. Other strong sectors since then have been airplanes, ships, cars, satellites, electricity, tractors, chemical fibres, cotton yarn, scrim, sugar, sulphuric acid, ethylene, integrated circuits, cell phones and computers. By 2040, these branches have intensified even more and China has been able to attract entire industry clusters, acquiring a critical mass of companies that can catalyze creativity, leading to rapid innovation processes and the ability to compete in a knowledge economy. One of the branches that suffered most from China's ascension has been the automobile industry. Even before 2000, many big European car producers had opened production sites in China. During the following years, many were enlarged in order to meet the increasing demand for cars in China. In the main, renowned European brands produced luxury cars *in situ* for those who could afford them. In 2040, however, cheaper cars and popular middle-class models using fuel cells are now produced by Chinese car-makers. These have also conquered the European and American markets, repeating and even topping the success story of Japanese car producers half a century before. Automobile production in Europe has dramatically decreased and many big production sites have been closed or transferred to Asia. As a result of cheap Chinese products on the world market, other traditional industries in Europe that were already under pressure have declined even further.

One example is the cotton- processing industry in the regions of Münsterland, Emsland, Gelderland, Swabia, Allgäu, Thuringia, Vogtland, Saxony, Kassel, East Switzerland and the Rhine Valley.

In the meantime, many older European manufacturing firms have closed. Not only have the products from Far East Asia been selling more cheaply in the European boutiques due to the higher production costs of domestic articles, far more important is the fact that due to cheap Chinese mass production delivered all over the world, the global export market for European enterprises has collapsed. Foreign trade or trade with other countries from the European Union has been reduced to a small remainder of goods, mainly food products.

In Europe, Chinese enterprises have also been able to nearly monopolize cheap versions of simple machines, toys, consumer electronics, textiles, shoes, cars, furniture, chemical products, watches, metal products and sports goods. Cheaper prices do not always equate to low quality. Chinese enterprises have also taken the lead in biotech, fibre optics, supercomputer manufacturing, and the luxury apparel and accessory market. Moreover, since 2015, China has become the world's largest producer of movies, computer games, music, and television programming, profiting from a large talent pool of highly creative performers and its rich history in theatre and the arts.

As salaries in Europe have fallen only modestly during the last few decades, due to the still very influential workers' unions, working in Europe has become more interesting for both qualified and unqualified Chinese workers, all of them fluent in English. They have obtained travel visas and work permits for all over Europe and can be found managing enterprises, at universities, and as migrant workers during the harvest season. The beauty of Europe, in contrast to the severely damaged environment of eastern and southern China, has attracted many Chinese businessmen to move. They are serving as managers in Chinese or (still) European enterprises.

Since the 2020s, telecom and transport companies have been taken over, leading to a decline in Western commerce in many other areas. The European Union has even been unable to stop a hostile Chinese takeover of some of the leading producers of weapons and military equipment. Chinese doctors and engineers have long since surpassed European standards, and they successfully offer their services all over Europe for lower fees than their European counterparts, a situation that has fuelled European unemployment.

In cities mainly affected by the drop in jobs and taxes, unemployment has risen significantly. Mass unemployment has occurred in the older industrialized regions and peripheral regions of Europe. In larger and smaller cities, middle-class and working-class households have suffered from gradual impoverishment as public funds for social security and unemployment insurance had to be reduced. Conversely, costs of living have developed in different ways: energy and related activities such as travel, transport, etc., have become very expensive, but living costs have dropped as people buy more cheap Chinese products than the more expensive European ones and rents on apartments and homes fall as well.

Living conditions in European countries in 2040 much resemble those of the US in the early 2000s. Undetermined work contracts are the exception and family members are working as 'Me corporations' (*Ich AG*). Work has lost its sense of self-fulfilment and has become a purely money-making activity. To have work is a question of survival, and it is taken wherever found. It is hard to describe one's profession when a person is distributing journals in the early morning, then driving a bus for elderly disabled persons until noon, selling ice-cream on sunny afternoons, cleaning dishes in a cocktail bar, and trying to sell flea-market articles on Internet auctions late at night. Only those who have the energy to live with such a patchwork of many small jobs that can change at any time have a chance to escape from working poverty. In another example, some former middle managers from banks and trade companies have found franchising opportunities in small shops for Chinese-owned enterprises designed for the European market and are running their own all-night city convenience stores, selling Chinese-brand articles and no-name products, or running massage and beauty parlours. Others tried their luck with exchange markets for used articles, but had to give up as such trading was transferred more and more to the Internet. Less flexible people have fallen victim to depression and continually decreasing unemployment benefits.

Along with new urban poverty, more accentuated segregation along income lines has developed. In previously neglected neighbourhoods, residence quality has continued to decrease. The abandoned buildings in the core of the cities are decaying as no one wants to invest in them or live there. However, Chinese investment corporations have begun to buy complete neighbourhoods for possibly profitable regeneration projects and constructing edifices for Chinese enterprises. The state-run Chinese Development Co-operation Agency has started development aid projects to overcome social segregation in the most problematic city centres in Europe. One positive outcome of smaller populations in most European regions and a lack of available money is that urban sprawl, one of the biggest problems of urban agglomerations of the late 2000s, has ceased. However, in the surrounding economic centres, many business offices and production sites have been abandoned.

The poorest people are living either in city centres or in anonymous housing estates in satellite settlements (*banlieux*). Since 2030, lack of purchase power has also led to empty malls and shopping centres, where the homeless struggle for space and seek shelter from street gangs. Crime, prostitution and drugs in the inner cities have aggravated segregation, causing wealthier families to flee to gated communities in the suburbs. In many cities, wasteland has become renatured: rabbits, wild dogs, foxes, wild pigs and deer populate many former city parks, now wilderness zones. Theme parks, however, have survived after hard times, due to an increasing number of Chinese tourists coming to Europe. Attractive regions and historical hotspots, such as the Swiss and Austrian Alps, Rothenburg ob der Tauber, Neuschwanstein, Heidelberg, Venice, Paris, the Côte d'Azur, Marbella, Barcelona and London have accentuated their tourist appeal and hotels (now run by Chinese investor groups) are fully booked in high season.

In order to overcome another important bottleneck for trade, the capacity of European seaports, Chinese investment firms, backed by the Chinese government, have started to take over European ports or buy parts of them to increase their capacity. Thus, in 2020, the City of Hamburg sold a part of its port to a Chinese authority. Only ten years later, in 2030, Chinese investors began to buy land in the Voorne region in the Netherlands in order to build a new port neighbouring Rotterdam's Europoort. Nearby Emden, a new port and the biggest one in Europe, also owned by Chinese companies, is due to open in 2050. Being gatekeepers to trade ships from China, European ports and their surrounding cities, such as Hamburg, Bremen, Rotterdam, Antwerp, London and Le Havre on the North Sea, as well as cities on the Baltic Sea (Gothenburg and Baltic cities), have prospered considerably by offering cargo discharge, storage and trans-shipping on vans, accompanied by several tributary services. The ports on the Mediterranean Sea have also been able to increase their amount of sea-cargo handling, but not to the same extent as the ports to the north. The same is true for European cargo airports, such as Frankfurt, Paris, London, Amsterdam, Berlin, Milan, Vienna and Zurich, as well as some other small regional airports, previously abandoned, but bought and refurbished by Chinese investors.

The competition between cities for new enterprises from profitable and job-creating branches has grown throughout Europe. The larger cities in Europe have been able to adapt. They have a large enough pool of highly skilled experts for innovation and research and development. These cities are the engines for economic development in Europe. Smaller cities, however, have suffered more, as they have mainly relied on handcraft, small enterprises in manufacturing, and agricultural production. In 2040, Chinese companies also largely dominate the service sector. The post-industrial era for European cities has come to a much faster end than projected. Europeans have been occupied with questions of EU enlargement and their fear focused on the clash of civilizations between the Western and the Muslim world for too long, overlooking what was happening in China and what effects this would have on their lives. The biggest potential Europe can offer is well-trained, highly skilled labourers in the service sector, banks, insurance and consulting companies, tourism and research industries. But due to low birth rates, this potential has thinned as well. In schools, Chinese has become the second foreign language after English, and many graduates are happy to find work in a Chinese European-based enterprise. However, many young people remain without a job or apprenticeship and share the destiny of the unemployed masses or try their luck in cultural activities (music, literature, painting), where they also have to compete with Chinese artists.

The overall mood in European cities in 2040 is depressive, and the remaining foreigners are suffering from the xenophobia. All over urban Europe, right-wing radicalism has found fertile soil, and new demagogues have appeared on the political scene, gaining more and more influence in national and local parliaments. Increasing urban poverty all over Europe has resulted in different socio-political reactions: in France, a new *levée en masse* occurred in 2035, which has since been put down several times by the police and the army, but the movement has become even stronger, spreading to Berlin, Madrid, Rome, Prague and Warsaw. It seems that in the near future, pan-European revolutions will be unavoidable.

Conclusion

This chapter presents a scenario of a rather undesirable possible future for Europe. The saying goes: Those who expect the worst are never disappointed. If their doom-laden scenario were to become reality, they can claim that they sounded the unheeded alert at an early stage. If the future were to prove different, or more positive than depicted in their gloomy scenarios, the authors can argue that the worst was only avoided because of reactions to their warnings and precautionary measures subsequently taken. However, we do not intend to be *weisenheimers*. Our aim is to sharpen awareness of possible development streams and to start a discussion on how European cities could react. We abstained from drawing a positive scenario for urban Europe in 2040. This will be the task of planners, politicians, stakeholder, and entrepreneurs – everyone in Europe – in the decades to come.

16 Hanbao

The Chinese Hamburg in 2035

Thomas Krueger

In a newspaper comment from September 2006 about the activities in Hamburg focusing on China, the author complained about the dominance of Chinese business and culture in Hamburg. He missed the self-confidence of the German. From his point of view, the so-called dialogue between Germany and China is characterized by fear on the German side.

The background of this commentary was that the conference languages at a recent Hamburg–Chinese business event were English and Chinese, not German. And the musicians, who played work by Hamburg-born composer Brahms at that conference, came from China. At the same time, the Chamber of Commerce is presenting a concept for a Chinese district. The proposal is to concentrate cultural, entertainment, business and other China-related facilities in the very centre of the city (see Figure 16.1).

Figure 16.1 Hamburg-Port near to the City (©Hafen Hamburg Marketing).

Briefly speaking, the central questions are: Are the Chinese on their way to conquering Hamburg economically? Will Hamburg in the future be a settlement or even a colony of the Chinese economy in Europe?

In this chapter, I want to inform you about the relationship between Hamburg and China today. After a very brief overview of the economic structure of the Hamburg Metropolitan Region, I want to point out some aspects which could be relevant for a Hamburgian development strategy in this 'Chinese Century'.

Hamburg and China today

In September 2006, significant economic and cultural activities took place to present and anchor the Free and Hanseatic City of Hamburg as a central gateway for Germany and northern Europe to and from China. The campaign 'China Time 2006', which was coordinated by the Senate of Hamburg, was intended to inform residents about China. About 250 activities and events under five main headlines took place:

1   policy, society and law;
2   education and science;
3   economy and environment;
4   culture and lifestyle;
5   sports.

Not only in the city centre, but across the entire City of Hamburg, people could not escape the different events focusing on China. Special campaigns concentrated on schools. The activities were well prepared and supported by the local and regional media.

In mid-September 2006, the Hamburg Chamber of Commerce organized the international conference 'Hamburg Summit: China Meets Europe', with high-ranking German and Chinese businesspeople. It was the second summit after 2004. Issues of the conference were, for example:

* EU–China trade relations;
* banking and finance in China;
* getting there: logistical challenges;
* China's emerging automotive sector.

Wen Jiabao, Prime Minister of the People's Republic of China, spoke at this conference before he met with the German Chancellor in Berlin.

What is the reason for this concentration of activities concerning China in Hamburg? Hamburg is traditionally the main port for the Asian and especially the Chinese trade with Germany and northern Europe. Over the last 20 years, the export volume has been exploding. At the beginning of the twenty-first century, trade with Asia-Pacific makes up half of the total harbour turnover, of which China again has a share of 50 per cent. That means one of four containers

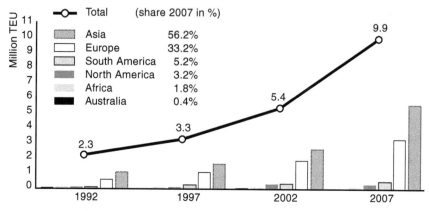

Figure 16.2 Container handling in the Port of Hamburg by continents in TEU 2006/7 (©Port of Hamburg Marketing).

handled in the Port of Hamburg is coming from or going to China. And, this trade is still increasing remarkably (see Figure 16.2).

According to a survey by the Hamburg Business Development Corporation (HWF), some 400 Chinese companies are located in Hamburg. This is the highest concentration of Chinese companies in Europe (Frankfurt has 190 and London 200 companies). For more than 15 years, China has been an important target of the activities of Hamburg's marketing. A town-twinning with Shanghai was established in 1986. Since 2002, German–Chinese bilingual teaching has been established in a secondary school. In 2005, some 600 Chinese students studied at the different universities in Hamburg.

There are two important aspects of the business infrastructure in Hamburg, i.e. the so-called 'hard location factors' that are attractive for companies trying to penetrate the German and European markets, for instance, the Chinese. At the end of this chapter I will come to the 'soft factors'.

Hamburg's economic structure

Hamburg is the main port for northern Europe, for the Scandinavians, Poland, the Baltic States, northwestern Russia and the Czech Republic, Slovakia and Hungary. So-called feeder-ships carry containers from or to the big transatlantic container ships, or railway lines connect the port with its hinterland. More or less locked to the port function is a wide range of logistic facilities and services, which are growing fast in the Hamburg region. The city is investing a lot of money in the port facilities.

Based on the specialized logistic infrastructure, Hamburg's economy has a traditional emphasis on wholesaling, distribution and marketing. Looking at its history from the industrial development of the nineteenth century up to the structural changes in the German economy, especially since the 1970s, Hamburg was primarily the main import centre for its hinterland. The German export sector is traditionally dominated by high-value and low-volume goods, especially machinery. In contrast to this, imports were dominated by raw materials and consumer goods, which are still moving via the harbour and are distributed by traditional wholesale and sale structures. For products with low or medium complexity for the German or European market that are still shipped by sea containers, the Hamburg economy offers a wide range of support. So this is a good place for Chinese export companies to settle and penetrate the German and European markets.

Connected with the strong logistic infrastructure and the highly developed network of wholesaling, distribution and marketing, is an urban economic culture – or if you like a business 'climate' or 'milieu' – of openness to international contacts and business, much as one will find in other ports and trading cities all over the world. People living in Hamburg are accustomed to being in contact and doing business with international people and institutions. This aspect may help Chinese businesspeople in selecting Hamburg for their first economic step in Germany and Europe.

In a similar way, Hamburg had a strong position in the trade with Japan from the 1960s up to the 1970s. But when the Japanese companies had established themselves more and more on the German and Western European markets, many of them moved to the hinterland, especially to the Rhine area and Frankfurt. Now, new businesses or products from Japan can use the experience and the widespread network of established Japanese companies across Germany and Europe.

Experts expect that with the growing import business from China in terms of volume and quality, the activities will be more and more oriented, and later relocated, to the German hinterland, i.e. to the metropolitan areas of Rhine–Main and Rhine–Ruhr, and the Württemberg and Munich regions. In addition, expansion is expected to spread to the Copenhagen–Malmo region, the large cities of the Baltic States, and the areas around Helsinki, Warsaw and Petersburg. Businesses will orient themselves to the big metropolitan areas, sales markets and technology partners. Concerning the traditional import functions of Hamburg, the strong position in trade with China will weaken in the next 10–15 years in relation to Chinese business in Germany and Europe in total.

But in absolute figures, transport and trade via the Hamburg region will continue to rise in the future. And if the regional stakeholders have creative ideas, are cooperative and act flexibly, there should be opportunities to develop new China-related businesses in the region. But what are the resources the Hamburg region could mobilize?

The Hamburg economy is not just harbour and trade, which are partly interlocked. There are also other important sectors, independent from the traditional businesses, which have an important role in the future development of the region.

About 100,000 people are still working in the industrial sector in Hamburg, which is 15 per cent of all employees. After sharp reductions, especially in the shipbuilding and food industries, which have their roots in the harbour function, the remaining industrial structure is highly diverse and characterized by companies that are highly specialized and well integrated in their production systems and markets. More than half of the employees in the industrial sector are producing high-technology products. An industry that is expanding significantly is the aviation industry with Lufthansa technology and Airbus production at its core. Perhaps you have already heard that Russia has bought a capital share of this company. China is very interested in cooperating from being a supplier up to production with Airbus Industries.

Let me come to another asset of the Hamburg economy: More than 15 years ago Klaus Kunzmann coined the term *Kulturwirtschaft* (i.e. cultural economy or creative industry), which became popular in the regional sciences. He demonstrated the importance of the creative industry for the development of the region. A recent study has found that Hamburg has 20,000 registered and 9,000 independent workers in the arts alone. Following a survey by the Chamber of Commerce, the entire creative industry, including publishing, TV, video and audio production, advertising, design and multimedia, account for more than 60,000 jobs in Hamburg. Particularly in the publishing sector, Hamburg has very strong position with the companies Springer, Bauer and Gruner+Jahr acting on an international level.

Together, the traditional port-related harbour, logistic, wholesaling, distribution and marketing clusters are estimated to include approximate 100,000 jobs in the city and 150,000 in the metropolitan region. The technical industries and the culture and media industries have more than 60,000 jobs each. In terms of export-basis theory, in Hamburg one-third of the local economy is oriented to each of the German, European or world markets (see Figure 16.3).

What are the perspectives? Which are the possible elements of a development strategy for Hamburg in the 'Chinese Century'? To answer this, it is useful to

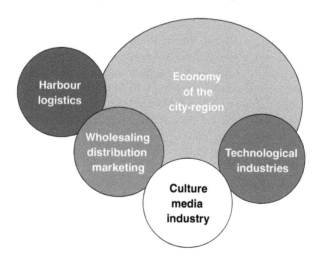

Figure 16.3 Current clusters of Hamburg's economy (©Krueger 2008).

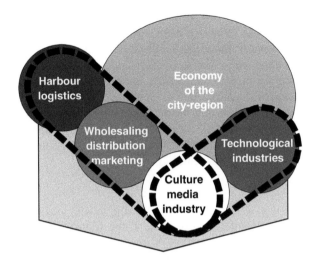

Figure 16.4 Structural interaction of Hamburg's economy in the future (©Krueger 2008).

make a distinction between the aspects we can influence on a regional level and the issues that are out of our hands (see Figure 16.4).

Out of our hands is the international flow of capital. Chinese companies can buy shares and control important businesses in Hamburg. And, hopefully, they want to! Foreign capital and control is not good or bad as such. It can exploit or strengthen former independent enterprises. In a situation of introduction into new markets and regions, the main interest of acquisition is to learn and to establish, not to cut down what you have just bought.

The key challenge of a metropolitan economy in the post-industrial world is to stay fit in the fields where you are engaged and to keep looking around to see which new developments and opportunities occur. The task is to develop and integrate knowledge and innovation to the existing chains and networks of value. What we need are, on the one side, management and technological competence and, on the other, culture and creativity. Both dimensions relate to the core economic processes and networks of the region. So the activities have to at least focus on the existing products and services, their production and distribution and their development context.

The Hamburg region has a traditional competence in logistic, distribution and marketing. In the future, the main interest of foreign companies, especially those from China, is surely not to produce in Germany. They want effective logistic solutions and access to the market. That's what they get in Hamburg now. When quality standards and product complexity rise, and as we can see, this process is very fast, the more knowledge about the specific context of use or consumption is needed. This is a field where knowledge of structures, cognition and interpretation are needed, in other words: cultural knowledge and communication. This is the core know-how of the culture and media industry, which is well developed in Hamburg.

On the regional level, we can't make or even support technological innovations. This field is of a national or European dimension. But in a similar way to the fields of logistics and trade, innovation in the industrial sector could be stimulated by developing interaction and innovative links between the technology industry and the culture and media industry.

Both developments can introduce new fields of activities, interactions and products that we don't know about yet. So my thesis is that the culture and media industries will become key industries for the regional development of regions like Hamburg in the twenty-first century.

'Hanbao'

If we look at the advantages Hamburg is offering to the Chinese, there is an excellent business infrastructure for the import of goods from China, as shown above. And if the expectation that culture and media industries will become key factors of regional development is correct, then Hamburg is an even better location for Chinese investments.

Up to this point, the analysis was restricted to more or less 'hard' economic factors. As we know, there are also 'soft' factors in locational behaviour. When we are looking at the target group in question, Chinese companies and their decision-makers who want to establish or expand their business in northern Europe, we have to consider the simple fact that it is easier to establish a company where other Chinese people and companies are already located, i.e. in Hamburg.

There is know-how and experience in managing the typical problems of newcomers from a certain, i.e. Chinese background. In the case of Hamburg, there are a lot of experienced lawyers, translators and other business-services available, which are important for a Chinese start-up.

There is a Chinese community with clubs, private schools, a Chinese newspaper, Chinese medicines and so on. This living infrastructure is integrated in a dense network of German associations and individuals who are engaged in improving contact and understanding.

As we saw at the beginning, the government and important institutions are trying to attract and support Chinese activities in Hamburg and to learn more about China. A lot of schools, universities and most of the cultural institutions are involved.

The friendly welcome from officials, the attention that companies, businesses and other institutions give to the China issue and the well-developed business infrastructure and environment for private life are especially relevant for a very important group of Chinese businesspeople: those who are in Hamburg for just a few weeks, some months or years, which are the majority. For them, being able to work and live in an environment that they partly know or can easily understand is a major attraction.

17 1950–2050

Sunset and sunrise over the Eurasian continent

Philippe Doucet

Each ordinary person is responsible for the rise and the fall of his/her country.

(Chinese proverb)

Our future is essentially unpredictable. Regrettably or not, it is up to us, human-kind, to shape our common future. By and large, it will be determined by our own decisions, behaviour and policy steps, many of which remain yet to be taken. True, some steps have already been taken and they will influence the course of events, but to an extent that can hardly be gauged. This is probably the reason why contemporary planning favours short-term visioning rather than the presumptuous long-term blueprint planning of the post-war era. Yet it remains stimulating to propose some long-term scenarios, each of which explores one among many fictitious courses of events. In no way should these be regarded as predictive models, but instead as provocative speculation intended to rouse alertness regarding the possible consequences of some strategic choices. The short story that follows is based upon one such scenario.

FENG Xiao Hong had spent the whole afternoon on a bench in Zhanyuan Garden. On such a nice spring sunny day, her habit was to bring along her portable Inter-net browser to a quiet and beautiful place to concentrate on one of these disserta-tions she often had to write. This studious and lovely young lady had no real reason to worry about her future, even though her relatively anxious and perfec-tionist nature sometimes inclined her to do so. She was born in 2030 in Shen-zhen. At the time, FENG Zhenbang, her 32-year-old father, a real maverick, was already a brilliant liberal industrialist in the nanotechnology business. LÀI Kuan-Yin, her Eurasian mother (born in 2002), was a psychologist employed in an occupational medicine centre (the number of such centres had soared in the Guangdong province from 2010 onwards). Xiao Hong had no brother, but she was the eldest of three sisters. This was her parents' deliberate choice, convinced as they were that the old single-child policy and the foolish popular preference for boys had to be contested.

Not surprisingly, the higher education of these three beloved daughters was a very serious matter in such an open-minded and well-to-do family. Exact sci-

This feeling of being welcome is reinforced by another element: In Chinese, Hamburg is spoken as *hanbao*. In the Chinese language and sound, this means castle. As you can see in the official crest of Hamburg, the people of Hamburg see their city as a castle too. I hope the Chinese never need a castle in Europe, but they find Hamburg's attributes in the fields of retirement, recreation, and support for their activities in Europe very welcome.

Reflecting on all these remarks and observations, we return to the two questions at the beginning of the chapter: Are the Chinese on their way to conquering Hamburg or Europe economically?, And: Will Hamburg be a settlement or a colony of the Chinese economy in Europe in the future? The answer to both is clear. It would make no sense for the Chinese to conquer Hamburg's economy because they are interested in the city's gateway function and its cultural transitory function to the markets of northern Europe. This function needs to be substantially of a German or European type to work. Markets are embedded culturally, now and in the future.

So in the 'Chinese Hamburg' of 2035, we will have, besides US, European and Russian stakeholders, if we are lucky, also Chinese stakeholders in strategic parts of the regional economy, i.e. in the logistics, wholesale and media clusters. And, we will have a well-developed business, culture and leisure infrastructure of a Chinese character throughout the region with focal areas and buildings that symbolize the anchoring of the Chinese culture in the city. There is no danger in this scenario. The competitive advantage of harbour cities is integration and innovation. The main task for the local governments of port cities like Hamburg is to maintain openness.

ences were not quite Xiao Hong's cup of tea. She felt much more attracted by humanities and literature. Therefore, she enthusiastically welcomed her parents' suggestion to study at NJU (the prestigious Nanjing University.) One could hardly imagine a better place in China to graduate in history, a discipline that much appealed to Xiao Hong. She was so gifted that her enrolment turned out to be nothing more than a mere formality.

For the course on contemporary history of this 2050–1 academic year, Professor YĬN Wou Ki asked Xiao Hong to write an essay comparing the evolution of urban and territorial development in Europe and China over the past century. In China, as everywhere, some academics have their head in the clouds: they do not realize how demanding they are with their poor young students. Not every professional could master such complex subject-matter as the history of planning in one country; how on earth could a young student manage to produce a comparative historical analysis of planning in two completely different societies?

While the sun was shining in Zhanyuan Garden, a storm invaded Xiao Hong's heart. She surfed on the Internet with powerful search engines, spotted hundreds of relevant sites, each mentioning an abundance of articles and book references. The list was endless, and only exacerbated Xiao Hong's feeling of helplessness. Professor YĬN's topic was definitely beyond her ken. She was on the brink of bursting into tears when her viewphone rang.

'Hello, honey!' said Kuan-Yin, 'How are things in Nanjing?'

'Er..., well, Mum, very well.... Or rather, to be honest, things could be better...' replied Xiao Hong, strangling a sob.

'It seems I'm ringing at just the right time! What's the trouble, my dearest dragonfly? How can I help?'

'You can't, Mum, you can't! Anyway, I'll never make it. I've made up my mind: I'm going to give up studying history at NJU. The level here is far too high for me, I'd better study something else anywhere else.'

With much patience and maternal empathy, Kuan-Yin listened to her daughter's detailed report on her awful afternoon and the accursed Professor YĬN.

'Oh, my poor little dragonfly!' said Kuan-Yin. 'You can't imagine how much I sympathize. I remember being in exactly the same kind of predicament when I was a student. But you know, things are not necessarily as grave as you may believe. Sometimes, I'm pretty sure, others among your fellow students also feel overwhelmed by events in similar circumstances. Then the golden rule is: no panic! For heaven's sake, do NOT panic! You're no less gifted than others. All you probably need is to change method. In your shoes, I'd give up surfing on the Internet and piling up book references you'll never read anyway. You'd better get some guidance from an experienced person, who could help you identify the key points. Why don't you ring your great-grandfather,[1] for example? He dedicated his whole brilliant career to spatial planning theory and practice. He is a *planoloog*, alumnus of the famous Technische Hogeschool Delft,[2] where he started studying in 1969. I'm ready to bet he'll be delighted to give you some tips, or even much more! After all, professional heuristics in contemporary history entails supplementing readings by live interviews of key witnesses, doesn't it?'

'Well, Mum, perhaps you're right. I'm not sure whether Great-grandpa can really help me overcome my deep ignorance of territorial development issues, but still, it's always so good to chat with him. For sure I've nothing to lose in ringing him up!'

'Can I stay on line? I also would like to hear what he's got to say about this.'

'What a weird question! Of course you can, Mum!'

Xiao Hong dialled Klaas De Hoop's number. After a few seconds, a trilateral videoconference was taking place between Klaas, his granddaughter and great-granddaughter.

'Well I never! What a nice surprise!' Klaas exclaimed, 'Both of you on my screen! You're probably calling about my 100th birthday party in October? Don't tell me you won't be able to come!'

'Don't worry, Great-grandpa,' said Xiao Hong. 'Of course we'll come. We are calling about another matter which I'll explain. But first, how are you and where are you?'

'I'm as fit as a fiddle. These new nano-robot drug injections I got last time I came to see you in China are simply miraculous. At your age, Xiao Hongetje,[3] I was far from thinking that I'd live to be a hundred! Now I can quietly carry on with my modern nomadic life. My houseboat is currently moored in Belgrade. I was eager to revisit this city as I hadn't seen it since Serbia joined the Union. Thereafter, I'll pursue my trip along the Danube River up to the Black Sea. Now, tell me why you called.'

Xiao Hong once more explained her dilemma, and her desperate attempts to grapple with the task set out by the accursed Professor YĪN.

'Your professor has been wonderfully well inspired, Xiao Hongetje! What a brilliant idea to make you explore such a fascinating and stimulating topic!'

'Please, Great-grandpa, don't poke fun at me!'

'I'm not poking fun! This topic is extremely interesting – maybe a bit tricky for a novice – but really interesting. You did very well to ring me up. I've got so much to say about territorial development and planning: this was my whole life! Let me begin.'

'Hang on, hang on, Great-grandpa! I'm opening my electronic notepad.'

'Are you ready now? Yes? All right. In 1969, my dear girls, when I set about studying urban and regional planning in Delft, this profession was highly regarded in Europe. At the time, the word "ecology" was unknown to the layman, and post-war Western societies developed an optimistic and Promethean relationship with the environment. This was especially true in the Netherlands, where a Promethean approach had already been a well-established tradition for centuries, culminating with the Pharaonic Delta Project launched in 1958 in response to the 1953 North Sea Flood disaster. This was, of course, an exceptional undertaking, but it exemplifies quite well the state of mind widely shared by governments and planning professionals in the post-war era. Man had more to shape the environment than to adapt to it, let alone to protect it. Rationalist thought was triumphing everywhere, especially in planning schools. Le Corbusier's most extreme views, for example those spelled out in his *projet pour une ville de trois millions d'habitants*, were still points of reference, even if more moderate models were also on the agenda.'

'Le Corbusier? Who is this guy?' asked Xiao Hong.

It took Klaas a while to acquaint Xiao Hong with completely antiquated modernist planning theories of the twentieth century. Then he concluded on this topic:

'As you can see, modernist planning, in the field of territorial development, prolonged the European prestigious Enlightenment rationalist tradition. Of course, its determination to control every tract of land through master planning, comprehensive land-use planning and proactive land policy, and particularly its ambition to transform society by reshaping its built environment did not remain unchallenged.'

'Sorry to cut you short again, Great-grandpa: "master planning", "comprehensive land use planning", "land policy", what do you mean exactly?'

Again, he didactically spelled out these jargon terms, much to Xiao Hong's and Kuan-Yin's contentment (the mother was no less curious than her daughter.) This done, he went on with his story.

'In the 1970s, things evolved, and continued to do so increasingly as the century drew to a close. As you know, a series of events, including the end of the gold-dollar convertibility, two oil crises, the demolition of the Berlin Wall and the Iron Curtain, the collapse of the USSR, etc. and also new technologies, deeply impacted society. Attitudes, theories and practices dramatically shifted in virtually all areas: economics, technology, culture, science, politics, etc. A completely new, more flexible, networked, knowledge-based, market-led and globalized society was emerging. Needless to say, this brought about considerable change in the planning profession as well. Modernist theories rapidly gave way to postmodern thought. The very word "planning" was regarded with suspicion. Any kind of economic planning was not far from being equated to Stalinist Gosplan's practice. This was not quite the case with urban and regional planning, but its credibility and respectability were clearly fading. An article published in 1959[4] to ridicule comprehensive planning and advocate the so-called "incrementalist" approach to policy decision-making processes was revisited and celebrated in various planning circles. The art of "muddling through" became a new, acceptable planning paradigm.'

Xiao Hong and Kuan-Yin were ill at ease with this new jargon, but they refrained from interrupting Klaas once more, to avoid having him lose the thread of his narrative. After all, they grasped the essence of his meaning: the planning culture was declining in Europe in the last decades of the twentieth century.

'True,' said Klaas, 'The importance of the long-term dimension was still emphasized by many good professionals, especially by the apostles of sustainable development. But, despite their ambition to accommodate economic, social and environmental policies in a consistent integrated policy approach, sustainability was mainly regarded in practice as the solitary domain of the environmentalists and less a responsibility for administrations dealing with economic or social affairs. As a matter of fact, integration of policies remained wishful thinking. Importantly as well, the Promethean planning approach of the post-war era was henceforth a part of the past. Any ambition to artificially reshape the environment by harnessing breakthroughs of modern science and technology was considered a dangerous sorcerer's apprentice game. Instead, the so-called "precautionary principle" became the First Commandment of the new sustainability faith.'

'Unless I'm mistaken,' intervened Kuan-Yin, 'All this must have represented a real professional challenge for you, Granddad! The models and ideals of your younger days were being treated rather roughly!'

'Yes, indeed!' replied Klaas, 'However, the planning profession, despite its loss of popularity, still had an important role to play, at least in dealing with local issues such as land use, planning permissions, etc. There also remained some room for "grand visions" (but no longer of the Promethean planning type, of course). For example, strategic planning documents were still elaborated, despite their very limited efficiency in terms of policy integration (which, by the way, contributed to further discrediting the profession). In the area of city planning, a remarkable new line of thought gave birth to numerous "sustainable city" or "eco-city" models. The cross-border and international dimension of planning also proved to be a promising area, with good prospects for further breakthroughs. Considering the steadily deeper interdependence between regions of different countries that characterized the last two decades of the century, there was growing recognition that planning in isolation, I mean within national borders, no longer made sense. Therefore, the European Union....'

Klaas broke off. He realized that Xiao Hong's eyelids were getting heavy. He looked at his watch.

'My goodness!' he said, 'I completely lost sight of the time lag. It must be after 1 a.m. in Nanjing! My poor Xiao Hongetje, you're certainly worn out. Why didn't you tell me?'

'I'm fine, I'm fine, Great-grandpa, please carry on, your story is simply fascinating.'

'No, no!' intervened Kuan-Yin, 'My graceful dragonfly is probably too shy to dare confess it, Granddad, but after the exhausting day she's had, I'm ready to bet she's going to drop off to sleep within five minutes if we carry on talking.'

'You're definitely right,' replied Klaas, 'Let's continue all this tomorrow. Please call me back at, say, 3 p.m. your time, after my breakfast. Cheerio, *slaap lekker*, and have sweet dreams!'

Back in her studio, Xiao Hong set her alarm clock for 10 a.m. and let herself drift deliciously into the arms of Morpheus. She awoke refreshed, indulged in a generous breakfast (she had skipped her dinner yesterday...), then surfed on the Internet, but no longer frenetically: this time she calmly focused on sites dedicated to planning terminology, to check the exact meaning of the various terms used by Klaas, which she carefully stored in her electronic notepad.

At 3 p.m. Chinese time, Klaas, Kuan-Yin and Xiao Hong resumed their videoconference as agreed.

'Hello, my dear girls, how far did I get yesterday?' asked Klaas.

'You were about to address the European Union, Granddad,' replied Kuan-Yin.

'Ah yes, I remember now! The European Union! What a sad story! As of the late 1980s, and increasingly more so in the 1990s, the attention of planning administrations and academics was drawn to the cross-border and European dimensions of territorial development. Now, this has no relation to the fruit industry, but oddly enough two celebrated publications[5] identified a "blue banana", a banana-shaped sub-area of Europe where driving forces of the economy tended to polarize, and a "bunch of grapes" model, of a more polycentric and cooperative nature, meant to counteract the polarization trend. At the time, a "roving band of planners" (as they were dubbed by a prominent colleague of mine who taught in the Netherlands),[6] who were actually a handful of enthusiastic planning officials, embarked on an exceptionally exciting exercise. They wanted to incorporate spatial planning into the formal EU policy agenda, not only to favour cooperation and coordination between regional and national planning strategies of the member states, but also to promote a better integration of various EU policies of territorial relevance (cohesion, environment, transport, etc.) Inside the European Commission staff, this initiative was backed up by a very small group of officials, especially by a former member of Jacques Delors's advisory board, who favoured ambitious visionary policy approaches. You can't imagine the tremendous amount of effort invested by these guys in persuading the various administrations concerned that all this was worth undertaking. They ultimately succeeded though. In September 1999, in Potsdam, after a decade of protracted negotiations, they managed to get the so-called "European Spatial Development Perspective (ESDP)", a territorial strategy for the EU, approved by the ministers of the 15 EU member states responsible for spatial planning. This was relatively unexpected, as the exercise had generated a good deal of scepticism from the outset.'

'Very well, Great-grandpa,' said Xiao Hong, 'But, if so, I don't quite understand why you announced a sad story. This looks more like the happy ending of a success story, doesn't it?'

'The elaboration and approval of the ESDP was indeed no sad story, you're right, Xiao Hongetje. What makes me sorrowful is what happened next, not only to European planning but also, and more importantly, to the European Union itself. A real tragedy!'

'Are you sure you're not laying it on a bit thick, Granddad?' asked Kuan-Yin, who was used to, and loved, her grandfather's lyrical temperament.

'Well, put it as you like, to my mind, it was a tragedy!' he replied. 'Please listen to the rest of my story, and then tell me if I'm exaggerating. Once adopted, the ESDP gave rise to mixed feelings. The community of planners were clearly "ESDP enthusiasts". This was no real cause for surprise, if you consider the renewed legitimacy conferred on the profession by the document. Moreover, all planners across Europe could communicate and exchange stimulating views and make progress together thanks to the excellent platform offered by the European Spatial Planning Observation Network, the technical arm of the ESDP process.

Planning administrations also welcomed the ESDP. However, they constantly stressed its specific status: a document of a strictly intergovernmental nature, a "non-EU document" of sorts, as planning was in no respect a policy competence of the Union. What a strange paradox: several EU policies of territorial relevance were addressed in the ESDP, but the EU as such was not allowed to coordinate these policies and integrate them into a consistent strategy! In so doing actually, planning departments of the member states, following their colleagues of many other national bureaucracies, were simply confirming the profound anxiety that any form of further deepening of European integration could generate at that time.'

'And what was the reaction outside planning circles? Did other administrations and the public take an interest in the ESDP?' asked Kuan-Yin.

'Some of them simply ignored it, while others wondered about the real use of such an esoteric and vague document. They were too unfamiliar with the planning jargon, and in any case, the ESDP had been drafted in a very soft and diplomatic style, avoiding explicit statements or precise policy objectives, as is the rule in any intergovernmental exercise of the sort. With a view to widening the debate and involving more people while circumventing the EU competency issue, the "Assembly of European Regions" coined the phrase "territorial cohesion" and managed to introduce it in the Amsterdam Treaty. Initially, this new concept appeared rather promising, but in fact lent itself to diverging interpretations: whereas idealist activists advocated "territorial cohesion" as a way to promote the integrated cross-sector approach that was so close to their hearts, others, more pragmatically, exploited this new fashionable concept to put forward their own, rather self-serving, cases. Every category of region (maritime, urban, mountainous, peripheral, rural, etc.) portrayed itself as the most deprived, hence laying claim to a large as possible share of the EU structural funds cake and other types of public subsidies, "for the sake of territorial cohesion".'

'Somehow, a dialogue of the deaf then?' asked Kuan-Yin.

'Definitely so!' replied Klaas. 'But also a manifestation, in the specific area of planning and regional policy, of a much more widespread and insidious societal disease that was corroding the EU at the turn of the century. Not only planning, but the entire European integration process was at stake. The great impetus given by the founding fathers in the post-war era had completely lost momentum. Building the European house was no longer seen as a positive-sum game. Instead, considerable concern, primarily based on nationalistic considerations, was expressed in many member states, especially on the occasion of the 2004 enlargement: "Don't we contribute too much to the EU budget? Do we get our money back? What's the use of all this Eurocracy in Brussels? Free movement of workers: why in my country, where so many people are on the dole? Aren't we losing our national identity?", etc. Of course, this new trend was resisted by the old proponents of a more united Europe, including the Union of European Federalists, whose influence was perceptible in the draft Treaty establishing a Constitution for Europe. The agreement reached in 2003 by the European Convention on this draft Treaty was rightly regarded as a big surprise. This major breakthrough, though, was rapidly turned into a major breakdown after its rejection by France and the Netherlands, two founding member states of the European Community. Henceforth, progressive and constant European decay proved simply inexorable.'

'Sad story, indeed, Great-grandpa!' said Xiao Hong, 'But how do you explain that Europe never managed to unite, whereas the federal model has become popular in so many other parts of the world?'

'Brilliant topic for your future PhD thesis, Xiao Hongetje!' replied Klaas with a wink of affectionate complicity, 'But as I'm no professional historian, I'd best refrain from proposing what could be an amateurish theory. Still, I may attempt to describe, rather than explain, the course of events as I witnessed them. In the first decades of this century, Europeans made a strategic mistake: they regarded socio-economic welfare and the improvement of European polity as two separate issues that could be tackled in parallel. In other words, they completely underestimated the high degree of dependence of welfare on polity. The disappointing outcome of the EU Constitution saga inclined EU leaders to concentrate on economic competitiveness, the so-called "Lisbon strategy", which the European Council had adopted in March 2000. The ambition was to make the EU "the most competitive and dynamic knowledge-driven economy by 2010".

'After several years, this objective turned out to be virtually unattainable. An attempt to re-launch the strategy was made in 2005. Various policy steps were put forward, in particular, the implementation of "national action plans", regarded as key instruments. Those aware of the pointlessness of the intergovernmental method – the ABC of European political culture – strongly criticized the move, making a fervent case for an EU economic government (as opposed to the then-fashionable economic governance). All to no avail. The debate had become lost in a cycle of sophisticated and unending rhetoric, discussing at length the merits of the "open coordination method", the "multi-level governance", the "enhanced cooperations" and a wealth of other newly coined phrases. As a matter of fact, the only use for this convenient phraseology was to defer, again and again, the tackling of the EU key dilemma: a strong European federation, or a club of independent dwarf states? The ambitious Lisbon Agenda was reconsidered in 2010, then again in 2020, always with sizeably lower targets. Yet these were never achieved. Finally, the Agenda was definitively forgotten and replaced by a negative growth strategy.

This dramatic about-turn was advocated by the European Malthusian Party, which had been progressively gaining considerable influence among EU leaders. On the institutional side, it succeeded in reforming the EU. Tactics- and content-wise, the line taken was exactly opposite to that of the European Convention. The sense of urgency gave way to a very patient and discrete step-by-step approach. No longer was there streamlining of the decision-making procedures; instead, there was a clear intention to make the EU more democratic while taking account of the steadily growing complexity of contemporary social life. EU policies were categorized in five distinct "pillars". In each pillar, a different decision-making procedure applied: four different types of qualified majority voting systems for the first four pillars, consensus for the fifth one. This was a bit subtle, but many people were pleased to see the old Eurocratic "community method" superseded by this wide array of new procedures. To make progress on non-EU policies, enhanced and semi-enhanced multi-level cooperations could also be initiated. A quadricameral system was born: the legislative power was henceforth shared between four assemblies, all on an equal footing, namely the Council, the European Parliament, the Committee of the Regions, and the Economic and Social Committee (whose membership was formally extended to various lobbies and other components of the civil society). All this was meant to secure a perfect transparency of decision-making while weaving closer ties between the EU and its citizenry. Bravo, the Europeans!' (He applauded.) 'How wonderful is your democracy! But a bit paralysed, I'm afraid!'

Xiao Hong and Kuan-Yin found it very hard to understand this Euro jargon apparently so familiar to Klaas. However, they did not ask him for further details, for fear of endless explanations. After all, they had grasped the essence of his account: in the first decades of the twenty-first century, the EU, far from uniting, opted for highly complex institutions and a weak position in the world. Despite her fascination with Klaas's erudition, Xiao Hong was getting a bit nervous, because it was high time to get back to Professor YĪN's topic: urban and territorial development in Europe and China. As if by chance, Klaas brought the conversation round to China when he concluded with:

'In a nutshell,' he said, 'Europe and China have evolved in two diametrically opposite directions over the first half of this century, especially after your Purple Revolution.'

'Ah! The Purple Revolution!' Kuan-Yin exclaimed. 'The wonderful years of my youth! Your dad and I, honey, joined the Free Democratic Party of China in 2020. It was at a meeting of FDPC activists that we fell in love. You should have seen your dad taking the floor: he was so handsome and eloquent! In 2025, TENG Zedong, our charismatic leader, called for mass demonstrations in every city of China to demand that a convention be summoned to elaborate a new constitution based on the principles of liberal democracy: an elective multiparty system, civil rights fully guaranteed, rule of law, etc. Surprisingly, some activists (but no leaders...) of the Communist Party enthusiastically took part in the demonstrations. Less than six months later, without the least bloodshed, a brand new constitution was drafted in a very clear and concise style, then submitted to, and adopted by, the Chinese people. The referendum gave a landslide victory to the "yes vote".'

'Interestingly, the constitution was not only of liberal-democratic, but also of federalist inspiration. It included a crystal-clear allocation of responsibilities between the federal government, federated entities, and local authorities. Elections were held shortly after. You can't imagine the emotion triggered by this event, especially among the elderly: so many voters freely electing their MPs for the first time in their long life! Despite the absolute majority won by the FDPC, TENG Zedong opted for a blue-red coalition cabinet: the first government of this new era brought together FDPC and Communist ministers. Actually, this rather unusual alliance wasn't unprecedented: such a "chalk-and-cheese" coalition had come to power in Mongolia as early as 2004. Of noteworthy innovation, however, was the capacity of this government to design and implement an extremely consistent and original policy agenda.'

'This agenda was based on TENG Zedong's political writings. He creatively revisited the modernist left-wing heritage of the European Enlightenment. To some extent, this had already been done one century earlier by President Mao, but on a completely different basis. This time, philosophical left-libertarianism[7] was the main inspiration, no longer the authoritarian Marxist-Leninist ideology. Two fundamental principles were asserted: first, individual liberty, free-market economy and unlimited private property rights on personal and man-made resources (mental and physical capacities, means of production, etc.); second, tight state control on the use of natural resources (including land). Theories of classic left-libertarian authors (for example, Thomas Paine, Hippolyte de Colins, Henry George, Léon Walras) and their contemporary intellectual heirs such as TENG Zedong, were popularized and taught in state schools.'

In no way was all this new to Xiao Hong. She had a complete grasp of Purple Revolution history, not only from having been taught it at school, but also because of her parents' lifelong commitment to it. Whenever her mother set about telling her favourite fairy tale, it was as if she was doing so for the first time.... When that happened, Xiao Hong knew that she had no other choice than to wait patiently until it was over. This time however, the never-ending story exasperated her, as she was desperately eager to hear something about Professor YĪN's topic. She kept heroically silent, but her slight pout of impatience did not escape Klaas's notice.

'Do you realize,' he said, cutting Kuan-Yin short, 'How deeply the Purple Revolution impacted on territorial development and planning in China?'

Xiao Hong was so grateful! She would have liked to throw her arms round Klaas's neck. What a pity that modern telecom technologies had not yet made virtual hugs possible!

'As your mother has just said, Xiao Hongetje, left-libertarianism entails strong state control on the use of natural resources. As fervently advocated by Léon Walras, for example,[8] land in China is owned by the state. By and large, this was already the case before the Purple Revolution: urban land was state-owned, whereas collectives (administered by public authorities anyway) owned the farmland. After the launch of the "open-door policy" in 1979, it became clear that some market mechanisms were needed to tackle the issue of land-resource allocation. Therefore, the land-policy reform of the late 1980s introduced a separation between land-use rights, which could be sold or transferred by land users, and land ownership, which remained a state monopoly.'

'The reform brought about positive results, but also negative side-effects, corruption in particular, as government officials were often bribed to grant land-use rights at low prices. Yet, it can be argued that this transition period of the "socialist market economy" was some sort of partial left-libertarian experiment, but only in terms of economic policy, of course: a market economy combined with state control of land. In terms of civil liberties, everything remained to be done, and was done by the Purple Revolution. What strikes me in this unprecedented story is that China avoided the pitfall that trapped so many countries of the former Soviet Bloc: the "privatize-everything" policy. Instead, the Purple Revolution succeeded in generating an extraordinarily efficient polity: liberal democracy, federal institutions, stimulation of entrepreneurship and a prosperous market economy in the productive sector, prudent public management of natural resources, a ban on land speculation through public land ownership, sale of land-use rights through auction, and allocation of the resulting income to public expenditures such as education and social welfare.'

'I assume that public land ownership has also allowed public authorities to carry out very efficient land-use and regional planning policies?' asked Xiao Hong.

'This goes without saying,' replied Klaas, 'And I'm going to expand a little bit on that. But first, I'd say that this evolution in China had a major territorial effect at the global level. Its buoyant and highly competitive economy attracted a considerable number of immigrants, especially a highly qualified workforce, for example, in the R&D sector. The trend was already perceptible at the beginning of the century. China appealed to some young open-minded professionals. Your grandma, Xiao Hongetje – I mean Gerda, my beloved daughter – ranked among them. After marrying T'Ien-Khuan, she set up a practice in Shanghai, specializing in eco-friendly architectural and urban design. She was, of course, involved in the development of Dongtan Eco-City, and many other such schemes that followed. Gerda belonged to a small group of forerunners. Later on, especially when the Malthusian negative growth strategy was adopted in the EU, a massive brain drain took place from Europe to China and other countries, for example, Brazil, India or even the good old United States, whose economy, though declining as well, was rather resilient.

Nowadays, the European population is polarized by two main social categories: a vast majority of poorly paid, low-skilled workers, and a group of idle, wealthy people, "*rentiers*", as they put it in French, whose main concern is to manage a fortune they simply inherited from their parents. But innovative companies have understood that they no longer have any future in this part of the world. Again, things are completely different in China, where "*rentiers*" are becoming a disappearing species since the first TENG Zedong government passed the 2027 Succession Duty Act, deeply inspired by Eugenio Rignano's thought.'[9]

'Well, Great-grandpa, all this is captivating,' Xiao Hong intervened, 'But apart from the development of eco-cities, I haven't heard much about spatial planning policies at this stage.'

'You're right, honey,' said Kuan-Yin, 'But you can easily guess what your venerated great-grandpa is going to demonstrate...'.

'That contemporary Chinese planning completely surpasses the European one?'

'European planning?' replied Klaas, 'What do you mean? Does this still exist? I doubt it! Be that as it may, the sharp contrast between European and Chinese territorial development is striking. To illustrate this, I'm going to give you some examples. With regard to urban development, the eco-city model, as I said, has become widespread in China. In Europe, it is also commonplace, but only in theoretical writings of some confidential specialized publications.... In reality, the European city pattern has been tailored to the needs of the new social divide: the historical centre has encroached on the former inner city to make room for "*rentiers*" and hordes of tourists, accommodated in luxury flats and air-conditioned hotels, whereas the poor have been relocated to the suburbs. There, campsites and other forms of shanty-towns alternate with the villas formerly occupied by wealthy families, now co-rented by two, three or more households, who have turned the luxury gardens into orchards and kitchen-gardens, with a shelter for their mules (a cheap means of transport of great appeal to commuters). No planning policy was needed to get this result. A simple *laissez-faire* approach achieved it.'

'Good heavens!' Kuan-Yin exclaimed. 'I didn't realize, to be honest, the gravity of the situation the last time I visited Europe!'

'That's probably because you only visited city centres, as so many tourists do!' replied Klaas.

Kuan-Yin kept silent. She took the criticism, a bit ashamed of her conformist style of travelling and promised herself to change her habits when exploring foreign countries in future. Klaas carried on.

'Now take the example of transport policy. Twenty years ago in China, modern technologies made it possible to equip every vehicle with a zero-carbon dioxide emission engine. The car industry had, of course, to comply with the new regulations, which made the use of such engines compulsory. Still, the traffic congestion issue was left unsolved. More importantly, the high number of car crashes was simply unacceptable. To improve safety while streamlining the traffic flow across the country, the federal government took radical steps. Most motorways were turned into HST rail tracks. Very strict speed limitations based on the nature of the vehicle were enforced, not through local speed controls carried out by the police on the roads, but through compulsory technical standards applied to the design of the vehicles. For example, the sale of all private vehicles (such as motorcycles, cars, vans, lorries, etc.) required a built-in technical device limiting their speed to a maximum of 40 km/h. Public surface transport, namely buses, coaches and trams, cannot exceed 65 km/h; the metro: 80 km/h; regional trains: 150 km/h; and intercity high-speed trains: 400 km/h.'

'You are pretty well informed, Granddad!' said Kuan-Yin, 'And I can confirm that these tough but very rational measures taken by the federal government have considerably improved our quality of life!'

'Meanwhile in Europe,' said Klaas, 'The situation has remained virtually unchanged: the interoperability of various national networks is still an irritating issue; much rhetoric to promote sustainable mobility but steadily less budgetary means to invest in waterways, railways and public transport; tens of thousands of fatal car accidents registered every year on the roads; and many confident car drivers are extremely suspicious about GMO food.'

'Oddly enough, Great-grandpa,' said Xiao Hong, 'While you are still worrying about GMOs in Europe, Chinese research centres have launched very ambitious genetic engineering schemes to experiment with artificial biodiversity regeneration techniques. It's China's turn to engage in Promethean projects! And how has regional policy evolved in Europe?'

'Here again, Xiao Hongetje, China and Europe have taken two completely opposite lines. Thanks to the federal system, regional policy is a relatively simple matter in China. It is clearly up to the federation to decide about the level of regional aid. Every five years, the federal parliament approves the regional policy budget, based on a constant monitoring of regional disparities. Then monies earmarked for less developed regions are simply transferred to the federated entities, whose elected authorities are fully responsible for the design and implementation of regional development schemes. Both economic development and physical planning are addressed in these documents, which are elaborated in consultation with local authorities. In Europe, the discussion of the regional policy budget is always protracted. The quadricameral system has favoured the involvement of many different so-called "stakeholders"! Every national government is eager not to contribute too much to the EU budget, whereas every interest group wants to obtain the biggest possible share of the structural-funds cake. So many people have been given a say that at the end of the day nobody really feels responsible for the decision made...'.

'In any case, the adoption of the negative growth strategy has unavoidably led to a considerable reduction of the regional policy budget. Regional disparities are doomed to increase. As to the implementation of operational programmes in the member states, the formal strategic approach that officially applies is nothing other than a sham concealing the fact that subsidies are actually granted to the most influential lobbies and cronies. This "bottom-up approach" is sometimes presented as the ultimate refinement of democracy.'

This time, Klaas's bitter irony cast a shadow over the conversation. Kuan-Yin and her daughter were gaping at Klaas. The essay asked for by Professor YIN was no longer Xiao Hong's main concern. This very long viewphone chat had left her with mixed feelings. On the one hand, her great-grandfather's insightful views decisively contributed to enriching her political culture, and this made her happy. On the other hand, she could not help feeling great compassion for Europeans. This was part of her humanist upbringing.

'Hey! Xiao Hongetje!' Klaas said suddenly, 'Are you all right? Cat got your tongue?'

'Er ..., no, Great-grandpa, not at all! I was simply meditating on all you've just said.'

'And are we allowed to know what came out of your meditations, young lady?'

'Two things. First, your story reminds me very much of my antiquity course. City-states of ancient Greece never managed to found a lasting federation. After the brief rationalist golden age of Pericles, they rapidly fell into decay, and other civilizations conquered the world. In spite of everything, the Greek civilization has always remained a major cultural reference, and Greek cities have remained popular tourist resorts. Second, most EU member states are far less populated than a Chinese province, and national borders are pure nonsense on the very small European continent. But thinking that through, I consider that the globe has become very small as well. All national borders are equally foolish, and it is high time to found a global federation of humankind.'

Notes

1 Kuan-Yin is referring to Klaas De Hoop (1951–), her grandfather. The ties of kinship between him and Feng Xiao Hong (2030–) are as follows: Feng Zhenbang (1998–) and Lài Kuan-Yin (2002–) are Feng Xiao Hong's father and mother respectively, Lài T'Ien-Khuan (1976–) and De Hoop Gerda (1977–) are Lài Kuan-Yin's father and mother respectively, De Hoop Klaas (1951–) is De Hoop Gerda's father.
2 Renamed Technische Universiteit Delft in 1986.
3 Klaas could not help adding an affectionate Dutch diminutive suffix to his great-granddaughter's first name.
4 See Lindblom (1959).
5 See Brunet (1989), and Kunzmann and Wegener (1991).
6 See Faludi (1997).
7 See Vallentyne and Steiner (2000a, 2000b).
8 See Walras (1880). See also Vallentyne and Steiner (2000a: 217–23).
9

> Eugenio Rignano (1870–1930) […] holds that people are fully entitled to the wealth that they produce, and thus have the right to give (and bequeath) it to others without taxation. He argued, however, that people who receive wealth by gift do not have an unrestricted right to further donate that wealth to others. Such wealth should be classified and taxed according to the number of times it has been donated since its initial creation (e.g. zero per cent for donor-created wealth, 50 per cent for donations of wealth previously received from the original creator, and 100 per cent for subsequent donations). This proposal was widely discussed in Great Britain and elsewhere after the First World War.
>
> (Vallentyne and Steiner 2000a: 225)

References

Brunet, R. (ed.) (1989) *Les Villes européennes*, Paris: DATAR/GIP RECLUS, la Documentation française.

Chung, C. J., Inaba, J., Koolhaas, R. and Leong, S. T. (2001) *Great Leap Forward*, Cambridge, MA: Harvard Design School.

Ding, C. (2003) 'Land Policy Reform in China: Assessment and Prospects,' *Land Use Policy* 20: 109–20.

Faludi, A. (1997) 'A Roving Band of Planners,' *Built Environment* 23(4): 281–7.

Faludi, A. and Waterhout, B. (2002) *The Making of the European Spatial Development Perspective*, London and New York: Routledge.

Guigou, J.-L. (1982) *La rente foncière – Les théories et leur évolution depuis 1650*, Paris: Economica.

Izraelewicz, E. (2005) *Quand la Chine change le monde*, Paris: Grasset, le Livre de Poche.

Kunzmann, K. R. and Wegener, M. (1991) 'The Pattern of Urbanisation in Western

Europe 1960–1990', *Berichte aus dem Institut für Raumplanung* 28, Dortmund: Universität Dortmund.

Le Corbusier, F. E. (1994) *Urbanisme*, Paris: Flammarion.

Lindblom, Ch. E. (1959) 'The Science of Muddling through', *Public Administration Review* 19: 59–79 (reprinted in S. Campbell and S. Fainstein (eds) (1996) *Readings in Planning Theory*, Malden, MA/Oxford: Blackwell).

Vallentyne, P. and Steiner, H. (eds) (2000a) *The Origins of Left-Libertarianism – An Anthology of Historical Writings*, New York: Palgrave.

Vallentyne, P. and Steiner, H. (eds) (2000b) *Left-Libertarianism and Its Critics – The Contemporary Debate*, New York: Palgrave.

Walras, L. (1880) *Théorie mathématique du prix des terres et de leur rachat par l'Etat* (mémoire lu à la Société vaudoise des sciences naturelles à Lausanne), in J. L. Guigou (1982) *La rente foncière: les théories et leur évolution depuis 1650*, Paris: Economica: 749–97.

Websites

www.asia-home.com/china/ (accessed 19 September 2008)

www.chine-informations.com/guide/categorie-expressions-et-proverbes-chinois-17.html (accessed 19 September 2008)

Dongtan   Eco-City: http://en.chinabroadcast.cn/811/2006/05/07/301@85444.htm (accessed 19 September 2008)

www.pnyv.org/index.php?id=34&tx_ttnews%5Btt_news%5D=277&tx_ttnews%5BbackP id%5D=8&cHash=c0c03521e4 (accessed 19 September 2008)

Union of European Federalists: www.federaleurope.org/ (accessed 19 September 2008)

Index

eBooks – at www.eBookstore.tandf.co.uk

A library at your fingertips!

eBooks are electronic versions of printed books. You can store them on your PC/laptop or browse them online.

They have advantages for anyone needing rapid access to a wide variety of published, copyright information.

eBooks can help your research by enabling you to bookmark chapters, annotate text and use instant searches to find specific words or phrases. Several eBook files would fit on even a small laptop or PDA.

NEW: Save money by eSubscribing: cheap, online access to any eBook for as long as you need it.

Annual subscription packages

We now offer special low-cost bulk subscriptions to packages of eBooks in certain subject areas. These are available to libraries or to individuals.

For more information please contact webmaster.ebooks@tandf.co.uk

We're continually developing the eBook concept, so keep up to date by visiting the website.

www.eBookstore.tandf.co.uk